Ab

Abraham's Dice

Chance and Providence in the Monotheistic Traditions

Edited by
KARL W. GIBERSON

OXFORD
UNIVERSITY PRESS

OXFORD
UNIVERSITY PRESS

Oxford University Press is a department of the University of Oxford. It furthers the University's objective of excellence in research, scholarship, and education by publishing worldwide. Oxford is a registered trade mark of Oxford University Press in the UK and certain other countries.

Published in the United States of America by Oxford University Press
198 Madison Avenue, New York, NY 10016, United States of America.

Library of Congress Cataloging-in-Publication Data
Names: Giberson, Karl, editor.
Title: Abraham's dice : chance and providence in the monotheistic traditions / edited By Karl W. Giberson.
Description: New York: Oxford University Press, 2016. |
Includes bibliographical references and index.
Identifiers: LCCN 2015023139| ISBN 978–0–19–027716–1 (pbk. : alk. paper) |
ISBN 978–0–19–027715–4 (cloth : alk. paper)
Subjects: LCSH: Chance. | Providence and government of God. | Abrahamic religions.
Classification: LCC BD595 .A27 2016 | DDC 123—dc23 LC record
available at http://lccn.loc.gov/2015023139

5 7 9 8 6 4
Printed by Webcom, Canada

Contents

Contributors

John D. Barrow is Professor of Mathematical Sciences in the Department of Applied Mathematics and Theoretical Physics at the University of Cambridge, and a Fellow of Clare Hall. He has also held the positions of Professor of Geometry and Professor of Astronomy at Gresham College, London, and was Director of the Astronomy Centre at the University of Sussex. Barrow directs Cambridge University's Millennium Mathematics Project, which focuses on increasing the teaching, learning, and appreciation of mathematics and its applications amongst students of all ages and the general public. He holds a DPhil in astrophysics from the University of Oxford and five honorary doctorates. One of Britain's leading public intellectuals, Barrow has received numerous international prizes. He is a Fellow of the Royal Society and of the Academia Europaea. He is the author of more than 500 research articles in cosmology and theoretical physics, and over twenty acclaimed books, including *The Anthropic Cosmological Principle, The Constants of Nature, The Book of Nothing,* and *The Book of Universes,* along with many reviews, web articles, and op-eds about science and mathematics. Barrow also wrote the play *Infinities,* which was premiered at the Piccolo Teatro, Milan, directed by Luca Ronconi, and which received the Italian Premi Ubu award for best play in the Italian theater in 2002 and the 2003 Italgas Prize for contributions to Italian culture. He delivered a series of centenary Gifford Lectures at Glasgow University in 1989 and received the 2006 Templeton Prize. He has lectured around the world at many prestigious venues including, 10 Downing Street, Windsor Castle, and the Vatican Palace.

Reinhold Bernhardt is professor of systematic theology at the University of Basel in Switzerland, holding the chair formerly occupied by Karl Barth. From 2006 to 2008, he served as dean of the Faculty of Theology. He is coeditor of the quarterly journal *Theologische*

Zeitschrift, an interdisciplinary and multilingual publication promoting cross-disciplinary theological dialogue. Bernhardt earned his PhD from the University of Heidelberg in 1990 with a dissertation titled "Der Absolutheitsanspruch des Christentums: Von der Aufklärung bis zur Pluralistischen Religionstheologie" (The absoluteness of Christianity: From the Enlightenment to the pluralistic theology of religions.) Bernhardt has written four books: *Was heißt "Handeln Gottes"? Eine Rekonstruktion der Lehre von der Vorsehung Gottes* (On divine action: A reconstruction of the doctrine of God's providence); *Wahrheit in Offenheit. Der christliche Glaube und die Religionen* (Truth in openness: The Christian faith and the religions); *Ende des Dialogs? Die Begegnung der Religionen und ihre theologische Reflexion* (End of dialogue? The encounter between religions and their theological reflection); and *Christianity without Absolutes.* Bernhardt has also edited ten anthologies, and written more than eighty articles for books or encyclopedias and more than fifty articles for scholarly journals.

James Bradley taught mathematics and computer science at Calvin College, Michigan, from 1986 to 2005 and served as Calvin's director of assessment and institutional research from 2005 to 2007. His work explores the relationship between randomness and probability, challenging the common perception that there is no purpose in the world because biology and physics show that reality is random. From 2000 to 2001, Bradley served as a William C. Foster fellow with the United States Department of State, consulting on the problems of arms control and missile defense. Long a leader in Christian explorations of the nature of mathematics, he is the coauthor of *Mathematics through the Eyes of Faith* and coeditor of *Mathematics in a Postmodern Age: A Christian Perspective.*

John Hedley Brooke is an Emeritus Fellow of Oxford's Harris Manchester College and a Distinguished Foundation Fellow at the University of Durham's Institute of Advanced Study. From 1999 to 2006, Brooke held the Andreas Idreos Professorship of Science and Religion and the directorship of the Ian Ramsey Centre at Oxford University. He has served as editor of the *British Journal for the History of Science,* as president of the British Society for the History of Science, and as president of the Historical Section of the British Association for the Advancement of Science. With Geoffrey Cantor, he delivered the 1995 Gifford Lectures at Glasgow University. He is currently Visiting

Professor at the University of Leeds. His books include the acclaimed and influential *Science and Religion: Some Historical Perspectives, Thinking about Matter: Studies in the History of Chemical Philosophy,* and (with Geoffrey Cantor) *Reconstructing Nature: The Engagement of Science and Religion.* More recently, he coedited (with Ronald Numbers) *Science and Religion around the World.* He contributed to *The Oxford Handbook of Natural Theology* and *Evolution, Games, and God.* He has written many articles, both scholarly and popular, and contributed to many edited volumes. Brooke is president of the Science and Religion Forum and recently served as president of the International Society for Science and Religion.

Oliver D. Crisp is professor of systemic theology at Fuller Theological Seminary. He is the author of eight books, and the editor or coeditor of another nine volumes. His most recent monograph is *Deviant Calvinism: Broadening Reformed Theology.* Crisp has published articles in professional journals such as *Religious Studies,* the *Journal of Theological Studies, International Journal for Systematic Theology,* and the *Journal of the American Academy of Religion.* He co-organizes the annual Los Angeles Theology Conference with Fred Sanders, is a founding editor of the *Journal of Analytic Theology,* and coedits the *Oxford Studies in Analytic Theology* series with Michael Rea.

Karl W. Giberson is Scholar-in-Residence at Stonehill College, where he also directs the Center for Science and Religion. He holds a PhD in Physics from Rice University. He has written or coauthored ten books, including *Oracles of Science: Celebrity Scientists Versus God and Religion*—which was translated into Italian, Spanish, and Romanian—and *Saving Darwin: How to Be a Christian and Believe in Evolution,* which the *Washington Post* called "one of the best books of 2008." His latest book is *Saving the Original Sinner: How Christians Have Used the Bible's First Man to Oppress, Inspire, and Make Sense of the World.* Giberson has published hundreds of reviews and essays in outlets that include the *New York Times, CNN.com, The Guardian, USA Today, LA Times, Salon.com, Discover,* the *Weekly Standard, Quarterly Review of Biology, Perspectives on Science and Christian Faith,* and *Books & Culture.* Giberson was the founding editor of *Science and Theology News,* editor-in-chief of *Science and Spirit* magazine from 2003 to 2006, and vice-president/president of the BioLogos Foundation from 2008 to 2010. From 2007 to 2009, he was the program director for the Venice Summer School on Science and Religion.

Byung Soo (Paul) Han is an assistant professor of systematic theology at the Asia Center for Theological Studies and Mission, and the director of the Institute for Reformed Theology in South Korea. He is also teaching in Central Reformed Theological Seminar during summer and winter breaks. He holds a PhD from Calvin Theological Seminary in historical theology focused on Reformation and Post-Reformation Reformed theology. Dr. Han has published four books, *Reformed Orthodox Theology: Prolegomena*, *Mirroring: Theological Meditation of Scripture*, *Symphonia Catholica: The Merger of Patristic and Contemporary Sources in the Theological Method of Amandus Polanus (1561–1610)*, and *Meditation: The Dignity of the Saints*. In addition, he has published three Korean translations of theological texts: Richard A. Muller's *After Calvin*, Willem van Asselt, Maarten Wisse, T. Theo J. Pleizier, and Pieter L. Rouwendal's *Introduction to Reformed Scholasticism*, and Willem van Asselt and Eef Dekker's *Reformation and Scholasticism*. He is translating Francis Turretin's *Institutio elencticae theologiae*, volume 1, into Korean.

Peter Harrison is an Australian Laureate Fellow and Director of the Institute for Advanced Studies in the Humanities at the University of Queensland, Australia. Previously, Harrison was the Andreas Idreos Professor of Science and Religion and Director of the Ian Ramsey Centre at the University of Oxford. He holds a PhD from the University of Queensland and a DLitt from Oxford, and he is a senior research fellow at Oxford's Ian Ramsey Centre. Harrison is the author or editor of six books. His first book, *"Religion" and the Religions in the English Enlightenment*, traces the roots of the discipline of comparative religion back to the Enlightenment. *The Bible, Protestantism, and the Rise of Natural Science* establishes a link between the rise of modern science and the Protestant approach to interpreting texts. *The Fall of Man and the Foundations of Science* demonstrates the religious underpinnings of scientific knowledge and inquiry. His newest book is *The Territories of Science and Religion*.

Jennifer Michael Hecht is a poet, philosopher, historian, and commentator. She is the author of many books, including the bestseller *Doubt: A History*, *Stay: A History of Suicide and the Philosophies Against It*, *The Happiness Myth*, ***The End of the Soul: Scientific Modernity, Atheism, and Anthropology in France***, and *The End of the Soul: Scientific Modernity, Atheism, and Anthropology*, which won Phi Beta Kappa's 2004 Ralph Waldo Emerson Award "For scholarly studies that contribute significantly to interpretations of the intellectual and cultural condition of humanity." Her first book of poetry, *The Next Ancient World,* won three national awards, including the Poetry Society of America's First Book award for 2001. Her latest poetry book, called *Who Said,* was published in November 2013. Hecht holds a PhD in the history of science and European cultural history from Columbia University (1995) and has taught in the MFA program at Columbia University and the New School in New York City. Hecht has also published in many peer-reviewed journals, and has delivered lectures at Harvard, Yale, MIT, Cal Tech, and Columbia University, as well as the Zen Mountain Monastery, Temple Israel, Saint Bart's Episcopal Church, and other institutions of learning. Hecht has been featured on many radio programs, served as one of the five nonfiction judges for the National Book Award in 2010. She is a member of the New York Institute for the Humanities.

Shaun Henson researches and teaches in Oxford University's Faculty of Theology and Religion. His interests are at the intersections of science, philosophy, and religion, teaching in areas like science and religion and Christian doctrine. Henson has recently collaborated on an international research project based at the London School of Economics, investigating God's Order, Man's Order, and the Order of Nature. A Church of England priest, he serves as Chaplain to St. Hugh's College, Oxford. His recent book is *God and Natural Order: Physics, Philosophy, and Theology.*

Alister E. McGrath holds the Andreas Idreos Chair of Science and Religion at Oxford University. He is the author of dozens of popular-level books, including *The Twilight of Atheism, The Dawkins Delusion?,* and *Why God Won't Go Away.* He recently published *C. S. Lewis: A Life,* a biography and collection of essays marking the fiftieth anniversary of Lewis's death. Like Lewis, McGrath began his academic career as an atheist before becoming a Christian apologist; McGrath earned a doctorate in molecular biophysics from Oxford in 1978 and a doctorate in divinity from Oxford in 2001. McGrath has written well over a hundred books and many academic texts, including *Christian Theology: An Introduction,* which has become one of the world's leading theological textbooks. In 2009, McGrath delivered the Gifford Lectures, titled "A Fine-Tuned Universe? Natural Theology and Anthropic Phenomena." McGrath is a Senior Research Fellow at Oxford's Harris Manchester College, a founding member of the International Society for Science and Religion, and a fellow of the Royal Society for the encouragement of Arts, Manufactures and Commerce.

Richard W. Miller is associate professor and director of the MA in Theology program at Creighton University. His research interests include reconciling the Christian doctrine of providence with evil and human suffering, God as Mystery, the implications of the doctrine of the Trinity for ontology, the thought of Karl Rahner and Thomas Aquinas as resources for contemporary theology, the moral implications of human-induced climate change, and the mission of Catholic Universities in light of the climate crisis. Miller has published in journals such as the *Heythrop Journal, New Blackfriars,* and the *Journal for Peace and Justice Studies.* He is a contributor to or editor of seven books, including *Suffering and the Christian Life, Women through the Ages: Women and the Shaping of Catholicism, Spirituality for the 21st Century: Experiencing God in the Catholic Tradition,* and *Lay Ministry in the Catholic Church: Visioning Church Ministry through the Wisdom of the Past.* Miller's edited volume *God, Creation, and Climate Change: A Catholic Response to the Environmental Crisis* received second place in the Faith and Science category for the 2011 book awards of the Catholic Press Association.

Sarah Ruden is a journalist, poet, translator, and writer on religion and culture. She was awarded a Guggenheim Fellowship in 2010 to translate Aeschylus's *Oresteia,* and she has also published translations of the *Homeric Hymns,* Virgil's *Aeneid,* and Aristophanes's *Lysistrata* and Apuleius's *Golden Ass.* She is currently working on a translation of Augustine's *Confessions.* In addition to translating, Ruden writes about religion: her book *Paul among the People: The Apostle Reinterpreted and Re-imagined in His Own Time,* contrasts Paul's egalitarian vision with contemporaneous Greek and Roman literature; and she is completing *The Voice, the Harp, the Book: A Translator on Beauty and Meaning in the Bible.* In 1996, she received South Africa's then-leading book prize, the Central News Agency Literary Award, for her collection of poems entitled *Other Places.* Sarah Ruden earned a PhD in classical philology from Harvard University, after which she spent ten years teaching, translating, and writing in South Africa. Her work there shed light on the role churches played and could play in alleviating post-apartheid problems.

Mustafa Ruzgar is an associate professor of religion at California State University, Northridge. Born in Turkey, he completed his BA in Islamic Studies at Uludag University in Bursa, Turkey. He received his PhD in Philosophy of Religion and Theology at Claremont Graduate University in 2008. Ruzgar's research interests and publications include themes in Islamic thought, contemporary philosophy of religion and theology, process philosophy and theology, religious pluralism, and interfaith dialogue. Ruzgar's most recent article, "An Islamic Perspective: Theological Development and the Problem of Evil," is published in *Religions in the Making: Whitehead and the Wisdom Traditions of the World*, edited by John B. Cobb Jr.

Michael Ruse is the Lucyle T. Werkmeister Professor of Philosophy and the Director of the History and Philosophy of Science Program at the University of Florida. Ruse has written numerous books, including *The Darwinian Revolution: Science Red in Tooth and Claw, Monad to Man: The Concept of Progress in Evolutionary Biology*, and *Can a Darwinian Be a Christian? The Relationship between Science and Religion*. Ruse specializes in the relationship between science and religion, emphasizing the creation versus evolution controversy and the problem of defining the boundaries of science. He frequently writes for widely read publications such as *The Guardian* and the *Huffington Post*. Ruse describes himself as an agnostic, claiming that both "new atheism" and "humanism" fail to represent his views. Ruse formerly taught at the University of Guelph in Ontario, Canada, for thirty-five years. He was a key witness in the 1981 trial of *McLean v. Arkansas*, which determined whether the Arkansas school system had the right to mandate the teaching of "creation science." In 1986, he was elected as a Fellow of both the Royal Society of Canada and the American Association for the Advancement of Science. Ruse holds honorary doctorates from four institutions: University of Bergen (1990), McMaster University (2003), the University of New Brunswick (2007), and University College London (2014).

Ignacio Silva is a Research Fellow at the Ian Ramsey Centre for Science and Religion and Harris Manchester College at the University of Oxford. He received his DPhil from Oxford for his work on divine action. Silva is a codirector of "Science, Philosophy and Theology in Latin America," a three-year research project at the Ian Ramsey Centre that aims to promote and document inquiry on science and religion in that region. Silva has written two books, *Saint Thomas Aquinas: On the Unity of the Intellect against Averroists* and *Indeterminism in Nature and Quantum Mechanics: Werner Heisenberg and Thomas Aquinas*. Silva is also coeditor of the series "International Perspectives on Science, Culture and Society" at Pickering and Chatto publishers. Silva has written several scholarly essays, including: "Revisiting Aquinas on Providence and Rising to the Challenge of

Divine Action in Nature" and "Thomas Aquinas Holds Fast: Objections to Aquinas within Today's Debate on Divine Action," which explore Aquinas's account of divine action and analyze the arguments for and against it; and "John Polkinghorne on Divine Action: A Coherent Theological Evolution" and "Great Minds Think (Almost) Alike: Thomas Aquinas and Alvin Plantinga on Divine Action in Nature."

PART 1

The Challenge of Chance

I

Chance, Divine Action, and the Natural Order of Things

Karl W. Giberson

THE HEARTBREAKING, INSPIRING, and deeply provocative story of Job in the Hebrew scriptures is beloved in the Western literary tradition. Google the phrase "a modern-day Job" and you get more than 50,000 hits, most of them referring to someone enduring an inexplicable and unfair series of personal struggles. When the *New York Times* reviewed the recent Russian drama *Leviathan*, they described the lead character, a middle-aged mechanic living in northern Russia, as a "modern-day Job," afflicted with "miseries" and "agonies" not of his own making.[1]

The original Job was a powerful, rich, fortunate man, blessed with ten children, many servants, and thousands of farm animals. He was the "richest man among all the peoples of the East," living in a time when good fortune was the natural consequence of personal righteousness.

Job's happy world came inexplicably crashing down one day as a series of messengers arrived one after the other, alerting the great and righteous man that his "servants were put to the sword"; that "lightning has fallen from heaven and has completely burned up the sheep"; that enemies had "raided the camels and drove them away"; and even that his children were killed while dining at the oldest son's house, when "a great wind came from across the wilderness, struck the four corners of the house, and it fell upon the young men and killed them." Eventually Job's troubles included being afflicted with leprosy "from the sole of his foot to the crown of his head." It was so terrible that he sat in ashes and "took a piece of broken pottery with which to scrape himself."

Job's tale has generated a vast literature exploring the meaning of the story and the lessons to be drawn from it. And not all interpreters read the story in the same way. But they all agree that the story raises deep questions about divine providence—the traditional and enduring belief that God works in the world according to some plan, the details of which may or may not be discernable to us. Certainly the disasters that befell the hapless Job fit no pattern of divine justice that he—or anyone but Satan, who caused them—could imagine. In the worldview of the ancient Hebrews, God blessed righteous men like Job with land, livestock, and healthy children. That was the providential order that God had set up. The wind that God sometimes caused to blow was not supposed to collapse the house over the heads of the righteous man's children.

The monotheistic traditions have long wrestled with the meaning of such apparently random events. In the story of Job, we have a proposed rationale for the disasters: God's taunting of Satan—actually "the Satan"—led to a sort of divine wager between them about how long Job's faith would last in the absence of rewards for righteousness and in the midst of great suffering. This "rationale" is not entirely satisfying, of course, and some scholars reject it outright. Jennifer Michael Hecht, whom we will meet in the pages to follow (chapter 2), argues that the Job story is a skeptical, even subversive, pushback on the ancient Hebrew theme that the world has a providential, moral trajectory that rewards the righteous.[2]

The story ends with Job admitting that "I have uttered what I did not understand, things too wonderful for me, which I did not know. . . . I have heard of You by the hearing of the ear, but now my eye sees You. Therefore I abhor myself, and repent in dust and ashes." The lesson is clear but seems forced and unsatisfactory, as anyone who has experienced the death of a child will attest.

The book of Job is the oldest book in the Hebrew scriptures, written before Genesis. It introduces our first sustained encounter between sovereign monotheism and the problem of evil. This tension—how can there be evil, or even randomness with uncertain consequences, if God is all-powerful?—remains unresolved, at least as a purely rational inquiry. The theme is not developed in the Hebrew scriptures, which are animated more by a powerful sense of moral order in which righteousness is consistently rewarded and disaster selectively falls on those who reject God's will.

The specifically Christian response to this early version of the problem of evil was the Incarnation. Sarah Ruden calls our attention to St. Paul's theological claim that God's incarnation in Christ renders the travails of this world irrelevant by guaranteeing eternal life to believers (chapter 5). Christians are admonished to endure in the face of hardship—even martyrdom—taking solace in the assurance that the Christ who suffered for them now suffers with them, but only for a moment. Even Job's suffering fades into insignificance in the light of Christ's provision of eternal bliss for the faithful. This is a satisfying argument for some, but questions remain about the details of the moral order and the degree to which it exhibits a rational, philosophically satisfactory pattern.

Intuitive and undeveloped ancient notions of divine sovereignty and the natural order were refined in the first centuries of the Christian tradition, as the Church Fathers developed their understanding of the Christian worldview. Thinkers like Augustine, influenced by their time and place, articulated Christianity within a Greco-Roman context, rather than a Jewish one. Well-developed pagan notions of chance, fate, providence, and divine action raised questions about a world created and ruled by a sovereign God. In a world ruled by the idiosyncratic, anthropomorphic, and all-too-finite gods of the Greeks and Romans, chance events posed no real threat to the divine "order," such as it was. But once those gods gave way to Judeo-Christian monotheism, genuine chance events posed problems. Surely there could not be *genuinely* chance events that God did not foresee. How can God be in full control if the natural order occasionally tosses up surprises? Theologian Richard Miller notes that Augustine's resolution of these ambiguities in a largely platonic context so diminished—and perhaps eliminated—genuine chance from the world that Christianity was critiqued for creating a new form of determinism (chapter 7). Indeed, the deterministic Calvinism that would develop centuries later drew heavily on such ideas from Augustine. Along another track, mathematician James Bradley argues that an Augustinian "Christian Platonism" allows us to locate random numbers in the mind of God, a move that creates space for God's providential control of events that, from a human perspective, have no apparent order (chapter 4).

During the High Middle Ages, Thomas Aquinas sought to reconcile the inherited Christian understanding with the newly encountered and more "scientific" Arab Aristotelian tradition. His far-reaching and influential resolution divided the causality of the natural world into primary and secondary versions. God's direct actions, like the creation of the world or specific miracles, were examples of *primary* causes in action, but the world, with its seasons and daily cycles, ran largely by *secondary* causes that, although created and sustained by God, had some autonomy. Because secondary causes were finite and contingent, their actions were not always entirely successful in accomplishing what they were created to do, and in these limited "failures" of secondary causes Aquinas opens space for natural events that do not unfold in entirely predictable ways. There may be, as Ignacio Silva argues (chapter 8), randomness or at least unpredictability in the world when finite and imperfect causes fail to produce their intended effects.

In opening the world to the actions of secondary causes, Aquinas created space for the investigation of those causes on their own terms. Initially referred to as *natural philosophy*, the investigation of nature's secondary causes is now called *science*. And, as we know, the investigation of randomness in the world has been a primary focus of science in the past century.

The scientific revolution inaugurated the first sustained exploration of the nature of secondary causes. The result, as John Hedley Brooke shows (chapter 11), was the famous clockwork universe of Isaac Newton. This picture of the world was so deterministic, with seemingly no room for genuine novelty, that many were inclined to restrict God's action to creation, asking if it was even possible for God to intervene in the course of human affairs with an unexpected miracle. This deism (a theology that affirmed God created the universe but does not—or perhaps cannot—influence it) that flourished in the so-called Enlightenment challenged Christianity in many ways, largely by rendering miracles problematic. On the other hand, the elegant design of the universe and its many creatures laid the foundation for a robust natural theology in which God's wisdom and providence could be seen in the wonders of creation. Newton famously saw grandeur in the elegant design of the solar system "which could only proceed from the counsel and dominion of an intelligent and powerful Being." Alister McGrath recounts the influential story of William Paley (chapter 12), who saw grandeur in the design of living organisms, a compelling view of the world he laid out in his book *Natural Theology* that deeply influenced the young Charles Darwin. The worlds of Newton and Paley, separated by over a century, were ones in which God's providential care was clearly visible in the *created* order but ambiguously present in human affairs, discernable only with the "eye of faith."

All this changed with the publication of Charles Darwin's subversive blockbuster *The Origin of Species*. The solid pillars on which natural theology had been resting for centuries began to crumble. The grandeur of living organisms, said Darwin, was not the result of intelligent and providential design but rather the conclusion of a messy process he called natural selection—a process with random chance at its heart. Furthermore, living organisms were not uniformly grand, and there were many features of the natural world that seemed rather dreadful to Darwin, like the way that the Ichneumonidae wasps laid their eggs inside caterpillars or how cats played with mice en route to killing them. "I cannot persuade myself," Darwin wrote to his friend Asa Gray in May of 1860, a year after his book was published, "that a beneficent & omnipotent God would have designedly created Ichneumonidæ with the express intention of their feeding within the living bodies of caterpillars, or that a cat should play with mice."[3]

The various issues surrounding divine providence developed gradually, however. Darwin, as we know, knew nothing of genes and mutations, and his claim that the novel features of organisms on which natural selection operated appeared randomly was little more than inspired speculation. As a result, it was decades before Darwinian randomness was widely accepted. The immediate response to *The Origin of Species* was to accept its claims about the common ancestry of all living things, but import non-Darwinian, teleological mechanisms to drive the process of change. Such strategies, of course, mitigated theological concerns.

The transformation wrought by Darwin's generation of naturalists was subtler than it appears, as historian Peter Harrison articulates in a remarkable chapter in this volume (chapter 13). The issue for Christian notions of divine action and providence was the relocation of the study of living things—including humans—from the realm of *observational science*, where providence seemed readily discernable in nature's marvelous contrivances, to the realm of *history*, where it could be seen only through the "eye of faith," as poor Job knew only too well. By making "natural history" genuinely historical, and populating that history with chance events operated on by a blind, pitiless, and often cruel process of natural selection, Darwin created a challenge to the Christian understanding of divine creation that remains unmet to this day. Evolution's dependence on randomness makes it all but impossible to see how God might be guiding the process, and Christians who have tried to articulate a viable theistic evolution—including me—have been frustrated in their efforts to find a plausible way to embed God's providential involvement in natural history. Philosopher Michael Ruse argues quite simply that it cannot be done (chapter 15).

Leading antievolutionist Ken Ham, in his writings and widely publicized 2014 debate with Bill Nye, explicitly retains the pre-Darwinian notion that the study of history—even natural history—is not scientific and thus outside the realm of empirical investigation. Ham's position, shared by most antievolutionists, is that one sees what one expects to see in history.

Sir John Herschel was one of Darwin's fiercest nineteenth-century critics, lampooning natural selection as the "law of higgledy-piggledy" for its reliance on chance. The exact character of Darwinian "chance," however, was not clear, nor did it need to be for his theory of evolution to work. The "chance" element in mutations, for example, refers only to the fact that mutations appear without regard for their value to the organism. A species of bird that would benefit from better eyesight is just as likely to have mutations producing longer beaks, and vice versa. The mutations could be completely nonrandom, in the sense that they were produced by deterministic processes, but they would appear random because they bore no relationship to the evolutionary needs of the organisms in which they appeared.

"Chance" and "randomness," in our long conversation about the nature of the world and God's role in it, have always been slippery concepts, understood in very different ways. Often used interchangeably, they typically refer to dramatic things that happened by "surprise," outside the normal course of events, like getting killed by a stray bullet or—as many experienced this year (2015) in New England—having one's roof collapse under the weight of repeated snowfalls. But they also refer to normal things that are unpredictable, like landing on Boardwalk in Monopoly, seeing an old friend at Disney World, or winning a lottery. But this simple perspective leaves important questions unanswered. Job was *surprised*, for example, that the wind collapsed the roof of the house where his children were having dinner and killed them. Likewise, we are surprised when we roll snake eyes several times in a row in a game of dice. And, if the dinosaurs had been capable, they would have been surprised at the comet that hit the earth seventy million years ago and drove them to extinction.

Such events, however, are only random in the sense that we cannot predict their outcomes. The carnage created by a vigorous wind is not predictable. Why was this house damaged rather than that one? Why was that tree left standing while those ones were toppled? But nobody doubts that the wind follows the laws of physics and, if we could know the situation more completely, we could predict many of the outcomes and the apparent randomness would disappear or at least be greatly diminished. The same is true for dice. We can easily imagine a high-tech programmable "dice-rolling machine" that, perhaps working in a vacuum, could roll dice predictably. The apparent random character of these examples derives entirely from our lack of knowledge of the relevant details. We don't know whether this or that unpredictable event is genuinely random; we only know that is how it appears to us. Most physicists would say that the roll of the dice is not random, but the movement of the electron is.

The apparent randomness in nature has often been connected to a divine plan that we cannot discern. It could be the case that some supernatural action, hidden from us, determines the outcome of what appear to be "chance" events. We encounter this in Job, for example, where inscrutable calamities are assumed to be a part of some pattern we cannot discern. Job has no knowledge that God and Satan are playing a game with his life. We find in antiquity and even today chance being used as the "mouthpiece of the gods." Biblical characters "cast lots" to divine God's will. Leading cosmologist John D. Barrow suggests that viewing chance as divine communication may be the reason it took so long for the theory of probability to emerge (chapter 3). It would be presumptuous and perhaps blasphemous to develop a "theory" about chance if chance was the way the gods communicated their will.

Chance and randomness moved to the center of the scientific radar in the early twentieth century. Physicists—with much wailing and gnashing of teeth—became convinced that electrons moved in *genuinely* random ways and not merely under the influence of complex hidden causes, like Saturn's irregular orbit being tweaked by the passing of Uranus before it was discovered. If real, the random behavior of electrons suggested a radically new world picture, one that became enshrined in the strange new theory of quantum mechanics. Physicists were understandably reluctant to abandon the traditional, largely Newtonian, view that everything in nature followed laws of some sort. Einstein, although he helped develop the quantum picture of the world, never accepted that the randomness disclosed by the theory was real. "God does not throw dice," he insisted, which was his way of objecting to the arrival of Herschel's "higgledy-piggledy" in his beloved and orderly field of physics.

In one of the most significant intellectual revolutions of all time, physicists established to their own shock and satisfaction that the randomness of quantum theory was indeed genuine. Quantum events, like the movement of an electron from one orbit to another within the atom or the passage of an electron through a barrier with multiple openings, were genuinely unpredictable—not because, as was the case with rolling dice or the wandering of Saturn, we don't know all the relevant information, but because the electron actually behaves in genuinely random ways. Two identical electrons in identical circumstances will do two completely different things. The same electron, returned to an earlier situation with the same options, will choose a different path than before, as if the electron had free will.

The quantum revolution was profound and wide-ranging because every physical object in the universe was composed of elementary particles ruled by the laws of quantum theory. This mysterious randomness permeates everything and is invisible only because the countless tiny quantum events average out, like the departure times of commuters that, although chosen freely each day, lead predictably to rush hours.

No topic in science has received the scrutiny and philosophical interrogation of quantum randomness. I can think of no better way to summarize the significance of this issue than to highlight an exchange between Robert Wright, one of America's leading nonfiction writers and passionate defender of the reality of transcendent purpose, and Daniel Dennett, probably America's leading philosopher, who rejects the transcendent. In a wide-ranging conversation, Dennett agreed with Wright's statement: "Events happen for which there is no cause in the physical universe." The "choice" made by an electron when it "randomly" moves to location A rather than B is indeterminate. This provocative claim implies that the unfolding course of nature, construed broadly, does not occur in a closed system of cause and effect. The universe has a decidedly unclocklike openness, with the future not fully embedded in the present.[4] But open to what?

The open, indeterministic character of the universe has provoked considerable discussion about divine providence in a world where the future is not merely the extension of the present. This understanding stands in dramatic contrast to the clockwork universe of the Newtonians, which created conceptual challenges for divine action. It was difficult to see, in a tightly constrained system of cause and effect, how God could act in the universe in ways that would not be disruptive and highly visible. One response to this concern was the deism discussed above. If the universe is "open," however, because of its quantum character, then perhaps God can still be an agent within that universe by influencing quantum events but not breaking the laws of physics. This, of course, is highly speculative, but it creates conceptual space for divine providence within a universe understood scientifically.

The greatest question about divine providence, however, is not whether it occurs within the causally open world of our quantum reality. That complicated question, as important as it may be, is for armchair philosophers. The greatest question is still the one with which Job wrestled: Is there such a thing as divine providence or do we live in a world indifferent to human suffering? Why do events that should have no meaning—a wind blowing on the house where our children are happily seated around the dinner table—produce the most tragic consequences? This volume closes with some reflections on the nature of tragedy by leading German theologian Reinhold Bernhardt (chapter 16).

Surveying the monotheistic traditions on any topic is a daunting task that would require several volumes. A single volume on "Randomness and Divine Providence" necessarily requires an aggressive selection process that inevitably excludes many thoughtful voices and valuable perspectives. In assembling the roster of contributors for the present volume, I tried to cover the important bases so that readers will get as comprehensive a picture of the topic as was reasonable, but still be mindful that there were aspects left out.

A Word about this Volume

The contributors to this volume are largely but not exclusively drawn from the Christian tradition, which is consistent with how this conversation is playing out in the English-speaking world. The traditions of the contributors also reflect the theological overlap between Christianity, Judaism, and Islam. This is not to say, however, that all of them write as religious believers. Nevertheless, there are voices I sought to include but that were not available for various reasons; both science and theology remain disappointingly male-dominated. And I came up dry seeking a scholar from outside the monotheistic traditions to give an overview of some of the other ways that religious traditions have addressed these questions.

These concerns notwithstanding, the present volume has an outstanding roster of contributors. Among the authors are six Gifford lecturers, two Templeton Prize-winners, a *New York Times* bestselling author, and all three of the scholars who have held Oxford University's prestigious Andreas Idreos Chair in Science and Religion.

All but three of the papers in this volume were presented in November 2014 at a conference at Stonehill College, Easton, Massachusetts, where I am a faculty member.

Acknowledgments

I want to thank my friend Jim Bradley, professor emeritus of mathematics at Calvin College, for encouraging me to get involved in this project and for helping shape both the proposal that supported it and the project itself. My colleague and confidant at Stonehill College, John Lanci, provided encouragement and advice on this project from beginning to end. Marie Kelly and Bonnie Troupe helped manage the details of the grant that supported the project. And I want to especially thank Stephanie DesRossiers, who managed the budget, using her sharp eye to keep everything under control.

Emily R. Herrington provided general editorial assistance. Her input can be seen on almost every page of this volume. Carol Ruppel copyedited the final versions of the chapters. My student assistant, Olivia Peterson, worked tirelessly on formatting footnotes, bibliographies, and just about anything else that was in editorial disarray. I want to thank my former student Carissa Schutz who, from atop the mountains in Mongolia where she is teaching English, created the index for the book.

This project reunited me with Cynthia Read, the editor for my earlier book, *The Oracles of Science*. It was a pleasure to work with her again. I would also like to extend a special thanks to Alphonsa James, who oversaw production, including copy editing, with a meticulous eye for detail. And thanks to Glenn Ramirez who kept the project moving from its rather chaotic beginning with a complex roster of contributors from around the world.

I especially want to thank the John Templeton Foundation for providing financial support for so many engaging projects in science and religion, including this one.

I am also grateful to Stonehill College, especially Provost Joe Favazza and Dean Maria Curtin, for supporting me in this project.

And finally, I want to dedicate this book to my students at Stonehill, whose curiosity, enthusiasm, and passion for service fill my professional life with so much meaning.

Notes

1. Manohla Dargis, "Life: Poor, Nasty, Brutish and (Probably) Short: 'Leviathan' Turns on a Modern-Day Job," *New York Times*, December 24, 2014, http://www.nytimes.com/2014/12/25/movies/leviathan-turns-on-a-modern-day-job.html.
2. See, for example, Jennifer Michael Hecht. *Doubt: A History* (San Francisco: HarperOne, 2003), 62–74.
3. Charles Darwin to Asa Gray, May 22, [1860], Darwin Correspondence Project, Letter 2814, http://www.darwinproject.ac.uk/letter/entry-2814.
4. Robin Wright interviews Daniel Dennett, https://www.youtube.com/watch?v=SsoaCWpNzSM.

2

Ancient Hebraic Voices of Chance and Choice over Fate and Justice

Jennifer Michael Hecht

THE ANCIENT JEWS stand out, to us and to their contemporaries, as having given the world a new conception of fairness. Those cultures that first noted this Hebraic idea surely each had their own sense that being good led to success and good luck, because a common version of success—being comfortable and loved—correlates well with a common version of good behavior: hard work, honest dealing, and generosity to the weak. And as with various other religions, the performance of piety was also correlated with success, such that people paid the gods in praise, trial, or sacrifice, to win special favor. What was new with the ancient Hebrews was the centrality of the idea that you could also please the heavens by being morally good.

In this world, for a man to be morally good begins with being a hard worker and being "upright." Upright means what it sounds like: you're not a falling-down drunk, you are honest and loyal in business, and you are a responsible family man. As many have noted, people are comfortable doing business with an upright man. The English political philosopher Thomas Hobbes said it most memorably. Without government, "the life of man, solitary, poore, nasty, brutish, and short."[1] For Hobbes that government must have a monopoly on the use of force, because if no one possesses the power to keep all the rest "in awe," there would be a "condition which is called Warre . . . of every man, against every man."[2] But when a society has no such structure, a commitment to being upright can also create trust and produce the life-sweetening riches of abundance, leisure, and culture.

Three other key virtues, beyond being upright, are being a good host, taking care of widows and orphans, and fearing God. Being a good host was especially important because in a world without hotels, or even roads, one could hope for safe traveling only if everyone was expected to be a generous—or at least benign—host. It would have been socially horrific for a host to kill a visitor, or even let him go hungry. Care of widows and orphans is also about sacrificing one's own goods or comfort to benefit the community. If men who have resources take care of widows and orphans, all can rest more easily about the future of their own families and their community. Again, in the short run, or individually, this may not correlate with all definitions of success (it costs time and money to feed orphans), but if a whole community takes up these values the result is likely to correlate with broad definitions of success. It is worth noting that the most consistently explicit notion of success or good luck is that the person has a lot of children. Other markers of success are land ownership, good harvests, cattle that are healthy and breed well, having a voice of authority in the community, and long life.

Would the world seem fair to members of a culture following these biblical rules? Perhaps so. Since the biblical ideas of goodness discussed above are social virtues, being good is indeed likely to correlate with doing well. But there will be problems. Life, as we all know, can be unfair. We are going to meet the ancient Hebrew's morally sensible world through its two stunning protest texts: Job and Ecclesiastes.

Through personal stories and intellectual contemplation, these books challenge the idea of a fair world and of success being correlated with goodness and piety. They declare with the acerbity of grief that catastrophic bad luck makes nonsense of providence, or indeed of any sense of order or divine justice. Cheaters sometimes win over upright individuals. Some people are born rich, live selfishly, and die aged and comfortable in bed, while some who live lives of service are beset with random misfortune. Beyond the common problems with the idea of providence, personal luck, endemic disadvantages, and hard times, the author of the book of Job's great insight is that even one case of unfair suffering can give lie to whole system. In reference to Job, Martin Buber wrote of the "inner infinity of the suffering soul."[3]

Many people think of the Book of Job as a story of patience and faith being rewarded in the end by an equally faithful God, but that's because people often discuss only part of the story. Many scholars and writers have, instead, engaged with the book as a challenge to the idea of divine fairness.[4]

The preeminent German poet Heinrich Heine, writing on Job, said "This book is the Song of Songs of skepticism."[5] A hundred years later, in the early twentieth century, the scholar Morris Jastrow wrote plainly that "the entire book has been manipulated in the interest of conventional orthodoxy." He continued: "We must at the outset recognize that the Book of Job in its original form was a skeptical composition—skeptical in the sense of putting a question mark after the fundamental axiom in the teachings of the Hebrew prophets of the ninth and succeeding centuries, that the government of the universe rests on justice."[6] Nahum N. Glatzer's wonderful compilation *The Dimensions of Job* contains essays on this theme from Jewish, Christian, and humanist traditions.[7] Katharine J. Dell's *The Book of Job as Sceptical Literature* is perhaps the best contemporary source for these interpretations.[8] Another perspective is offered in my own book *Doubt: A History*.[9] Here we will take a close look at the story as it unfolds into these greater theological and philosophical questions.

Job

"There was a man in the land of Uz, whose name was Job; and that man was perfect and upright, and one that feared God, and eschewed evil. And there were born unto him seven sons and three daughters." That's how the book opens and I read it as one sentence: Job was honest, was not a fool, he was fearful of God, he stayed away from things he should not be doing—and he was rewarded with ten children. He also had thousands of sheep and camel, oxen and asses, and a very great household of servants and workers, such that he was "the greatest of all men of the east." When the story begins, Job's children are all grown and doing fine; we hear that the brothers send for their sisters to join them feasting and drinking wine. Job is happy and grateful, and when he gives his praise to God, we are told, he does it a few extra times to cover any possible stray unspoken blasphemy by one of his sons. Thus the book of Job pulls off one of the trickiest literary creations: a persuasive vision of a happy and rewarded life. Judaism had not yet posited an afterlife when this book was written, so this is the whole equation. Be good and you will have a pretty good life.

The scene now switches to an otherworldly counsel. "Now there was a day when the sons of God came to present themselves before the Lord, and Satan came also among them." It is a wonderfully strange little piece of theology. God asks Satan where he's been and Satan says he's been walking around Earth. God, who seems to have been anticipating that answer, asks if Satan got a look at Job, and wasn't he impressive? "Hast thou considered my servant Job, that there is none like him in the earth, a perfect and an upright man, one that feareth God, and escheweth evil?" Satan says that Job is only devoted to God because he has so much. God accepts the challenge casually, telling Satan to investigate Job's faithfulness under pressure. Don't physically hurt him, God cautions, but do whatever else you want.

In one of the most sublime of biblical passages, a messenger is sent to Job telling him that the Sabeans have slit the throats of his servants in the field and carried away his oxen and asses. "While he was yet speaking," another messenger arrives, and reports that fire has come down from the sky and burnt to death all of Job's shepherds and all his sheep. Another messenger arrives, and again while the last one has not yet finished speaking, tells Job that the Chaldeans have killed the remainder of his working hands and stolen all of his camels. Finally, while the last messenger is still speaking, yet another comes and says that a huge wind came in from the mountains and toppled the hall in which all Job's children were feasting together, and all are dead. Job tears his clothes, shaves his head, and on his knees declares, "The Lord gave, and the Lord hath taken away; blessed be the name of the Lord." This is not at all a claim that the Lord is just, but Job accepts the divine caprice. He is faithfulness itself.

The Job author switches scenes again to find God pleased with Job, but the devil is still unconvinced and teasing, "Skin for skin, yea, all that a man hath will he give for his life." He is asking God if he can torture Job physically. God agrees, but tells him not to kill him. The devil limits himself to Job's skin, but it is bad. He covers Job with "sore boils," putrid and stinking. This is the devil's last gesture in the Book of Job and in the Hebrew Bible.

As for Job, once you reek, things go downhill fast. From the highest height, Job is now a pariah in total misery. We hear not a word of protest from him. The Book of Job highlights the reality of suffering, of innocent suffering, such that it becomes difficult to make excuses for it. Is it possible to fit innocent anguish into a rational moral world while you are in its presence? Job's losses do not drive him into moral chaos. Job accepts the chaos or caprice that hurt him, and can cope with the disaster without rebellion. Everything changes when Job's friends attempt to make moral sense of his suffering.

The story now turns to its symposium, which begins when three of Job's prosperous, pious friends come to see him in his misery. When they set eyes on him they cannot believe it is the man they knew. In sympathy with his ruin, they rip their clothing and put ashes on their heads. For seven days and seven nights no one says a word. At last Job breaks the quiet, lilting out a stinging account of his grief. The poetry is famously up to the task. It is beautiful and insightful in its description of inner torment, but it also repeats itself in a way that at times is more liturgical than literary, perfect for the reader who is feeling anguish, and a bit repetitive for the more aesthetic observer. The great howl begins with his wish that the day he was born had never seen existence, or that he was murdered at birth like a "hidden untimely infant" who never sees light. It continues at that level of torment and despair.

Job's friends do not like to hear him speaking this way. They remind him of all the wisdom he has handed out to others over the years and ask him to now accept his loss. The first to speak, Eliphaz the Temanite, lays out for us the perspective of rational justice: "[W]ho ever perished, being innocent? or where were the righteous cut off? Even as I have seen, they that plow iniquity, and sow wickedness, reap the same. By the blast of God they perish, and by the breath of his nostrils are they consumed." It is not only that God accomplishes this rational moral world, it is also that virtue yields a better life: "For wrath killeth the foolish man, and envy slayeth the silly one. I have seen the foolish taking root: but suddenly . . . His children are far from safety, and they are crushed in the gate, neither is there any to deliver them." (Note the stakes here; either your children are welcomed into a good host's care or they are beaten to death by guards for approaching the gate.) Eliphaz also believes God gives hope to the poor and stops iniquity. God is so good, he concludes, that: "happy is the man that God correcteth."

This is perhaps not what you want to hear when you have just lost your children. Job knows his own innocence and goodness, and the true calamity of his own grief. He responds as a man shocked that these people think he is still living in their universe, with things like fairness and good. He furthers his description of the extent of his pain and his yearning for death. He seems to discover, as he speaks it, that he is daring to accuse God of cruelty. He is daring it, he says, because life is already impossibly shattered and since death ends everything, and he already yearns for death, what can God do? "As the cloud is consumed and vanisheth away: so he that goeth down to the grave shall come up no more." Job says he has nothing left to fear. "Therefore I will not refrain my mouth; I will speak in the anguish of my spirit; I will complain in the bitterness of my soul."

Job's fierce lament is varied and compelling. He rages at God for giving him terrifying dreams so he cannot even rest in sleep. What kind of cruel ironic mind could decide that even when unconscious we should be harried by nightmares? Job repeats as a refrain that he wishes he were dead. He accepts bad luck, but asks why his misery must follow him through the night and then meet him in the very moments he awakens. Why are grief and depression so relentless? Here is one of the only times Job seems to admit to having done anything wrong at all, and it is almost sarcastic. He is addressing God directly here:

> How long wilt thou not depart from me, nor let me alone till I swallow down my spittle? I have sinned; what shall I do unto thee, O thou preserver of men? why hast thou set me as a mark against thee, so that I am a burden to myself? And why dost thou not pardon my transgression, and take away mine iniquity? for now shall I sleep in the dust; and thou shalt seek me in the morning, but I shall not be.

Job is almost triumphant that he will at last escape God with death. Again, this issue of forgiveness is not typical of his concerns, he rarely suggests that he might have done anything needing pardon, but it brings up, for us, what will become a central Christian question, "Why doesn't God just forgive us and take us all to heaven?" It is not the central question here, because Job does not feel guilty in any way that matches what has happened to him. He does not want forgiveness, he is furious and somewhat beyond caring.

The next speaker, Bildad the Shuhite, cannot bear this nihilism. Job must somehow deserve his fate. "Doth God pervert judgment? or doth the Almighty pervert justice?" he rhetorically demands. We readers, of course, know that in Job's case, yes, without question, God perverts judgment and justice. Bildad also offers that Job's children may have sinned against God, and been cast away for it. He advises Job to supplicate God, to continue to try to trade on his good record. For him Job's punishment proves Job's crime: "If thou wert pure and upright; surely now he would awake for thee, and make the habitation of thy righteousness prosperous."

Again Job's response is to try to get his friend to realize how bad this really is. It is constant torture, he explains. It is not one day at a time, but one moment at a time: "He will not suffer me to take my breath." Still not directly addressing God, Job tells his friends what he will say unto God: "Thou knowest that I am not wicked . . . Remember, I beseech thee, that thou hast made me as the clay; and wilt thou bring me into dust again? Hast thou not poured me out as milk, and curdled me like cheese?" Here Job is adding the omniscience and omnipotence problem to the moral one: Shouldn't God know Job is good and give him what he deserves?

His listeners are stunned, and now the third friend, Zophar the Naamathite, voices his outrage: "Should thy lies make men hold their peace? and when thou mockest, shall no man make thee ashamed?" Zophar tells Job that God's secrets amount to double the knowledge that is possessed by humans. God is so far beyond them that, "Know therefore that God exacteth of thee less than thine iniquity deserveth." Not only does the punishment prove the crime, but God's reputed goodness proves that you deserved worse than you got. Job should just return to the fold and expect, eventually, to be made comfortable again.

Job too is outraged. He starts slow. He tells them they are all very wise, but that he too has understanding. Then he points out some of the cruelest aspects of life on Earth: He "taketh away the understanding of the aged." That is a keen observation. If we allow ourselves to think of the unfairness of the world, that one is glaring. "He increaseth the nations, and destroyeth them . . . He taketh away the heart of the chief of the people of the earth, and causeth them to wander in a wilderness where there is no way. They grope in the dark without light, and he maketh them to stagger like a drunken man." Job indicts the facts of life. What a strangely cruel catastrophe is aging as we humans do it, forgetting. How bizarre that a generation gets cut down in war, or lives without livelihood or hope. We stagger in pitch-dark ignorance, like drunks.

And he returns to descriptions of his misery. Again, the speech feels repetitive, but his words aim at an impossible task, to represent the ultimate in human anguish. Any theory of rational morality for the universe must seek to make suffering part of a fair ecosystem, yet the fact of real suffering can sometimes make these rationalizations seem obtuse and arrogant. Job shifts now to addressing God directly and asks for a confrontation: "[M]ake me to know my transgression and my sin. Wherefore hidest thou thy face, and holdest me for thine enemy? Wilt thou break a leaf driven to and fro?"

All his children are dead, all at once, from a sudden natural disaster. How can you put that kind of grief into any system of fairness?

Eliphaz tries to counter that immensity of pain with the immensity of the world that human beings cannot know, and with the fact of our endlessly disgusting animal nature. It doesn't work because while it is true that many people can be convinced that they are base, not everyone can. Job does not feel that way. I imagine Job's friends had some hidden secrets that they projected onto Job, such that they could not quite imagine him possessing true innocence.

"Miserable comforters are ye all," Job says to his friends, and adds, "what emboldeneth thee that thou answerest?" Which is to say: How dare you? "I also could speak as ye do: if your soul were in my soul's stead." Which is to say: Your perspective is situational. Soon Job is back to the repetitive gorgeous litany of devastation: "He teareth me in his wrath, who hateth me: he gnasheth upon me with his teeth; mine enemy sharpeneth his eyes upon me. . . . [H]e hath also taken me by my neck, and shaken me to pieces, and set me up for his mark. His archers compass me round about . . . ; he poureth out my gall upon the ground. . . . He runneth upon me like a giant. I have sewed sackcloth upon my skin . . . My face is foul with weeping, and my eyelids are the shadow of death; Not for any injustice in mine hands: also my prayer is pure."

Job starts to tell us more about his life before the disaster, and if it sounded good before, it sounds like paradise as he goes on. We learn that he was so highly respected that at town gatherings they waited until he arrived to begin and when he spoke even the old men were silent. He was the pinnacle of this community's version of wisdom and now he is outside its paradigm. He says to his sagacious visitors, "I cannot find one wise man among you." What is Job's new plan? "My days are past, my purposes are broken off, even the thoughts of my heart. . . . If I wait, the grave is mine house: I have made my bed in the darkness. I have said to corruption, Thou art my father: to the worm, Thou are my mother, and my sister." It is a solid plan. Can't really go wrong.

> He hath put my brethren far from me, . . . my familiar friends have forgotten me. . . . My breath is strange to my wife . . . Yea, young children despised me; I arose, and they spake against me.

The friends continue to talk for a while, with only a few new points. Zophar the Naamathite champions the idea that the wicked do win . . . but then later they lose. "The triumphing of the wicked is short, and the joy of the hypocrite but for a moment." Indeed, "though his excellency mount up to the heavens, and his head reach unto the clouds; Yet he shall perish for ever like his own dung." Furthermore, though the wicked man dines on gems, he will soon vomit them up. It is an important logical device because it helps negotiate the fact that we have all seen cheaters win and good women wither. Zophar is sure the wicked can't win for long: "The increase of his house shall depart, and his goods shall flow away . . . This is the portion of a wicked man." It is a sad little compromise: the world is fair, just don't expect it to look fair in any given now.

Now Job lets fly his ultimate response to fairness, beginning with the fantastic line: "Suffer me that I may speak; and after that I have spoken, mock on." Followed by the equally poignant, "Mark me, and be astonished, and lay your hand upon your mouth." He says that even he is trembling in fear over what he is about to say. He is going to contradict all the prime moral virtues of his society, and say what he actually sees.

> Wherefore do the wicked live, become old, yea, are mighty in power? Their seed is established in their sight with them and their offspring before their eyes. Their houses are safe from fear, neither is the rod of God upon them. Their bull gendereth, and faileth not; their cow calveth, and casteth not her calf. They send forth their little ones like a flock and their children dance.

Eliphaz tries to assert that Job was wicked enough to be punished but he hasn't got much to go on, blaming Job for things for which it is logically impossible to be innocent: "Thou hast not given water to the weary to drink, and thou hast withholden bread from the hungry." Job shakes that off and in what I imagine as pickle-faced derision says that even with everything he has said, "my stroke is heavier than my groaning."

Job says that life should be bad for people who cheat. The thieving, betraying person should not have been born or should die fast: "The womb shall forget him, the worm shall feed sweetly on him; he shall be remembered no more, and wickedness shall be broken as a tree. For he prays on the barren who do not bear and does no good for the widow." This man, who "does no good for the widow," is allowed to prosper, while Job is destroyed despite his careful generosity. It is a perversion of justice. Job tells us he has not forgotten that the universe is beyond him, inscrutable, as well as terrifying. He maintains respect for the force that made the world, but if the world doesn't turn against the wicked, it means that if you want justice, you need humanity.

Sharing one's wealth, looking after widows and orphans, and being a good host are mentioned often in Job's critique, but Job had other ways of defining good and bad as well. He believed that greed would have deserved some punishment: "If I have made gold my hope, or have said to the fine gold, Thou art my confidence." It is worth noting that greed is a mistake that will make you miserable without any supernatural help. Also, he nods, he would have deserved censor for egotism: "If I rejoiced because my wealth was great, and because mine hand had gotten much." What else does a good man try to avoid? "If I rejoiced at the destruction of him that hated me." That's a good one. But Job says he didn't do it. If I had done any of this, says Job, "Let thistles grow instead of wheat, and cockle instead of barley." The close of this section is clearly marked, "The words of Job are ended." He'll speak again, but the critique is over.

There's a speech here by a young man, Elihu, which scholars think was added later. It defends God's greatness and unknowability. The intrusion builds tension for the big reveal, which is that the Hebrew God does the thing he's most famous for not doing. He shows up. And talks. In fact we know he's talking before we know how he appears: "Then the Lord answered Job out of the whirlwind." Yet despite the talk, God never answers Job's question. He instead issues a tirade that is as gorgeous as it is surprising, but entirely avoids Job's issues.

All Job's fine points about being good, all the observations about the wicked, God ignores. If the two major reasons to believe in the Hebraic God are science (how did all this get here?) and wishes (the dream of a fair world), God disregards the wishes and offers a breathtaking panorama of the science. He repeatedly reminds Job that humanity could not have made this world. We do not have the more modern adjectives of majestic God here, instead we are vividly schooled in how lovely, interconnected, bizarre, and impressive is the natural world. The argument is nothing other than an insistence on the otherworldly imagination it would require to dream up an ostrich—not just its weird giant flightless birdness, but also, specifically, that it responds to danger to its children by putting its head in the sand.

The great science questions continue, as God asks, "Where wast thou when I laid the foundations of the earth? declare, if thou hast understanding." And: What is the earth standing on? The next questions are: How big is earth? When there is a flood, what makes the water recede again so that we can live? What keeps the ocean from breaking out of its bounds and flooding us? How does snow work? How about hail? What sets the schedule for the flooding of the great rivers? Why does it rain in the wilderness where there is no one to make use of it? Why waste the rain? Where does rain come from, and where dew, and where ice? Could you make the stars? Do you know how many months a goat gestates or how the eagle knows how to find dead meat? Consider the myriad bizarre yet somehow regular and regulated systems of nature. It is enormity and complexity beyond comprehension.

Job folds. He is in awe. He apologizes for his insolence. "I have heard of thee by the hearing of the ear: but now mine eye seeth thee. Wherefore I abhor myself, and repent in dust and ashes."

God is not pleased with the friends, but he does not tell us precisely why. He is mad at them, "for ye have not spoken of me the thing that is right, as my servant Job hath." God tells them to go to Job and fulfill a burnt offering, "Lest I deal with you after your folly, in that ye have not spoken of me the thing which is right, like my servant Job." Thus it is twice articulated by God that they were wrong and Job was right. Job was right. God is emphatic about it. Then God gives Job twice as much as he had before. In the end all his family and friends came to him, bemoaned his suffering, "and comforted him over all the evil that the LORD had brought upon him: every man also gave him a piece of money, and every one an earring of gold." It is a bit of an *It's a Wonderful Life* final scene, in which everyone shows up and chips in and the poor man is no longer poor, and in some sense never was. But where were all these friends before?

God said twice that where the friends spoke wrongly, Job spoke correctly. The friends said God was fair and to be trusted, Job said God was not fair, did not punish the wicked, nor help the weak, nor reward the good. God rejects all of the religious descriptions of him, though some had him as quite unknowable. God shows interest in none of the theories. Perhaps we are to infer that he liked Job's honesty. There is comfort, too, in seeing the bad for what it is. Also, God's speech reminds us that as bad as the world is, it is also wondrous and delightful.

It seems to me that the Book of Job is part of a robust tradition of accepting unfairness and death and learning to live a rich life anyway. It is correlated with occasional profound despair. In the book, people do not speak of life as meaningless, they speak of it as vastly, crassly unjust, vicious, irremediably unforgivable. It is overflowing with meaning, it's just not fair.

Surely, back when Job was healthy, wealthy, and beloved he had noticed that some of the other rich people were neither good nor pious. He must have known that the poor and unlucky did not deserve their suffering. But we are to see that it doesn't truly penetrate his consciousness until it hits his own flesh, "My flesh is clothed with worms and clods of dust; my skin is broken, and become loathsome." Until you have been tested—really tested—be careful what you say about the fairness of this world. In the face of other people's suffering, work hard to be empathetic or you will miss all sorts of truth.

The nuance and bravery of this book has been praised in the most extraordinary terms. The English author Thomas Carlyle called Job "The oldest choral melody as of the heart of mankind," adding, "There is nothing written, I think, in the Bible or out of it, of equal literary merit."[10] Daniel Webster described it as "The most wonderful poem of any age and language." Thomas Wolf wrote, "The most tragic, sublime and beautiful expression of loneliness."[11] And the poet Nelly Sachs, writing about the Holocaust, said:

> Job, you have cried through all vigils
> but one day the constellations of your blood
> shall make all rising suns blanch.[12]

WE CANNOT PINPOINT when our second minority report, Ecclesiastes, was written, but it was a few hundred years later, most likely in the latter part of the third century BCE. By this time in history there is an idea of an afterlife in Judaism, but it is vague and not at all uniformly accepted. Here it is explicitly rejected, so the question of the fairness of life is still assessed in terms of this world. There is an innocence and earnestness about the Book of Job that is gone by the time of this masterpiece of the more cosmopolitan Hellenistic age. Where Job is a howl in the wilderness, Ecclesiastes is a wry smile and world-weary sigh.

Of course, just as with Job, people have found ways to read Ecclesiastes that push back against its secularism, and its claims that the world is fundamentally unfair, and that other than companionship, love, good work, and good food and drink, much of life's envied experiences and accomplishments are overrated. James Crenshaw, one of the foremost scholars of wisdom literature, has written several books highlighting the strange realism of Ecclesiastes amid the rest of the Bible. He concludes, "There may indeed be some truth in the claim that the confrontation between Hebraism and Hellenism produced a compromise position, best exemplified by Qoheleth [the Hebrew form of the title]. However, the Jewish tradition alone had its share of ambiguities, and these disparities between religious conviction and actual reality found expression in Qoheleth's realism."[13] Biblical scholar Mark R. Sneed begins his recent book on the subject with these words:

> Biblical scholars must face reality. In terms of the canon, Qohelet is the "odd book in" as James Crenshaw describes. The book is easily the strangest in the Bible.[2] It can aptly be described as a "frightening guest . . . in the canon." Gerhard von Rad refers to "the farthest frontier of Jahwism where Ecclesiastes pitched his camp." Similarly, C. L. Seow describes the book as being on "the margins of the canon." Qohelet's conception of God is especially troubling for most readers, past and present.[14]

Walter Kaufmann wrote that we do not know "whether the author of Ecclesiastes retained any faith in God."[15]

Ecclesiastes

> There is a vanity which is done upon the earth; that there be just men, unto whom it happeneth according to the work of the wicked; again, there be wicked men, to whom it happeneth according to the work of the righteous.
>
> Ecclesiastes 8.14

The Ecclesiastes author introduces himself as "the Preacher" and it is customary to call him that in Hebrew, Koheleth. As with Job, we can surmise from the text a good deal about the common moral theory against which Koheleth wrote. From the above epigraph we can see that good things are expected to happen to good people, and bad things to bad people. We can also see that despite this being an accepted, indeed, assumed rule, it is obvious that life doesn't really work that way. Koheleth does not feel he needs to give named specifics, as if he were arguing something conceptually unlikely; he counts on his listener to be able to think of examples.

He counsels that we should accept mortality, and his descriptions of it are patient but blunt: "For that which befalleth the sons of men befalleth beasts;" he tells us, "even one thing befalleth them: as the one dieth, so dieth the other; yea, they have all one breath; so that a man hath no preeminence above a beast: for all is vanity. All go unto one place; all are of the dust, and all turn to dust again." Our membership in the animal kingdom is one of the strongest pieces of evidence that we are entirely natural beings. Without the other animals, our experience of thought and love might be so strange in the world that it would be reasonable to think of it as supernatural and not too much of a stretch to wonder if it had a nonphysical quality to it. With all the other animals around us (all with versions of feeling and thought, all dying pretty convincingly when their bodies die) it seems obvious to many that human death is final, too. In Ecclesiastes we are told that if we think death is the end for animals, we should take seriously the idea that it's the end for us too. Koheleth advises us to make peace with injustice.

The primary virtues are still about being upright, hardworking, honest, loyal, and generous to the needy. Koheleth wonders if these are associated with good results. We may ask ourselves, along with him: Do the chief virtues of the Hebrew Bible correlate causally with success? It seems true that if a man is not upright, does not labor, steals, betrays, and hurts the weak, he is likely to "pay for it," that is, to be punished or at least to lose other people's trust and friendship. It also seems true that countless honest, loyal, hard-working, clean-living people have toiled, suffered, and died without much recompense.

Job's conversation started in questions of bad luck; Koheleth dwells more on economics. As many have observed, even if life could be fair in some imagined first generation, it stops there. One person may get riches for his labor, but whoever inherits his estate may well benefit without having labored. I'm offering a little chunk of Ecclesiastes here to show how it roams around and weaves ideas together. This passage begins as Koheleth acknowledges that the fool walks around like a blind man, while the wise can see—but he quickly adds that even this huge advantage doesn't really matter.

> For there is no remembrance of the wise more than of the fool for ever; seeing that which now is in the days to come shall all be forgotten. And how dieth the wise man? as the fool. Therefore I hated life; because the work that is wrought under the sun is grievous unto

me: for all is vanity and vexation of spirit. Yea, I hated all my labour which I had taken under the sun: because I should leave it unto the man that shall be after me. And who knoweth whether he shall be a wise man or a fool? yet shall he have rule over all my labour wherein I have laboured, and wherein I have shewed myself wise under the sun. This is also vanity. Therefore I went about to cause my heart to despair of all the labour which I took under the sun.

Koheleth gives a lot of attention to whether the hard work it takes to succeed is really worth it. He has a vivid insight that people work their lives away, never seeing the sun, such that if they lived a thousand years their experience on earth would be the same. Everyone goes to one place in the end, whether they work themselves raw or not. Man arrives into life naked and leaves naked and takes nothing of his labor with him. And this having spent his whole life working in darkness and tortured by envy and wrath.

Koheleth sounds weary of any claims about justice, especially the simple idea that the good will be rewarded. He reminds us that no one is all good or all bad, "For there is not a just man upon earth, that doeth good, and sinneth not." There are many passive sins, and sins inherent in perspective. Many of us are evil, for example, in someone's eyes. None of us have shared everything with everyone, nor would that be a clear moral good. For Koheleth, trying to sort out who really deserves success is all vanity; there is no clear goodness, let alone reward for it. This leads him to two enormous conclusions. First, there is his famous hedonism: "Then I commended mirth, because a man hath no better thing under the sun, than to eat, and to drink, and to be merry." Second is his equally famous belief in a static world: "The thing that hath been, it is that which shall be; and that which is done is that which shall be done: and there is no new thing under the sun." Life is so crooked that it is appropriate to give up on any big ideas of success. You can't really change anything—things just cycle through their phases.

If the world is not divinely made fair, is it at least meritocratic? Does victory go to talent and skill? Do the wise get bread? It didn't look that way to Koheleth. "I returned, and saw under the sun, that the race is not to the swift, nor the battle to the strong, neither yet bread to the wise, nor yet riches to men of understanding, nor yet favour to men of skill; but time and chance happeneth to them all." When you don't have bread sometimes it is hard not to blame yourself about it, and when you win prizes it is hard to not feel rewarded, but he doesn't think there are any such correlations.

As a crucial piece of evidence of injustice, Koheleth points to periods of general suffering. The common suffering in bad times, he explains, is a keen indication that individuals do not get what they deserve. Koheleth confronts the problem of a good generation of people wasted, ruined, on an era of decline and disaster. "For man also knoweth not his time: as the fishes that are taken in an evil net, and as the birds that are caught in the snare; so are the sons of men snared in an evil time, when it falleth suddenly upon them." Ancient Judaism developed with a dramatically different response to this problem, an idea of communal guilt. In a time of general suffering, the Babylonian Captivity, they surmised that all must have disappointed God by insufficient ritualized piety. When the crime in question is impiety and there are debates about the nature of piety, the category is endlessly elastic—you can always find fault with yourself (and thereby protect your god). Koheleth had nothing like this in his essay on the nature of the world. Pious deeds are not suggested, indeed they are contraindicated. As with the Book of Job, goodness in Ecclesiastes is mostly about how you treat others.

"The Preacher" tells us his personal story. He was king over Israel in Jerusalem and he spent all his time seeking wisdom, which he thought was his task. But after seeing a bit of life, he gave up. "I have seen all the works that are done under the sun; and, behold, all is vanity and vexation of spirit. That which is crooked cannot be made straight: and that which is wanting cannot be numbered." Things are too bad to fix and what is needed is beyond us. He speaks about human suffering and his own sadness. He does not seem to have expected God to fix his sorrow, but here he laments secular solutions too. His hard-won wisdom and knowledge did not make him happier. "For in much wisdom is much grief: and he that increaseth knowledge increaseth sorrow."

He tried living for mirth and pleasure but it was too crazy and useless for him. He tried giving himself to wine. He got depressed. He decided to try everything, first turning to grand productivity, building houses, gardens, and orchards, and he enjoyed the attendant pleasures of success: "I gat me men singers and women singers, and the delights of the sons of men, as musical instruments, and that of all sorts. So I was great, and increased more than all that were before me in Jerusalem: also my wisdom remained with me." He was happy and rejoiced in his labor and indulged his desires. Then he started to feel bad again, concluding again that "all was vanity and vexation of spirit, and there was no profit under the sun."

The story of his life is about losing what sense of justice he had. He has come to believe that you cannot win. If you are kind you will be dealt the same blow as if you are cruel, and if you follow religious tenets you are just as likely to suffer and die as if you ignore them. If you break an oath to God you can expect pretty much the same future as someone who does not. "All things come alike to all: there is one event to the righteous, and to the wicked; to the good and to the clean, and to the unclean; to him that sacrificeth, and to him that sacrificeth not: as is the good, so is the sinner; and he that sweareth, as he that feareth an oath."

Koheleth says our hearts are full of evil, and madness, and then we die. The complexity of the world is beyond us. There's nothing to do "but for a man to rejoice, and to do good in his life."

He returns to the fact of real people suffering real oppression again and again. He considers their subjugation; he says that he saw their tears, and saw that no one was helping them, "they had no comforter." The other side had power, and power wins. For Koheleth that is unbearable. Realizing that he believed the oppressed truly had no comforter made him feel that it is better to be dead than living, and better yet would be to have never been born, and thus never see the evil work that is done. He is anguished by "the oppression of the poor, and violent perverting of judgment and justice."

The grotesque cruelties of life are strong arguments for him, and no underlying sense redeems them. Even piety is not worth the trouble and can be dangerous. His advice is to play it safe and be a survivor.

> All things have I seen in the days of my vanity: there is a just man that perisheth in his righteousness, and there is a wicked man that prolongeth his life in his wickedness. Be not righteous over much; neither make thyself over wise: why shouldest thou destroy thyself? Be not over much wicked, neither be thou foolish: why shouldest thou die before thy time?

It is a sophisticated conception of the world. Job had mentioned that even when the world gives people wealth, the money does not always make them happy. Koheleth too finds that another problem with the idea of a sensible moral world is that goods are not always good—especially because the rich man keeps toiling away while a growing entourage consumes his winnings. There is no easy relationship between getting more and having enough. "He that loveth silver shall not be satisfied with silver; nor he that loveth abundance with increase: this is also vanity." When you get rich, people use you. One of the only things Koheleth calls "evil" is that "riches kept for the owners thereof to their hurt." As Shakespeare would echo, "The sleep of a labouring man is sweet, whether he eat little or much: but the abundance of the rich will not suffer him to sleep." Success is a bit of a failure.

We can see nihilism in this, but also a wisdom we might usually associate with Greek philosophers or Zen monks. There is an element of working toward detachment. For Koheleth, life has reliable organization, "to every thing there is a season, and a time to every purpose," but as much as that offers order, it also offers a kind of moral relativism: there is a time to kill. There is a time to gather stones together, and a time to refrain from embracing, a time to lose, a time to cast away, a time to hate, and a time of war. There is a time to die. In this list no ill is absolute. In such a system, even the "wrong" is right for its moment.

On an interpersonal level, relativism and acceptance of competing values encourages positive social sensitivity. Real justice is explained to be more complicated than our hurt feelings often suggest. When someone angers you with some behavior, he recommends, ask yourself if you sometimes behave that way yourself. "Also take no heed unto all words that are spoken; lest thou hear thy servant curse thee: For oftentimes also thine own heart knoweth that thou thyself likewise hast cursed others."

As in Job, justice is firmly rejected as a regulating principle of the world. Yet also like Job, meaning is robust for Koheleth. By "meaning" I include the experience of having values, caring enough to offer advice, loving your spouse, taking your work seriously, trying to do some good, and holding life dear. Koheleth richly manifests investment in all of these in the great crescendo of Ecclesiastes. It begins from the very root question of the human condition: Is this life better than death? He says it is.

> For to him that is joined to all the living there is hope: for a living dog is better than a dead lion. For the living know that they shall die: but the dead know not any thing, neither have they any more a reward; for the memory of them is forgotten. Also their love, and their hatred, and their envy, is now perished; neither have they any more a portion for ever in any thing that is done under the sun. Go thy way, eat thy bread with joy, and drink thy wine with a merry

> heart. . . . Live joyfully with the wife whom thou lovest all the days of the life of thy vanity, which he hath given thee under the sun, all the days of thy vanity: for that is thy portion in this life, and in thy labour which thou takest under the sun. Whatsoever thy hand findeth to do, do it with thy might; for there is no work, nor device, nor knowledge, nor wisdom, in the grave, whither thou goest.

It is an amazing passage. Koheleth asks, wryly, "For what hath the wise more than the fool?" but the wisdom he offers has been remembered as helpful indeed—for several millennia. Do your best work now, because it is now or never, but don't work too hard for success because that game is not worth it. The thought of death is a tonic here, as it is in other wisdom and enlightenment literature. Since our envy dies with the body, we might as well let it go now.

Understand, he says, that the paradigm will shift after your life in ways that will negate your intentions, so do not torture yourself for some ideal. The constant turnover of life, endlessly shifting in its repetitions, suggests, for Koheleth, that we see ourselves within the context of the ages, and relax a little. Don't even try to be overmuch good, or to have it overmuch good. "For who knoweth what is good for man in this life, all the days of his vain life which he spendeth as a shadow? For who can tell a man what shall be after him under the sun?"

IT IS INTERESTING to consider the major religions as answers to the question, "What would it look like if the world were fair?" It is fascinating to see all the virtues human beings decide upon, all the punishments, and the rewards, the ways to conceptualize the struggle with problematic habits, and the ways to buy back into the world of goodness. The honing of ideas of morality, integrity, empathy, courage, and self-love, are masterful parts of the religious legacy.

It is also worth remembering that many people, very often within the religion, express serious doubts about providence. They may rail about the lack of divine justice, like the Job author, or like Koheleth, set the matter aside and try to talk about our actual situation. Koheleth's better question is, "What kind of fairness, contentment, joy, wonder, and love are possible in this world, as it is?" It is frightening to acknowledge that in some ways right-and-wrong is a mammalian concept, and while true in society, it is not true in the way measurements are true. Within human life, morality, it seems to me, is as true as love. Both feel elusive at times, but both are real. As I have argued before: The feeling of meaning is sufficient to the definition of meaning. In this real world, whatever people may believe, many of them want to be good, just because they are human. That is a lot to work with. I do not at all dismiss morality nor has it really become any harder to define; we have always had to figure it out as we go, and we do now. Having some commandments makes things simple in some ways, but our ten are rather intuitive: It is wrong to kill, bad to covet, and you should listen to mom and dad. And having your code written in stone, or certified by God, can make it hard to rethink parts of it and upgrade your behavior.

Acknowledging that outside the human world right-and-wrong does not exist any more than love is both bracing and enthralling. It allows us to see, if only fleetingly, what a mix of intention and chaos is our situation. We ought to be impressed that we came up with morality at all, and that we try for it. We also might accept that we all explode out of it, in our ways and in our time. The Roman author Terence wrote, "I am human; nothing human is foreign to me." In the humanist tradition, the great good then is to know yourself, learn to see the world as it is, and try to see it outside of one's ego, and outside of invented systems.

In the more than two thousand years following the origins of these texts, Judaism and Christianity would discover many new ways to parse morality, guilt, shame, goodness, redemption, and other nuances of right-and-wrong in majestically complex and often beautiful systems that insist the world is fair. But Jews and Christians would also have reference to the stunning visions of Job and Ecclesiastes, and for those who crave reality and truth above order and safety, these books would be much beloved.

Notes

1. Thomas Hobbes, *Leviathan*, ed. Richard Tuck (New York: Cambridge University Press, 1996), 89.
2. Ibid., 88.
3. Martin Buber, *On the Bible: Eighteen Studies*, ed. Nahum N. Glatzer, intro. Harold Bloom (New York: Schocken, 1982), 191.
4. Nahum N. Glatzer, ed., *The Dimensions of Job: A Study and Selected Readings* (New York: Schocken, 1969).
5. Katharine J. Dell, *The Book of Job as Sceptical Literature* (Berlin and New York: Walter de Gruyter, 1991).

6. Morris Jastrow, *The Book of Job: Its Origin, Growth and Interpretation, Together with a New Translation* (London: J. B. Lippincott, 1920), 26.
7. Glatzer, *Dimensions of Job.*
8. Dell, *Book of Job as Sceptical Literature.*
9. Jennifer Michael Hecht, *Doubt: A History* (New York: HarperOne, 2003).
10. Glatzer, *The Dimensions of Job*, ix.
11. Ibid.
12. From the poem "Chorus of the Stars," in the collection *Chorus of the Night.* Reproduced in the original and in translation in William H. McClain, "The Imaging of Transformation in Nelly Sachs's Holocaust Poems," *Hebrew University Studies in Literature* 8, no. 2 (1980): 281–300.
13. James L. Crenshaw, *Urgent Advice and Probing Questions: Collected Writings on Old Testament Wisdom* (Macon, GA: Mercer University Press, 1995), 509.
14. Mark R. Sneed, *The Politics of Pessimism in Ecclesiastes: A Social-Science Perspective* (Atlanta, GA: Society of Biblical Literature, 2012).
15. Walter Kaufmann, *The Faith of a Heretic* (Garden City, NY: Anchor, 1968). For more on how to understand Ecclesiastes within the canon, see Martin A. Sheilds, *The End of Wisdom: A Reappraisal of the Historical and Canonical Function of Ecclesiastes* (Winona Lake, IN: Eisenbrauns, 2006). For a modern look at various interpretations, see Doug Ingram, *Ambiguity in Ecclesiastes* (New York: Continuum, 2006).

Selected Bibliography

Buber, Martin. *On the Bible: Eighteen Studies.* Edited by Nahum N. Glatzer, introduction by Harold Bloom (New York: Schocken, 1982).

Crenshaw, James L. *Urgent Advice and Probing Questions: Collected Writings on Old Testament Wisdom* (Macon, GA: Mercer University Press, 1995).

Dell, Katharine J. *The Book of Job as Sceptical Literature* (Berlin and New York: Walter de Gruyter, 1991).

Glatzer, Nahum N., ed. *The Dimensions of Job: A Study and Selected Readings* (New York: Schocken, 1969).

Hecht, Jennifer Michael. *Doubt: A History* (New York: HarperOne, 2003).

Hobbes, Thomas. *Leviathan*, ed. Richard Tuck (New York: Cambridge University Press, 1996), 89.

Ingram, Doug. *Ambiguity in Ecclesiastes* (New York: Continuum, 2006).

Jastrow, Morris. *The Book of Job: Its Origin, Growth and Interpretation, Together with a New Translation* (Philadelphia and London: J. B. Lippincott, 1920), 26.

Kaufmann, Walter. *The Faith of a Heretic* (Garden City, NY: Anchor, 1968).

McClain, William H. "The Imaging of Transformation in Nelly Sachs's Holocaust Poems." *Hebrew University Studies in Literature* 8, no. 2 (1980): 281–300.

Shields, Martin A. *The End of Wisdom: A Reappraisal of the Historical and Canonical Function of Ecclesiastes* (Winona Lake, IN: Eisenbrauns, 2006).

Sneed, Mark R. *The Politics of Pessimism in Ecclesiastes: A Social-Science Perspective* (Atlanta, GA: Society of Biblical Literature, 2012).

3

Chance, Uncertainty, and Unknowability in the Universe and Beyond

John D. Barrow

Historical Attitudes to Chance and Providence

Eight years ago I visited the city of Tainen, the ancient capital of Taiwan, and was taken on a sightseeing visit to one of the ancient temples. There I witnessed a fascinating sequence of events. A man, about thirty years of age, knelt before the shrine and cast two small wooden objects on the floor. When he saw the outcome he went to a tall canister by the side of the shrine and pulled out a long thin stick on which were inscribed a sequence of Chinese characters. He then prayed and returned to the shrine and cast the two wooden objects on the floor again. The whole sequence of events was then repeated once more before he took his coat and departed, seemingly happy. My student guide explained to me that this young man was seeking divine guidance about an important decision he had to make, possibly regarding marriage. The wooden objects were simple asymmetric dice and the outcome of casting them was how the god would answer him. Perhaps two "heads" was "yes," two "tails" was "no," and one "head" and one "tail" was a notice to seek more guidance. That guidance was obtained by drawing the long yarrow stick from the canister. This told him what was still required of him—perhaps a donation to the temple or a promise to engage in some good works—and having accepted it he returned and threw the dice again. Eventually, the outcome gave the answer he was seeking.

What I had witnessed in Tainen was a vestige of the ancient view of chance as the mouthpiece of the gods. This idea is persistent even in the Judeo-Christian tradition. We read in the story of Jonah that the seafarers caught in the storm cast lots in order to determine who was responsible for the evil events that had fallen upon them "and the lot fell on Jonah."[1] In the Acts of the Apostles, Matthias was appointed in preference to Barsabbas as the thirteenth apostle, to replace Judas Iscariot, by the drawing of lots. In these and many other possible references we see that "chance" is one way in which God was believed to make God's choices known and a means by which those choices can be discerned without being influenced by human bias. This type of chance, therefore, has nothing to do with randomness: it was the definite act of God, foreseeable by the deity but not by us.

This interpretation of chance can be found in relatively modern times. Some pietist traditions in the eighteenth and early nineteenth centuries used the drawing of lots in order to make many decisions about their church life and worship: selecting which passages of scripture were to be read, who were to be elders, or even where church buildings should be located. In November 2012, the traditional drawing of lots was used to select Egypt's Orthodox Coptic pope, Theodorus II, in the final stage of the election process after voting by clergy and laity has narrowed the number of candidates to three. The "winning" name was selected from the three out of a glass chalice on the altar by a blindfolded boy.

Cleromancy, the drawing of lots for divination, has a long Jewish history. In the Old Testament period we see a tradition of divination by the chief priest who would keep two stone tokens within his robe (the *ephod*) which he could draw out in order to obtain God's answer to a question. These devices were called the Urim (meaning "cursed" or "guilty") and Thummim (meaning "faultless" or "innocent"). None of these devices survive and there is uncertainty about exactly how they were used. Yet their role seems clear. In the Book of Samuel[2] we read that "Saul inquired of the Lord, but the Lord did not answer him, not by dreams nor by Urim nor by the prophets." The prophet Ezra's account of the selection of righteous priests to return to Israel from their captivity in Babylon reveals that they were to be chosen by the use of the Urim and Thummim and "The governor instructed them [i.e., the prospective returning priests] not to eat any of the sacred food until there was a priest who could consult the Urim and Thummim."[3] I have multiplied the examples, and we could have looked for similar ones in different monotheistic traditions, in order to show how cleromancy might be the reason why there was no ancient mathematical theory of probability and chance. We see arithmetic, algebra, geometry, and the study of motion in sophisticated ancient cultures, but no theory of probability. The association of chance with the voice of the gods would have been sacrilegious and so perhaps a major taboo. It would be tantamount to foreseeing or foretelling the will of the gods—putting them under the control of human calculation.

This explanation is not the only one imaginable for the lack of an ancient theory of chance, despite the ubiquity of games of chance. Another explanation could be that one key concept was missing: that of equally likely outcomes.[4] The oldest gaming devices were irregularly shaped bones. No general theory is possible for all of them. The gambler in the marketplace will play his mark with his chicken bone. He alone understands, by experience, the biases in the fall of his asymmetrical gaming device. No theory of it will help a person win against another neighbor with a different chicken bone.

Later, the appearance of symmetrical dice, which migrated to Europe from their originating cultures in Mesopotamia with the returning Crusaders, and playing cards, which arrived in Europe in the fourteenth century, introduced games of chance that involved symmetrical objects and sequences of equally likely outcomes. With this key concept in place it becomes possible to devise a mathematical theory of probability.

There were two interesting threads of theological and natural theological history that implicitly drew conclusions about probability. The first was the attitude toward accounts of apparently miraculous events: were the witnesses reliable? The second was the attitude toward apparent fine tuning of nature in ways that that were seemingly helpful to humanity. Sometimes this was called the "design argument" and it was used as a natural theological argument for the existence of God or as a pre-Darwinian explanation for adaptation in the natural world.[5] This second thread is implicitly about probability because it assumes that the special circumstances seen in nature where environments appear tailor-made for their inhabitants are too improbable to have arisen naturally, or by chance. They require the deliberate hand of God to engineer them. It is interesting to examine one example of each thread which allows some precise mathematics to be used.

David Hume (1711–1776) had argued that it was more likely that the witnesses of supposedly miraculous events were deceived (or even sought to deceive) in their testimony than that the miracle they recounted had truly occurred.[6] In his maverick unofficial[7] *Ninth Bridgewater Treatise* of 1837, the distinguished mathematician and pioneering computer scientist Charles Babbage took great issue with Hume's imprecise arguments on this matter and showed how it could be precisely formulated and answered using Bayes's theorem.[8]

In general, Bayes's theorem teaches us that the probability of A given evidence B, denoted by $P(A|B)$, is related to the initial degree of belief in the truth of A, $P(A)$; the degree of belief in B given that A is true, $P(B|A)$; and the degree of belief that B is true, $P(B)$, by the formula

$$P(A \mid B) = P(B \mid A)\, P(A) / P(B) = P(B \mid A)\, P(A) / [P(B \mid A)\, P(A) + P(B \mid not\ A)\, P(not\ A)]$$

If n independent witnesses each tell truth with probability p (so $0 \le p \le 1$), and $A = Q$ is the prior probability that a miracle did occur, then the posterior probability of a miracle having occurred given the evidence of the n witnesses [i.e., $P(A \mid B)$] is

$$Q_n = Qp^n / [Qp^n + (1-Q)(1-p)^n].$$ [9]

If Hume wants $Q_n > ½$, that is, they are more likely to be right than wrong, then this is always possible for some large enough n if $p > ½$. If, instead, Hume is read as demanding that it be more probable that a miracle occurred than that the n witnesses were mistaken, then we require $Q > 1 - Q_n$. This is always possible for some large enough n if $p > ½$. Babbage's favored interpretation of Hume was simpler, that the probability of n witnesses concurring in falsehood or misinformation be less than the chance of miracle truly happening. This requires $(1 - p)^n < Q$, which can always be satisfied for some n for any value of the probability p.

Babbage showed how Hume's speculations can be made precise by using probability theory. However, Babbage's mathematical arguments still contain weak assumptions. The witnesses were assumed to be identical and statistically *independent*, so that the probability that n of them tell the truth is p^n if p is the probability that one of them tells the truth. This condition is unlikely to be true in the situations that Babbage is addressing.

He is also assuming that witnesses are as likely to be truthful when they say there was a miracle as when they say there was no miracle. But most questionable of all is his assumption that either the miracle truly occurred or that all of them are mistaken (or lying). There is a third option: they could be truthfully reporting an event that has another nonmiraculous explanation.

Our second example comes from a development in the history of the design argument. The problem of the design argument for many was that it appeared to advocate a "best of all possible worlds" view of the things around us without being able to exhibit the "other" worlds, except in a highly anthropocentric way, or to say what was meant by "best."

In 1744, the French scientist Pierre-Louis Maupertuis presented a striking response to these objections to the French Academy of Sciences.[10] He showed that Newton's cause-and-effect laws of motion could be derived by using a teleological perspective. Consider the case of a ball rolling down a hill, which Newton would describe as a mass moving in response to a gravitational force. We start by setting the initial and final states—location, speed, etc.—for how we want motion to start and end. We then require that a particular mathematical quantity called the "action" is minimized. (The action is calculated by adding up the sums of the momenta at each point along the path. This continuous summation is called the integral.) When we do this we discover, remarkably, that the path followed by the motion is the same as would be followed by applying Newton's laws of motion to the same initial state. Of all the paths that the rolling ball could take, it chooses the one where it ends up with the smallest possible value of the action.

The two solutions of the problem of motion, using either deterministic Newtonian laws or the teleological principle of action minimization, turn out to be physically equivalent, but they are philosophically completely different. Maupertuis believed that he had made a major contribution to natural theology by this mathematical discovery—a discovery that led to many important advances in our understanding of the behavior of nature. If someone asked what the "other worlds" were, then he would respond that they were the worlds where motion is not described by paths of minimal action. Asked what he meant by the "best" of all possible worlds, he would reply that it was the world with minimum action. Thus, Maupertuis found a way to inject metaphysics into physics and provide a different context for evaluating how likely it was that particular laws of nature would exist by formalizing the idea of an optimal universe.[11]

Is the World Simple or Complicated?

Our belief in the simplicity of nature springs from the observation that there are regularities which we call "laws" of nature. The idea of laws of nature has a long history rooted in monotheistic religious thinking and in ancient practices of statute law and social government.[12]

Laws reflect the existence of patterns. We might even define science as the search for patterns. We observe and document the world in all possible ways, but while this data-gathering is necessary for science, it is not sufficient. We are not content simply to acquire a record of everything that is, or has ever happened, like cosmic stamp collectors. Instead, we look for patterns in the facts, and some of these patterns we have come to call the laws of nature, while others have achieved only the status of bylaws. Having found (or guessed—for there are no rules at all about how you might find them) possible patterns, we use them to predict what should happen if the pattern is also followed at all times and in places where we have yet to look. Then we check if we are right (there are strict rules about how to do this!). In this way, we can update our candidate pattern and improve the likelihood that it explains what we see. Sometimes the likelihood gets so low that we say the proposal is regarded as "falsified," or so high that it is treated as "confirmed" or "verified," although strictly speaking neither conclusion is ever possible with certainty. This process is called the "scientific method."

At first, physicists after Newton were content to find the laws that dictated how changes would occur in space and in time from some starting configuration. Later, these laws of change were often found to be equivalent to a statement that some quantity—like the total energy or electric charge—did not change. This way of looking at the world in terms of conserved quantities, or invariances and unchanging patterns, would prove to be extremely fruitful. Since 1973, this focus upon symmetry has taken center stage in the study of elementary-particle physics and the laws governing the fundamental interactions of nature. Such theories are called "gauge theories."[13] All the currently successful theories of four known forces of nature—the electromagnetic, weak, strong, and gravitational forces—are gauge theories. Particular gauge theories govern the behavior of particular subsets of all the elementary particles according to their shared attributes. Each theory is based upon the preservation of a pattern which requires that a force of nature exists and this force dictates many aspects of its behavior and the identities of the particles it acts on.

The generation of preserved patterns for each of the separate interactions of nature has motivated the search for a unification of those theories into more comprehensive editions based upon larger symmetries. Within those larger patterns, smaller patterns respected by the individual forces of nature might be accommodated, like jigsaw pieces, in an interlocking fashion that places some new constraint upon their allowed forms. So far, this strategy has resulted in a successful, experimentally tested unification of the electromagnetic and weak interactions, and a number of purely theoretical proposals for a further unification with the strong interaction ("grand unification"), and candidates ("superstrings" and "M theory") for a fourfold unification with the gravitational force to produce a so-called Theory of Everything, or TOE.[14] It is this general pattern of explanation by which forces and their underlying patterns are unified and reduced in number (hopefully) by unifications, culminating in a single unified law. This way of thinking lies at the heart of the physicist's perception of the world as "simple."[15]

At first, it was hoped that one of these theories would turn out to be special: a clear candidate for the true Theory of Everything. Unfortunately, things were not so simple and the single underlying theory may have as many as 10^{500} realizations in which the laws of physics governing our low-energy stage in the history of the universe would be different. Deciding how these sets of low-energy laws are chosen in actuality appears to be the result of a random breaking of the theory's underlying symmetry. This is very strange. The old vision of a Theory of Everything that began with Einstein, was that the laws of nature would turn out to be "rigid," uniquely and completely prescribed by the requirement of logical self-consistency.[16] Instead, we find that there is a vast landscape of potential self-consistent realizations of them. This landscape has a formidable difficult and abstract mathematical structure, very little of which has been understood so far. We have also discovered that its exploration is a computationally " 'hard" problem which no fast computer program can explore for us.[17]

The simplicity and economy of the laws and symmetries that govern nature's fundamental forces are not the end of the story. When we look around us, we never observe the laws of nature; rather, we see the *outcomes* of those laws. The distinction is crucial. Outcomes are much more complicated than the laws that govern them because they do not have to respect the symmetries displayed by the laws. By this subtle interplay, it is possible to have a world which displays an unlimited number of complicated asymmetrical structures yet is governed by a few, very simple symmetrical laws. This is one of the secrets of the universe.

Suppose we balance a ball at the apex of a cone. If we were to release the ball in a quantum vacuum, then the law of gravitation will determine its subsequent motion. Gravity has no preference for any particular direction in the universe; it is entirely democratic in that respect. Yet when we release the ball, it will always fall in some particular direction, either because it was given a little push in one direction, or as a result of quantum fluctuations which do not permit an unstable equilibrium state to persist. So here, in the outcome of the falling ball, the directional symmetry of the law of gravity is broken. This situation teaches us why science is often so difficult and beset by uncertainties. When we observe the world, we see only the broken symmetries manifested as the outcomes of the laws of nature; from them, we must work backwards to unmask the hidden symmetries which characterize the laws behind the appearances. If the symmetry breaking that leads to the observed outcome is of quantum origin, then the outcome will be intrinsically random and unpredictable, like the decay of a single radioactive nucleus.[18] One of the most striking things about cosmology is that such microscopic random symmetry breakings in the very early stages of the universe's history can determine its large-scale properties today.

This distinction between laws and outcomes influences the perspective of different scientists on the world. The particle physicist works closest to the laws of nature themselves, and so is especially impressed by their unity, simplicity, and symmetry. But the biologist, the ecologist, or the meteorologist is occupied with the study of the complex outcomes of the laws rather than with the laws themselves. As a result, it is the complexities of nature, rather than her laws, that impress them most. Their viewpoint is Aristotelian rather than Platonic, focusing on the visible features of the world rather than the hidden harmonies that express themselves in these features. This separation also manifests itself in the two different styles of design argument—one from laws (introduced by Newton via Richard Bentley[19]), the other from outcomes (which can be seen in Paley,[20] although it is much older)—that are to be found in old natural theological discussions.[21]

Until the late 1970s, physicists focused far more on the study of the laws than the complex outcomes. This is not surprising. The study of the outcomes is a far more difficult problem, one that requires the existence of powerful interactive computers with good graphics for its full implementation. It is no coincidence that the study of complexity and chaos in that world of outcomes has advanced hand in hand with the growing power and availability of low-cost personal computers since the late 1970s. It has created a new methodology of experimental mathematics dedicated to the simulation of complex phenomena with an array of diverse applications.

Disorganized Complexities

Complexity, like crime, comes in organized and disorganized forms. The disorganized form goes by the name of *chaos* and has proven to be ubiquitous in nature. The standard folklore about chaotic systems is that they are unpredictable. They lead to out-of-control dinosaur parks and out-of-work meteorologists. However, it is important to appreciate more fully the nature of chaotic systems than the Hollywood headlines.

Classical (that is, nonquantum mechanical) chaotic systems are not in any sense intrinsically random or unpredictable. They merely possess extreme sensitivity to ignorance. We cannot predict the weather to high precision tomorrow because we don't know the state of the weather everywhere with perfect accuracy today. As James Clerk Maxwell was the first to recognize in 1873 (in a reflection on free will and determinism), any initial uncertainty in our knowledge of a chaotic system's state is rapidly amplified in time.[22] This feature might make it seem hopeless even to try to use mathematics to describe a chaotic situation. We are never going to get the mathematical equations for weather prediction 100 percent correct—there is too much going on—so we will always end up being inaccurate to some extent in our predictions after some future time.

Another important feature of chaotic systems is that, although they become unpredictable when determining the future from a particular uncertain starting value, there may be a particular stable statistical spread of outcomes after a long time, regardless of how it started out. They can have very stable and predictable average behaviors. As a simple example, take a gas of moving molecules in a room (their average speed of motion determines what we called the gas "temperature") and think of the individual molecules as little balls. The motion of any single molecule is chaotic because each time it bounces off another molecule, any uncertainty in its direction is amplified exponentially. Anyone can check this phenomenon by observing the collisions of pool or snooker balls. In fact, the amplification in the angle of recoil, θ, in the successive (n + 1st and nth) collisions of two identical balls is well described by an equation

$$\theta_{n+1} = (d/r)\theta_n,$$

where d is the average distance between collisions and r is the radius of the balls (typically d/r is about 200). Even the minimal initial uncertainty in θ_0 allowed by Heisenberg's uncertainty principle is increased to exceed $\theta = 360$ degrees after only about fourteen collisions, since the solution of our equation is $\theta_n = (d/r)^n\theta_0 \approx 200^n\theta_0$. This means that any initial uncertainty in position is amplified by a factor of 200 at each collision. Very soon we know nothing of use from the equation about the molecule's location because the uncertainty has grown bigger than the whole room. Nonetheless, although all the molecular motions are individually chaotic, we can still have simple rules like Boyle's Law, which governs the pressure P, volume V, and temperature T—averaged properties—of a confined gas of molecules, with PV/T = *constant*. The lesson of this simple example is that chaotic systems can have stable, predictable, long-term, average behaviors. This insight needs to inform the discussions about whether "running the tape of evolution" again would come with similar results—statistically similar is not the same as identical.

Organized Complexities

The advent of small, inexpensive, powerful computers with good interactive graphics has enabled large, complex, and disordered situations to be studied observationally—by looking at a computer monitor. Experimental mathematics is a new tool that has discovered how chaos and order can coexist in a curious symbiosis. Imagine sand continuously falling, grain by grain, to create a growing sand pile. The pile evolves under the force of gravity in an erratic manner. Sandfalls of all sizes occur, and their effect is to maintain the overall gradient of the sand pile in a temporary equilibrium, always just on the verge of collapse. The pile steadily steepens until it reaches a particular critical slope and then gets no steeper. The critical slope is maintained by the chaotically unpredictable avalanches of sand. This self-sustaining process was dubbed "self-organising criticality" by its discoverers, Per Bak, Chao Tang, and Kurt Wiesenfeld, in 1987.[23] The adjective "self-organising" captures the way in which the chaotically falling grains seem to arrange themselves into an orderly pile. The title "criticality" reflects the precarious state of the pile at any time. It is always about to experience an avalanche of some size or another. The sequence of events that maintains its state of large-scale order is a slow local build-up of sand somewhere on the slope, then a sudden avalanche, followed by another slow build up, a sudden avalanche, and so on. At first, the infalling grains affect a small area of the pile, but gradually their avalanching effects increase to span the dimension of the entire pile.

At a microscopic level, the fall of sand is chaotic, yet the result in the presence of a force like gravity is large-scale organization. If there is nothing peculiar about the sand that renders avalanches of one size more probable than all others, then the frequency with which avalanches occur is proportional to some mathematical power of their size (the avalanche formation is said to be a "scale-free" process).[24] There are many natural systems, like earthquakes, and man-made ones, like stock market crashes, where a concatenation of chaotic local processes maintains a semblance of equilibrium in this way. Order develops on a large scale through the combination of many independent chaotic small-scale events that hover on the brink of instability. Complex adaptive systems[25] thrive in the hinterland between the inflexibilities of determinism and the vagaries of chaos. There, they get the best of both worlds: out of chaos springs a wealth of alternatives for natural selection of sift, while the rudder of determinism sets a clear average course toward islands of stability.

Uncertainty in Cosmology

Cosmology introduces new forms of uncertainty and indeterminacy into science and amplifies the problems which are merely familiar minor irritations elsewhere in our scientific methods. As Donald Rumsfeld famously warned us, there are known unknowns and there are unknown unknowns. But in cosmology there are also *unknowable unknowns*.

In astronomy, we cannot experiment on the universe. We can only observe it. This lack changes aspects of the scientific method, and in the absence of being able to conduct experiments with freely changeable inputs, we look for correlations (a theory might predict that all big galaxies are elliptical, for instance). Popper's dogma of falsification doesn't help much (in fact, it doesn't in most other areas of science) because we cannot be sure what it is we have falsified—was the experiment done correctly? Was there a bias in obtaining the data? Our observations always test bundles of known and unknown hypotheses and none of the latter can ever be falsified with complete certainty (if only because the experiment might be done wrongly). All we can ever do is change the *likelihood* (in Bayes's sense) of a hypothesis being true.

Cosmology also has to face the existence of special biases in space and time. When we take large samples of the universe in order to carry out statistical analyses of, say, how uniform it is, we are limited by a feature known as "cosmic variance." This concept reflects the fact that when we take very large samples, or compare features that are widely separated in angle on the sky, the number of statistically independent samples of large size that we can obtain is limited. This restricts the extent to which we can reduce errors and uncertainties by taking large samples, as we do in other areas of statistical science. Our knowledge of the average level of variation in the universe on large scales will always be limited by this irreducible level of uncertainty, which is quite significant in magnitude and inversely proportional to the fraction of the whole sky included in the survey.

Another worrying cosmological problem, which has gradually become more important, is the realization that indirect evidence persistently shows that about 23 percent of the universe must be in some dark form that cannot be ordinary atomic matter, but is most likely in the form of a new type of weakly interacting neutrino-like particle that we hope will soon be discovered by the Large Hadron Collider at CERN. The ordinary luminous matter in the universe, out of which stars, planets, and people are made, is therefore just a small trace effect. The stars themselves are also not typical representatives of the distribution of matter in the universe. They are located at places where the density of matter became very high—high enough for nuclear reactions to ignite and light to shine. It is sobering to think that thousands of years of astronomical observation of the night sky, with all the folk-lore and speculation about the universe that went with it, was based upon a rather special subsample of the whole cosmos. A bias in the evidence we were able to collect, in this case optical light by our eyes, created a very biased view of what the universe is like.

There are also biases in time. The finiteness of the speed of light ensures that we observe only the past: observe an object one billion light years away and it means that the light left it one billion years ago. The finite light travel time since the observed universe began expanding about

13.7 billion years ago means that there is a visibility horizon which defines our "visible universe" (which is not equal to 13.7 billion light years but is about three times bigger because of the effect of gravity and the expansion of the universe). This distance is the farthest from which we can receive light rays today with perfect instruments. Observational astronomy is confined to gathering information about the visible universe inside our horizon to inform our mathematical descriptions of it. The entire universe (which may be infinite or finite—we don't know) is far bigger. We can never know if the entire universe had a "beginning" or is destined to have an "end," whether it is finite or infinite in size, whether it began in a chaotic or an ordered state, or whether it will one day start to contract. All we can hope for is steadily increasing knowledge about the visible universe, but whether our knowledge will still ultimately be bounded, we can't tell. Thus we see that the finiteness of the speed of light ensures that we can only see a finite portion of the universe. All the information we gather with telescopes from distant objects, such as quasars, is telling us what these objects were like long ago when the light left them: our observations are of the past.[26] This fundamental limitation causes uncertainty in our quest to understand the universe.

Inflation and the Multiverse

The standard modern picture of the evolution of the visible universe is that provided by the inflationary universe theory, which was first proposed by Alan Guth in 1980.[27] This theory proposes a small modification to the old picture of the expanding universe, but one which has far-reaching consequences. In the old picture the universal expansion was always decelerating, regardless of whether it would continue forever or one day be reversed into contraction. Once the expansion began, the mutual gravitational attraction between the universe's material constituents was the only force they would feel. It opposes the expansion energy and so decelerates the expansion. Inflation introduces the idea that in the very earliest stages of the expansion history there was a very brief period of *accelerated* expansion, which requires gravity to become predominantly repulsive. This new idea arose in 1980 because investigations of new theories of particle physics at very high energies seemed to give rise to new types of particle (dubbed "scalar fields"[28]) which behaved in a way which, if they formed, would quickly become the dominant density. They exerted negative pressure (tension) but had positive density. They exhibited repulsive gravity because their gravitational effect upon each other was determined by the density plus three times their pressure. This pressure could be negative and as a result, the expansion would accelerate until these particles decayed into other types of gravitationally attractive matter and the short period of accelerated expansion would then end.

This simple possibility had a host of elegant consequences. The accelerated expansion gave the universe an expansion rate very close to the critical rate that separates indefinite future expansion from eventual recollapse—just as we observed our universe to be. It also ensured that, no matter how irregular and anisotropic[29] the expansion was prior to the onset of the acceleration, it would be smooth and almost completely isotropic afterwards. The brief period of acceleration, which typically goes exponentially rapidly in time, also allows our entire visible universe to be the expanded image of a far smaller primordial region than if the expansion had always decelerated. A very brief period of acceleration suffices to expand the whole of our visible universe from a region that was only 10^{-25} cm in diameter when the acceleration began. Crucially, this region is small enough for light signals to cross in the time 10^{-35} s., and so any unevenness in the density can be smoothed out by energy transport processes as regions with differing energies get thoroughly mixed until everything is uniform.[30]

If inflation had not occurred, then the visible universe would have expanded from a region a few millimeters in size at the time 10^{-35} s. This region is far too large for light signals to cross and so the uniformity of our universe today would be very difficult to understand: the visible universe would be composed of a vast number of regions that had never exchanged light signals during their past history. According to inflation, all the large-scale features of the universe we observe today are direct reflections of those possessed by the tiny causally connected patch of space that it expanded from.

This simple idea had one further remarkable payoff that allowed the idea to be tested by observations. The little patch we expanded from could never have been made perfectly smooth. Heisenberg's uncertainty principle ensures that there must always have been some irreducible level of quantum random fluctuation in its density and temperature from place to place. These fluctuations would subsequently be inflated up in scale by the surge in expansion and should be present in the universe today. They could provide the first natural explanation of why there are small irregularities in density around the universe from place to place that gradually amplified before separating out from the overall expansion to form galaxies and clusters of galaxies.[31] Most remarkably of all, we can calculate the statistical patterns expected in the initial quantum fluctuations and so predict the detailed temperature patterns that they should imprint on the background radiation from the early universe that we detect all over the sky today. Three space missions (COBE, WMAP, and, most recently, Planck) have detected and mapped these temperature variations in increasing detail. There is a compelling detailed agreement between the predictions of the simple inflationary scenario about how the level of fluctuation should vary with scale over the sky and the observations. This agreement means that we have a direct observational probe of events that occurred when the universe was about 10^{-35} s. old. It persuades us to take the basic inflationary universe theory very seriously.

What we have just described focuses on the fate of one tiny patch of space near the beginning of the expansion—the patch that grows by expansion to encompass (perhaps by a huge factor) the whole of what we call the visible universe today. But what about the other parts of space beyond that initial patch? Each region roughly equal size to "our" patch will also undergo inflation. Since this is ultimately a quantum process, there will be a stochastic variation in the amount of inflation that each patch undergoes and in the times when it starts and ends. Ultimately, atom-based life will be able to evolve only in patches that expand for at least a few billion years, so that there is time for stars and carbon and "observers" to form.

The overall effect of this "chaotic inflation" is rather like heating up a foam of random bubbles: some bubbles will expand a lot and some very little. The change it creates to our picture of the universe's global geography is very significant. We expect the universe to be smooth with small variations only out to the scale dictated by the amount of inflation our patch underwent. We predict that if we were to go farther away, then we would eventually find the universe to be very different in structure, reflecting the quantum randomness and different initial conditions across the entire universe when inflation began.

While there have always been skeptical philosophers cautioning that we can't be sure the universe is the same beyond our visible horizon as it is within it, this is the first time that a cosmological theory has positively predicted that this should be the case. A further elaboration makes the history of the universe even more complicated than its geography. Andrei

Linde subsequently noticed that quantum fluctuations ensure that small inflating patches generally produce internal conditions for some of their subregions that will undergo further inflation.[32] This is a self-reproducing fractal branching process called "eternal inflation" that appears to have no end. This possibility gave rise to the picture (and the terminology) of the "multiverse," in which the universe consists of an infinite number of these inflating regions at all times. We inhabit one of them where inflation has been completed in the past. Others, in fact most others, are predicted to be inflating still today.

This complexification of our picture of the universe as a whole in space and time means that traditional big questions (like "did the universe have a beginning?") now have an even more nuanced answer. Our visible universe will have had a beginning of some quantum sort from the patch of space that inflated to produce our extended astronomical region, but the entire self-reproducing eternal inflationary multiverse need have no beginning and no end.[33]

This whole multiverse picture is rather disconcerting in many respects. It puts us in our place within an infinite universe of great complexity whose global properties may be very different from those we observe "locally" in our visible part of it. We don't know how far beyond our present horizon the conditions inherited from our inflated patch extend. In principle, we could start to see weird differences appearing on different sides of the sky next week if the structure of the adjacent inflated patch impinges upon us. But this would require an extraordinary coincidence in the amount of inflation that our patch experiences. The most likely state of affairs is that there was hugely more inflation (pick a number at random and it is likely to be a very large one) and it will be trillions of years before any evidence of other inflated patches could be seen. However, although we may never see these other universe-sized regions in the multiverse, their absence doesn't mean that we cannot falsify this theory. It might predict that something should be seen in every inflated region. If we don't see it in our universe, then this absence would falsify the theory without the need to see the other "universes."

This brief description of the various elaborations of the inflationary universe theory shows how microscopic intrinsic quantum randomness gets amplified and enlarged in extent by the expansion of the universe. When we discover an unusual feature of the universe, it is natural to try to explain it as a direct outcome and reflection of the laws of nature and the numerical values of the constants of physics. However, it might be that it is just a random outcome of the laws that arise by symmetry breaking near the beginning of our universe's expansion history and has no deeper explanation. Indeed, the values of the constants of physics, or even the number of dimensions of space that have become large, might arise in whole or in part in this way. The mysterious numerical value of the cosmological constant[34] Λ, which is responsible for the observed acceleration of the universe's expansion today,[35] is a case in point. Maybe a deep theory will one day explain this strange number, but maybe it arose at random in the early universe and there is nothing more we can say except that it must be found to have a value that allows galaxies, stars, and life to exist. In fact, this last condition for there to be any "observers" turns out to be very stringent as was first pointed out by Barrow and Tipler in 1986,[36] long before the evidence for a nonzero Λ was discovered in 1999.[37] A value of Λ of about 10^{-120}, just ten times larger than observed, would prevent galaxies forming in the usual way because the accelerated expansion becomes too rapid for condensations to separate out from the universal expansion.

We could invent a historical parable to make an analogous point. Imagine that in 1660 someone suggested to Johannes Kepler that the number of planets in the solar system just arises at random. To Kepler this statement would have been anathema. For him, the number of planets was a deep reflection of the symmetries and Pythagorean harmonies in the universe—in effect, it was a law of nature. Today, no planetary astrophysicist would try to predict the number of planets in the solar system. It is a historical accident influenced by objects unpredictably merging, breaking up, and leaving the system. There are many other stable things we can predict about planetary systems, but the number of planets they contain is not one of them. One of the challenges for cosmologists in the future will be to determine which aspects of the universe arise from random symmetry breakings early in its history and which are imprinted predictably by the laws of nature. Einstein had hoped that essentially everything determining the universe, including the constants of physics, would be uniquely and completely determined by the one and only possible "unified theory" of everything. We know now that nature doesn't seem to be like that. In addition to the vast array of "universes" in the multiverse, there are a vast number of self-consistent outcomes of laws and constants of nature for the low-energy, late-time period of the universe, thirteen billion years after the expansion began, in which we must necessarily live. So far, we don't see how to predict which one of these self-consistent outcomes we should see, although we can set about finding one (or more) realizations that closely correspond to the universe that we see.

In the absence of a definite prediction of what outcome of the multiverse we should find ourselves inhabiting, we might hope that our key tool for dealing with uncertainty—probability—could help us. We would like to be able to predict the probability distribution of outcomes from chaotic and eternal inflation so that we could see whether a universe like the one we see is likely or unlikely, and whether universes that permit the evolution of observers (say by expanding long enough without accelerating so as to contain stars) are special or not. Unfortunately, performing such calculations has proved impossible so far, regardless of the philosophy of probability (frequentist or Bayesian) adopted. Trying to add up the universes with a particular property and divide by the total number of universes yields different answers, depending on the order in which they are counted. This is called "the measure problem" and is bigger than the issue of outcomes in the inflationary universe scenario. It would not be an exaggeration to say that we don't know the a priori probability measure for anything in cosmology. We cannot rigorously say that some property of the universe is in any sense likely or unlikely.

An Uncertain Future

Finally, we should note that the far future of the universe is not only ultimately bleak for the survival of life as we know it, but also for astronomy. The structure of the universe will become increasingly inaccessible to astronomers in the far, far future. The present acceleration of the universe will eventually create an absolute horizon in about 100 billion years' time. We (or at least our descendants) will never be able to receive light rays from beyond it and gradually the whole panoply of galaxies we see around us will expand out through this horizon and never be seen again. Future astronomers will not be able to observe the expansion and acceleration of the universe that we see today and will have no knowledge of other galaxies. Gradually, when the universe is only fifty times its present age (and long before all the hydrogen-burning stars die) the microwaves from the hot beginnings of the universe will cool and increase in wavelength so they will be unable to penetrate the interstellar medium in our galaxy.[38]

All the evidence we have of the hot "big bang" and the structure of the universe will become unavailable to those future astronomers. They will read old books and astronomical journals to learn of the structure of the universe that their predecessors could see but they cannot. Our epoch of cosmic history is not only conducive to the emergence of life, but it allows understanding and a degree of certainty to be gained about the structure of the visible universe that will be denied to astronomers in the far, far future.[39]

Notes

1. Jonah 1:7; Michael D. Coogan, ed., *The New Oxford Annotated Bible*, 4th ed. (Oxford: Oxford University Press: 2001), 1303.
2. 1 Samuel 28:6
3. Ezra 2:63
4. Ian Hacking, *The Emergence of Probability* (Cambridge: Cambridge University Press, 1975).
5. John D. Barrow and Frank J. Tipler, *The Anthropic Cosmological Principle* (Oxford: Oxford University Press, 1986), chap. 2.
6. David Hume, *Writings on Religion*, ed. Antony Flew (La Salle, IL: Open Court, 1992), 70.
7. Charles Babbage, *The Ninth Bridgewater Treatise: A Fragment* (London: John Murray, 1837).
8. This important statistical theorem was published posthumously for the nonconformist Reverend Thomas Bayes FRS (d. 1761) in "An Essay towards Solving a Problem in the Doctrine of Chances," *Philosophical Transactions of the Royal Society* 53 (1763), 370–418, by his friend Richard Price. It is reprinted in *Biometrika* 45, nos. 3–4 (1958): 296–315.
9. I draw on D. J. Bartholomew's excellent discussion in "Probability, Statistics and Theology," *Journal of the Royal Statististical Society Series A* 151, no. 1 (1988): 137–178.
10. Pierre Louis de Maupertuis, *Œuvres*, vol. 4 *Accord de différentes loix de la Nature qui avoient jusqu'ici paru incompatibles* (Hildesheim: Olms, 1965), 3 (first published in 1768), and *Œuvres*, vol. 1, *Essai de cosmologie* (Hildesheim: Olms, 1974), 5 (first published in 1768).
11. Further discussion of the status of his claims can be found in Barrow and Tipler, *Anthropic Cosmological* Principle, section 3.4. Although causal and action principle formulations of classical physics appear to be identical, this is no longer the case in quantum physics, where the action formulation has become the standard approach via the Feynman sum-over-histories formulation of quantum theory. During the early nineteenth century, some French

scientists even claimed that the presence of vestigial organs and the discovery of fossils was evidence of failed worlds with nonminimal action! (see P. Janet, *Final causes*, transl. William Affleck (Edinburgh: T. & T. Clark, 1878), 148–149.

12. This civil and theological background can be traced in John D. Barrow, *The World within the World* (Oxford: Oxford University Press, 1988), 58–60 and references therein.
13. Juan Maldacena, "The Symmetry and Simplicity of the Laws of Physics and the Higgs Boson," *arXiv*, July 7, 2015, http://arxiv.org/pdf/1410.6753v2.pdf.
14. Four fundamental forces are known, of which the weakest if gravitation. There might exist other, far weaker forces of nature. Although too weak for us to measure (perhaps ever), their existence may be necessary to fix the logical necessity of that single Theory of Everything. Without any means to check on their existence we would always be missing a crucial piece of the cosmic jigsaw puzzle; see John D. Barrow, *New Theories of Everything: The Quest for Ultimate Explanation* (Oxford: Oxford University Press, [2001] 2007), and Brian Greene, *The Elegant Universe* (London: Jonathan Cape, 1999).
15. John D. Barrow, *Theories of Everything: The Quest for Ultimate Explanation* (Oxford: Oxford University Press, 1992), and John D. Barrow, "Simple Really: From Simplicity to Complexity . . . and Back Again," in *Seeing Further*, ed. Bill Bryson, 361–384 (London: Harper Collins, 2010).
16. Albert Einstein, *The Meaning of Relativity*, trans Edwin Plimpton Adams, 6th ed., (London: Methuen, 1956), and Hubert F. M. Goenner, "On the History of Unified Field Theories," *Living Reviews in Relativity* 7 (2004), http://relativity.livingreviews.org/Articles/lrr-2004-2/.
17. Frederik Denef and Michael R. Douglas, "Computational Complexity of the Landscape: Part 1," *Annals of Physics* 322, no. 5 (2007): 1096–1142.
18. Arthur Beiser, *Concepts in Modern Physics*, 6th ed. (New York: McGraw Hill, 2002).
19. Newton's correspondence with Bentley and Bentley's resulting Boyle Lectures can be found in *Isaac Newton's Papers and Letters on Natural Philosophy*, ed. I. Bernard Cohen and Robert E. Schofield, 2nd ed. (Cambridge, MA: Harvard University Press, 1978).
20. William Paley, *Natural Theology* (1802), ed. Matthew D. Eddy and David M. Knight (Oxford: Oxford University Press, 2008). For further analysis of Paley's treatment of design in laws of nature (in the second part of his book, aided by Brinkley) as well as in outcomes, see Barrow and Tipler, *Anthropic Cosmological Principle*, 76–83.
21. Ibid., chap. 2.
22. Lewis Campbell and William Garnett, *The Life of James Clerk Maxwell* (London: Macmillan, 1882), 434–444, paper read in Cambridge on October 31, 1876.

23. Per Bak Chao Tang and Kurt Wiesenfeld, "Self-Organized Criticality: An Explanation of the 1/*f* Noise," *Physical Review Letters* 59 (1987): 381–385, and Per Bak, *How Nature Works: The Science of Self-Organized Criticality* (New York: Copernicus, 1996).
24. Closer examination of the details of the fall of sand has revealed that avalanches of asymmetrically shaped grains, like rice, produce the critical scale-independent behavior even more accurately because the rice grains always tumble rather than slide.
25. Claudius Gros, *Complex and Adaptive Systems: A Primer* (New York: Springer, 2013).
26. George F. R. Ellis, S. D. Nel, R. Maartens, W. R. Stoeger, and A. P. Whitman, "Ideal Observational Cosmology," *Physics Reports* 124, nos. 5–6 (1985): 315–417.
27. Alan H. Guth, "Inflationary Universe: A Possible Solution to the Horizon and Flatness Problems." *Physical Review D* 23 (1981): 347–356.
28. The recently discovered Higgs boson is an example, although not one that we believe could have produced inflation in our past.
29. Anisotropic universes expand at different rates in different directions; isotropic universes expand at the same rate in all directions.
30. John D. Barrow, *The Book of Universes: Exploring the Limits of the Cosmos* (London: Bodley Head, 2011).
31. G. W. Gibbons, Stephen W. Hawking, and S. T. C. Siklos, *The Very Early Universe* (Cambridge: Cambridge University Press, 1983) (Nuffield workshop), and report by John D. Barrow and Michael S. Turner, "The Inflationary Universe: Birth, Death and Transfiguration," *Nature* 298, no. 5877 (1983): 801–805.
32. A. Linde, "Eternally Existing Self-Reproducing Chaotic Inflationary Universe," *Physics Letters B* 175, no. 4 (1986): 395–400.
33. It can have a beginning but this is not required. There is a theorem due to Arvind Borde, Alan H. Guth, and Alexander Vilenkin, "Inflationary Spacetimes Are Incomplete in Past Directions," *Physical Review Letters* 90, no. 15 (2003), that is sometimes interpreted as requiring the universe (even the eternal inflationary universe) to have a beginning. This theorem must, however, be interpreted with care. This type of result has been known for a long time and would require even the steady-state universe to have a beginning. It was discussed in Barrow and Tipler, *Anthropic Cosmological Principle*, 107, in this context who pointed out that all paths of light rays are incomplete to the past of a steady state universe.
34. The Newtonian counterpart of Einstein's cosmological constant is the addition of a second term proportional to separation, r, to the inverse-square attractive force of attraction, proportional to $1/r^2$
35. The universe began accelerating again when it had expanded to about 75 percent of its present extent. Although the effect is like that of inflation the cause cannot

be the same as in the very early universe. It is believed to be the manifestation of the quantum vacuum energy density that pervades the universe. However, why this energy has the particular numerical value that it does (approximately 10–121 in Planck units) remains something of a mystery, although there have been some attempts to explain it, see for example John D. Barrow and Douglas J. Shaw, "New Solution of the Cosmological Constant Problems," *Physical Review Letters* 106, nos. 10–11 (2011).

36. Barrow and Tipler, *Anthropic Cosmological Principle*, 412–414.
37. Because previous observational upper bounds and this anthropic upper bound forces Λ to be so small, there was a feeling amongst particle physicists and many cosmologists that its actual value was probably exactly zero and there was some fundamental principle still to be found that forced it to be so. The discovery that it was nonzero was therefore a considerable surprise.
38. Lawrence M. Krauss and Robert J. Scherrer, "The Return of a Static Universe and the End of Cosmology." *General Relativity and Gravity* 39, no. 10 (2007): 1545–1550; Tony Rothman and George F. R. Ellis, "The Epoch of Observational Cosmology," *The Observatory* 107 (1987): 24–29.
39. John D. Barrow, "The Far, Far Future," in *The Far-Future Universe: Eschatology from a Cosmic Perspective*, ed. George F. R. Ellis, 23–40 (Radnor: Templeton Foundation Press, 2002).

Selected Bibliography

Babbage, Charles. *The Ninth Bridgewater Treatise: A Fragment* (London: John Murray, 1837).

Bak, Per, Chao Tang, and Kurt Wiesenfeld. "Self-Organized Criticality: An Explanation of the 1/*f* Noise." *Physical Review Letters* 59, no. 4 (1987): 381–385.

Bak, Per. *How Nature Works: The Science of Self-Organized Criticality* (New York: Copernicus, 1996).

Barrow, John D. *The Book of Universes: Exploring the Limits of the Cosmos* (London: Bodley Head, 2011).

Barrow, John D. "The Far, Far Future." In *The Far-Future Universe: Eschatology from a Cosmic Perspective*, edited by George F. R. Ellis, 23–40 (Radnor: Templeton Foundation Press, 2002).

Barrow, John D. *New Theories of Everything: The Quest for Ultimate Explanation* (Oxford: Oxford University Press, 2007)

Barrow, John D. "Simple Really: From Simplicity to Complexity . . . and Back Again." In *Seeing Further: The Story of Science, Discovery, and the Genius of the Royal Society*, edited by Bill Bryson, 361–384 (London: Harper Collins, 2010).

Barrow, John D. *Theories of Everything: The Quest for Ultimate Explanation* (Oxford: Oxford University Press, 1992).

Barrow, John D. *The World within the World* (Oxford: Oxford University Press, 1988).

Barrow, John D., and Frank J. Tipler. *The Anthropic Cosmological Principle* (Oxford: Oxford University Press, 1986).

Beiser, Arthur. *Concepts in Modern Physics.* 6th ed. (New York: McGraw Hill, 2002).

Coogan, Michael D., ed. *The New Oxford Annotated Bible.* 4th ed. (Oxford: Oxford University Press, 2010).

Einstein, Albert. *The Meaning of Relativity.* Translated by Edwin Plimpton Adams. 6th ed. (London: Methuen, 1956).

Ellis, George F. R., S. D. Nel., R. Maartens, W. R. Stoeger, and A. P. Whitman. "Ideal Observational Cosmology." *Physics Reports* 124, nos. 5–6 (1985): 315–417.

Gibbons, G. W., Stephen W. Hawking, and S. T. C. Siklos, *The Very Early Universe* (Cambridge: Cambridge University Press, 1983).

Greene, Brian. *The Elegant Universe* (London: Jonathan Cape, 1999).

Gros, Claudius. *Complex and Adaptive Systems: A Primer* (New York: Springer, 2013).

Guth, Alan H. "Inflationary Universe: A Possible Solution to the Horizon and Flatness Problems." *Physical Review D* 23 (1981): 347–356.

Hacking, Ian. *The Emergence of Probability* (Cambridge: Cambridge University Press, 1975).

Janet, Paul. *Final Causes.* Translated by William Affleck (Edinburgh: T. & T. Clark, 1878).

Krauss, Lawrence M., and Robert J. Scherrer. "The Return of a Static Universe and the End of Cosmology." *General Relativity and Gravity* 39, no. 10 (2007): 1545–1550.

Campbell, Lewis, and William Garnett. *The Life of James Clerk Maxwell* (London: Macmillan, 1882).

Maupertuis, Pierre Louis de. *Œuvres.* Vol. 4, *Accord de différentes loix de la Nature qui avoient jusqu'ici paru incompatibles* (Hildesheim: Olms, 1965). First published in 1746

Maupertuis, Pierre Louis de. *Œuvres.* Vol. 1, *Essai de cosmologie* (Hildesheim: Olms, 1974). First published in 1750.

Newton, Isaac. *Isaac Newton's Papers and Letters on Natural Philosophy.* Edited by I. Bernard Cohen and Robert E. Schofield. 2nd ed. (Cambridge, MA: Harvard University Press, 1978).

Paley, William. *Natural Theology.* Edited by Matthew D. Eddy and David M. Knight (Oxford: Oxford University Press, 2008). First published in 1802.

Rothman, Tony, and George F. R. Ellis, "The Epoch of Observational Cosmology." *The Observatory* 107 (1987): 24–29.

4

Random Numbers and God's Nature

James Bradley

1 Introduction

Christianity has long applied philosophical reflection to theological questions, a tradition this chapter follows. Its philosophical subject is mathematical randomness; its theological subject is the nature of God. I start with mathematical Platonism,[1] an ancient stream of thought that views numbers as transcending physical reality—a view which has occupied a prominent place in much Christian thought about mathematics. I then join this traditional view of numbers and God to recent insights into mathematical randomness from theoretical computer science. Joining these streams—one ancient, one recent—yields the surprising conclusion that randomness, defined in a particular way, is part of the nature of God. I then explore some of the implications of this idea for our understanding of God's nature, the physical world, and tragic "chance" events.

2 Are Numbers Real?

Mathematical Platonism views the objects mathematicians study—familiar ones like numbers or less familiar ones like groups and manifolds—as objectively and timelessly existing, transcending individual human minds. This view is also known as *realism*, for its claim that numbers, like rocks and clouds, have a real existence—what philosophers would call an *ontological reality*.[2] Not all mathematicians are Platonists, however. Some are *nominalists* or *formalists*, two approaches that deny that mathematical objects are real, claiming instead that they are linguistic conventions—we agree among ourselves that a trio of apples will be identified as "three" apples, but this is merely the name we give to that trio and has no reality on its own. Other mathematicians are *antirealists* in the tradition of Kant, and see mathematical objects as patterns used by human minds to structure the reality they perceive. For them, mathematical objects do have ontological status—reality—but this status resides in the common structures of the human mind. Mathematics educators are often *constructivists*; they study the processes by which learners construct mathematical knowledge. They then identify the reality of mathematical objects with this process of construction. Although many variations on these and other perspectives can be found, most mathematicians tend toward some form of Platonism.[3]

Paul Benacerraf, a philosopher of mathematics, notes that Platonism has a "location problem": If numbers exist apart from human minds, where are they located? Many Christian thinkers respond that numbers are located in the mind of God and have been from eternity.[4] Let's look at this claim.

The Pythagoreans, a community of scholars (some would say a religious cult) around the turn of the fourth century BCE, were the first people known to reflect philosophically on mathematics. We have no written record of their work, so scholars depend on secondary sources and agree that the Pythagorean perspective on mathematics originated when they discovered that music was mathematical. If one takes two identical stringed instruments and plucks strings with lengths in the ratio of 2:1, the sounds blend in a pleasing way. Strings whose lengths are in the ratio of 3:2 and 4:3 also sound pleasing together. These ratios were called respectively the octave, fifth, and fourth; the entire twelve-tone scale of Western music is based on these ratios. The Pythagoreans generalized the discovery that numerical ratios underlie the sensory phenomenon of pleasing sounds to the idea that the sensory world we perceive is grounded in an immaterial world accessible to the intellect but not to the senses; for the Pythagoreans the principal characteristic of this unseen world was number.

The Pythagoreans deeply influenced Plato, whose central concept is his theory of forms—intelligible, abstract objects "corresponding to general terms such as 'just,' 'large,' 'triangle,' 'fire,' 'horse.'"[5] Plato is ambiguous, however, about the relationship of mathematics to the forms. Dominic O'Meara, professor and chair of Metaphysics and Ancient Philosophy at the University of Fribourg, writes, "In the *Republic*, for example, mathematics concerns objects that relate to the transcendent realm of Forms as images of the Forms. But what is not altogether clear is whether mathematical objects exist as image-like realities, or merely in the sense that they are the way that the mathematician thinks immaterial objects."[6] In the *Republic,* Plato claims geometry turns us away from the world of perception to contemplation of the intelligible and eternal. In his final book, *Timaeus,* Plato describes the creation of the world by a benevolent creator god who takes preexisting matter and makes it good by shaping it to resemble the forms. The god uses mathematics in this shaping process. Ian Mueller writes that Plato had "a comprehensive picture of the cosmos divided into a higher divine, intelligible world and a lower human, sensible world, and saw the task of the individual, on which his well-being, his divinization, depends as a matter of somehow attaching himself to that higher world. A, and I suspect the, crucial link between these worlds is mathematics."[7]

Aristotle was Plato's student, but differed from him dramatically on ontology, seeing no need to posit a *separate* world of forms. Aristotle argued that mathematics is the study of the mathematical properties of physical objects with no ontological status distinct from that. These two views—that mathematics transcends the physical world and that it is immanent in the physical world—have been the principal alternatives around which all discussions of the nature of mathematics have revolved.

The question remained: Where exactly was mathematics located? If Plato's forms existed, where were they? Subsequent thinkers identified mathematics more explicitly with the divine nature. Nicomachus of Gerasa (ca. 60 AD–ca. 120 AD) wrote an *Arithmetic Theology* identifying numbers with various deities in the Greek pantheon. Plotinus (204–270 AD) and Proclus (412–485 AD), known as Neoplatonists, refined and clarified Plato's ideas, locating the life of the divine in an eternal "soul" and interpreting mathematics as elaborations of concepts inherent in the nature of soul. However, the first known work locating mathematics in the nature of the Christian God is Augustine's *On Free Choice of the Will,* written at the end of the fourth century.[8] In book 2 of this work, Augustine dialogues with an interlocutor, Euvodius, seeking to articulate a proof of God's existence. His proof proceeds from a demonstration that there exist realities outside of the human mind that are higher than it. His primary example is numbers, although he is not writing about the nature of mathematics or even according it the prominence that Nicomachus and the Neoplatonists gave it. Rather, he locates all the Platonic forms as well as mathematics in God. Augustine saw "ideas" as "certain original and principal forms of things, i.e., reasons, fixed and unchangeable, which are not themselves formed and, being thus eternal and existing always in the same state, are contained in the Divine Intelligence."[9]

We have no evidence of significant additions to this conversation until the twelfth century. Aristotle's works, lost to Western scholarship during the first millennium, were reintroduced to the West from the Islamic world in the early twelfth century. They were enormously influential and much of Thomas Aquinas's work reconciles Christian thought with the insights of Aristotle. Aquinas writes little about mathematics, however, with the exception of one section on infinity in his *Summa Theologiae*.[10] After Aquinas, many scholastics went beyond Aristotle's denial of mathematics' transcendence and became *nominalists*[11]—while Aristotle thought of the forms as existent but *in* objects (and such that we can abstract them from objects), nominalists thought of the forms as merely names (*nomina*).

Johannes Kepler, Isaac Newton, and Gottfried Wilhelm Leibniz—principal figures of the sixteenth-century scientific revolution—held views similar to Augustine's. Kepler (1571–1630), famous for showing that the orbits of the planets were elliptical, argued that geometric shapes were ideas in God's mind. Since God thinks correctly about them, if we too think correctly about them, we are thinking "God's thoughts after him." Isaac Newton (1642–1727) saw his work on gravitation as explaining those ideas in God's mind that provided the basis of God's relationship with the physical universe. Gottfried Leibniz (1646–1716), with Newton the founder of calculus, argued that God could not abolish mathematical truths without abolishing God's self.

Philosophical reflection on mathematics and theology declined during the eighteenth-century Enlightenment, and with the secularizing of science in general and mathematics in particular, conversations about the relationship of mathematics to the divine have become uncommon in the community of professional mathematicians. Some contemporary Christian philosophers, however, remain interested. Alvin Plantinga, for example, has clearly articulated the Augustinian perspective on numbers.

> if the number 7 or the proposition *all men are mortal* exist necessarily, then God has essentially the property of affirming their existence. That property, therefore, will be part of his nature. Indeed, for any necessarily existing abstract object O, the property of affirming

> the existence of O is part of God's nature. It is thus part of God's nature to say, "Let there be the number 1; let there be 2; let there be 3. . . ." . . . God hasn't *created* the numbers; a thing is created only if its existence has a beginning, and no number ever began to exist . . . other mathematical entities—the reals, for example—stand in the same relation to God and humankind as do the natural numbers. Sequences of natural numbers, for example, are necessary beings and have been created neither by God nor by anyone else. Still, each such sequence is such that it is part of God's nature to affirm its existence.[12]

Christian Platonism in mathematics remains relevant today, even though it is currently out of fashion. Consider the following three claims in support of Christian Platonism: (1) God desires to reveal God's nature; (2) God is triune; and (3) Some truths are "necessary"—that is, they cannot fail to be true in any possible world; such truths are part of God's nature.

(1) God's desire to be revealed in creation is evident throughout the Old Testament and culminates in the New Testament with the Incarnation. John's Gospel makes this point: "No one has ever seen God; but, the only Son, who is in the bosom of the Father, has made him known."[13] The Incarnation does not guarantee that all conclusions we draw about God are true, but it does assure us that God wants to be understood by humans.

(2) God is triune and would have been triune even if God hadn't created anything. "Threeness" is a numerical notion that applies to God and would have applied even apart from creation. From this perspective, "numerical laws" cannot be merely laws of creation. If God is necessarily triune, then we must conclude that some numerical notions apply to God.

(3) This is Plantinga's argument quoted above. Necessary truths include those of logic (such as *modus ponens*—if A implies B is true and A is true, then B is true) and arithmetic (such as 5 + 7 = 12). They are not contingent—not even God could make them be otherwise and be faithful to God's own nature. Since they are necessary, God must have known them eternally and must have affirmed their existence as necessary truths. This is the same as saying they must have been eternally in God's mind.

There are also three arguments from natural theology for locating mathematics in the mind of God: (1) the indispensability argument; (2) the argument for universality; and (3) the a priori argument.

(1) Mathematics is indispensable for doing science. Not only is mathematics necessary to do measurements and articulate formulas for laws of physics and chemistry, but frequently manipulations of these formulas yield surprising predictions that turn out to be true. This close linkage between mathematics and the physical world gives credence to the idea that God used mathematical ideas to provide patterns for creation, as Kepler suggested. But if God used mathematical ideas to provide patterns for creation, a natural conclusion is that these ideas were present in God's mind at creation.
(2) Mathematics is universal. While culture does affect the way we develop mathematics, many different cultures have independently developed similar mathematics. The universality of mathematics implies that it transcends human minds; where else could it be located than in "God's mind"?
(3) Some argue that mathematical truths such as 2 + 2 = 4 are known from experience: we observe that two apples combined with two more apples result in four apples and we generalize from that. But it does not seem to accord with our sense of how we acquire mathematical knowledge or how we use it to describe things outside our experience, like curved space or gravity. Mathematics seems to be explorable on its own terms, apart from experience. Augustine argued that small children have an intuitive understanding of infinity even though infinity is outside human experience. And not everything combines according to the laws of arithmetic. While 1 apple plus 1 apple may be two apples, one drop of mercury plus another is still just one drop of mercury. Where, then did our certain knowledge that 2 + 2 = 4 originate? It is certainly reasonable to claim that such knowledge is a priori, and a Christian can therefore say it comes from God.[14]

There are arguments against *Christian* Platonism as well. Paul Benacerraf (cited earlier) does not entertain the possibility that God exists. So for him there is no place to locate a transcendent mathematics. Alternatively, Sir Roger Penrose is an enthusiastic Platonist, but he minimally affirms the transcendent existence of mathematics without locating it in the mind of a deity.[15] At the opposite end of the spectrum, perhaps God is so transcendent that suggesting God has ideas or thoughts is an inappropriate anthropomorphism. The latter perspective does not deny the possibility that mathematics consists of ideas in God's mind; rather, it says we can *never know* that because God is so dissimilar to us that there is no conduit from God's mind to ours. Of course, the assertion "We cannot know that mathematics consists of ideas in God's mind" is not the same as "We know that mathematics cannot consist of ideas in God's mind."

The cautions that critics of Christian Platonism advocate deserve respect. Nevertheless, I find the arguments for Christian Platonism compelling, particularly the argument from necessity: (1) God is omniscient, (2) hence God must have always known mathematical truths, (3) such truths are necessary, (4) thus they are not contingent on God's will, and (5) hence such truths must have been in God's mind forever. I am thus going to assume that Christian Platonism is true. But I want to note that it provides only a partial account of the nature of mathematics—its beauty, ubiquity in nature, and comprehensibility by human minds all originate in God as well.

3 Random Numbers

Words like "random," "uncertain," "unpredictable," and "chance" have many meanings, on Main Street, where they are a part of popular but informal discourse; in the more formal world of philosophy; and in the more precise world of science and mathematics, where they typically have a mathematical formulation. The discussion here will be informal; the appendix presents some mathematically precise formulations.

In popular discourse "random" means: *not having a governing design, method, or purpose; without order; without cause.* This popular meaning arises from classical notions of chance discussed elsewhere in this volume. It excludes any association of randomness with divine providence—a random event in this sense is without design or purpose and thus cannot be caused by God, at least as traditionally understood in the Abrahamic traditions.

Philosophical and scientific definitions differ—often dramatically—from the popular definition but also vary among disciplines. Some philosophers use "chance" to refer to natural processes and "random" to refer to numbers.[16] Mathematicians use the word "random" but typically do not use the word "chance" in a technical way. By "random" they mean unpredictable and they typically use "random" to describe processes in which multiple outcomes can occur and each is associated with a probability that gives the likelihood of that outcome.

Physicists use "random" in the sense of unpredictability—as in a coin toss—but also use it to mean "without cause"—this does not apply to a coin toss but does apply to elementary particles. In quantum mechanics, these particles are described mathematically by an equation for waves—spread out and often undulating like a water wave—but they behave like traditional particles when observed, being located in one place, like a baseball. The humble electron illustrates the simplest example of this randomness. Electrons are like tiny magnets that can point up or down in reference to the measuring apparatus. When they are measured, the magnet always points one way or the other—no "sideways" option—and no causative factor has ever been found that can account for the direction of the magnet that is actually observed. In fact, physicists have shown that if such a factor exists, it must be completely different from anything we currently understand.

Biologists also make extensive use of the term "random" to mean unpredictable, but they also use it in a quite different way. In evolutionary biology, mutations are considered to be random, not because they have no cause, but because no correlation exists between the occurrence of mutations and the needs or opportunities of individuals or species. As helpful as immunity to AIDS may be, this need does nothing to produce mutations that would confer that immunity. If such mutations do occur, natural selection can favor them and, via enhanced reproduction, spread them throughout the populace, but the mutations will not arrive just because they are needed.

Computer scientists approach randomness via random *numbers* rather than random events. But the term "random number" is not the same as that used by experimenters for whom a random number is one generated by a process that makes any of a *collection* of numbers equally likely, as occurs when tossing a single die. Rather, computer scientists take a *single* number and ask if it is random. In the binary, "base 2," language used in computers, where "1" and "0" are the only options, all numbers are strings of 1's and 0's. Consider, for example, the numbers .1010101010101010 . . . and .0111110011110110111. Intuitively, the latter seems more random since predicting the next digit appears impossible. (The latter number was, in fact, generated by flipping a coin, which confirms that the next digit would be unpredictable.) Computer scientists ask what "random" means for such numbers.

The first attempt to formulate a concept of randomness for sequences of numbers was by Richard Von Mises in 1919. This approach starts with the idea that for a random number written in binary, each consecutive bit should be equally likely to be a 0 or a 1. Thus, as we look at increasing numbers of bits, the bits will come closer to being half 0's and half 1s—this is called the law of large numbers. However, there are strings—.1010101010101010101010 . . . for example—that satisfy the law of large numbers (being half 1's and half 0's) but are not random. So Von Mises focused on substrings. If one picks the substring found in positions {1, 3, 5, –} of .1010101010101010101010 . . . one gets the string .111111 . . . , which is clearly not half 0s and half 1s. This result, according to Von Mises, shows that .1010101010101010101010 . . . is not random. He calls any selection process that can be described by a rule like "look at every other bit" an "acceptable selection rule." He then says that a random number is one for which all substrings selected by acceptable selection rules satisfy the law of large numbers. This was a good start to defining randomness for numbers, but it didn't solve the problem because it provided no way to decide which rules were acceptable.

In 1936, Alan Turing (1912–1954) defined what has today come to be known as a Turing machine. Turing's goal was to develop an abstract, unambiguous formalization of the process of evaluating a mathematical function (such as $x^2 + 2x + 1$). While not a physical machine, Turing's "machine" was a careful description of a step-by-step process, what we commonly call an "algorithm."[17] Turing's concept heavily influenced the development of actual computing machines that took place in the decade following. Mathematicians and computer scientists generally regard Turing's efforts as successful; the "Church-Turing thesis," named for Alonzo Church (1903–1995) and Turing, asserts that any operation that can be carried out on an actual computer can (at least in principle) be carried out on a Turing machine. Thus Turing machines provide an abstract setting in which one can ask and answer theoretical questions about what computers in principle can and cannot do. Von Mises wrote before the concept of Turing machine had been defined. Its introduction made it possible to say which selection rules are acceptable, namely the ones that can be formulated as a Turing machine.

Starting with the work of Per Martin-Löf in 1966, computer scientists have formulated a detailed theory of randomness for numbers; the theory extensively uses Turing machines. It includes numerous definitions of what it means for a number to be random, what it means for one number to be more random than another, and many other nuances. The features of this theory that are of the most interest to us here, however, are:

(1) Three definitions of "random" that have been shown to be equivalent,
(2) The fact that using these equivalent definitions, it can be shown that, in a mathematically precise sense, almost all numbers are random.

The definitions are intuitively appealing and can be made mathematically rigorous—and when mathematicians formulate a concept in more than one intuitively appealing way and the definitions are subsequently shown to be equivalent, it reinforces the belief that they have successfully captured a significant idea. What follows is a brief, intuitive explanation of each concept; a more technical explanation can be found in the appendix. The three concepts are described below:

Irreducibility

Consider two bit strings: 10101010101010101010 and 011111001110110111. The first has an obvious pattern; the second was generated by flipping a coin twenty times. The first can be generated by this algorithm:

Repeat 10 times: output '10'

The second, however, requires an algorithm like

Output '011111001110110111'

That is, the second string cannot be reduced to one shorter and simpler than itself. The underlying intuition is that a string of *n* bits is random if any algorithm able to generate it requires at least n bits, that is, the string is irreducible. Infinite strings are random if they cannot be reduced to finite expression.

Martin-Löf Randomness

A string like 10101010101010101010 has an obvious pattern; a string like 011111001110110111 does not. Of course, a string could look like it has a pattern near its beginning but then become patternless. Martin-Löf randomness captures the idea that a string which is not random has a finite pattern and maintains that pattern throughout a possibly infinite length. A random string is one that lacks a pattern.

Constructive Martingales

Suppose a string of bits is revealed one bit at a time. The intuitive idea behind the martingale concept of randomness is that there is no betting strategy that would enable one to profit by predicting the next bit. That is, randomness defined in this way corresponds in a meaningful way with unpredictability.

In short, the underlying intuition behind these three concepts of random numbers is that a number is random if it is irreducibly infinite, has no finite pattern, and is unpredictable. The key point for us in this chapter, however, is that random numbers are numbers. Thus:

> *If numbers have indeed existed in the mind of God from eternity, randomness is and always has been part of God's nature.*

I will explore the theological implications of this idea in the next section and the scientific implications in the section following that.

4 *Theological Implications*

What does the idea that randomness is part of God's nature tell us about God? First, let's consider what it does *not* tell us. The popular concept cited above is that randomness means not having a governing design, method, or purpose; without order; without cause. This popular concept is what makes the idea that randomness might be part of the divine nature seem strange or shocking. But algorithmic randomness is quite different from the popular concept of randomness and *is* informative about God's nature—even under a Christian theology which has always affirmed that God has designed the world, acts with method and purpose, and is orderly. Unlike popular notions of randomness, under the mathematical hypothesis of numbers being ideas in God's mind, the properties of random numbers are necessary properties of God's nature[18] and can enrich our understanding of God's infinitude. Before we can see what these properties add, though, we need to see how systematic theologians have historically understood divine infinitude. Here is a typical list of divine attributes to provide a context for the analysis that follows.[19]

The Nature of God

Divine sufficiency (primary and essential attributes of God inapplicable to creatures and not communicable to creatures):

- uncreated
- infinite
- one

The divine majesty (relational divine attributes displaying God's way of being present, knowing and influencing the world):

- omnipresence
- omniscience
- omnipotence

The Character of God

The divine thou (active and interpersonal attributes belonging to the divine-human relationship and analogous to personal experience):

- incomparably personal
- spiritual
- free

The divine goodness (moral qualities intrinsic to the divine character):

- holiness
- goodness
- compassion

In this taxonomy, infinity is one aspect of God's sufficiency; however, Christian thinkers' understanding of God's infinitude has varied over time and across religious traditions. The notion that God is infinite seems to have first appeared in Christian writings among early Gnostics. Augustine wrote that God is infinite in wisdom and is unbounded not in the sense of being suffused throughout space, but rather God is infinite "in another way," although he did not comment on what this way is.[20] Thomas Aquinas devoted Question 7 of the first part of his *Summa Theologiae* to God's infinitude. He conceived of it as meaning that God is not limited in any way and is infinite in perfection in the sense that God's perfection cannot be diminished or increased. He wrote that God is unique in being infinite, that no bodily thing can be infinite, and that there cannot be an actually infinite number. This latter notion originated in Aristotle's idea of "potential infinity"—for example, integers increasing without bound but not reaching a limit.[21] Some medieval scholars distinguished extrinsic and intrinsic infinity. The concept of "extrinsic infinity" was based on the integers continuing without limit; "intrinsic infinity" was based on the notion of a finite space being infinitely divisible. They suggested that God's infinitude is intrinsic not extrinsic; this seems to be a way to affirm divine infinitude while avoiding the notion that God is infinite in extent—but this was ambiguous about the relationship of intrinsic infinitude to God's nature. John Calvin's concept of God's infinitude was "beyond our senses." Many theologians have pointed out that God's infinitude is not separable from other attributes—it is part of what it means for God to be omnipresent, omniscient, and omnipotent. Some pointed out that God's infinitude, when applied to time, is God's eternality; when applied to space, it is God's omnipresence. Herman Bavinck emphasized that God's infinitude applies to character attributes as well as sufficiency and majesty, and in this way is quite different from a quantitative notion of infinity.[22] The principal common theme, however, that runs through these notions is "without limit." And the etymological basis of infinity is "unlimited."

I can see two ways that the idea of divine randomness can enrich our understanding of God's infinitude: (1) it can serve a pedagogical role by providing images that enable us to form clearer concepts of divine infinitude, thereby enriching our worship; and (2) it can introduce aspects of divine infinitude that had not been previously noted.

(1) The integers provide an image that many theologians have used to illustrate God's infinitude. The concepts of randomness discussed here follow that tradition—an infinite number that is irreducibly random is one that cannot be described by repetition of a finite string; a Martin-Löf random number lacks a pattern that can be generated by any (necessarily finite) algorithm. Both of these concepts provide images of the idea that God cannot be described in terms of any finite thing—no *complete* description of God is possible.

(2) The martingale definition of randomness introduces an aspect of the divine nature that I have not seen discussed in connection with the doctrine of divine infinitude, namely the element of surprise or mystery. Random numbers are mysterious, such that no matter how many bits of one have been revealed, the next bit is still unpredictable. Saying that such numbers exist in the mind of God provides an image of the idea that one may indeed understand aspects of God truly and may learn more, but never come to the point where there are not further aspects of God that are surprising. Put differently, no matter how much knowledge one has of God, God's mystery remains unfathomable.[23]

In summary, discussions of divine infinitude that are informed primarily by the image of the integers lead one to the idea that God is unlimited, but not much more. A comprehension of divine randomness extends this understanding, nuances it, and enriches it.

5 *Implications for the Material World*

Some properties of physical objects (weight and length, for example) correspond to numbers in meaningful ways—the process of combining two weights or two lengths corresponds to addition; cutting an object into two equal parts corresponds to division by two. Numbers provide precise and meaningful measurements of such properties and enable comparisons between objects. (They are not as helpful in dealing with properties that do not act in ways that correspond to numbers—love and guilt, to pick two examples.) Mathematical functions (an abstraction originating in numbers) can be used to describe relationships between quantifiable properties; they provide a deductive framework for scientific theories, enabling prediction and control of the behavior of physical entities.

However, mathematics (defined broadly to include numbers as well as more advanced topics such as algebra and calculus) plays another critical role beyond enabling measurement and scientific theorizing. It provides images that often shape the thinking of human communities, even entire cultures. One example noted in the previous section is that the integers shaped many theologians' concept of God's infinitude. Most importantly here, however, is that Isaac Newton's mathematical formulation of the laws of gravitation shaped the European Enlightenment in the eighteenth century. Newton saw these laws as explaining how God worked in the material world; subsequent scholars kept the mathematics and dropped divine action. A famous example of this latter perspective is the apocryphal story of a conversation between the mathematician Pierre-Simon Laplace and the French emperor, Napoleon. Commenting on a book by Laplace, Napoleon supposedly pointed out that Laplace had written a lengthy study of the physical universe but had never mentioned God. In the story, Laplace replied, "Sir, I had no need of that hypothesis."

Laplace provided a notably clear articulation of scientific determinism, having written,

> We may regard the present state of the universe as the effect of its past and the cause of its future. An intellect which at a certain moment would know all forces that set nature in motion, and all positions of all items of which nature is composed, if this intellect were also vast enough to submit these data to analysis, it would embrace in a single formula the movements of the greatest bodies of the universe and those of the tiniest atom; for such an intellect nothing would be uncertain and the future just like the past would be present before its eyes.[24]

Newton's laws of motion provided Laplace and others with the image that shaped the Enlightenment view of the world—mechanical, deterministic, and under the control of inviolable laws of nature. It shaped expectations of what understanding the world meant and how scholarship should proceed in the search for that understanding. For example, Charles Darwin was inspired by Newton's laws in his search for laws governing speciation in evolutionary biology.[25] So images that originate in mathematics may have broad implications for our collective understanding of the material and spiritual world.

However, with the discovery of quantum mechanics and genetic mutation in the twentieth century, the Enlightenment view of a mechanistic material world collapsed. Among physicists, the idea that the universe was governed by deterministic laws was replaced by the idea that a fundamental indeterminism lay at the root of the properties of elementary particles. Among biologists, a consensus developed that the diversity of living organisms found on earth was the result of random mutations. These concepts nourished a widely held perspective that the universe was without meaning, purpose, or direction. An eminent paleontologist, Stephen Jay Gould, for example, famously wrote that if we were to rewind the tape of evolution back a million years and run it again, it would produce a very different world than the one we live in because so many aspects of plants and animal biology are the result of chance. [26] So the currently reigning image of the physical world is one deeply influenced by the image of random processes—and a popular interpretation of this idea equates randomness with purposelessness and meaninglessness.

My principal objective in this section is to examine how the interpretation of this image would change if randomness were seen as originating in God's nature. However, a question needs to be addressed first: is there any connection between algorithmic randomness (the kind I have argued is found in God's nature) and randomness observed in the material world? For reasons I will expand on below, I posit that it is reasonable to believe the following:

First, that God used mathematical concepts (located in God's mind) in creating the physical universe and that is why mathematics is so effective in science. As above, this is a long-held idea of Christian Platonism and while God is under no constraint to use this particular aspect of the divine nature in the physical world, it would be no surprise if God did.

Second, algorithmic randomness and the mathematical concept of random process are quite similar—both formalize the intuitive notions of unpredictability, absence of pattern, and irreducibility. The principal difference is that an algorithmically random number is infinite in length and a list of the outcomes of a random process is necessarily finite. However, if coded as base 2 numbers by some coding method, the finite list of outcomes can be viewed as the beginning of a random string of infinite length. That is, random sequences in the material world can be viewed as truncations of infinite random sequences in the divine nature. Charles

Darwin and others have suggested that the presence of random processes in nature is evidence of a lack of intelligent control of the physical world.[27] While a correspondence between divine randomness and the outcomes of finite processes does not demonstrate the existence of intelligent control, it does show that absence of intelligent control cannot be inferred from the presence of randomness.

Now let's return to the main question: How would seeing randomness as rooted in God's nature affect an interpretation of the world that has been shaped by our knowledge of existing random processes?

(1) Randomness in the physical world should come as no surprise—infinitude is part of God's nature. Hence, it is reasonable to expect that many aspects of the world would be unpredictable and exhibit an absence of finite patterns.
(2) Rather than randomness being seen as evidence against providential care for the world or as impersonal, unguided "chance," randomness would be seen as an expression of God's transcendence, variety, mystery, and the subtlety of God's wisdom in ordering and managing the world; it would not be seen as an absence of divine control but rather as a subtle form of divine management that allows freedom within constraints. For example, random mutations could be seen as a way to allow species to explore all of the opportunities available in the genetic space surrounding their gene pool. Natural selection then identifies the discoveries that improve a species' adaptation.
(3) There are physical situations in which randomness is undesirable, such as, for example, static corrupting the electronic transmission of a message. But in the case of the diffusion of nutrients in the body or the operation of the human immune system, it plays a central role in preserving life. Genesis 1:31 says, "God saw all that he had made, and it was very good." The word "good" here would be seen as including randomness.
(4) The existence of divine randomness establishes a distinct mindset for how we approach the natural world. Rather than seeing it as either a determined system or a meaningless system, it would be seen as a never-ending source of surprise and wonder.
(5) We should not expect to find a "theory of everything," as such a theory would be a finite account of a world created by an infinite creator.

6 Conclusion

Sections 4 and 5 examined the implications of divine randomness for our understanding of God's nature and our understanding of the material world. One major area remains to which we can apply this understanding of randomness—the presence of what are commonly called chance events in people's lives. Such events are of greatest concern when they are tragic.[28] For example, a person is waiting at a traffic light during a storm. The wind blows over a tree; it falls on the car and kills the driver. But a slight difference in the position of the car or a few seconds' difference in the arrival time at the red light would have meant no accident at all. Does an understanding of divine randomness have anything to offer to our understanding of such events? I am going to suggest it does, but only when coupled with two key Christian doctrines—the doctrine of *creatio ex nihilo* and the doctrine of the atonement. Note that this analysis applies only to certain types of natural evil—not to evil that is the result of human moral failure.

Creatio ex nihilo (creation from nothing) is the doctrine that God did not use preexisting matter in shaping the world, as Plato believed, nor is the material world an extension of God's essence, as pantheists believe. Rather, creation from nothing entails that the material world is wholly other from God; in creating entities, God gave each of them characteristics and properties of their own. Each is capable of being a causative agent in its own right[29]—God does not control their every action, although Christian theologians have typically asserted that God concurs in (i.e., permits) all causative actions by secondary agents. This view does not deny that God is in control—it simply says that God exercises control not by micromanaging (occasionalism) but in other ways including establishing properties, capabilities, and limitations for creatures. It follows from this understanding of *creatio ex nihilo* that the world contains an enormous number of agents acting independently within their own capabilities and limitations. The result is the occurrence of events that are random in the sense of being unpredictable; these events may seem disorderly, but the aggregate of the actions of such agents typically exhibits a high degree of order. As David Bartholomew put it, "God can have it both ways"—that is, have both the freedom associated with randomness and the order associated with structure.[30]

So what can we say then about the person killed by the falling tree? First, God did not take the person's life, nor is God directly responsible for the death. God does permit the death but only in the sense that God honors the distinct identity given to all of creation—by not micromanaging or stepping in every time a creature acts in a way that can harm another. Second, events like a car and a tree trying to occupy the same space at the same time will necessarily happen. They are a consequence of making a complex world and giving creatures the capability of being independent causative agents—such events are not the direct result of human moral failure, and events analogous to this occurred in the world before human beings existed, so neither are they a generic result of human sin. Third, seeing such events as inevitable may make God seem heartless and without compassion for those who are harmed by them. However, they need not be seen that way—such events are rare and God does not leave us alone in them. God enters into and shares our suffering. God does not take away such suffering but also does not abandon us to it. That is, God sets a very high value on the freedom given to creatures, and the possibility of such events is a necessary consequence of freedom, but God couples that freedom with compassion.

Putting all this together then, the bottom line is that randomness need not be seen as a threat or as evidence of purposelessness or meaninglessness. Rather, it originates in the divine nature; points to God's mystery and transcendence; expresses God's desire to give each creature an identity, capabilities, and freedom; and is, in many ways, an incredibly beautiful and subtle tool used to carry out God's good will in the world.

Appendix

This appendix presents a technical discussion of the three concepts of randomness introduced in section 3.

KOLMOGOROV COMPLEXITY

Consider two bit strings:[31]

10101010101010101010
01111110011110110111

The first has an obvious pattern; the second was generated by flipping a coin twenty times.

The first can be generated by this algorithm:

Repeat 10 times: output "10"

The second, however, requires an algorithm like

Output "011111001110110111"

The underlying intuition behind Kolmogorov randomness is that a string of n bits is random if any algorithm able to generate it requires at least n bits. The precise definition is a formalization of this intuition.

The first problem one encounters in attempting to formalize this intuition about randomness is that an algorithm has to be written in some language. However, languages differ, so the length of an algorithm depends on the language in which it is written. But randomness should depend on the bit string, not on the language someone might use for writing algorithms.

The Church-Turing thesis provides us warrant for disregarding all formal or informal programming languages that could be used for writing algorithms and focusing solely on algorithms formulated as Turing machines.

The next step is to introduce another of Turing's concepts—the **universal Turing machine**. There are lots of Turing machines—one for every computation that could ever be carried out. A universal Turing machine is one that can simulate any specific Turing machine—it's an algorithm that can carry out any other algorithm.

Turing machines produce outputs, but they also require inputs. Thus if x denotes an output string and y an input, we can define the **Kolmogorov complexity of x relative to y** (denoted **$K(x|y)$**) as the length of the shortest program on a universal Turing machine that outputs x from input y. In essence, it measures the shortest path to x given the information y. The universal Turing machine allows us to define randomness in a way that is independent of algorithmic language. Let $d(x)$ denote the length of x—i.e., the number of bits in it. Then we say that a finite string is **Kolmogorov random** if $K(x|d(x)) \geq d(x)$.

Now consider numbers in the unit interval [0,1]. These can be written in base 2 as infinite strings of bits (for example, .10101010101010101010 ... or .011111001110110111 ...). Because these are infinite in length, we cannot apply the definition for finite strings. It would seem natural to define randomness for infinite strings by saying that for any n, its first n bits are Kolmogorov random; however, it is possible for a string to satisfy this definition and still be produced by a Turing machine. A stronger definition based on the concept of **prefix-free Kolmogorov complexity** (where prefix-free refers to a restricted class of Turing machines) does give a class of random numbers that are equivalent to those given by the next two concepts. The specific details defining that class are too technical to address here; for more information, see the work by Downey and Hirschfeld.[32]

Martin-Löf Randomness

The first precise definition of randomness for sequences of bits was given by Per Martin-Löf in 1966.[33] His approach is based on the intuition that random numbers should be "common" or ordinary. Thus he took the idea of a test for a pattern and abstracted it.

There are two difficulties in testing a bit string to see if it has a pattern. First, the idea of "pattern" is not precise, and second, with only countably many exceptions, bit strings that represent real numbers in [0, 1], are infinite in length. Thus a particular string might seem to have a pattern near its beginning, but that pattern may disappear further on. Martin-Löf's definition formalizes the notion of a string "having a pattern" by saying it belongs to a **computably enumerable set**—there is an algorithm (i.e., a Turing machine) that can enumerate the members of the set. The definition addresses the issue of an apparent pattern in the prefix of a string that does not continue by introducing the idea of a **Martin-Löf test**—a sequence $\{U_n\}$ of computably enumerable sets whose measure $\mu(U_n) < 2^{-n}$ for all *n*. A collection, *C*, of strings is defined to be **Martin-Löf null** if there is a Martin-Löf test $\{U_n\}$ such that $\subseteq \cap_n U_n$. A string, *A*, is **Martin-Löf random** if it is not Martin-Löf null. That is, being Martin-Löf null formalizes the idea of successively looking further and further out in the string and still finding that it has a pattern.

For example, suppose a bit string, *A*, has the property that it is zero in positions 1, 2, 4, 8, . . . 2^n—A is clearly not random since an easily definable substring consists entirely of zeroes. Let U_n be the set of all strings that have a zero in positions 1, 2, 4, 8, . . . , 2^n. Then $\{U_n\}$ is a Martin-Löf test—each is computably enumerable and has a measure less than 2^{-n}. The latter is true because [0, 1] has measure 1 and as each of the *n* bits is specified to be zero, the measure of the set being specified is divided by 2. Thus *A* is Martin-Löf null and the test verifies our intuition—that it is not random.

Note that each Martin-Löf null set has measure zero. Furthermore, because they are computably enumerable, there are only countably many Martin-Löf null sets. Thus the collection of all numbers that are Martin-Löf null has measure zero and the Martin-Löf random numbers have measure 1. This is the precise sense in which almost all numbers are random. Martin-Löf randomness is equivalent to Kolmogorov randomness.[34]

Constructive Martingales

The intuitive idea behind the martingale concept of randomness is this: Suppose a string of bits is revealed one bit at a time.[35] There is no betting strategy that would enable one to profit by predicting the next bit. That is, randomness corresponds in a meaningful way with unpredictability.

To formalize this idea, let's again begin with an example. Consider the two bit strings we looked at before:

10101010101010101010
01111110011110110111

Suppose these strings are being revealed one bit at a time. Consider a betting strategy, say "Whatever the value of the previous bit, I'll bet that the opposite bit will come up next." Suppose also that the payoff will be that we gain one unit of money every time we are right and lose one unit every time we are wrong. Consider the first string. For its first bit, we just have to guess—we may win or lose. But after that, we will win every time and, if the game continued forever, we would win an infinite amount of money. For the second string, however, we would sometimes win and sometimes lose. In fact, for this particular string and strategy (after the first bit) we would win seven times and lose twelve times.

So, suppose we have an unknown infinite bit string. A **martingale** is a betting strategy on the revelation of its bits. We associate a payoff function, *d*, with the martingale where d maps finite bit strings into the real numbers. That is, *d* keeps a running total of the wins and losses as each bit is revealed. The concept of martingale does not put many restrictions on the allowable payoff functions—only that they satisfy a **fairness condition**: Suppose *w* denotes the first *n* bits of the martingale: *w*0 denotes those *n* bits with the prediction that the *n* + 1st bit revealed will be 0; *w*1, the same *n* bits with the prediction that the *n* + 1st bit will be 1. The fairness condition is usually written $d(\mathrm{w}) = \frac{d(\mathrm{w}\,0) + \mathrm{d}(\mathrm{w}\,1)}{2}$. The idea is that whatever one might gain by predicting correctly is exactly balanced by what one would lose from guessing incorrectly. Thus, suppose a casino managed this game and took a fraction of every bet. For instance, if you guess incorrectly you lose 1.00, but if you guess correctly, you gain 0.99. Such a policy would violate the fairness condition and no betting strategy could be a martingale. [Such games are modeled by the concept of **supermartingale**, but I am not going to pursue that here.]

A martingale **succeeds** on a particular bit string if, allowed to run forever, it would yield an infinite positive payoff. A **constructive martingale** is one that can be generated by a Turing machine—that is, it can be produced by an algorithm. Algorithmic information theorists have proven that a bit string is Martin-Löf random if and only if no constructive martingale succeeds on it. Thus all three definitions of randomness are equivalent.

Notes

1. *The Stanford Encyclopedia of Philosophy* has an extensive article on mathematical Platonism.
2. Ontology is a branch of philosophy concerned with the essential nature of beings or things that exist.

3. In *The Mathematical Experience* (Boston: Houghton Mifflin, 1981), 321–322, Philip J. Davis and Reuben Hersh suggest that most mathematicians are Platonists in practice but if pressed philosophically, retreat to formalism.
4. "Mind of God" here is used metaphorically; it does not include an assumption that God has a mind in the same sense as human beings do. Rather it means that God has always known these objects and they are part of God's nature.
5. Ian Mueller, "Mathematics and the Divine in Plato," in *Mathematics and the Divine: A Historical Study*, ed. T. Koetsier and L. Bergmans (Amsterdam: Elsevier, 2005), 101.
6. Dominic J. O'Meara, "Geometry and the Divine in Proclus," in *Mathematics and the Divine: A Historical Study*, ed. T. Koetsier and L. Bergmans (Amsterdam: Elsevier, 2005), 138.
7. Mueller, "Mathematics and the Divine in Plato," 117.
8. Quotes here are from the translation by Thomas Williams (Indianapolis, IN: Hackett, 1993).
9. Augustine. *Fathers of the Church, Volume 70: Eighty-Three Different Questions* (Baltimore, MD: Catholic University of America Press, 1982).
10. *ST* 1. 7, 1–4.
11. Edith Dudley Sylla, "Swester Katrei and Gregory of Rimini: Angels, God, and Mathematics in the Fourteenth Century," in *Mathematics and the Divine: A Historical Study*, ed. T. Koetsier and L. Bergmans, 249–271 (Amsterdam: Elsevier, 2005).
12. Alvin Plantinga, *Does God Have a Nature?* (Milwaukee, WI: Marquette University Press, 1980), 142–143.
13. John 1:18, RSV
14. This argument is based on James Bradley and Russell Howell, *Mathematics through the Eyes of Faith* (New York: HarperOne, 2011), chap. 9.
15. See Roger Penrose, *Shadows of the Mind* (Oxford: Oxford University Press, 1994).
16. See the article "Chance versus Randomness" in the *Stanford Encyclopedia of Philosophy*, www.plato.stanford.edu for a more complete discussion of this distinction.
17. A precise definition can be found on the Internet or in any introductory text on computing theory.
18. Note that this analysis does not simply give analogies taken from nature; rather it provides propositions that are necessary truths about God, subject to the limits of human language.
19. Based on Thomas C. Oden, *Classic Christianity: A Systematic Theology* (New York: HarperOne, 1992), 36–37. The terminology used in this taxonomy is Oden's.
20. *Confessions*, book 7, chapter 14.

21. Following the work of Georg Cantor, mathematicians today would say that Aquinas was incorrect. Not only are there actually infinite numbers, there are infinitely many of them of infinitely many different sizes. For Aristotle, numbers were quantitative aspects of physical things. Aquinas seems to have used this Aristotelian concept in saying there cannot be an actually infinite number, although he does not explicitly mention Aristotle when he says this. This is one place where Christian Platonism enjoys a decided advantage over Aristotelianism. Seeing numbers as ideas in God's mind removes the conflict Aquinas saw between God being uniquely infinite and there being actually infinite numbers—actually infinite numbers can exist because they participate in the divine infinitude. For a discussion of Cantor's work and its theological implications, see Christian Tapp, "Infinity in Mathematics and Theology," *Theology and Science* 9, no. 1 (2011): 91–100.
22. Bavinck, 159–160
23. When presenting this concept at a recent conference, one conferee commented, "My tradition has always focused on God's covenantal faithfulness, but you are asking us to see God very differently." I found it quite heartening that the analysis of divine randomness opened a new understanding of God for this person.
24. Pierre-Simon Laplace, *A Philosophical Essay on Probabilities*, first published as *Essai Philosophique sur les Probabilités* (Paris: Mme Ve Courcier, 1814).
25. For example, see Curtis Johnson, *Darwin's Dice: The Idea of Chance in the Thought of Charles Darwin* (Oxford: Oxford University Press, 2015).
26. Stephen Jay Gould, *Wonderful Life* (New York: W. W. Norton, 1990), 48–51.
27. Johnson, *Darwin's Dice*, 66.
28. For more discussion on the meaning of "tragic" in such situations, see Reinhold Bernhardt, "Closing Reflection" in part four of *Abraham's Dice in the Flow of Life: The Experience of the Tragic and Its Theological Interpretation*.
29. This idea originates with Aquinas; an occasionalist would not agree.
30. David J. Bartholomew, *God, Chance and Purpose: Can God Have It Both Ways?* (Cambridge: Cambridge University Press, 2008).
31. The discussion of Kolmogorov complexity presented in the appendix is based on Uwe Schöning and Randall Pruim, *Gems of Theoretical Computer Science*, trans. Randall J. Prium (Berlin: Springer, 1995), chap. 8, and Alan L. Selman, *Complexity Theory Retrospective* (New York: Springer, 1990), chap. 7.
32. Rodney G. Downey and Denis R. Hirschfeldt, *Algorithmic Randomness and Complexity* (New York: Springer, 2010), section 3.5.
33. For this concept, I have drawn heavily on ibid., section 6.2.
34. See ibid. for the proofs of the theorems cited here and in the discussion of martingales that follows.

35. This explanation is also based on ibid., section 6.3.

Bibliography

Augustine. *Fathers of the Church, Volume 70: Eighty-Three Different Questions.* (Baltimore, MD: Catholic University of America Press, 1982). ProQuest ebrary. Web. 4 January 2016.

Augustine. *On Free Choice of the Will.* Translated by Thomas Williams (Indianapolis, IN: Hackett, 1993).

Bavinck, Herman. *The Doctrine of God.* Translated and edited by William Hendriksen (Edinburgh: The Banner of Truth Trust, 1977), 154.

Bradley, James, and Russell Howell. *Mathematics through the Eyes of Faith* (New York: HarperOne, 2011).

Downey, Rodney G., and Denis R. Hirschfeldt. *Algorithmic Randomness and Complexity* (New York: Springer, 2010).

Gilson, Étienne. *The Christian Philosophy of Saint Augustine* (London: Victor Gollancz, 1961).

Mueller, Ian. "Mathematics and the Divine in Plato." In *Mathematics and the Divine: A Historical Study*, edited by T. Koetsier and L. Bergmans, 99–122 (Amsterdam: Elsevier, 2005).

Oden, Thomas C. *Classic Christianity: A Systematic Theology* (New York: HarperOne, 1992).

O'Meara, Dominic J. "Geometry and the Divine in Proclus." In *Mathematics and the Divine: A Historical Study*, edited by T. Koetsier and L. Bergmans, 133–147 (Amsterdam: Elsevier, 2005).

Penrose, Roger. *Shadows of the Mind* (Oxford: Oxford University Press, 1994).

Schöning, Uwe, and Randall Pruim. *Gems of Theoretical Computer Science.* Translated by Randall J. Prium (Berlin: Springer, 1995).

Selman, Alan L. *Complexity Theory Retrospective* (New York: Springer, 1990).

Sylla, Edith Dudley. "Swester Katrei and Gregory of Rimini: Angels, God, and Mathematics in the Fourteenth Century." In *Mathematics and the Divine: A Historical Study*, edited by T. Koetsier and L. Bergmans, 249–271 (Amsterdam: Elsevier, 2005).

Tapp, Christian. "Infinity in Mathematics and Theology." *Theology and Science* 9, no. 1 (2011): 91–100.

5

The Natural Science of Greek Philosophy and the Social Science of Judaism Become the Super-Providence of Paul

Sarah Ruden

My Master, my Light, at this point doesn't your truth
enjoy a good laugh at human expense?

AUGUSTINE

PAUL OF TARSUS, the most important early exponent of what was to become Christianity, represents both a nexus and a breaking point in the development of thinking about chance and providence. He was born to two traditions—the Greco-Roman and the Jewish. These cultures were fairly similar in positing extensive determinism (or the idea that all events are caused by means external to human will) and yet insisting that, in everything that ultimately mattered, fate could and should be negotiated through human knowledge and will—under the guidance of learned authority. But Paul left behind him a momentously influential vision of nearly the opposite. The death and resurrection of Jesus had created—or just shown—a sort of super-providence, a hugely enhanced version of the Jewish God's abiding care for all people. For the first time in known Western history, the vagaries of life on earth—let alone the workings of the universe in detail—were not even supposed to be of any great interest.

Paul's views in this regard had an immense impact on modern Western culture. Individualism, egalitarianism, artistic and intellectual exploration, and even experimental and observational science could likely not have reached such striking states of development had Paul's basic teachings not first overridden elaborate and longstanding beliefs about the mechanisms of the universe. Though the prevailing monotheisms of the modern era (Judaism, Christianity, and Islam) retain much in common from their shared heritage (including from the philosophy-based sciences of antiquity) and from their parallel and sometimes overlapping evolution, Christianity is, in its fundamentals, absolutely unique in its assertions about the events built into the structure of the universe and what they mean for individual human beings. This viewpoint is especially evident in Paul's writings. Though Paul's intention may have been to focus his followers' minds on the helplessness and triviality of their earthly existence, as opposed to God's immense, inscrutable power and unfailing, eternal care for them, one practical result of Paul's teachings over time seems to have been the opposite: a space substantially empty of human authority was created, in which people felt licensed to understand and act as they wished.

Greco-Roman and Jewish thinking varied greatly in how they viewed the divinity's design of locked-in cause-and-effect mechanisms as well as the divinity's involvement with earthly events. The two modes of thought also varied greatly in degrees of resemblance to modern forms of scientific determinism, such as belief in the power of existing genetics over future events. But both Greco-Roman and Jewish thinkers tended to agree strongly that human beings—given expert guidance—could understand the mechanisms well enough to be self-determining actors at least at the ethical level. Paul made gestures toward both of the old systems (especially the Jewish one), but these seem mainly rhetorical, incompatible with his own experience and beliefs, and apt to fall away readily from a cohesive view of the new sect he promoted.

Paul's personal background is critical to understanding this change. His Greek education and his upbringing in the Roman provincial port city of Tarsus (on the southern coast of what is now Turkey) in the early first century CE would have brought him, on one side, into the quasi-scientific realm of Greek philosophy, where practitioners pictured—and projected through public discourse and popular literature—near-perfect webs of physical cause and effect that humans could understand if not control. In fact, Stoicism and Epicureanism, the great duo of philosophical religions during this period, each taught (though in different ways) that if a human being came to know—as he could—the ways the universe necessarily worked, he could avoid certain personal vulnerability to outside forces, or greatly lessen their effects, transcending the ordinary human lot.

I write "philosophical religions," as this is conventional, but the movement here was really away from religion. Stoicism asserted that a form of divinity played a permeating role in determinism, but since the philosophy characterized this divinity as an implacable energizing substance (*pneuma*, or wind, breath, or spirit), whose actions throughout the universe (*phusis*, usually translated as "nature") were all informed by *logos* (reason) and could be grasped in turn by developed human understanding, religious thinking about fate in the traditional sense did not operate here. The believer did not imagine herself—or any group of people—in a relationship with a god (providential or not) as much as fitting, through her studies and efforts, into a pantheistic god's universe. The ideology (along with others) was literally a science if we rely on the Latin derivation of that word (from *scientia*, "knowledge" or "skill"). The still-recognizable scientific principle of cyclical oneness in change informed Stoic "virtue," often shown in popular accounts as steadiness in the face of changing fortune, and particularly as that ultimate declaration of independence from fortune, principled suicide. An influential strain of Stoicism held that only the sage would at last achieve oneness with the universe.

The Epicureans pursued a sort of scientific determinism in a more direct way, relegating the gods of the Greco-Roman heritage to a distant, inactive realm and propagating an atomic theory of causation: because single atoms had swerved to strike others (events for which the Epicureans, famously, offered no persuasive explanation), setting off immense chain reactions, all physical causation was connected, and its mechanisms could be deduced through observation. But people could withdraw themselves from much of the universe's agitation (both physical and mental, as there was no barrier between the two)—say, by not going to sea, where storms threatened. The right choices along these lines required them to eschew passions such as greed, ambition, and sexual infatuation, which might well drive them into stressful exertion and danger; instead, they should embrace simple pleasures, including plain food and friendship. Above all, the understanding that life is entirely material should free their minds from surplus anxieties, so that they could happily face even death as an endless, dreamless sleep.

The entwining of natural-science determinism and an ethic of individual self-determination in Stoicism and Epicureanism made these philosophies deeply humanistic. In fact, all major strains of Greek philosophy (except misanthropic Cynicism), from the pre-Socratic of the Archaic period (the eighth into the fifth centuries BCE) to the Neoplatonic of late antiquity (when philosophy competed and merged with Christianity), partook of a similar unshadowed rationalism. Even the ancient movement called Skepticism did not correspond well to our cautious, rather gloomy modern "skepticism," but served instead as a favored methodology for many physicians.[1] Causality was supposed to be fixed and graspable to a great extent, but not so as to throw a gloom over individual destiny and social relations: on the contrary, both of these were seen as liberated and enlightened through philosophy. They were not, for example, assigned a future as immutable as that of the weather, as in some forms of modern determinism that claim a scientific basis. And the role of personal divinity was pushed to the background if not clear out of the picture, so that troubling questions of divine power and intention in the shaping and direction of the world could not assert themselves.

Paul was also, at least in his young adulthood, a pious Jew, a Pharisee and an adherent of the Jerusalem Temple. The traditional, mainstream type of ancient Judaism, which he appears to have favored, leaves no evidence of interest in the natural sciences or in the formal logic that we most readily associate with intellectual pushback against the idea of a chaotic, unknowable universe. (I exclude from "traditional" and "mainstream" ancient Judaism both the withdrawn, ascetic sects such as the Essenes and the Alexandria-centered variety of intellectualizing, which was so heavily influenced by Greek philosophy as to form almost a subset of it.) However, the concept of providence was so well developed in this strain, and so pervasive, so short of exceptions in Scripture and in the interpretation of scriptural law—in which, by the way, the Pharisees specialized—that we could speak of a Jewish "science" of history, a laboratory whose findings shaped all of ordinary Jewish life. God's providential responses to righteous behavior were supposed to be as regular and predictable as a modern "law of nature."

This view allowed for no randomness under a just, all-controlling God, and also salved human ignorance and weakness with near-comprehensive rules for living and worshipping. If God's dispensations seemed unjust or merely incomprehensible, this was because events were still unfolding.

Unique in the ancient world, to the wonder or scorn of outside observers, this belief in holistic providence apparently developed through the Jews' particular fortunes, never far from the edge of disaster even when David's and Solomon's kingdoms flourished around the tenth century BCE. The Jewish (previously the Israelite, and before that the proto-Israelite) experience of conquest and near-conquest at the hands of massive foreign powers went back at least to the reign of the Egyptian pharaoh Merneptah in the thirteenth century BCE and probably much further, but the Jewish community had succeeded in harnessing its identity to the toughness of oral tradition and written literature lasting many generations.

Most arrestingly, the learned Jewish elite survived the sack of Jerusalem and the destruction of Solomon's temple (586 BCE) through successive exiles by the Babylonian conquerors themselves. Some were sent back by the Babylonians' own later conquerors, the Persians, to witness the rebuilding of the Temple (begun in 538 BCE) and the reestablishment of the Jewish nation under Persian sponsorship. The Persians also sponsored the same scholars (and others who never returned from Babylon) as they edited an authoritative digest of Jewish scripture, the basis of what we call the Bible.

Determinism therefore seems a critical force in the evolution of Jewish ideology. Materially and geographically quite vulnerable, the Jews must have puzzled early on about their conspicuous continuity among so many Semitic peoples and among the wider array of Mediterranean and Middle Eastern empires, and also about their ability to preserve such a distinct and impressive religion. The scriptures, without question an important vehicle for this preservation, were an important forum for treating these questions. There, the logic of the Jewish people's relationship with God, a relationship of interlocking chosenness, promise, rescue, law, recalcitrance, punishment, repentance, and redemption (a word that in Hebrew, as well as in Greek and Latin translation, is associated with buying back from captivity or slavery) was registered and constantly reiterated, with disobedience and its consequences forming a repeated cycle in scriptural history, poetry, and prophecy. Within this system, tight but open-ended, the nation was supposed to negotiate its fate. At the same time, a Jewish individual's relationship with God under scriptural regulation entailed many everyday opportunities and hazards. Rules related to purity and uncleanliness, for example, shaped the way many ordinary activities were carried out.

Thus it may not be an absurd exaggeration to see a kind of observational, almost statistical, reasoning in Jewish thought: *We are repeatedly overrun, but we repeatedly return to our law, and we repeatedly emerge with our identity as people of the law intact; therefore, we confidently project the same cycle of events into the future.* An element of quite credible empiricism (bordering on experimentation) comes into the assertion: *We intensively and stubbornly cultivate written religious law; our neighbors do not, and this appears to make an important difference in the survival of our unique culture.* And as Jewish misfortunes worsened in the age of extremely brutal, religiously quite unfriendly Greek and Roman dominance starting in the late first millennium BCE, it must have made some sense, as a stepped-up effort at self-determinism within this largely deterministic schema, to redouble study of the law and its application in a search for safety against apparently worsening divine wrath. This effort helped spawn the Mishnah, the first extant body of scriptural commentary, set down in its present form around 200 CE.

It also would have made sense to project redemption to the end of history and the afterlife: justice would surely arrive with the apocalypse, if there were no way to imagine justice arriving soon on earth to reward current zealous proponents of the law. The Dead Sea Scrolls, with writings collected and composed during the period of Greek and earlier Roman domination, testify to preoccupation with the end of the world in these terms.

In fact, a link between deterministic thinking about piety and the apocalypse on the one hand, and political and military stress on the other, seems to be beyond any doubt. For example, in the biblical book 2 Maccabees 12:38–45, about events in the early to mid-second century BCE, the binding together of historical events with eternal causation and the negotiation of destiny through obedience to the divine law is set out neatly in a short narrative. After a major battle, the leader Judas and his surviving victorious army purify themselves and return to the battlefield to retrieve their dead. All of these, they find, are wearing forbidden pagan amulets under their tunics, an impiety that, it is surmised, must be the cause of their deaths. The survivors pray for the forgiveness of this sin, and Judas takes up a large expiation offering on behalf of the slain, "taking account of the resurrection" (verse 43).[2]

The Pharisees also envisioned the righteous being resurrected at the end of historical time and granted eternal life, though it took vigorous interpretation to extract support for this idea from classical Hebrew Scripture as a whole, where treatment of the afterlife is scattered and equivocal. The Pharisees, however, with their mission of applying the law among the people at large, could hardly advocate the thoroughgoing providential determinism of the utopian Essenes (nor, for that matter, the belief in complete free will espoused by the elite Sadducees); instead, the Pharisees seem to have articulated and practiced a limited determinism: knowledge and effort allowed an individual to achieve the self-determination that mattered by conforming to all of God's immutable dispensations.[3]

Mainstream ancient Jewish religion, in connection to determinism, is therefore oddly similar in outline to ancient Greek philosophy. In both, a very broad description of ineluctably interwoven cause and effect did not intrude on the most vital human sphere: human beings were self-determining where it really counted, and they could vindicate their fate through the grasp and application of knowledge that was to a vital extent transparently logical and readily persuasive, though it was handed down from learned authority.

In the six New Testament letters or Epistles scholars have attributed to Paul with the most confidence,[4] and according to the third-person depiction of his ministry in the Acts of the Apostles, Paul used language, motifs, and themes from these two views of fate. How could he not have? Intellectual culture at the time tended to offer a narrow dichotomy: the Greco-Roman and Jewish. (The Roman Empire's subjugated peoples included many with ancient learning and cultivation, but, classed as barbarian and outlandish, these peoples and their thinking seem to have been almost as obscure to the cosmopolitan mind as they are today. Influences such as Babylonian astrology and Egyptian mystery religion, tightly amalgamated into Greco-Roman culture, did not create any significant range in the typical popular international viewpoint.)

On the evidence of his writing—in a version of *Koinē* or common Greek much more sophisticated than the one used in the Gospels—and of the pagan authors he cites,[5] Paul enjoyed a good standard pagan education, but in the Greco-Roman world there was only one kind of education above basic literacy and numeracy. For boys of citizen-class families,[6] schooling concentrated on literature and rhetoric and culminated in philosophy—not that Paul would likely have had a full dose of this. Acts 17:16 shows him at Athens (which provided the closest thing to university education in the ancient world), reacting in middle age to the myriad shrines as if he is a first-time visitor to the city. Instead, as an adolescent or a young man Paul voyaged to Jerusalem for his extended training and professional development, and he is shown naming the distinguished Pharisee Gamaliel as his teacher there (Acts 22:3).

However, his home city of Tarsus, a port on the southern coast of what is now Turkey, was thoroughly Hellenized and Romanized, wealthy and cosmopolitan. In such provincial cities during the established Roman Empire, there was literally a marketplace of ideas: rhetoricians and philosophers performed in public, so that any boy whom menial work did not confine all day could pick up some intellectualism.

But again, and critically, that intellectualism, especially in explanations of fate, ran along deep, well-worn tracks and offered few easy detours, in contrast to our wildly pluralistic modern Western thought. The Greeks and Romans, though loyal to their myths and rituals, some of which probably dated back to the period of early agriculture or even further, prided themselves on increasingly rising above the *do ut des* ("I give so that you'll give") idea of a relationship with the gods that their traditional religion offered. Educated people from the pre-Socratic philosophers to the Roman satirists and beyond looked down on the crudities of mythology (in which gods tended to appear as rapacious as humans with equal power would likely be) and naïve reliance on the efficacy of rites, blaming both on gullibility, superstitious terror, and wish-fulfillment fantasies, and deploring both for lack of applicable moral content. Certainly for a young man like Paul, whose alien religion would have separated him altogether from reliance on Greco-Roman storytelling and worship as ways to understand the workings of the universe, philosophy was the only possible source for parallel explanations in his pagan education.

Jews, for their part, could not step outside of their ancestral formulations about fate without becoming virtual Hellenistic philosophers (such as Philo of Alexandria), on the one hand, or proponents of randomness, on the other. Probably under the influence of Epicureanism, Ecclesiastes toys at length with the idea that the future is arbitrary and unknowable and conventional effort wasted, and the book consequently enjoins enjoyment of the present. But in the extant, canonical version of Ecclesiastes, the final chapter returns to pieties and concludes: "Fear God, and keep his commandments; for that is the whole duty of everyone. For God will bring every deed into judgment, including every secret thing, whether good or evil" (12:13–14). This ending accords with the Book of Job's culminating speech (chapters 38–41) about God's marvelous, diverse, and mysterious creation, a speech humbly accepted by the tortured and bereaved Job, then ratified by his friends' penance for speaking on behalf of the divinity and by Job's restored prosperity (chapter 42). Nihilistic assertions in the Book of Job are effectively cancelled out in this way.

The upshot in both Ecclesiastes and Job is the impossibility of accepting that God is not in control of everything except personal human choice. Even Ecclesiastes, far from its end, prompts, "In the day of prosperity be joyful, and in the day of adversity consider, God has made one as well as the other" (7:14). The sphere of the unknown is made clear in the wind-up of that very verse: "so that mortals may not find anything that will come after them." While ancient Jews might freely express puzzlement about God's purposes, they did not go as far in their professed uncertainty as to speculate in a modern way on whether God really exists or has sufficient power or benevolence or interest to shape fate overall. Randomness, in their literature, is seen only from an individual, despairing human perspective and shows the great distance between the human and divine condition. In effect, this is an affirmation of God's reign over fate.

Paul was likely brought up to see in a favorable light only these two quite stereotyped, somewhat similar versions of determinism, the mainstream Greek and the mainstream Jewish, and he had an actual professional commitment to one version. Pharisees taught and advised among the poorer and less-educated classes, constantly purveying the quid pro quo of conditional divine providence to those Jews who must have been the most susceptible to skepticism, as they were on the giving end of religious conformity—much unlike the wealthy Temple hierarchy. The Mishnah is closely associated with the Pharisees' teaching, and in this compendium we find statements exactly suited to an equilibrium envisaged between spheres of determinism and self-determination and to the Pharisees' drive to reconcile providence with free will. It may be in a parody of the sect's didactic certainties that in Matthew 19:16–22, Mark 10:17–22, Luke 10:25–37, and Luke 18:18–25, Jesus is approached by an individual asking what he must do to achieve eternal life. In no case does Jesus give a practical, circumscribed answer (what specific kinds of conformity to God's will can achieve the ultimate reward from God) but rather an extremely challenging one, in effect a demand that the inquirer become a different person altogether.

A great irony is that Paul had to use the Greek and, especially, the Jewish systems' terms and expectations[7]—if for no other reason than simply because there were no others available that had anywhere near equal currency and prestige—to describe a major break with both systems. For Paul, the death and resurrection of Jesus had effected a sort of super-providence.

The death and the resurrection that had already taken place were the ultimate free gift (traditional translation: "grace") to mankind. The entire human species was granted not only forgiveness of sins but elevation above faulty mortal nature to a substantial spiritual reform on earth, and to perfection, immortality, and eternal communion with God in the afterlife—in exchange for nothing but acceptance of the gift, that is, acknowledgment that it had happened (usually translated as "faith"). No elaborate knowledge was required as to what actions would bring positive and negative outcomes, neither were there any demands for adherence to a body of authoritative dictates. Instead, the Way of Christ was supposed to be a matter of surrendering to a counterintuitive belief in God's perfect love of degraded humankind, a love exceeding that for an only son, and powerful enough to override humans' inevitable shortcomings.

But how is a modern scholar to establish Paul's preference for a sort of offhand, dismissive view of determinism, when this preference is nowhere explicitly laid out in his letters, and at most merely implied? In fact, this may have been a view to which Paul came reluctantly, or about which he was embarrassed, as it would have put him at odds with mainstream intellectual leaders of his time—including his former self, the Pharisee. Both Pharisees and philosophers confidently *led* in describing destiny in extensive terms and giving instructions for its management, but Paul's claim to leadership was, repeatedly, only that he was a terrible sinner, saved by the same evident but unaccountable providence as everyone else (albeit with a special missionary purpose manifested later).[8]

At any rate, Paul's intricately argumentative use of Hebrew scripture in particular (especially in Romans, where his metaphysics are most plainly laid out) suggests that sometimes he felt that there was still an elaborate quid pro quo going on in individual, community, and international life; that this mechanism aimed toward the fulfillment of the universe's purposes; that he could understand this mechanism; and that if he could not figure out how to explain it persuasively, all would be lost. However, his own most impressive experiences and the basic sense he made of them were at war with these notions, and clearly won.

It may help to give a broad account of Paul's position on determinism, which drove him toward positing a super-providence. This is perhaps best expressed in his statement that the Jews have supernatural criteria (they look for "signs" or miraculous interventions to show them what to believe and do), and that the Greeks pursue philosophy or wisdom (the quasi-scientific systems I have described above), but that "we" only "proclaim Christ crucified" (1 Corinthians 2:22–23). That is, we make known a single event that changes everything, superseding vast systems to explain causality.

Jesus had flashed in the pan, as it were; after the Romans crucified him along with violent felons, his following was terrified and nearly immobilized, and apparently dwindled almost to nothing. But within a couple of days of the crucifixion, the story went, his remaining followers met him again, not as a vision or a ghost, but as a solid, living person, in dialogue with them, eating, and with the marks of his ordeal witnessed by the whole group together (Luke 24:39–42; John 20:15–29).[9]

The Gospels present in retrospect an elaborate build-up to and rationale for the events surrounding the crucifixion, including genealogies going back to Abraham and through Adam to God (Matthew 1:1–17; Luke 3:23–38), to affirm the will of God in a momentous new dispensation. But Jesus's followers' immediate ambivalence and confusion manifest too. All four Gospels agree that some of Jesus's female followers were the first witnesses of something very surprising at the tomb—and this is probably not the kind of narrative folklore that male authors would spontaneously come up with. Moreover, Mark, likely the earliest Gospel, emphasizes the sheer shock and bafflement after the discovery (16:6, 8, 11, 13, 14); and the peremptory ending of Mark (appearing between the verses marked 8 and 9 in modern Bibles), in conflict with the longer ending (verses 9–20), may show early editorial efforts to resolve real-life shock and confusion into a more conventional story of a holy man's ascent into heaven.

Given the followers' religion and culture, they must have been stumped at anything like this happening, most particularly as it assaulted the traditional Jewish idea of providence, which (as noted above) was essential for making sense of individual and communal life. First of all, Jesus was painfully, alarmingly unqualified for resurrection, especially after his death on the cross, and his followers would have had to grope to make any sense of his identity and purpose.

Certain leaders in Jewish history, under the general rubric of "prophets," were marked out for lives of outstanding service and instructiveness, with missions that followed clear divine commands. Though they often suffered because of their obedience, they had the satisfaction of possessing self-aware roles in the divine plan that would be recognized also by the faithful, at least in retrospect. Prophets are presented as living scripture; if they do not appear as voicing the rationale of God's will mainly through instruction and preaching, as, for example, Amos does, then they illustrate it, as, for instance, Elijah does by ascending to heaven at his death in a miraculous chariot, vindicating all his ordeals. In any case, prophets' words and their lives were supposed to be unambiguous lessons.

The characterization of the messiah in Scripture was of course forward-looking: this man, out of all kings and priests anointed with holy oil (the translation of the Hebrew *messiah*—and the Greek *christos*), was the Lord's chosen, the successor of David, the savior of the nation. The messiah would demonstrate providence in an absolute and undeniable way, establishing a divinely blessed kingdom that would have no end. It went without saying that this was not a merely metaphysical scenario but instead would entail the defeat or assimilation of the chosen people's earthly enemies. The messiah, too, was to be living scripture, and his coming would be the ultimate teachable moment. This is the category into which Jesus's identity settled.

This understanding must have been a great strain at first for his followers. Aside from any other doubts about Jesus's qualifications (and there would have been terrible doubts if the accounts of his disregard for the purity laws are at all reliable[10]), crucifixion hardly fits into extant visions of messianic (or prophetic) mission and would have contradicted any signs of a special destiny that Jesus showed during his life, such as his healings and wise sayings. Crucifixion's history and archaeology are gruesome.[11] The runaway slave-gladiator (gladiators were a notoriously demeaned class of persons) Spartacus and his followers had been the best known of the (very numerous) crucified persons in antiquity, and at the time they held nothing like the mythic status they were to gain in the modern world; rather, they were known mainly as dangerous but failed insurrectionists.[12] Particularly because crucifixion was a normal punishment for disturbance of public order by people without respected status or fixed legal rights, it apparently inspired few feelings in the general public beyond fear, helpless pity, and disgust, imposing near-oblivion on any publicity a life had enjoyed and shame on any previous popularity.

Jesus's death and his resurrection would therefore have been, in his followers' eyes, set at opposite ends of the spectrum of expectations for prophets. Prophets enjoyed great divine favor and thorough justification—but no prophet had ever been reported resurrected in the flesh, on earth, on his own merits. Nor was the messiah expected to achieve this. Why had the crucified Jesus, of all people, been able to?

From the start, therefore, the Jewish establishment must have been threatened and offended by efforts to include the Way within Judaism. The story behind the new movement made less sense than the destruction of the Temple in 70 AD and showed less of a familiar way forward. (The Temple, after all, had been destroyed centuries before, but the Ezra-Nehemiah account of religious and national regeneration explained how such a catastrophe, a punishment for national sinfulness, was survivable.)

This is why the high priest had James, the most popular of Jesus's followers who remained in Jerusalem, executed even though he lived according to the strictest rules of Jewish piety. Ideology, not conduct, brought his demise.[13]

In sum, so critical was a fixed idea of providence in explaining causality, both in the broad sweep of history and in daily life for the Jews, that if it were insistently asserted that a questionable character had been crucified and had risen from the dead because he was the messiah—then all basic calculations of why anything happened must be threatened.

Modern scholars suggest this in acknowledging the political disappointments that Jesus's fate and its aftermath forced on the hopeful: he had not come in order to throw off Roman rule and establish a tangible "kingdom of heaven" on earth (or if he had come with that purpose and failed, he could hardly be said to have come from God). But the problem must have been more than this. According to the way Jesus's followers were explaining his death and resurrection, Judaism both forward-looking and backward-looking could not exist. The religion worked by setting out God's will in minute particulars and offering the means of compliance, and thus of self-determination, within the known terms of God's providence. Proto-Christians rushed to take that framework and all its contents away.

If the Book of Acts' account of Stephen's death is at all accurate—and the event was witnessed by many, not just by Paul—then it seems evident that a vigorous, if not to say devastating, critique of traditional Jewish intellectualism had come to the fore just a few years after Jesus's death.

The speech given to Stephen in Acts 7 contains a scripture-based précis of divine care and guidance throughout Jewish history and indicates that the Jews have blown it—they've ended history by killing "the Righteous One" himself (verse 52). The righteous one had normally been defined as a fulfiller of the law. But clearly, in this speaker's (or writer's) opinion, the law is somehow annulled or outdated by this person. Stephen's answer from the crowd of Jews is an immediate application of the law. Paul guards the cloaks (verse 58)—of "witnesses," so this is depicted as a lawful killing, as prescribed by Deuteronomy 17:7—and he is in accord with how it turns out (Acts 8:1).

Shortly after, however, comes Paul's Damascus Road experience, changing him, through mysterious divine intervention, from a persecutor of Jesus's followers to a convert who will become a great leader among them. Paul's teachings in substance always accord with that experience: God's action is absolutely unpredictable; God's favor absolutely undeserved; God's new, overriding providence largely incomprehensible.

With conceivable transactions with the divine gone, Jewish society's whole providence-invoking structure would have collapsed. No functionary, not even the high priest, could have counted his position or his work necessary. Why should he—or his ancestors or his descendants—have the assignment, and not someone else, as salvation was a free gift to all mankind? And what would have been the point of doing anything at all in the Temple, as salvation had already arrived? For hundreds of years, teachings like Micah's (6:6–8), that the sacrifice God truly loved was virtuous behavior and a reverent attitude, had been influential—but what would be the point of those merits either?

The underlying logic of Paul concerning providence (I write "underlying" because nowhere does he lay out the logic on its own, but rather incorporates it in his doctrine of salvation) is that God had taken near-complete care of humankind in spite of their shortcomings. The gift already given should relieve them of all anxiety about the vagaries of human life[14] and make suffering for their faith the ultimate earthly privilege, a chance to testify that God alone can bring them real deliverance.[15] But by the same token, they were not to push back even against an unhappy marriage or slavery,[16] as if they thought such destinies mattered in the end—which they were to expect any day. For those following "the Way," all calculation of personal destiny must be ruled out.

This attitude is of course impossible; the degraded human condition—the tangible index to the extent of God's mercy—cannot exist free from the calculating ego, but like all other shortcomings, it is bought off by Christ's sacrifice. Paul, in fact, makes a joke of the paradox with his repeated play on boasting: he cannot help but boast, but should be indulged in his boasting, because he knows he has nothing in himself to boast about and so is in effect boasting of his own nothingness and God's infinite power and mercy.[17] The upshot is that he treats the choice whether to boast or not as comically trivial—though regulation of the ego along set lines is in most religions considered a basic, essential task, a virtual map of the self-determination allowed and desirable. This extreme manifestation of the proto-Christian ideology practically wiped self-determination off the agenda; it was possible—Paul never claimed it wasn't—it just wasn't a legitimate concern.

As for practical rules, standards, and advice for proto-Christian communities, providence was supposed to be, so to speak, built in. Yet it is everywhere plain that Paul favors Jewish morality, especially in matters of sex. The Jewish classification of male homosexuality as an abomination to be punished by death (Leviticus 18:22 and 20:13) surely helps inform Paul's tirade in Romans 1 against the acts as prevalent and tolerated in Greek and Roman culture; he even adds, "They know God's decree, that those who practice such things deserve to die" (verse 32). Interestingly, language with a Stoic tinge—which Paul uses elsewhere in discussing social norms[18]—enters in too: homosexuality is "unnatural" and heterosexuality "natural" (verses 25–27). It does look as if philosophy also influenced Paul's opinions on what people should do, and why.

But Paul's other clear reference to homosexuality, in 1 Corinthians 6:9–10, his threat that "male prostitutes" and "sodomites," among others, will not inherit the kingdom of heaven, is curiously followed up:

> And this is what some of you used to be. But you were washed, you were sanctified, you were justified in the name of the Lord Jesus Christ and in the spirit of our God.
>
> "All things are lawful for me," but not all things are beneficial. "All things are lawful for me," but I will not be dominated by anything. "Food is meant for the stomach and the stomach for food," but God will destroy both one and the other. The body is meant not for fornication but for the Lord, and the Lord for the body. And God raised the Lord and will also raise us with his power. (1 Corinthians 6:11–14)

Underlying most of Paul's statements about morality (some of which, quoted in textual or ideological isolation, serve conservative Christians as favorite proof-texts) is a similar reasoning. The mitigation of sinful human nature, even amounting to the disappearance of homosexuality (Paul does not indicate whether this is the desire or merely the practice), is bound up in salvation. Human planning, will, and action do not get credit, because divine providence has hugely expanded to cover everything ultimately important.

As I wrote at the beginning of this chapter, the Pauline idea of providence had a decisive effect on the shape of Western culture. First of all, it was conducive to both egalitarianism and individualism. Since there was no longer any essential human authority to act as intermediary between determinism and self-determination, intellectual capacity and social position had no sure value for leadership, and would appear negative if the would-be leader had the natural pride that would risk focusing his attention on his personal superiority instead of on salvation. In early Christianity, each one of the faithful was supposed to be at liberty to "work out [his] own salvation with fear and trembling" (Philippians 2:12), as Paul phrased it.

Christianity's freer and more equal footing had many implications, even after the church established steep hierarchies. The confidence believers gained from the wide and sturdy umbrella of their destiny would have licensed a great deal of independent and assertive intellectual development in whichever direction they desired. Thus in Christian cultures, rapid and daring intellectual moves have been extremely striking. Many modern religious thinkers and historians have remarked on the rapid shift from "pure" Pauline Christianity to extensive and diverse theological elaborations. Stoic and Neoplatonic philosophy contributed to an unprecedented flowering of systematic thinking, with its early culmination in Thomas Aquinas's *Summa Theologiae*, and its later one in Karl Barth's commentary on Romans. This varied intellectual development must have been in part because individuals felt licensed to come into the empty intellectual space Paul had created and to act as they pleased there; on principle, the space was supposed to stay empty—but it wasn't going to, given human nature, especially human nature delighting in inherent chosenness.

Paul himself had already done the same sort of thing in, for example, reassuring those worried about community members who had died before the Second Coming (1 Thessalonians 4:13–18), thereby propagating if not inventing the doctrine of literal resurrection in the flesh for all of the faithful. The style and structure of Paul's writing—including the abruptness and glibness of these assertions to the Thessalonians, inserted between exhortations to live unobtrusively and inoffensively (verses 11 and 12) and reminders that they can have no idea when the Second Coming will actually occur (5:1–3)—certify that he wasn't deeply committed to what he wrote on such occasions; however, the leaders who succeeded him (who, not incidentally, came for the most part from the philosophizing pagan world) were eased by the characteristic freedom of this new religion into the conviction that their pronouncements were essential, and so moved away from the religion's original terms. They argued for the indispensability of extensive doctrine, of professional clergy, and, eventually, of many official rites. These could be written into

Christian doctrine, even as conditions of salvation, because there was so little there before.

Since, however, the simple Pauline system remained at the core of Christian theology and was extant in the evangelist's letters, it was also inevitable that it would embolden people to attack elaborations as well as to build them, and before and during the Reformation and beyond it, many returned toward Pauline essentials, if only to use them for new starting points. No religious movement in the history of the world has been more fertile in ideas, and in my view it could not have been so without the space cleared in the intellectual forest by Paul.

The theological dynamism made possible by Pauline metaphysics is perhaps most clearly seen in the progress of Augustine's thought. In the fourth century CE, systematic scriptural study was by no means an ordinary part of Christian practice. Though raised by a ritually devout Christian mother, Augustine was largely left to sift through abstract precepts by himself and struggled for years with the concept (grounded in Stoicism and elaborated by the Gnostic Manichees) that divinity was material—what else could it logically be?

Augustine took up the study of the Vulgate Old Testament only in his late teens, but it did not advance his understanding; rather, it seemed to show God's will either as inconsistent or as inconsistently expressed by God's various servants. Neoplatonism proved helpful, as did the study of Paul. These experiences loosened the argumentative knots in Augustine's mind, and his conversion was deeply emotional: God, necessarily incomprehensible, was the all-transcendent beauty that Augustine adored and that accepted him in exchange for his submission and devotion—and his feelings would not change but only intensify as he lay dying in a city under siege by the Vandals. God, though he was the fountainhead of being, was not to be held accountable by the human mind for any particular thing that happened.

But it was no coincidence that this attitude in Augustine led not to intellectual quietism, but instead to a decades-long flood of—largely theoretical—writing: polemical letters and tracts, sermons, scriptural commentaries, the mighty *City of God,* as well as the *Confessions,* which is largely a history of the author's thought. In effect, Pauline Christianity allowed a formidable thinker to shake off and discard centuries of restraints on statements about how the universe worked and to make his own way forward.

As noted at the opening of this chapter, Pauline Christianity's basic formulations reached well beyond religion in influence. It is not a coincidence that the Scientific Revolution was grounded in the same geography as Christianity. Not every celebrity of the new thinking was Christian, but Spinoza, Newton, and others—though in different ways—all adjusted themselves *against* existing dogma and moved beyond it, and it proved to have little power to slow them down. The unexpungeable license to speculate, to reason, to formulate for oneself continued to mean a busy, broad, and deep filling-in of the enormous gap in authority that Paul had endorsed and acted on again and again in his ministry. Ironically, the natural sciences and other studies that reject metaphysics altogether have their ancestor in the ideas developed by history's greatest religious innovator.

Judaism and Islam, so similar to Christianity in many respects, seem to offer a telling contrast in this one: though they fostered extremely rich intellectual creativity, they did not make room for *independent* innovation—institutional, cultural, ideological, technological—on anywhere near the scale of the Christian world's. The reasons for this could be debated at length, but one I believe to be very powerful is that in these religions there was never, let alone in the charter period, any ceding of human authority as intermediary between other humans and the divine. "Do all of this, and the following good things will result; avoid all of that, in order to avoid punishment both temporal and eternal," and "The universe, including human society, was created in these detailed ways and for these detailed purposes" are statements that, in structuring a religion, have a profound and long-lasting effect; so does the absence of these statements.

Notes

1. Pythagoreanism, with its vegetarianism and belief in reincarnation, perhaps comes the closest to an actual philosophical religion, but the final book of Ovid's epic poem *Metamorphoses*, which presents Pythagorean cosmology, makes it clear that in this philosophy too a vision of determinism—and self-determination through knowledge of deterministic mechanisms—reigned.
2. All Biblical quotations are from Michael D. Coogan, ed., *The New Oxford Annotated Bible*, 4th ed. (Oxford: Oxford University Press, 2010).
3. This is quite explicitly expressed in the part of the Mishnah entitled *Pirkei Avot* ("Chapters of the Fathers"): "Rabbi Akiva [active in the late first and early second

centuries CE] said, 'All is foreseen, but freedom of choice is given'" (3:15). But modern scholars are most heavily dependent on the *Jewish Antiquities* (13.5.9) of the Romanized Jewish historian Josephus for a characterization of these sects in regard to their attitude toward destiny.

4. In the order in which they stand in the Bible (though this is far from representing the order of their composition), these are Romans, 1 and 2 Corinthians, Galatians, Philippians, and 1 Thessalonians. For an accessible summary of the debate over authenticity, see John McRay, *Paul: His Life and Teaching* (Grand Rapids, MI: Baker Academic, 2003), 263–281.
5. In 1 Corinthians 15:33, he appears to quote Menander; in Acts 17:28 he quotes a Greek philosopher so obscure than modern scholars cannot identify him firmly, and passes on to a verse from the learned Stoic cosmologist Aratus.
6. Whether Paul was actually a Roman citizen is not certain, though Acts (25:10–12) ascribes to him the privileges of one; but at any rate only a well-assimilated family of means and standing could have educated him to the level he evinces.
7. Romans 15:4 is Paul's notation of his constant citation of and argumentation from Jewish scripture: "For whatever was written in former days was written for our instruction."
8. It is telling that Paul, in his remarks about his most conventional miraculous, revelatory experience (one that he probably believed showed him God's plans for the future, if not the rationale behind these), is derogatory. He notes, for example, that he has been extracted to the "third heaven," where he was imparted visionary knowledge—something like this was probably a routine claim for holy men of the time—but he asserts that the experience does not matter; circles jokingly around the idea of "boasting" of it; places the account in the third person; denies knowing whether it was an actual physical event or not; writes that he must keep the revelations to himself; insists that people must judge him merely by his ordinary words and actions; and passes on to the story of God placing a "thorn in his flesh" (the interpretation of which phrase has been controversial ever since) and keeping it there in spite of pleas to remove it, in order to prevent him from "being too elated" and to induce a rejoicing in "weakness" that in itself is "strength" (2 Corinthians 12:1–10).
9. These two Gospels are thought to be later, so their more forensic details may have been added on.
10. See, for example, in Mark (recalling, again, that this is probably the earliest extant Gospel), the passage 7:18–23, in which Jesus appears to renounce the critical dietary restrictions. Jerome H. Neyrey, "The Idea of Purity in Mark's Gospel," *Semeia* 35 (1986): 91–128, contains a full list of Jesus's violations according to this book.
11. See John Dominic Crossan's summary in *The Birth of Christianity: Discovering What Happened in the Years Immediately after the Execution of Jesus* (San Francisco: HarperSanFrancisco, 1998), 541–545.

12. Plutarch *Crassus* 8, Florus 2.8.8, Appian *Civil Wars* 1.116.
13. Josephus *Jewish Antiquities* 20.9.1.
14. 1 Corinthians 7: 29–31: "from now on, let even those who have wives be as though they had none, and those who mourn as though they were not mourning, and those who rejoice as though they were not rejoicing, and those who buy as though they had no possessions, and those who deal with the world as though they had no dealings with it. For the present form of this world is passing away."
15. It is with elation that Paul in Romans 8:36 quotes Psalms 44:22: "Because of you we are being killed all day long."
16. 1 Corinthians 7:12–16 and 21–24. To take such decrees as self-contained matters of Christian law is, by the way, strikingly mistaken: the overarching principal is clearly articulated at 1 Corinthians 7:17: "However that may be, let each of you lead the life that the Lord has assigned, to which God called you. This is my rule in all the churches"; and further at verse 24: "In whatever condition you were called, brothers and sisters, there remain with God."
17. 1 Corinthians 1:31 and 15:10, 2 Corinthians 11:16–17, Galatians 6:14.
18. 1 Corinthians 11:14.

Selected Bibliography

Armstrong, Karen. *The Bible: A Biography* (New York: Grove Press, 2007).

Bowden, Hugh. *Mystery Cults of the Ancient World* (Princeton, NJ: Princeton University Press, 2010).

Coogan, Michael D., ed. *The New Oxford Annotated Bible.* 4th ed. (Oxford: Oxford University Press, 2010).

Crossan, John Dominic. *The Birth of Christianity: Discovering What Happened in the Years Immediately after the Execution of Jesus* (San Francisco: HarperSanFrancisco, 1998).

Crossan, John Dominic, and Johnathan L. Reed. *In Search of Paul: How Jesus's Apostle Opposed Rome's Empire with God's Kingdom* (New York: HarperCollins, 2004).

Goodman, James. *But Where Is the Lamb? Imagining the Story of Abraham and Isaac* (New York: Schocken, 2013).

Hecht, Jennifer Michael. *Doubt: A History* (New York: HarperOne: 2004).

Long, A. A., and D. N. Sedley, eds. and trans. *The Hellenistic Philosophers.* Vol. 1, *Translations of the Principle Sources, with Philosophical Commentary* (Cambridge: Cambridge University Press, 1987).

McRay, John. *Paul: His Life and Teaching* (Grand Rapids, MI: Baker Academic, 2003).

Neyrey, Jerome H. "The Idea of Purity in Mark's Gospel." *Semeia* 35 (1986): 91–128.

Satlow, Michael L. *How the Bible Became Holy* (New Haven, CT: Yale University Press, 2014).

Vermes, Geza. *Christian Beginnings: From Nazareth to Nicaea* (New Haven, CT: Yale University Press, 2012).

White, L. Michael. *From Jesus to Christianity: How Four Generations of Visionaries and Storytellers Created the New Testament and the Christian Faith* (San Francisco: HarperSanFrancisco: 2004).

Wills, Garry. *What Paul Meant* (New York: Penguin, 2006).

Wilson, A. N. *Paul: The Mind of the Apostle* (New York: W. W. Norton, 1997).

PART 2

Theological Conversations

6

Chance and Providence in the Islamic Tradition

Mustafa Ruzgar

Introduction

Chance has often been considered nonexistent in major theistic worldviews. Theologies that attribute absolute power or control to God or pseudo-independence to humans and nature see chance and providence as binary opposites. In Islamic thought, this emphasis has partial support from the Qur'an. The Qur'anic universe works with full purpose, harmony, divine guidance, and providence. It is, as Fazlur Rahman puts it, "one firm, well-knit structure with no gaps, no ruptures, and no dislocations. It works by its own laws, which have been ingrained in it by God, and is, therefore, autonomous; but it is not autocratic, for, in itself, it has no warrant for its own existence and it cannot explain itself."[1] Because the existence of nature and its laws have been attributed to God's initiative, the Qur'an depicts the universe in such a way that the entirety of it contains signs for God's "presence in the universe."[2]

The term that denotes the meaning of "sign" is *ayah*. Although it is conventionally used to refer to the verses of the Qur'an, Muslims have a deeper understanding of the term by applying it to everything in nature "since all things are God's creatures."[3] Because nature contains signs for God's presence, God's creative activity indicates more than the mere existence of things. As a purposeful Creator, God ingrains order, meaning, and purpose in creation in such a way that it becomes possible to find God through contemplation of nature. This is a central theme frequently highlighted in the Qur'an and has been interpreted as presupposing that it is more rational to think the universe was created by a purposeful creator, not by mere chance,[4] leading to the belief that chance and providence mutually exclude each other.

With regard to purposefulness of the universe, Rahman nicely summarizes the Qur'anic perspective in detail:

> God does not create as a frivolity, pastime, or sport, without a serious purpose. It is incompatible with the power of the Powerful and the mercy of the Merciful that He should produce toys for amusement or as sheer whim—a blind Fate can do this but God cannot: "Those [are believers] who remember God standing and sitting and lying down and reflect upon the creation of the heaven and the earth [and say]: Our Lord! You have not created all this in vain" (3:191); "We have not created the heaven and the earth and whatever is between them in vain" (38:27); "We have not created the heaven and the earth and whatever is between them in sport. If We wished to take a sport, We could have done it by Ourselves [not through Our creation]—if We were to do that at all" (21:16–17); finally, with regard to the creation of man, "Do you then think that We have created you purposelessly and that you will not be returned to Us? The True Sovereign is too exalted above that" (23:115); "Does man think that he will be left wandering [at his own whim]?" (75:36).
>
> Thus, not only does the Qur'ān part company with atheists and those who believe that the universe is a product of chance and a play of matter, but also with all those who believe that God produced the universe as a sport. . . . Also, if the world is a sport, all talk of guidance and misguidance and judgment in the Qur'ānic sense (not in the sense of the rules of the sport!) is not only beside the point, but a massive delusion.[5]

Inspired by relevant Qur'anic passages, many Muslim thinkers have perspectives similar to Rahman. They often see necessary connections among order, purpose, and denial of chance.

This perceived opposition between chance and providence has led to ways of thinking that do not necessarily serve the initial purpose of safeguarding God's purposefulness, however. Often, providence has been thought of as the absolute control of God to the degree of undermining human freedom or some measure of autonomy in nature. God's power has frequently been characterized as coercive, not persuasive, and in absolute control of every single event at all moments, supernaturally if necessary. Equating providence with divine power in this way has been one of the main reasons for anti-Darwinian sentiment in the Muslim world. Darwin's allowance of chance events inspired a significant number of Muslims to reject his theory in its totality, sometimes leading to perceptions that any evolutionary approach, whether theistic or not, is unfavorable.

Views that undermine human freedom and some autonomy in nature create challenging problems for theistic traditions because of their tension with religious or moral responsibility. Some have offered the solution of considering freedom and autonomy as free gifts from God. According to this, humans act in ways that are not entirely controlled by God, and natural events occur with pseudo-independence. This solution is not entirely successful, though, because the logic of "gift" indicates a God who could suspend freedom and autonomy at any moment, if wished.

Alternative views to this dominant approach, which grant more freedom to humans and autonomy to nature, arguably have the potential to allow for some degree of chance and thus, for theistic evolution. Such views have been available in Islamic thought, but often only at the periphery of conventional views. It is true that mere occurrence of chance in nature in such a way as to reject divine influence contradicts the purposeful universe of the Qur'an as outlined. However, some believe the Qur'anic universe displays a more dynamic structure, and this chapter gives a brief account of Islamic theology, philosophy, and mysticism that is relevant to issues of divine providence and randomness.

Randomness and Providence in Islamic Thought: Theology, Philosophy, and Sufism

Islamic intellectual heritage—in the forms of theology, philosophy, and mysticism—displays a deep commitment to the general ideals of the Qur'anic universe in terms of order, meaning, and purpose, and to God's agency in terms of power and creativity. In varying degrees, these ideals have implicitly or explicitly motivated most interpretations. On issues that directly or indirectly relate to these ideals, such as human freedom and destiny, Muslim thinkers have entertained diverse positions, sometimes in direct opposition to each other. Proposals that identify "an Islamic position" on such issues should be critically examined, in light of the historical situatedness of dominant interpretations, the influences of politics, and the richness of competing alternatives during the formative years. Randomness and providence is no exception.

Theologians

Free will and determinism exemplify one of the pivotal issues for early theologians. The discussions during the Umayyad dynasty (661–750) and earlier were not purely abstract speculations devoid of political developments. Interactions with and influences from outside cultures and religions played their role in contributing to these discussions as well.[6]

Around the middle of the eighth century, the school of theologians known as the Jabarites represented extreme deterministic views. Jahm Ibn Safwan (d. 745) is often considered to be the one who substantiated the idea of predeterminism as part of Islamic theology, although the view that everything was strictly predetermined by God as part of God's plan was articulated by some before him.[7] He "repudiated categorically the concept of 'created power,' or human ability to carry out their designs in the world, and attributed power in every shape or form to God."[8] Because of their belief in strict predeterminism and their rejection of free will, the Jabarites rejected religious responsibility as well as divine punishment and reward. They substantiated their arguments by believing that "if the creator of the universe was both omnipotent and omniscient then the ultimate authority for everything was vested in Him and as a result, the ultimate responsibility was His."[9] Believing in free will would be a form of *shirk* [associating gods with God] because of its acceptance of humans as associates in the act of creation.[10]

Against these deterministic views, which justified moral laxity and political oppression, the school known as the Qadarites held views that emphasized free will and religious responsibility. According to them, accountability for good or bad actions solely belongs to human actors, not to God. Although there is much ambiguity in the origination of the term Qadarite and its association with other theological schools, such as the Mu'tezilites, the Qadarite movement signified a growing interest among Muslims in seeing God's providence through a less deterministic lens.[11]

While both groups wanted to justify their views on the basis of the Qur'an, because of the Qur'an's practical intent, one may identify passages that appear to support contradictory positions. The Qur'an is "essentially a religious and ethical document" that emphasizes "faith-in-action," thus "pure theory [in the Qur'an] is minimal."[12] However, it is clear in its emphasis on the order and purposiveness of the universe, human responsibility, and overall divine providence.

Another school, the Kharijites, also believed that human beings are free and responsible for their actions. They held the extreme view that anyone who committed a "grave sin" and did not regret and seek forgiveness is guilty of becoming non-Muslim, whose blood is justified to be shed—and they often acted on their convictions. Their beliefs were heavily influenced by political conditions. According to the Kharijites, the Muslim community "had the right to depose or even assassinate a Caliph deemed guilty of a grave sin, political or other."[13] From their standpoint, "[t]he Umayyads and their officials ... are responsible for their sins and misdemeanors, and are unworthy of the sovereignty they exercise; they may also be lawfully opposed when opportunity offers."[14] Though political in essence, their justifications ultimately related to issues of free will and responsibility.

Against the Kharijites, the Murji'ites entertained a philosophy of "postponement of judgment" on matters of membership to the Muslim community, as "they asserted that the question of whether those who had committed grave sins belonged to the 'people of Paradise' or the 'people of Hell' could not be answered by men but must be left to God's decision on the Last Day."[15] Any definitive judgment, they reasoned, contradicts the belief that God is the only one who knows "the rightness and wrongness of actions."[16]

Most of the views outlined so far have to do with issues that relate to God's power and providence. While free will defenses may imply tensions with divine power, none of these schools in principle has rejected it.

One group that vigorously maintained views that have been perceived as contradictory to divine omnipotence—the Mu'tezilites—are sometimes labeled as the rationalists of Islamic theology. A primary doctrine among Mu'tezilites was the "justice" of God. "By 'justice' they meant that Allah is *obliged* to reward the righteous and to punish the transgressor."[17] In other words, "Allah cannot give good reward to an evil-doer, nor can He punish a pious person."[18] Otherwise, Allah would not be just. Because of the binding emphasis they put on divine justice, some interpreters have suggested that Mu'tezilite views limited God's power.[19] Although this view has some plausibility, the Mu'tezilite perspective is strictly limited to the issue of divine justice—it does not extend to an overall limitation in God's power. In fact, the Mu'tezilites were as keen on preserving God's omnipotence as their contemporaries. As Majid Fakhry argues, some of the Mu'tezilite views surpassed "in [their] extremeness the teaching of their avowed antagonists, the Ash'arites, and [are] inspired by precisely the same theological motive: namely, the safeguarding of the absolute and unqualified omnipotence of God."[20]

Their belief in divine justice and religious responsibility inspired the Mu'tezilites to support free will and reject predeterminism. Otherwise, they reasoned, "the idea of hell and heaven becomes farcical."[21] They famously stated that human actions are created by humans, not by God—we are the authors of our own actions.

Mu'tezilite rationalism peaked in the belief that the sources of goodness and badness are not strictly to be sought in God. Something is good or bad because of its inherent goodness or badness, which can be discovered by reason alone. It is not good or bad because of God's saying so. Although God's wisdom and justice require that God could command only what was right and prohibit what was wrong, in reality, what reason discovers coincides with what God says.[22] This belief of the Mu'tezilites puts reason on equal level with revelation in discovering moral truth,[23] which was highly difficult for the orthodoxy to accept.

The orthodox theological position has been largely represented by the Ash'arites, whose influence has dominated Muslim thought to this day.[24] Their beliefs were almost the exact opposite of the Mu'tezilites' on a number of issues, ranging from divine justice and free will to the value of reason. Its founder, al-Ash'ari (d. 941), gave a limited role to reason. Without help from revelation, he believed, not all issues could be resolved through reason alone. Although al-Ash'ari's view did not entirely eliminate the role of reason, some of the later Ash'arite scholars arguably limited its value more.[25]

As a movement concerned with contesting antiorthodox views, one of the fundamental tenets of Ash'arite thought is its unwavering emphasis on the belief in God's absolute power. Ash'arites rejected the Mu'tazilite belief that good and bad can be discovered by reason alone and that God is under compulsion to command what is commendable and prohibit what is reprehensible.[26] They resolved what seemed to be this Mu'tazilite limitation of God's power by insisting that "God is under no compulsion of any kind, so that whatever He commands is by definition right and what He prohibits, wrong."[27] Power belongs only to God, they believed. Human power is derivative and is "subject to the will and power of Allah. Man can only have so much freedom as Allah grants him and also in the manner that Allah wills."[28]

On the subject of free will, the Ash'arites rejected the Mu'tazilite idea of absolute freedom in human actions (the belief that humans are the authors of their own actions). They also differed from the Jabarite belief in absolute predeterminism. The Ash'arite solution was a search for a middle ground that would do justice to religious responsibility without jeopardizing God's providence, power, and agency. How they achieved this is a complicated theory known as the doctrine of *acquisition*, which essentially was an attempt to "reconcile Divine Omnipotence with human responsibility."[29] As C. A. Qadir comments, however, it is difficult to develop a consistent theory that allows for authentic human freedom when God is conceived of as all-knowing and all-powerful.[30]

The belief in the absolute power of God was "further supported by an atomistic theory of nature denying causation and potentialities in natural bodies and providing for the direct efficacy of God for the production of events, whether physical or mental."[31] Although atomistic conceptions existed in al-Ash'ari's own works,[32] this theory was perhaps most comprehensively developed by al-Baqillani (d. 1013). Al-Baqillani's views reinforced certain Ash'arite convictions, including those about revelation, the contingency of the universe, the absoluteness of God's power and the derivativeness of nondivine power, the affirmation of miracles, the rejection of laws of cause and effect due to God being the cause of everything, and the belief that God is the only power to create existence and provide harmony in it.[33] The occasionalist metaphysics of atoms and accidents, according to Majid Fakhry, "accorded well . . . with the Qur'anic concept of God's omnipotence and His sovereignty in the world, for it belonged to God alone to create or recreate the atoms and accidents which made up physical objects in the world and to cause them to cease as He pleased and when He pleased."[34]

Although similar to the Ash'arites in its basic outlook, the theology of al-Maturidi (d. 945) attempted a further reconciliation between divine power and human freedom—it emphasized God's power but did not reject the "efficacy of the human will and, in some of its later developments, the absolutely free human production of acts was unequivocally stated."[35] Al-Maturidi gave more room to reason than the Ash'arites and more room to revelation than the Mu'tezilites.[36] Yet the majority of Maturidis rejected the idea that God creates through cause and effect because, they thought, such a view limits God's power.[37]

The formative years of Islamic theology reveal rich and diverse intellectual activity with strong advocacy of the basic Qur'anic doctrines. Even the schools that were most emphatic about the use of reason have been motivated by this primary impulse. Although there was no outright disagreement on the order and purposiveness of the universe and the necessity of God's power and providence, subsidiary issues found diverse and often competing advocates.

Without conceding to the Mu'tazilite alternative, some contemporary Muslim scholars see Ash'arite notions as problematic. The Ash'arite-Mu'tazilite dichotomy, they suggest, is unproductive—each possessing unique problems for an authentic Muslim worldview. For example, with regard to human actions and destiny vis-à-vis God's sovereignty, Fazlur Rahman states: "God and man are not rivals therein—as the later Mu'tazilite and Ash'arite theologians thought, so that the former made man the sole agent and denied God's role totally in order to make men 'completely responsible,' while the latter denied any power to man in order to safeguard the 'omnipotence of God.'"[38] Both aspects, according to Rahman, are part of the realities of moral life, and the Qur'an retains "both sides of the tension."[39] Part of the reason why the Qur'anic balance has often been distorted is the lack of an adequate worldview that consistently reconciled divine providence with human freedom (or with pseudo or real autonomy of nature and a dynamic world with open future). In this context, it is valuable to address Muslim philosophers who arguably offer a more systematic approach to existing problems.

Philosophers

Writing in the context of Islam,[40] Muslim philosophers have been keen on accepting and expounding the main Qur'anic outline of the orderliness (rationality) of the universe. Having been influenced by various external sources, such as Greek philosophy, they express their beliefs in philosophical terminology to understand God, nature, and the God-world relationship. Among the views advocated by Muslim philosophers have been contingency of the universe and the phenomenal world, God as the first and necessary cause, and the rational structure of the universe.

Al-Kindi (d. ca. 866), the first genuine Muslim philosopher, paid attention to the appearance of order in the universe, its harmony, its organization, and the interrelatedness of its components, arguing that such order points to God's existence.[41] Metaphysics, according to al-Kindi, tackles issues that relate to "the True One, who is eternal and infinite."[42] It is clear from al-Kindi's perspective that God's providence pervades everything as God is the creator (ex nihilo) and preserver of everything. Though he was influenced by Greek philosophy, al-Kindi believed that "time and motion are finite and the world, as the product of God's creative power, must have a temporal beginning and end."[43] These beliefs of al-Kindi reflect his deep commitment to the teachings of the Qur'an.

Unlike al-Kindi, Abu Bakr al-Razi (d. 925/935) believed that "the world was created in time out of preexisting matter."[44] Matter is eternal and the concept of creation ex nihilo is "logically untenable," according to him.[45] Al-Razi posits "five eternal beings whose interactions framed the world we know: God, Soul, time, space, and matter. In the beginning these five coexisted."[46] Because of this and other views, al-Razi has often been charged with having commitments other than to main Islamic beliefs and has often been described as one of the least orthodox of Islamic intellectuals.

Al-Farabi (d. 950), like al-Kindi, elaborates on the "First Being, the cause of all existing things, and of His essential attributes."[47] He upheld an emanational (*sudur*) account of existence, according to which the most perfect being, the First Being, gives rise to the less perfect, all the way down.[48] All creation exists in a causal relationship to, and is linked with, the First Being, who holds all the perfect attributes and characteristics.[49] Although some aspects of his theory of emanation are difficult to reconcile with orthodox views of creation and existence, al-Farabi's association of politics and ethics with metaphysics reflects his commitment to Islamic doctrines about human beings and their relation to God, the universe, and other humans.[50]

Ibn Sina (d. 1037), like al-Farabi, adopted an emanational cosmology. And like al-Razi, he believed in the eternality of the cosmos, but differed from him by attributing "contingency" to it. For him, the existence of matter "depends (eternally) on the act of God."[51] He distinguished between contingency and necessity and argued that the Necessary Being is different from the contingent universe.[52] "He [defined] the necessary in *al-Shifā'* as 'that which, conceived in itself, must necessarily exist,' and in *al-Najāt*, less tautologically perhaps, as 'that being which, if it is supposed not to exist, an absurdity will ensue'; unlike the contingent which, whether we suppose it to exist or not, would entail no such absurdity."[53]

After famously proving the existence of the Necessary Being from the contingency of the world,[54] Ibn Sina detailed some of the negative and positive attributes of this Necessary Being, which highlights his commitment to Islamic teachings—attributes such as absolute unity (that necessitates no composition, including the composition of essence and existence); indefinability; having no accidental property; and being pure good, pure reason, and pure truth.[55] The Necessary Being's knowledge entails everything, but since his essence "entails no multiplicity or change," He knows everything universally.[56]

Despite these diverse opinions and sources, the overall discussion here so far reveals that both theologians and philosophers have been trying in their own ways to be loyal to the basic Qur'anic doctrines on a number of issues relevant to randomness and providence, such as creation, God, God-world relationship, the orderliness of the universe, and free will. However, after the rise and dominance of Ash'arite theology, clear differences can be identified between what the philosophers at large emphasized and how these points of emphasis have generally been perceived.

Arguably, Muslim philosophers' impact on Islamic thought was "marginal"[57] for the reason that many Muslims have been suspicious about the methodology and implications of the philosophical metaphysics. For example, the Ash'arite notions of God's absolute and supernatural power, as well as the limited role the Ash'arites attributed to reason,[58] are generally in conflict with the philosophers' acceptance of the "efficacy of secondary causation and the continuity of nature," their attempts to rationally explain the workings of the universe, and their doubts about God's miraculous power.[59] The general philosophical suggestion that "there are things which [God] cannot do once he has decided to produce a certain sort of world with particular kinds of creatures in it" constitutes "no restriction on God's power"[60] goes against the heart of Islamic orthodox belief. Arguably, the famous attack by al-Ghazali (d. 1111) on the philosophers' general convictions has intensified orthodox persuasions.[61] The doctrine of God's absolute and miraculous power, inherent in the Ash'arite denial of "necessary causation," has become the dominant approach among Muslim thinkers.[62]

Sufis

Sufism, the mystical tradition of Islam, reveals extraordinary diversity and richness through numerous figures, methodologies, and practices. In a short chapter like this, it is impossible to undertake a figure-by-figure analysis to unearth Sufi approaches to randomness and providence. However, as a general observation it is reasonable to state that the Sufi tradition has been comparatively more uniform in underlining divine providence and the improbability of chance in the universe. Trust in God's predestination has been one of the most important Sufi themes emphasized by different schools and individuals, finding its way into the psychology of Muslims even today. It is illuminating to observe that, rightly or wrongly, many modernist Muslims have criticized Sufism exactly on this point—its power to motivate Muslims into accepting different degrees of fatalism that brings about laziness.[63]

Despite their diversity, Sufis have consistently detailed and reinforced the main Qur'anic doctrines about God and the world. One of the constant themes regarding divine providence has been the belief that God's act of creation is not finished; it is continuously renewed at every moment.[64] In principle, the idea of continuous creation could be interpreted in ways that may reduce God's agency in the world. However, in the hands of Sufis, it indicated just the opposite—God's absolute agency at any moment of creation. Because of this, there cannot be any randomness that implies actions or places from which divinity is absent.

Sufis see in nature signs that lead its contemplators to God—a frequently emphasized notion in the Qur'an and well ingrained in Muslim minds. Their perception of nature goes beyond its mere materiality. "Sufis contemplate nature, seeing in its forms, life, and rhythms spiritual realities that are of the greatest importance not only in themselves but also for us as wayfarers on the path to spiritual perfection."[65] Transcending the material level of existence, they see in nature the reflection of God, sometimes even coming close to pantheistic perspectives.

Darwin, Evolution, and Chance

The intellectual heritage outlined so far brings to light a few points pertinent to Muslims' reception of Darwin's evolutionary theory. First, despite a rather comprehensive worldview detailed in the Qur'an, it may prove problematic to try to identify a particular system or thought strictly and exclusively with the adjective "Islamic." Spread over centuries, Islamic intellectual history is fertile and diverse. Over time, naturally, certain interpretations and dogmas have prevailed and even crystallized, such as Ash'arite theology and some Sufi tenets and attitudes, as well as rejection of some philosophical views and methodologies. As a result, the idea of predestination and varying degrees of fatalism, the doctrines of absolute divine power and creation out of nothingness, and rather weak versions of human freedom have gained more currency than their alternatives, leading to widespread emphasis among Muslims of the impossibility of randomness in varying degrees.

Theological, philosophical, and mystical approaches that draw upon this perspective in terms of free will, destiny, divine and nondivine power, natural laws, and creation highlight the need for a more dynamic understanding of a universe with genuine freedom, an open future, causality, and divine influence. Despite clues in Islamic thought about the possibility of such a universe, the dominant Muslim theology is in tension with such dynamism, creating challenges for the acceptance of an evolutionary universe.

The alternative theories that had the potential to challenge this overall picture have become unfavorable because of the common belief that they fail to correspond to overall Qur'anic perspectives. In this milieu, a positive reception of a theory (Darwin's) that allows chance events at the expense of divine agency in the universe was impossible. Since the introduction of the theory to the Muslim world in the second half of the nineteenth century,[66] Muslims have displayed ambivalent approaches to it due to its irreconcilability with divine influence, regardless of its scientific implications. The ambivalence was reinforced by the absence of a worldview that supports unconventional themes or beliefs. Despite minor attempts to reconcile Darwinian theory[67]—or more general approaches that are sympathetic to evolution but not necessarily to Darwin or the possibility of chance[68]—with the Muslim faith, antievolutionary views have been stronger among Muslim intellectuals and within the Islamic educational curricula.[69]

Writing about Darwin's theory, Hüseyin Aydın explains the problem succinctly: inasmuch as evolution uses causality, there is no contradiction to a theistic perspective because mere causality does not exclude teleology, and inasmuch as it uses chance or randomness, which rejects any divine decision and determination,[70] it is in direct contradiction to a theistic God, because chance or randomness not only excludes causality, but also teleology.[71] The Qur'anic universe is overwhelmingly teleological, not only about the organic world but also the inorganic. For Muslims, rejection of such teleology equals rejection of God—and Darwin's theory just does that.[72] Using chance as a justification for atheistic or materialistic interpretations of Darwin, as many proponents of atheism do, strengthens the conviction that allowing chance in the evolutionary process necessarily negates God. Hence, Muslim critics of evolution and its atheistic interpreters are often found in agreement: chance and divine providence are irreconcilable.

Theistic Evolutionism and the Need for a More Dynamic Universe: Process Thought and Islam

As discussed above, the Qur'an offers a well-defined perspective on chance, orderliness, and providence—a perspective which always depicts a purposeful universe full of meaning, order, and divine influence, and thus seems largely incompatible with Darwinian evolution. Accordingly, Muslims have adopted various positions on Darwin's theory. Many Muslims simply reject it in its totality. Some accept evolution, or a version of it, while avoiding the issue of randomness. And some Muslims believe that religion is separate from science, preventing any tension between science-based randomness and religion-based providence.

There is, however, another alternative that focuses on a theistic evolutionism without rejecting God or divine influence. This alternative has been voiced especially by some Western authors, most of whom construct their versions of theistic evolutionism around the language of chance (I will expand on these views below).[73] However plausible these interpretations are within their respective religious communities, many Muslims may feel skeptical about them as long as chance is understood as referring to no purposive or teleological divine influence and guidance. Even the proposal that it is God who initially introduced the element of chance into evolutionary history may not be convincing because chance, by definition, excludes purposive guidance. For a Muslim, then, it may prove more useful to drop the language of chance and focus instead on aspects that make a theistic evolutionism possible.

New perspectives on theistic evolutionism voiced by these Western authors provide promising indications for the possibility of reconstructing a genuinely Islamic approach by utilizing notions inherent in, but on the peripheries of, Islamic intellectual history. These approaches may grant more power and freedom to nondivine entities without contradicting, and arguably being in more agreement with, the Qur'anic universe. This thoroughly evolutionary model is particularly, and uniquely, possible for Islamic thought because of the availability of Muslim thinkers and schools that advocated notions of freedom, nondivine power, evolution, and even nonsubstantial metaphysics.

The most systematic account of theistic evolutionism has been developed by Whitehead-inspired[74] process theologians, which is both evolutionary and theistic through and through. Process theology focuses on an event-based unfinished creation where nondivine entities possess an irreducible power of self-determination and the power to influence others, allowing genuine freedom with an open future, with God's providence continuously working through *persuasion* rather than *coercion*. Process theologian Marjorie H. Suchocki notes that this approach "uses evolution to deepen its understanding of creation as call and response. The world is formed in and through its response to God, not only "in the beginning" but today and tomorrow as well. The God of creation is the God of providence."[75]

As David Ray Griffin summarizes, "process philosophy's naturalistic theism . . . portrays God as the creator of this evolutionary cosmos—but not in such a way as to be indictable for its evils."[76] In other words, process theologians' naturalistic theism provides a "viable version of theistic evolutionism," disagreeing with the "nontheistic account of evolution given by neo-Darwinism."[77] The theory called panexperientialism, which sees "nature [as] composed of prehensive occasions of experience," explains "how divine influence could lead to progressive change" in order to "bring about more complex societies in which higher values can be realized."[78]

According to other key elements of process thought, the world is not created from absolute nothingness. The world is dynamic, not fixed or finished, with an open future and novel possibilities. Process theologians conceptualize God's power not in absolutist or supernaturalistic terms. Divine power works persuasively to bring about the best possibilities, not coercively. Nondivine entities are not merely passive respondents to God; they possess nonderivative twofold power—the power of self-determination and the power to influence others. Understanding evolution within this framework gives important clues for solving the problem of evil as well, the occurrence of which is tied to some metaphysical principles with which God works.[79]

The basic tenets of the process approach do not necessarily conflict with the main Qur'anic worldview and some of its historical interpretations as found in the Mu'tezilite conception of freedom and the philosophical approaches to natural laws. Moreover, there have been prominent Muslims intellectuals who advocated uniquely process-like views, some of them being directly inspired by Alfred North Whitehead. Muhammad Iqbal (d. 1938), for example, developed a dynamic worldview based on "constant change and creation."[80] He was considerably inspired by Whitehead, both of whom understood reality as not being composed of substances but events. An event-based approach can be found among other Muslim thinkers before Whitehead and Iqbal, such as in Mulla Sadra (d. 1640), who sees everything in the universe being in constant becoming, rejecting fixed or finished things. Essentially, both Sadra and Iqbal base their views on the Qur'an, arguing that its various verses inform a worldview that is more dynamic than traditionally assumed. Many of Iqbal's other views are related to process thought, such as his interpretations of divine power and the problem of evil.

Conclusion

Justifiably, chance and divine providence have been conceived as two contradictory terms by Muslims. Because evolution (Darwinian or neo-Darwinian) is often associated with chance, Muslim intellectuals have generally been skeptical about it. Rejecting chance, nevertheless, does not necessarily require rejection of evolution. A theistic version of evolution is possible on the grounds of four sources from Islamic intellectual history: (1) the Qur'anic emphasis on orderly and purposive creation, (2) views derived from thinkers who attribute genuine power and freedom to human beings as well as more autonomy to nature, (3) a rich tradition of evolutionism since the formative days of Islamic thought, and finally (4) the event-based worldviews developed by thinkers such as Mulla Sadra and Muhammad Iqbal.

Although the implications of the theistic evolution described above would still be in tension with some of the prevailing interpretations of Islamic theology (as instigated by the Ash'arites and others) on issues such as God's power, natural causes, and human reasoning and freedom, these views do not necessarily represent the "religion" itself. Islamic intellectual history has been considerably rich and diverse. Moreover, there is no doubt that the future will be marked by novel ideas and syntheses that will add to this richness and diversity.

Notes

1. Fazlur Rahman, *Major Themes of the Qur'an* (Chicago and London: University of Chicago Press, 2009), 3.
2. Farid Esack, *The Qur'an: A Beginner's Guide* (Oxford: Oneworld, 2009), 66.
3. Sachiko Murata and William C. Chittick, *The Vision of Islam* (St. Paul, MN: Paragon House, 1994), 54. For more information on the meaning of "sign" and its different usages, see the section titled "Interpreting the Signs," 54–57.
4. For more detail on order, contemplation, and chance, see Rahman, *Major Themes of the Qur'an*, 10–11. A number of other Qur'anic terms reveal similar perspective on the meaning of nature and the place of chance in it. For example, the Qur'anic term *qadar* means both "power" and "measuring out." Though the meanings relate to each other in the Qur'anic usage, especially the second one, measuring out, points to the fact that the universe is not a product of blind chance. The agent of *qadar*, God, measures things out in certain degrees with order and purpose. The universe works according to natural laws, but these laws have been created by God. Similarly, the Qur'anic term *amr* also indicates the same meaning of measuring out. *Amr* means "command" and God as the ultimate "command/er" creates the nature in such a way that the "laws of nature express the Command of God." For more information on *qadar* and *amr*, see ibid., 12–14.
5. Ibid., 7–8.
6. For examples and a summary account of the interaction between politics and theology before and during the Umayyad dynasty, and for the examples and influences of foreign sources, see Mahmoud M. Ayoub, *Islam: Faith and History* (Oxford: Oneworld, 2005), 160–165, and Fazlur Rahman, *Islam* (Chicago: University of Chicago Press, 1979), 85–94.
7. İrfan Abdülhamid, "Cebriyye [Jabarites]," in *TDV İslâm Ansiklopedisi* [*TDV Encyclopedia of Islam*] (İstanbul: Türkiye Diyanet Vakfı [Turkey Diyanet Foundation], 1993), 7: 206.
8. Majid Fakhry, *Islamic Philosophy, Theology and Mysticism: A Short Introduction* (Oxford: Oneworld, 1998), 15.
9. C. A. Qadir, *Philosophy and Science in the Islamic World* (London, New York, and Sydney: Croom Helm, 1988), 44.
10. Abdülhamid, "Cebriyye [Jabarites]," 207.
11. For more information on the Qadarite school, see İlyas Üzüm, "Kaderiyye [Qadarites]," in *TDV İslâm Ansiklopedisi* [*TDV Encyclopedia of Islam*] (İstanbul: Türkiye Diyanet Vakfı [Turkey Diyanet Foundation], 2001), 24: 64-65.
12. Rahman, *Islam*, 85.
13. Fakhry, *Islamic Philosophy, Theology and Mysticism*, 12.

14. W. Montgomery Watt, *Islamic Philosophy and Theology* (Edinburgh: Edinburgh University Press, 1962), 31.
15. Ibid., 33.
16. Qadir, *Philosophy and Science in the Islamic World*, 47.
17. Ibid., 48 (emphasis mine).
18. Ibid., 51.
19. Qadir, for example, maintains that the Mu'tezilite perception of divine justice cannot be accepted from an orthodox perspective because of its rejection of Allah's omnipotence. He further supports his interpretation by citing one of the Mu'tezilite scholars, al-Nazzam (d. 845), who asserted that God's goodness limits his omnipotence in such a way that God cannot do evil. For more information, see ibid., 48–53.
20. Majid Fakhry, *Philosophy, Dogma and the Impact of Greek Thought in Islam* (Aldershot: Variorum, 1994), 95.
21. Qadir, *Philosophy and Science in the Islamic World*, 50.
22. Fakhry, *Islamic Philosophy, Theology and Mysticism*, 16.
23. Rahman, *Islam*, 88, 90.
24. Qadir, *Philosophy and Science in the Islamic World*, 60.
25. Ibid., 62.
26. Fakhry, *Islamic Philosophy, Theology and Mysticism*, 16.
27. Ibid., 16.
28. Qadir, *Philosophy and Science in the Islamic World*, 64.
29. Rahman, *Islam*, 92.
30. Qadir, *Philosophy and Science in the Islamic World*, 64.
31. Rahman, *Islam*, 93.
32. Watt, *Islamic Philosophy and Theology*, 107.
33. Qadir, *Philosophy and Science in the Islamic World*, 66–69.
34. Fakhry, *Islamic Philosophy, Theology and Mysticism*, 4.
35. Rahman, *Islam*, 93. For a more detailed comparison between the Ash'arites and Maturidis on the efficacy of human will, see Yusuf Şevki Yavuz, "Mâtürîdiyye [Maturidis]," in *TDV İslâm Ansiklopedisi* [*TDV Encyclopedia of Islam*] (İstanbul: Türkiye Diyanet Vakfı [Turkey Diyanet Foundation], 2003), 28: 173–174.
36. Yavuz, "Mâtürîdiyye [Maturidis]," 166.
37. Ibid., 169.
38. Rahman, *Major Themes of the Qur'an*, 15.
39. Ibid.
40. Oliver Leaman, *A Brief Introduction to Islamic Philosophy* (Malden, MA: Blackwell, 1999), 13–14.
41. Qadir, *Philosophy and Science in the Islamic World*, 81
42. Fakhry, *Islamic Philosophy, Theology and Mysticism*, 25.
43. Ibid., 25.

44. Ibid, 31.
45. Fakhry, Majid, *A History of Islamic Philosophy* (New York: Columbia University Press, 1970), 121.
46. Lenn E.Goodman, "Muhammad ibn Zakariyyā' al-Rāzī," in *History of Islamic Philosophy*, ed. Seyyed Hossein Nasr and Oliver Leaman (London and New York: Routledge, 2001), 203.
47. Fakhry, *Short Introduction to Islamic Philosophy, Theology and Mysticism*, 40.
48. Ibid., 41.
49. Fakhry, *History of Islamic Philosophy*, 136.
50. Ibid, 135–136.
51. Goodman, "Muhammad ibn Zakariyyā' al-Rāzī," 204.
52. Fakhry, *Short Introduction to Islamic Philosophy, Theology and Mysticism*, 50.
53. Ibid.
54. For more detailed information, see ibid.
55. Ibid., 51.
56. Ibid., 50–51.
57. John L. Esposito, *Islam: The Straight Path* (New York and Oxford: Oxford University Press, 2011), 91.
58. Fakhry, *Short Introduction to Islamic Philosophy, Theology and Mysticism*, 68–69.
59. Leaman, *Brief Introduction to Islamic Philosophy*, 39–41.
60. Ibid., 40–41.
61. For more information on al-Ghazali's criticisms, see Fakhry, *Short Introduction to Islamic Philosophy, Theology and Mysticism*, 70–72.
62. Ibid., 72.
63. For a brief discussion on the modernist critiques of Sufism, see Carl W. Ernst, *The Shambhala Guide to Sufism* (Boston and London: Shambhala, 1997), 200–205.
64. Seyyed Hossein Nasr, *The Garden of Truth: The Vision and Promise of Sufism, Islam's Mystical Tradition* (New York: HarperOne, 2008), 45.
65. Ibid., 47.
66. Veysel Kaya, "Can the Quran Support Darwin? An Evolutionist Approach by Two Turkish Scholars after the Foundation of the Turkish Republic," *Muslim World* 102, no. 2 (2012): 357.
67. There have been numerous Muslims who adopted evolutionary perspectives in conceiving creation and nature before Darwin. Drawing upon John M. Coulter's tripartite periodization of the history of evolution, Fatih Özgökman situates these approaches in the first period—"speculation." The most extensive study on such figures is conducted by Mehmet Bayrakdar, whose investigation includes, but is not limited to, the following figures: al-Cahız (d. 868/869), al-Biruni (d. 1051), Ikhwan al-Safa [Brethren of Purity], Ibn Tufayl (d. 1185/86), Jalaluddin Rumi (d. 1273), Ibn Miskawayh (d. 1030),

and Ibn Khaldun (d. 1405). For more information, see Fatih Özgökman, *Tanrı ve Evrim* [*God and Evolution*] (Ankara: Elis Yayınları, 2013), 41, 43–44, and Mehmet Bayrakdar, *Islam'da Evrimci Yaratılış Teorisi* [*Evolutionary Creation Theory in Islam*] (Ankara: Kitabiyat, 2001), 31–117.

68. For example, after metaphorically interpreting the story of "Adam and Eve" and reiterating the possibility of "humanlike" creatures before Adam, Ahmed Hamdi Akseki concludes that from a religious point of view there is no clear evidence of the exact time for the emergence of human beings. Moreover, he interprets the Qur'anic concept of creation in evolutionary terms, even using "divine selection" to describe it (as opposed to "natural selection"). In a similar way, Süleyman Ateş, a prominent Turkish Muslim scholar, accepts "natural selection" as a "natural law made by God." God, according to Ateş, "created the universe through a reliance on the law of evolution." But neither Akseki nor Ateş deals with the issue of randomness directly. For more information, see Kaya, "Can the Quran Support Darwin?," 357–370.

69. Taner Edis, "Modern Science and Conservative Islam: An Uneasy Relationship," *Science and Education* 18, nos. 6–7 (2009): 886.

70. Hüseyin Aydın, *İlim Felsefe ve Din Açısından Yaratılış ve Gayelilik (Teleoloji)* [*Creation and Teleology from the Perspective of Science, Philosophy, and Religion (Teleology)*] (Ankara: DİB Yayınları, 2012), 145. Taner Edis makes similar observations by quoting Adem Tatlı and Muhammet Altaytaş, both of whom emphasized the irreconcilability of chance (in Darwin's theory) with notions of a conscious plan, wisdom, guidance, and purpose. For exact quotations, see Edis, "Modern Science and Conservative Islam," 887, 894–895. Şemseddin Akbulut's book *Darwin ve Evrim Teorisi* [*Darwin and Evolutionary Theory*] (İstanbul: Yeni Asya Yayınları, 1985) constitutes a prime example of the degree that the role of "chance" plays in general rejection of Darwin. After identifying "chance" as the most important element of Darwin's theory, Akbulut focuses on disproving the theory by disproving the possibility of chance throughout the book.

71. Aydın, *İlim Felsefe ve Din Açısından Yaratılış ve Gayelilik (Teleoloji)* [*Creation and Teleology from the Perspective of Science, Philosophy, and Religion (Teleology)*], 130–136. Fatih Özgökman agrees that randomness and teleology are mutually exclusive in *Tanrı ve Evrim* [*God and Evolution*], 9.

72. Aydın, *İlim Felsefe ve Din Açısından Yaratılış ve Gayelilik (Teleoloji)* [*Creation and Teleology from the Perspective of Science, Philosophy, and Religion (Teleology)*], 130; Özgökman, *Fatih, Tanrı ve Evrim* [*God and Evolution*], 14.

73. Attempts to reconcile chance and divine providence have taken different forms. After stating that genuine chance has been proven by modern physics in a number of theories that illustrate a future with possibilities—an open

future—Elizabeth A. Johnson concludes that evolution and chance have been working hand in hand since the beginning. This collaboration between evolution and chance, according to her, does not require excluding God from the universe. Instead, the richness, novelty, and freedom we observe in nature do point to a God who uses chance for an open and free future. Like-minded theists extrapolate from the notion of chance and its compatibility with a theistic God against those who use chance as a sufficient reason for atheism. Leading Christian theologians Peter van Inwagen and John F. Haught, using different justifications, find chance compatible with divine providence. According to van Inwagen, evolution is a small part of God's design and the fact that evolution includes the element of chance does not mean that the entirety of the universe is reducible to it. According to Haught, because the Christian God is primarily associated with love and because love requires freedom, God allows a certain degree of chance in the universe. Accordingly, the future is not predetermined. God does not interfere with the evolutionary process in a forcible way, nor does God forcibly control or guide it. Johnson's, van Inwagen's, and Haught's views are summarized in Özgökman, *Tanrı ve Evrim* [*God and Evolution*], 209–212.

74. Alfred North Whitehead (1861–1947) was an English mathematician and philosopher whose concept of reality has been profoundly important to process theology.
75. Marjorie H. Suchocki, "Process Theology and Evolution," in *Evolution and Faith*, ed. Bas van Iersel, Christoph Theobald, and Hermann Häiring (London: SCM Press, 2000), 61.
76. David Ray Griffin, *Reenchantment without Supernaturalism: A Process Philosophy of Religion* (Ithaca, NY: Cornell University Press, 2001), 204.
77. Ibid., 205.
78. Ibid., 213.
79. According to process theologian David Ray Griffin, evil occurs as a result of the necessary order of things that are metaphysically irreversible. In creating our world, he argues, God "necessarily worked with some pre-existent actualities." He adds that there are some "eternal, uncreated, necessary principles (beyond purely logical truths) about the way these actualities can be ordered which limit the sorts of situations that are really possible"; Griffin, "Creation Out of Chaos and the Problem of Evil," in *Encountering Evil: Live Options in Theodicy*, ed. Stephen T. Davis (Atlanta, GA: John Knox Press, 1981), 104. For an account of a process-inspired Muslim perspective on the problem of evil, see Mustafa Ruzgar, "An Islamic Perspective: Theological Development and the Problem of Evil," in *Religions in the Making: Whitehead and the Wisdom Traditions of the World*, ed. John B. Cobb, 72–97 (Eugene, OR: Wipf and Stock, 2012).

80. Mustafa Ruzgar, "Islam and Deep Religious Pluralism," in *Deep Religious Pluralism*, ed. David Ray Griffin (Louisville, KY: Westminster John Knox Press, 2005), 171.

Selected Bibliography

Abdülhamid, İrfan. "Cebriyye [Jabarites]." In *TDV İslâm Ansiklopedisi* [*TDV Encyclopedia of Islam*], vol. 7 (İstanbul: Türkiye Diyanet Vakfı [Turkey Diyanet Foundation], 1993).

Akbulut, Şemseddin. *Darwin ve Evrim Teorisi* [*Darwin and Evolutionary Theory*] (İstanbul: Yeni Asya Yayınları, 1985).

Aydın, Hüseyin. *İlim Felsefe ve Din Açısından Yaratılış ve Gayelilik (Teleoloji)* [*Creation and Teleology from the Perspective of Science, Philosophy, and Religion (Teleology)*] (Ankara: DİB Yayınları, 2012).

Ayoub, Mahmoud M. *Islam: Faith and History* (Oxford: Oneworld, 2005).

Bayrakdar, Mehmet. *Islam'da Evrimci Yaratılış Teorisi* [*Evolutionary Creation Theory in Islam*] (Ankara: Kitabiyat, 2001).

Black, Deborah L. "Al-Fārābī." In *History of Islamic Philosophy*, edited by Seyyed Hossein Nasr and Oliver Leaman, 178–197 (London and New York: Routledge, 2001).

Edis, Taner. "Modern Science and Conservative Islam: An Uneasy Relationship." *Science and Education* 18, nos. 6–7 (2009): 885–903.

Ernst, Carl W. *The Shambhala Guide to Sufism* (Boston and London: Shambhala, 1997).

Esack, Farid. *The Qur'an: A Beginner's Guide* (Oxford: Oneworld, 2009).

Esposito, John L. *Islam: The Straight Path* (New York and Oxford: Oxford University Press, 2011).

Fakhry, Majid. *A History of Islamic Philosophy* (New York: Columbia University Press, 1970).

Fakhry, Majid. *Philosophy, Dogma and the Impact of Greek Thought in Islam* (Aldershot: Variorum, 1994).

Fakhry, Majid. *Islamic Philosophy, Theology and Mysticism: A Short Introduction* (Oxford: Oneworld, 1998).

Goodman, Lenn E. "Muhammad ibn Zakariyyā' al-Rāzī." In *History of Islamic Philosophy*, edited by Seyyed Hossein Nasr and Oliver Leaman, 198–215 (London and New York: Routledge, 2001).

Griffin, David Ray, "Creation Out of Chaos and the Problem of Evil." In *Encountering Evil: Live Options in Theodicy*, edited by Stephen T. Davis, 101–119, 128–136 (Atlanta, GA: John Knox Press, 1981).

Griffin, David Ray. *Reenchantment without Supernaturalism: A Process Philosophy of Religion* (Ithaca, NY: Cornell University Press, 2001).

Kaya, Veysel. "Can the Quran Support Darwin? An Evolutionist Approach by Two Turkish Scholars after the Foundation of the Turkish Republic." *Muslim World* 102, no. 2 (2012): 357–370.

Leaman, Oliver. *A Brief Introduction to Islamic Philosophy* (Malden, MA: Blackwell, 1999).

Murata, Sachiko, and William C. Chittick. *The Vision of Islam* (St. Paul, MN: Paragon House, 1994).

Nasr, Seyyed Hossein. *The Garden of Truth: The Vision and Promise of Sufism, Islam's Mystical Tradition* (New York: HarperOne, 2008).

Özgökman, Fatih. *Tanrı ve Evrim* [*God and Evolution*] (Ankara: Elis Yayınları, 2013).

Qadir, C. A. *Philosophy and Science in the Islamic World* (London, New York, and Sydney: Croom Helm, 1988).

Rahman, Fazlur. *Islam* (Chicago: University of Chicago Press, 1979).

Rahman, Fazlur. *Major Themes of the Qur'an* (Chicago: University of Chicago Press, 2009).

Ruzgar, Mustafa. "Islam and Deep Religious Pluralism." In *Deep Religious Pluralism*, edited by David Ray Griffin, 158–177 (Louisville, KY: Westminster John Knox Press, 2005).

Ruzgar, Mustafa. "An Islamic Perspective: Theological Development and the Problem of Evil." In *Religions in the Making: Whitehead and the Wisdom Traditions of the World*, edited by John B. Cobb, 72–97 (Eugene, OR: Wipf and Stock, 2012).

Suchocki, Marjorie H. "Process Theology and Evolution." In *Evolution and Faith*, edited by Bas van Iersel, Christoph Theobald, and Hermann Häiring, 53–61 (London: SCM Press, 2000).

Üzüm, İlyas. "Kaderiyye [Qadarites]." In *TDV İslâm Ansiklopedisi* [*TDV Encyclopedia of Islam*], vol. 24 (İstanbul: Türkiye Diyanet Vakfı [Turkey Diyanet Foundation], 2001).

Watt, W. Montgomery. *Islamic Philosophy and Theology* (Edinburgh: Edinburgh University Press, 1962).

Yavuz, Yusuf Şevki. "Mâtürîdiyye [Maturidis]." In *TDV İslâm Ansiklopedisi* [*TDV Encyclopedia of Islam*], vol. 28 (İstanbul: Türkiye Diyanet Vakfı [Turkey Diyanet Foundation], 2003).

7

Chance and Providence in Early Christianity

Richard W. Miller

IN 313, THE emperor Constantine declared freedom of worship for all "so that 'whatever god may be in heaven, he may be propitious to us and those over whom we rule.'"[1] This edict mandated that property confiscated from Christians had to be returned to them and amounted to toleration, indeed wholesale acceptance, of Christianity within the empire. In 361, shortly after the accession of the emperor Julian to the throne, Christians in the city of Caesarea made it clear that they simply could not return the favor—they were not going to show tolerance to the goddess Tyche, who was the goddess of luck or chance, and destroyed the only remaining temple dedicated to her.

The destruction of the temple dedicated to Tyche, according to the influential Christian theologian Gregory of Nazianzus (329–390 CE), "amounted to a declaration of freedom from the tyranny of random chance and luck."[2] For, in the words of the Christian ascetic Macrina (ca. 327–380 CE): "If life begins in consequence of an accident of *tyche*, the whole course of it becomes at once a chapter of such accidents of *tyche* from beginning to end."[3]

While some Greek and Roman philosophers held that the existence of everything was due to chance (e.g., Epicurus), the long tradition in Greek thought of wrestling with chance (*tyche*) in its poetry, plays, and philosophy had less to do with reflection on cosmological origins than it did with the unpredictable and random elements of human experience, though the two notions were related. William Greene, in the introduction to his classic book *Moira: Fate, Good, and Evil in Greek Thought,* ably describes the experience from which the concepts of luck, fate, and providence emerge in their earliest treatments in Western civilization: "The spectacle, and still more the experience, of life's vicissitudes has always been the parent of perplexity. Disappointed hopes, the prosperity of the wicked, the suffering of the innocent, even the little ironies of circumstance, invite men to question whether the ultimate power in the universe is good or evil."[4]

From its earliest poetry through its later philosophy, Greek and Roman thought wrestled with the question of good and evil through its investigations of chance, fate, and providence. In this chapter I first sketch some salient features of this constellation of concepts which became the context within which early Christian thinkers developed their doctrine of divine providence. Second, I articulate the Christian response to the problem of chance as an answer to the atomist Epicurus and examine the Christian concept of creation *ex nihilo* in relation to Epicurus and Plato. Third, I trace the Christian response to the most serious charge against Christianity; namely, that it was a new form of determinism. Finally, after offering a critical examination of a problematic assumption that runs through early Christian accounts of God's providence, I suggest an alternative approach that will help contemporary Christian thinkers formulate a doctrine of providence that takes seriously chance and contingency.

Chance, Fate, and Providence: The Greco-Roman Background

The Greek word *tyche,* which we translate as "chance" or "luck," appears in earliest Greek literature. In Homer (ca. 700 BCE), human beings are not "pushed around by inexplicable happenstance,"[5] whereas in Hesiod (ca. 700 BCE) and the lyric poets, "Tyche appears as an external, palpable, quasi-personified force, distinct from *Moira* [Fate, Destiny], sometimes neutral or even benevolent, more often malign."[6] Over the following centuries the influence of *tyche* "becomes progressively wider in scope, more irresistible, more fatal in every sense"[7] such that one of Sophocles's (ca. 400 BCE) characters asks, "How am I, a mortal, to fight against godlike Tyche?"[8]

By the fourth and third centuries BCE, an anthropocentric perspective begins to take hold of the Greek and Roman world, as evidenced in the sophist Protagoras's famous line—"man is the measure of all things"—such that "man had moved boldly into more and more areas hitherto dominated by the old gods, and the gods had, when appealed to, offered unpredictable help, or, worse, no help at all."[9] With the diminishment of the ties to the old gods, *tyche* took hold of the Greek imagination. Indeed, in the Hellenistic Age (330–30 BCE), according to Michael Grant, "tens of thousands of people were gripped by an unreasonable, dismal, desperate conviction that everything in the world was under the total control of Tyche: Fortune, Chance, or Luck.[10] There was a deep-seated feeling that men and women were adrift in an uncaring universe, and that everything was hazardous, beyond human control or understanding or prediction. And so the cult of Chance swept conqueringly over the Mediterranean."[11]

The philosopher Epicurus (341–240 BCE) vehemently dismissed the idea that *tyche* was a goddess. He did not deny the reality of chance; rather, he wanted to depersonalize chance and understand it in a more rational way. Epicurus denied that the gods were concerned with human beings and strongly criticized the superstitious fear of the gods, which "were a cause of needless anxiety and a threat to the tranquility of mind which he prized."[12] Like the earliest atomists, Leucippus (ca. fifth century BCE) and Democritus (ca. 460 to late 300s BCE), he thought that the basic constituents of the world were tiny, indivisible solid bodies that moved through empty space (our modern term for this concept is "atom," which came from the Greek word *atomos* meaning indivisible). Epicurus maintained that atoms, analogous to falling terrestrial bodies, fall eternally along parallel lines through infinite space. To avoid any hint of determinism, as human free choice was his chief philosophical concern, he argued that atoms spontaneously swerve from their straight line of descent. The later atomist Lucretius (ca. 99–55 BCE) is our best source for Epicurean teaching on the swerve:

> When the atoms are being drawn downward through the void by their property of weight, at absolutely unpredictable times and places they deflect slightly from their straight course, to a degree that could be described as no more than a shift of movement. If they were not apt to swerve, all would fall downward through the unfathomable void like drops of rain; no collisions between primary elements would occur, and no blows would be effected, with the result that nature would never have created anything.[13]

Epicurus held that the universe is eternal and "atoms have fallen, swerved, and collided for all eternity."[14] While the universe as a whole is eternal, particular worlds come into existence and go out of existence. The swerve generates collisions which cause more collisions of atoms which then combine to form worlds. With infinite space and an infinite number of atoms swerving and colliding eternally, an infinite number of worlds are generated. The "swerve of an atom has no cause in events previous to its occurrence; it is in principle unpredictable and random."[15] As such, for Epicurus, our world came into existence devoid of purpose.

Epicurus provides an account neither of how atoms happen to be in motion nor of how the swerves can be random, uncaused events. As such he contradicts one of the central principles of his philosophy—"nothing arises from nothing" and "an uncaused event in a tightly deterministic system such as atomism is an absurdity."[16] Epicurus was willing to pay such a high philosophical price because it was not cosmology that was his chief interest; rather, it was ethics. He sought to save human freedom by representing a human being "as partially determined (in his organic functions) and partially free (in his ethical capacity)."[17] It was this doctrine of the swerve that allowed Epicurus to save human freedom, though his understanding of human freedom is hardly recognizable to us. "It is," as Lucretius summarizes Epicurus's teaching, "this slight deviation of the primal bodies, at indeterminate times and places, which keeps the mind as such from experiencing an inner compulsion in doing everything it does and from being forced to endure and suffer like a captive in chains."[18] Thus "ethical choices are the result of random atomic events occurring in the psyche and brought to consciousness in 'the will.' "[19]

While Epicurus's impersonal and rationalized understanding of *tyche* had influence among those with a philosophical bent, the wider public adhered to a personified understanding of *tyche,* which loomed ever larger in their lives. Once the idea prevailed that whether one prospered or suffered was not the result of individual industry and choice, but was entirely accidental, then human beings were increasingly seen not as rulers of their histories but rather as subjects dominated by blind chance. Once *tyche* was viewed as reigning over human life, *tyche* morphed into "a deterministic fate (*heimarmenē*)."[20] As one of the characters in the play by Menander (ca. 342–ca. 291 BCE) "despairingly cries: 'Each single thought, each word, each act of ours is just Chance. All you and I can do is sign on the dotted line.' "[21]

Unpredictability is anathema to the human mind, so it is not surprising that human beings searched for something stable amidst the unreliability of life. They thus turned to what they saw as fixed and unchangeable to make sense of their lives, namely the course of the planets and the stars. While distant, the planet and stars were not understood to be unconnected to earth: "the sun makes the vegetation grow and die, and causes animals to sleep . . . and the moon appears to control the tides like a magnet."[22] If the moon had such power that it could move the sea, it seemed only reasonable that it could affect human lives.[23]

While the stars were not blind and deaf as *tyche* because they operated by fixed laws, they did not allow for human agency. Human beings were now "ruled by the unfeeling, unchanging, inescapable heavenly spheres," which impelled them as irresistibly as the celestial spheres were moved. In avoiding the unpredictability of *tyche* by turning to the immutable and fixed motions of the planets to make sense of human life, Hellenistic Greeks and Romans were pushed into a kind of fatalism where human free choice yielded to the immutability of the stars, which predestined all that would happen.

The Greco-Roman mind "sought to escape from the oppression of this cosmic mechanism to free itself from the slavery in which *Ananke* [i.e., necessity] held it."[24] One path to liberation was through the personification of the heavenly bodies as fitting objects of worship who could be placated through prayers. Another path toward liberation "was to find out, by enquiry, what the powers had in store; and then to discover how to determine, arrange, and time one's own future activities so as to avoid subjecting oneself to [the gods'] most hostile intentions."[25] Out of this need emerged a highly influential class of astrologers who, through the study of the patterns of the stars at the time of a person's birth (or conception), could allegedly foresee the person's destiny. But that was not all; astrologers could help their clients outmaneuver the stars by planning their activities around the purported time when the celestial bodies were going to exert their influence. While pagan philosophers like Cicero (106–43 BCE) and later Plotinus (204/5–270 CE) vehemently attacked astrology,[26] it was still widely practiced in the fifth century CE, such that Augustine of Hippo (354–430 CE), in reflecting on how serious sins can seem trivial because they are so common, laments in his *Enchiridion on Faith, Hope, and Love* (ca. 419–422 CE) that astrology is so common and openly practiced that "we are afraid not only to excommunicate a lay person for them, but even to degrade a cleric."[27] Indeed, as late as 633 CE, the problem of clergy involvement with astrology was widespread enough that it was condemned at the fourth Council of Toledo.[28]

Yet astrology was not the only form of determinism in Hellenistic and Roman thought. Probably the most influential philosophical system of the Hellenistic age was Stoicism. Founded by Zeno of Citium in Athens (ca. 300 BCE), Stoicism was brought to Rome in the second century BCE, was taught formally until the third century CE, and was still influencing the thought of Christian thinkers through the early Middle Ages. For Stoicism, "chance, *Tyche,* became no more than a label for yet-undiscovered causes."[29] Chance was not an indication that there were really chance or random events; rather, *tyche* referred to our lack of knowledge of the cause of an event. In his dialogue *On Divination,* Cicero summarizes the thought of Posidonius (ca. 135–ca. 50 BCE), an influential Stoic of Middle Stoicism:

> Reason compels us to admit that all things happened by Fate. Now by Fate, I mean the same that the Greeks call *heimarmene,* that is, an orderly succession of causes wherein cause is linked to cause and each cause of itself produces an effect. . . . Therefore nothing has happened which was not bound to happen, and, likewise, nothing is going to happen which will not find in nature every efficient cause of its happening. . . . He who knows the causes of future events necessarily knows what every future event will be.[30]

The causal nexus that unites all events in the universe "is identified with both fate and providence."[31] Stoics were pantheists—"God is mind, God is matter, and God is the universe."[32] For Stoics, "the entire universe, or God, constitutes one living organism, at the same time sentient, rational, and material, existing in and of itself. The universe is its own creative force and its own source of growth, change, and activity. God, or the universe, is not only its own cause; it is the one cause and explanation of all things."[33] The rational structure of the universe or God is the divine Logos and all things are governed by the divine Logos. This governance of all things according to reason is what Stoics understood as divine providence. Yet God is not transcendent, but is utterly immanent as the rational order of the universe. We are now a long way away from *tyche* as an oppressive force personifying the unpredictable and the resulting oppressive fatalisms; rather, "fate . . . is rationalized and identified with the good will of the deity."[34]

For Stoic ethics, which was central to the Stoics' system, human free will was absolutely necessary, but it was unclear how they could maintain it. Indeed, the Stoics were often criticized for their denial of free will, especially by the leading Aristotelian philosopher Alexander of Aphrodisias, active in the late second and early third centuries CE. Alexander was part of a long line of philosophers in the ancient world who strongly defended human free will, including Plato, Aristotle, Carneades, and Plutarch. The most common defense of free will was that if everything was determined by fate or the configuration of the stars, then we could not make sense of our social and legal practices of exhorting virtue and punishing vice. For if human actions were determined by some outside force, how could society reward some people but blame and punish others when they were in no way responsible for their actions?

While the Stoics offered the most comprehensive account of providence, Plato's ideas on creation and providence, especially in his work *Timaeus,* were part of the intellectual air that early Christian thinkers breathed. Christian thinkers saw such affinity between Plato's work on creation and the Hebrew Scriptures that some of them accused Plato of taking his ideas from the Hebrew Scriptures.[35] In his *Timaeus,* Plato held that the "world is the product of Intellect (Anaxagoras' *nous*) personified in the figure of a divine craftsman (demiurge)."[36] The demiurge formed the world out of formless matter, which was unordered chaos, "in the likeness of an eternal model," because the demiurge "was good, and any good being wants anything else to be as good as it can be."[37] The goal of the demiurge was to fashion a world that is "as good and as beautiful as the character of the materials out of which it is made will allow."[38] The demiurge must persuade the formless matter, but this cannot be carried out perfectly because there is a residual of brute fact that cannot be made perfectly orderly and rational. The preexisting chaos upon which the demiurge imposed order is called *Ananke* (i.e., necessity) and this necessity "being itself without purpose is the substratum of phenomena."[39] Divine providence is the act of ordering the preexisting chaos. As such, divine providence is responsible for all that is good and beautiful, while the recalcitrant material substratum is responsible for all the imperfection, negativity, and evil in the world.

Christian Responses to Epicurean Chance and Plato's Demiurge

Eusebius (260–340 CE) composed perhaps the most systematic and comprehensive account articulating the superiority of Christianity over pagan philosophy through both advancing his own arguments and collecting the arguments of his Christian predecessors. In his refutation of the ideas of Epicureanism, he draws upon the writings of the Christian Dionysius of Alexandria (d. 264 CE). Dionysius points out through a series of rhetorical questions, of which I excerpt only one, that the perfection of the cause cannot be less than the effect:

> Now in a general and summary way I ask who made this whole tabernacle [the human being] such as it is, lofty, erect, of fine proportion, keenly sensitive, graceful in motion, strong in action, fit for every kind of work? The irrational multitude of atoms, say they. Why, they could not come together and mould an image of clay, nor polish a statue of marble, nor produce by casting an idol of silver or gold; but men have been the inventors of arts and manufacturers of these materials for representing the body. And if representations and pictures could not be made without intelligence, how can the real originals of the same have been spontaneous accidents? Whence too have soul, and mind, and reason been implanted in the philosopher? Did he beg them from the atoms which have no soul, nor mind, nor reason, and did each of them inspire him with some thought and doctrine?[40]

Not only could an effect not be greater than its cause but, as the great fourth-century theologian Gregory of Nyssa (ca. 330–395 CE) showed, as an underlying theme running through his argument in his *Hexaemeron* (the work of creation in six days), human beings could not know and understand the order and structure of the world if the world had come into existence by chance, for if there were no order, there was no intelligibility.[41] In addition, Epicureanism did not, according to the *Hexaemeron* of St. Ambrose (ca. 339–397 CE), provide a sufficient explanation for the continuous existence of this world in its order and structure. Such an explanation for the order and structure of the universe could be found only in the Author and Ruler of the cosmos.[42]

While Christians employed philosophical arguments to refute Epicureanism, the foundation for their understanding of creation came out of their reading of the opening chapters of Genesis. Drawing upon Genesis, Christians maintained that "the world is not random or disordered, it came into being not by chance or spontaneously, but by God's wisdom and love."[43] While Plato's *Timaeus*, which had the greatest influence on Greek and Roman accounts of the origin of the world, held that a demiurge had formed the world out of formless matter, the Christian held that God had created all that exists out of nothing (creation *ex nihilo*). This means that nothing exists prior to God bringing it into being and all that exists is utterly dependent for its existence on God.

Perhaps the earliest articulation of this line of thinking comes from Theophilus of Antioch (late second century): "The power of God is manifested in this, that out of things that are not he makes whatever he pleases."[44] Theophilus and other early defenders of Christianity "recognized that the coeternity of God and matter was inconsistent with the sovereignty and freedom of God."[45] Basil of Caesarea (330–379 CE) succinctly summarizes the doctrine of creation and the doctrine of God's transcendence of the world, "The creator of the universe, whose creative power is not bound by one world but transcends all bounds, brought into being the vast extent of the visible world solely by the movement of his will."[46]

Not only did God bring all things into existence, but God sustained all things in existence. In his commentary on Genesis, St. Augustine responds to an unnamed view that was current at his time, which held that God's providence ruled the heavens (i.e., "the loftier parts of the cosmos . . . that extend upward from the upper limits of this grosser atmosphere"[47]), yet the lower part of the atmosphere which is nearest to us "is the plaything . . . of chance and fortuitous upheaveals."[48] Augustine recognized that the happenings in this lower atmosphere nearest to us appear to be from chance: "Nothing, I agree, appears to be so rolled around by chance as all these storms, this frequent turbulence that affects the constantly changing face of the sky—which too is not improperly classified under the heading of 'earth.' "[49] Those who argue that earth is dictated by chance not only appeal to "the unpredictable irregularity of storms"[50] but also appeal to the "good and bad fortunes of human beings, which happen to them in total disregard of their deserts."[51]

Prior to attending to the particulars of these two arguments, Augustine addresses the underlying issue central to belief in creation from nothing;

namely, if God withdrew his activity in our lives, then chance would not be the source of what happens—rather, nothing would exist at all, for everything is dependent upon the wisdom and love of God. In responding to the two arguments, Augustine maintains that the "marvelous ordering of the bodily organs of any living creature"[52] in the lower part of the cosmos (i.e., earth), which is evident to "any person of average intelligence and sense,"[53] shows that God governs the lower part of the cosmos. Yet Augustine maintains that it is not only the bodies that God governs but also the order and arrangement of human lives. Some do not see God governing their lives because they expect the progress and arrangement of their lives to be clearly visible as the order of bodies is clearly visible. When the invisible order is not visible to them, they mistakenly assume that it does not exist.

Early Christian thinkers held, through their reading of Scripture, that God not only guided and ordered the natural world according to God's plan of providence, but God also guided human history and was intimately involved with the lives of human beings. While the term "providence" (from the Latin *providentia* and the Greek *pronoia*) is not strictly a biblical term (it was used in Stoic and Neoplatonic philosophy), and there are only a limited number of instances in which the substance of God's loving and purposeful guidance of the world and human history is captured by a single term, the idea can be found in one form or another in every book of the Bible. The New Testament teaching continues the Old Testament vision of God's activity as lovingly, wisely, and powerfully guiding their history. The New Testament, however, adds to the Old Testament the conviction that God's activity is centered in the sending of God's son as the source of the world's salvation and sending the Holy Spirit as the one who communicates that salvation. The depth of the Father's love for his creatures is expressed and revealed through the sending of the preexistent Word, who was with the Father in the beginning and through whom "all things came into being" (John 1:3) in the world "so that we might live through him" (1 John 4:9).

It is against this scriptural background that Augustine responds to the belief among some that God governs the natural world but is remote from human lives. In his response, Augustine quotes John's gospel (John 5:21) where Jesus says, "The Father abiding in me . . . performs his works; and as the Father raises the dead and brings them to life, so too the Son brings to life whom he will."[54] In Paul's letter to the Ephesians (1:3–13), he suggests that the whole purpose of God (i.e., the Word) becoming human was for human beings to become adopted children of the Father through Jesus Christ and thus share in the Father's life through Jesus Christ. This is the plan (*oikonomia* or economy) "set forth in Christ for the fullness of time" where all things in heaven and on earth will be gathered up or recapitulated through Jesus Christ. Early Christian theologians spoke of the economy (in the Latin West they referred to this as the *dispensatio* or dispensation) in terms of God's divine plan of salvation. Moreover, because of the centrality of God's redemptive activity, the term "economy" (or dispensation in the West) was a common way of speaking of God's providence in early Christianity since it signified the divine plan for the redemption of the cosmos.

God was seen here not as a removed and distant creator who set the cosmos in motion; rather, God in God's very self as Father, Son, and Holy Spirit was intimately involved and creatively bringing God's creation to fulfillment. Irenaeus of Lyon (135–200 CE), for instance, thought that God's creative activity was inseparably tied to God's salvific activity, such that God created human beings in the image and likeness of God and then brought human beings closer to God so that human beings could share in God's eternal life in a "community of union" with God.[55]

For Irenaeus and many other early Christian theologians, one only understood creation (the beginning) and the course of the unfolding of human history when one understood the end for which all things were created. It was not chance then that animated the origin and course of creation and history, but God's providence. This was not a God who was identified with the universe itself, as in Stoic thought, but was a transcendent God. While transcendent, God was not distant but utterly immanent and was intimately involved in nature, the individual's life, and all of human history. This was the God of Jesus Christ, who is a God with us (Emmanuel).

Is Christianity a New Determinism?

While Christians addressed themselves to the question of chance as represented in the thought of Epicurus, the refutation of chance as the explanation of the origins and course of the world was not the central problem they had to deal with in formulating a doctrine of providence. For once Christians accepted that God was the beginning and end of all things, then God's activity seemed to take over as an explanation for everything.

This led to the problem of how to hold onto human free choice and responsibility in light of the doctrine of God's providence. While Christians had allies—among them many pagan philosophers—in their criticism of the Epicurean teaching on chance, Christians were under attack by some pagan philosophers for promoting a new form of determinism. Minucius Felix, a Christian apologist from North Africa writing in the late second and early third centuries, describes this charge: "Others says that all our actions are due to fate; you [Christians] say, similarly, that they are due to god. This entails that it is not of their own free will that human beings desire to join your school; they have been chosen (*electos*). Therefore the judge that you fashion is unjust; he punishes human beings not for their intentions (*voluntatem*) but for their lot in life."[56]

Justin Martyr (d. 165), who was the first Christian thinker to mention and defend free choice,[57] responded to such charges by arguing that determinism is not consistent with the scriptural teaching that God gives rewards or punishments according to one's actions.[58] Justin had also argued that Christianity is true because the events of Christ happened just as they were predicted in the Old Testament. Yet God's foreknowledge implied in prophecy seemed to indicate that Christianity is a new form of determinism because "the prophetic Spirit speaks of things that are going to happen as having already happened."[59] Prophecy seems to suggest that the future is fixed and determined like the past.

While God's foreknowledge appears to entail a new form of determinism, it was precisely the doctrine of God's foreknowledge that Justin and the theological tradition through the early writings of Augustine drew upon to argue for the possibility of free choice and human responsibility. According to Justin, the God of Jesus Christ does not predetermine human actions; rather, God foresees how human beings will freely act and announces it beforehand through God's prophets.[60] The implication of Justin's response is that the plan of providence is fixed because God knows what every person will do in every possible circumstance and God governs the world through God's foreknowledge.

The problem of prophecy was not the only problem a Christian had to contend with in arguing for both human free choice and the justice of God. There were many biblical texts that suggested that God elects some and punishes the rest. In this vein, chapter 9 of Paul's Epistle to the Romans "acquired unwanted notoriety and was surely known to pagan critics of Christianity."[61] The passage on predestination in Romans 8:28–30 was interpreted through the lens of Paul's examples in Romans 9 that emphasized God's sovereignty. These verses created serious difficulties for early Christian theologians which cast a long shadow over the whole history of theological reflection on God's activity in relationship to human free choice.

At the end of Romans 8 (8:28–39), Paul maintains that nothing can separate us from the love of God in Christ Jesus. In Romans 9, however, Paul confronts the problem that the coming of Christ seemed to exclude the Jews, who were the objects of God's love and to whom God gave the "adoption, the glory, the covenants, the giving of the law, the worship, and the promises; ... [and] the patriarchs."[62] The question then becomes: has the word of God failed? Responding to this quandary, Paul draws upon biblical texts and metaphors that indicate that God arbitrarily wills, and thus is responsible for, both human flourishing and human diminishment. Paul tells the story of God's choice of Jacob over Esau even before they had been born (9:13) and responds to the question of the justice of such a choice by citing Exodus 33:19: "I will have mercy on whom I have mercy, and I will have compassion on whom I have compassion" (9:15). He further supports this understanding of God's arbitrary will by invoking the story of God hardening Pharaoh's heart (9:17–18). In response to the question of how God can find fault with human beings if God's will is irresistible, Paul introduces the image of a potter and suggests that the clay is in no position to question the potter (9:19–21). These texts, in the view of Robert Wilken, "presented almost insurmountable obstacles" for early Christian commentators in their efforts to preserve human free choice.[63]

In responding to the difficulties posed by Romans 9, the common approach of theologians through the early writings of Augustine was to ground God's election of those to be saved in God's foreknowledge in order to hold onto human freedom and responsibility while simultaneously preserving God's wisdom, goodness, justice, and sovereignty. These theologians held that God foreknows what a particular person would do in every possible circumstance, including what they would do if God gives them God's grace. Based on this knowledge, God elects those who God knows will respond favorably to God's grace. For example, in his commentary (the first complete commentary) on Romans, Ambrosiaster (writing between 366 and 384) maintains that God chose Jacob over Esau because God foreknew what each of them would become; the Word of God had not failed because God's promises were carried forward through Jacob. God's "foreknowledge chose the one and rejected the other. And in the one whom God chose, his purpose remained, because nothing other than what God knew and purposed in him, to make him worthy of salvation, could happen."[64] In this way, God's election was not frustrated. The sovereignty and infallibility of God's election was preserved.

While there are scores of texts that could be cited, the particularly fecund text of Diodore of Tarsus (d. ca. 390) provides an illustrative example of how early Christian theologians preserved the purpose, wisdom, goodness, and justice of God's actions and human free responsibility. Here Diodore is interpreting Paul's image of the potter and the clay (Romans 9:19–21):

> Do not dare to condemn God or imagine that he showed mercy on one and hardened another by accident, for it was according to the power of his foreknowledge that he gave each one his due. Nor is he guilty because he knew in advance what would happen, but rather each of those who were foreknown in this way is responsible for his own actions, whether good or evil.[65]

In this way, divine election is not arbitrary and irrational, but rather is guided by God's knowledge or wisdom. God elects and gives grace to those who were foreknown to accept that grace. The scriptural testimony of 1 Timothy 2:4 that God wills the salvation of all people is also preserved. The divine goodness is reflected in God's will to save all people and the divine justice is reflected in that God elects those who merit salvation through their free choice. Moreover, divine sovereignty is preserved because God's election is infallibly efficacious in that God elects and gives grace only to those foreknown to accept the gift. Since it is assumed in this tradition that divine sovereignty requires that God's election cannot be frustrated in individual instances, God's providential plan entails knowing all the choices creatures would make in any particular set of circumstances.

Augustine's early *Commentary on Propositions from the Epistle to the Romans* (394–395), echoed the arguments of this common tradition. However, within eighteen months of writing his commentary on Romans, he initiated a significant change in his thinking that would have an enormous impact on the history of Christian theology. Augustine changed his mind in a letter responding to various questions of his friend Simplician. The shift came in rereading Romans 9, especially Romans 9:16, in its assertion that divine election depends not on human will or exertion but on divine mercy. In his earlier account, Augustine preserved divine sovereignty by suggesting that God's act of election was not frustrated because God elected only those whose assent to God's call in faith was foreknown. In that account, however, God's election was not absolute. It was conditioned by the creature's free response. God's election depended on the human being responding in faith to God's call, known prior to the person's actual choice.[66] Thus the person's acceptance of God's call was necessary for faith and conversion.

Augustine, however, in rethinking Romans 9:16 argued that this explanation would undermine Paul's teaching because it suggests that the mercy of God is not sufficient of itself but requires the consent of the human will. "Clearly it is vain," Augustine wrote, "for us to will unless God have mercy. But I do not know how it could be said that it is vain for God to have mercy unless we willingly consent."[67] The problem is that if divine grace is not sufficient of itself, then Paul's statement that God's election "depends not on human will or exertion, but on God who shows mercy"[68] could be reversed to say that divine election does not depend on God who has mercy, but on human will or exertion.[69] Augustine concludes that to be true to Romans 9:16 one must hold that divine election depends entirely upon God's grace, and in no way on the human will.

In 426 and 427, Augustine wrote several works to monks in North Africa and Gaul in response to objections to his new predestinarian theory of God's election. In his *On Rebuke and Grace*, which was written to the monks of Hadrumetum in North Africa, Augustine extends the principles he developed in his letter to Simplician to the perseverance in faith. Here he argues that not only is the gift of conversion utterly dependent upon God's election but so also the gift of perseverance in faith. This theory of divine election, of course, has its dark side. For Augustine, those whom God does not elect are condemned because of the sin they inherited from Adam and Eve.

The turn in Augustine's thinking toward the absolute sovereignty of God's will that took place in his letter to Simplician is also reflected in Augustine's treatment of divine providence in his later magisterial work *The City God* (413–426), which was written to explain the fall of the Roman Empire. In book 5 of *The City God,* Augustine shows the close resemblance between the Christian understanding of divine providence and the Stoic understanding of fate:

> It is beyond doubt, however, that human kingdoms are established by divine providence. If anyone ascribes them to fate because he

> uses the term "fate" to mean the will and power of God, let him hold to his meaning but correct his terminology. . . . There are some, however, who use the word "fate" not for the position of the stars at the moment of a thing's conception or birth or beginning but rather for the chain and sequence of all causes, due to which everything that happens happens. There is no need to go into heavy battle with these people over what is, after all, a merely verbal controversy. For they ascribe this order and chain of causes to the will and power of the supreme God, who is most rightly and properly believed both to know all things before they happen and to leave nothing unordered. All powers are from him, although not the wills of all. Thus what they call fate is most especially the will of the supreme God, whose power extends invincibly through all things.[70]

Augustine recognizes the difficulties this line of thinking raises for human free choice, but he vehemently attacks a possible alternative—namely, Cicero's attempt to preserve free choice by rejecting divine foreknowledge. Augustine concludes that Cicero's position was not an option for Christians: "the religious mind chooses both [i.e., human free choice and divine foreknowledge], confesses both, and confirms both in its religious faith."[71] As we have seen, the Stoic understanding of an interlinked chain of causes allowed them to hold that the future was fixed and could be known by one who knows the causes of future events. In Augustine's reading, Cicero maintained that divine foreknowledge entailed a fixed future and so there was no possibility of human free choice. To preserve free choice, Cicero denies foreknowledge. Augustine strongly rejects Cicero's position indicating that astral determinism is a more tolerable position than denying foreknowledge.

Augustine tries to hold together divine foreknowledge and human free choice by maintaining:

> even if there is a fixed order of all causes for God, it does not follow that as a consequence, nothing depends on the choice of our will. In fact, our wills are themselves included in the order of causes that is fixed for God and contained in his foreknowledge. For human wills are causes of human actions, and so the one who foreknew all the causes of things certainly could not have been ignorant of our wills, among those causes, since he foreknew them to be precisely the causes of our actions.[72]

While human wills are in the order of causes, for Augustine, unlike Stoic pantheism, God is transcendent and God is not subject to the order of causes; rather, all created causes are dependent on God for their existence and power. Thus Augustine says:

> Our wills . . . have just as much power as God willed and foreknew that they would have. Whatever power they have, then, they have most assuredly, for he whose foreknowledge cannot fail foreknew that they would have the power to do it and would do it. That is why, if I wanted to apply the term "fate" to anything at all, I would prefer to say that the fate of the weaker is the will of the stronger, who has him in his power, rather than that the order of causes (which the Stoics call fate, not in the usual sense but in a sense of their own) does away with the choice of our will.[73]

For Augustine, an action is necessary (could not be otherwise) in two senses. First, when it is compelled by something external. The will of the human being is not compelled in this way by God. Second, an action is necessary (could not be otherwise) when it is caused by an internal tendency; for instance (Augustine's example) God living eternally is necessary, it could not be otherwise, but it is not compelled from outside of God. According to Augustine, by the sin of Adam and Eve the whole human race has become a mass of perdition and while God in his justice does not have to save anyone, God in God's infinite mercy chooses some to inherit eternal life, while justly allowing others to fall into eternal damnation. Those who are not saved have a necessitating internal tendency that moves them toward wickedness and those whom God has chosen and to whom God has given God's grace have a necessitating internal tendency toward choosing goodness. Since this internal tendency is not an external compulsion, Augustine regards the will that is moved by this internal tendency as "free." It is in this sense that Augustine can claim that the human being has free will, yet her choices and actions could never be otherwise than they will be. Although for both the Stoics and Augustine a human being's action could not be otherwise, Augustine thinks that his theology of a transcendent God who empowers the human being by operating within the human being coupled with his doctrine of original sin allows for human free will. While the Stoic doctrine that human beings are compelled by an external cause "does away with the choice of our will."[74]

Despite Augustine's efforts to preserve free choice, if one cannot do otherwise and thus does not have a choice between alternatives, then real free choice is absent. Augustine recognized this at the end of his life when he reflected on the turn in his thinking in his letter to his friend Simplician, which profoundly colored his doctrine of God for the rest of his life: "I, indeed, labored in defense of the free choice of the human will; but the grace of God conquered."[75]

A Critical Look at the Doctrine of Providence in Early Christianity

In dealing with the obstacles presented by Romans 9, early Christian thinkers focused on the examples of individuals that Paul presented in in Romans 9—God choosing Jacob over Esau, God hardening Pharaoh's heart, God is like a potter with clay. When early Christians focused on these examples, they assumed that God's election must be understood in terms of individual instances. Once one makes this assumption, then the infallibility of God's sovereign providence and predestination requires that God's election or decrees cannot be frustrated in individual instances. This assumption leaves one with only two possible theological options: (1) ground God's sovereign providence in God's knowledge, which was the traditional position through the early writings of Augustine, or (2) ground God's sovereign providence in God's will, which was Augustine's position beginning with his letter to Simplician. If one grounds God's sovereign providence in God's knowledge, then one must hold that God exhaustively knows what every human being would do in any set of circumstances, for God's infallibly efficacious election of those who are saved requires that God know how creatures would respond if offered God's grace.

The central problem with those who ground God's sovereignty in God's knowledge of what creatures would do is the problem of what grounds this knowledge of God. A free choice involves the determination of a creature's power of acting to one way of acting. Prior to this determination to one way of acting, the creature is capable of choosing from a number of possible ways of acting. It is through the free creature determining itself to one way of acting that the subject actualizes one among numerous possibilities open to it so that what was merely possible becomes actual and as such becomes knowable. Antecedent to this determination to one way of acting, there is nothing actually there to be known. The determination to one way of acting as the condition of the possibility of the knowability of a free choice cannot be grounded in the human will because it has not yet acted. In order to preserve the free choice of the creature, the free act can be grounded neither in the circumstances nor in God's divine decree. Thus the free choice is ungrounded. It has no being. As such it is unknowable. These accounts are incoherent because they require that God know what is undetermined and thus unknowable.

If one grounds God's sovereign providence in God's will, then one has to hold that God's election is not conditioned by God's foreknowledge and God chooses prior to foreseen merit those whom God will save. In this way, God's sovereignty is in no way conditioned by creatures. This view, however, puts into question human freedom and responsibility. This view also substantially alters one's understanding of God's wisdom, goodness, and justice. The wisdom of God's election becomes impenetrable because the actions of creatures are not part of the reason for their election. God's goodness flowing from God's universal salvific will is diminished. This is illustrated by Augustine, who reinterprets the received tradition coming from 1 Timothy 2:4 that God wills to save all people. In his novel interpretation of the verse, Augustine maintains that God's will to save all people means either that those who are saved are those God wills to save or that God wills to save some from every class of human beings. God's justice is also altered. For Augustine, God does not will the salvation of all people and justly elect those whom God knows will respond favorably to God's grace; rather, by the sin of Adam and Eve, the whole human race has become a mass of perdition or a damned mass corrupted in its root. By the standards of justice, God does not need to save anyone, but God in mercy chooses to destine some for eternal life, the rest God justly lets go to eternal damnation. In his grounding God's election in God's sovereignty, Augustine limits the love of God.

The problem with the accounts reviewed in this chapter is twofold. First, they have misinterpreted the difficult texts in Romans 9. Prominent contemporary biblical scholars argue that when Paul writes about God's election and predestination of Israel, "his emphasis is on corporate Israel despite the examples of individuals that he uses."[76] Second, they have focused too exclusively on those texts in Scripture that emphasized God's sovereignty. A more fruitful approach involves reviewing the whole of Scripture to examine the relationship between God and the world, between divine and human activity, between the plan of God and the unfolding of history.[77]

John H. Wright, SJ (1922–2009), wrote a two-volume work on the teaching of the Old and New Testaments on the doctrine of providence, paying particular attention to the "biblical teaching about God as Lord of nature and Lord of history, and about the interaction of divine and human freedom in accomplishing God's purpose in the world."[78] In his examination of the whole of Scripture, Wright discovers amidst the great diversity of biblical texts and stories an identifiable pattern of interaction between God and creation that is repeated over and over. This pattern of divine-human interaction is typified by three moments: (1) God's absolute, free divine initiative in creation and redemption; (2) human beings' free response, in obedience and faith or sin and unbelief; (3) God's response to the human response, in a judgment of blessing or condemnation. Integral to this pattern of divine-human interaction are four themes that run through the whole of Scripture and which are crucial to a proper understanding of divine providence: the omnipotence and infallibility of the divine government, the frustration of God's plan in the face of free human resistance, the adaptability that characterizes God's dealings with human beings, and the collective and communal quality of God's purpose and the means for attaining God's purpose.

While all of these themes must be considered in constructing a theology of providence and predestination grounded in the biblical witness, the key scriptural theme for reconciling the other three themes is the insistence that there is a communal quality to God's purpose and the means for attaining God's purpose. Although there was development in the biblical understanding of God's final purpose for God's creatures, the communal, collective, and social character of the end of God's activity (i.e., the ultimate flourishing of the people of God) remained primary from the beginning of the Old Testament through the New Testament. In the New Testament, Jesus proclaims and inaugurates the establishment of the kingdom of God as the realization of God's providential plan. The kingdom is not "an inevitable but incidental consequence of having many individuals attain salvation."[79] Instead, "the constitution of the kingdom is primary; the individual by his fidelity to God's call can guarantee his entrance into this kingdom."[80]

Once we recognize that the infallibility of God's salvific purpose is understood in communal and corporate terms, we can maintain the infallibility of God's saving purpose while recognizing the biblical account of

God's plan being frustrated in individual instances and the adaptability of God's dealing with human beings. We can then begin to overcome the insoluble theological problems created by the assumption that God's sovereign providence requires that God's election or decrees cannot be frustrated in individual instances and construct an understanding of divine election, which is a moment within the plan of providence, along the following lines. God does not elect some for salvation and exclude others; rather, God wills the salvation of all creatures and makes the salvation of all creatures truly possible. Which particular created persons will respond in loving acceptance to God's offer of salvation and which will refuse depends on the free creatures. This capacity for particular created persons to refuse God's call does not mean that God's purpose of realizing a society of the blessed united to God in love and friendship can ultimately be frustrated. God does not know what creatures would do antecedent to giving being to the free creature's choice; rather, God knows antecedent to the free choices of creatures that the means for realizing a society of the blessed will be infallibly effective. These means for salvation can be frustrated in individual instances, but not for the community as a whole.

Conclusion

Early Christian thinkers vehemently rejected the idea that origin of the universe and the course of human life were dictated by chance, luck, or fortune. Yet it was not chance that was the chief difficulty for Christians in articulating a coherent doctrine of providence; it was rather that Christian understandings of the truth of prophecy, which entailed divine foreknowledge, and God's sovereignty appeared to place Christianity in line with the other determinisms of the day—*tyche* as it morphed into an oppressive fate, astral determinism, and Stoic determinism. In contrast, the scriptures are pervaded with the testimony that God calls human beings to God's self and human beings respond to that call. This dialogical relationship presupposes human free choice. Early Christian thinkers, in trying to preserve prophecy and divine sovereignty, assumed that God's sovereignty required that God's election or decree cannot be frustrated in individual instances. Once one makes this assumption concerning God's sovereignty, one has only two theoretical options—ground God's sovereignty in God's foreknowledge or ground God's sovereignty in God's will. These two options played themselves out in early in Christian thinking.

In the tradition prior to Augustine's letter to Simplician, Christian writers grounded God's sovereignty in God's foreknowledge. This position, however, is incoherent because it requires God's knowing what is unknowable. Augustine challenged the tradition of grounding God's sovereignty in God's foreknowledge not because it implied that God knows what was unknowable, but because he thought it limited God's sovereignty. Thus, Augustine grounded God's sovereignty in God's will, which led him to maintain that God predestines some to salvation antecedent to their free choices. This view had cascading negative repercussions for the doctrines of God's goodness, wisdom, and justice. In addition, human free choice, as the possibility open to one to choose between alternatives, was eviscerated.

Augustine is perhaps the most influential figure in the history of Western theology and his focus on God's sovereignty, including the infallibility of God's decrees in individual instances, casts a long shadow over Western theology and gave rise to multiple controversies, including the "predestinationist controversies of the ninth century, the double predestinationist theories of the Calvinists, Jansenism, and the *de auxiliis* controversy between Jesuits and Dominicans in the sixteenth and early seventeenth centuries."[81] If contemporary Christian thinkers are going to formulate a coherent doctrine of providence in a world that appears to be shot through with contingency and chance, then they will have to drop the problematic assumption that God's sovereignty requires that God's election or decrees cannot be frustrated in individual instances. Rejecting such an assumption is more in line with the relationship of divine and human activity that is found throughout the whole of Scripture. Once theologians recognize that a doctrine of providence must include not only the infallibility of the divine government but also the frustration of God's plan in the face of free human resistance, the adaptability that characterizes God's dealings with human beings, and the collective and communal quality of God's purpose and the means for attaining God's purpose, then they will be better equipped to develop a doctrine of providence in line with contemporary scientific thought.[82]

Notes

1. Henry Chadwick, *The Church in Ancient Society: From Galilee to Gregory the Great* (Oxford: Oxford University Press, 2001), 187.

2. Gregory of Nazianzus, *Oration* 18.34. Original Greek text is in Jacques-Paul Migne, *Patrologiae cursus completus: Series Graeca*, vol. 35 (Paris: J. P. Migne Imprimerie Catholique, 1857–66), 1029. (References to this series abbreviated as *PG*, with volume number.) Summarized by Jaroslav Pelikan, *Christianity and Classical Culture: The Metamorphosis of Natural Theology in the Christian Encounter with Hellenism* (New Haven, CT: Yale University Press, 1993), 160.
3. As quoted by Pelikan, *Christianity and Classical Culture*, 152, who is quoting Gregory of Nyssa in *On the Soul and Resurrection* (*PG* 46:117)
4. William Chase Greene, *Moira: Fate, Good, and Evil in Greek Thought* (Cambridge, MA: Harvard University Press, 1944), 5.
5. Peter Green, *Alexander to Actium: The Historical Evolution of the Hellenistic Age* (Berkeley: University of California Press, 1990), 400.
6. Ibid., 401.
7. Ibid., 401.
8. Ibid., 401.
9. Ibid., 398.
10. During this period Tyche was conflated with the goddess Fortuna in Rome as a Roman cult to Fortuna emerged.
11. Michael Grant, *From Alexander to Cleopatra: The Hellenistic World* (New York: History Book Club, 2000), 214.
12. Christopher Stead, *Philosophy in Christian Antiquity* (Cambridge: Cambridge University Press, 1994), 42.
13. Lucretius, *On the Nature of Things*, trans. Martin Ferguson Smith (Indianapolis, IN: Hackett, 1969), 2.217–24, 40–41.
14. David Furley, "Cosmology," in *The Cambridge History of Hellenistic Philosophy*, ed. Keimpe Algra, Jonathan Barnes, Jaap Mansfeld, and Malcolm Schofield (Cambridge: Cambridge University Press, 1999), 424.
15. Ibid., 424.
16. George K. Strodach, *The Philosophy of Epicurus* (Chicago: Northwestern University Press, 1963), 24.
17. Ibid., 24.
18. Lucretius 2.289–93, as quoted by Strodach, *Philosophy of Epicurus*, 24–25.
19. Ibid., 25.
20. Green, *Alexander to Actium*, 586.
21. Grant, *From Alexander to Cleopatra*, 215.
22. Ibid., 219.
23. See Green, *Alexander to Actium*, 597.
24. Franz Cumont, *Astrology and Religion among the Greeks and Romans* (New York: G. P. Putnam's Sons, 1912), 160.
25. Grant, *From Alexander to Cleopatra*, 221.
26. See Green, *Alexander to Actium*, 596.

27. Augustine, *The Augustine Catechism: The Enchiridion on Faith, Hope, and Love*, ed. Boniface Ramsey, trans. and notes Bruce Harbert, *The Works of Saint Augustine: A Translation for the 21st Century*, vol. 1 (Hyde Park, NY: New City, 1999), 21.80, 102.
28. See Tim Hegedus, *Early Christianity and Ancient Astrology*, Patristic Studies 6 (New York: Peter Lang, 2007), 186.
29. Green, *Alexander to Actium*, p. 634.
30. Cicero, *De Divinatione*, 1.125–127, in Cicero *De Senectute, De Amicitia, De Divinatione*, trans. W. A. Falconer, Loeb Classical Library (Cambridge, MA: Harvard University Press, 1923), 361. I have transliterated the original Greek.
31. Marcia L. Colish, *The Stoic Tradition From Antiquity to the Early Middle Ages*, vol. 1, *Stoicism in Classical Latin Literature*, Studies in the History of Christian Thought, ed. Heiko A. Oberman, vol. 34 (Leiden: E. J. Brill, 1985), 31–32.
32. Ibid., 23.
33. Ibid., 24.
34. Ibid., 32.
35. Theodoret of Cyrus, *A Cure of Pagan Maladies*, trans. Thomas Halton, Ancient Christian Writers 67 (New York: Newman, 2013), 6, 33, 143.
36. Donald J. Zeyl, "Introduction" in Plato, *Timaeus*, trans. Donald J. Zeyl (Indianapolis, IN: Hackett, 2000), xxxiv.
37. Ibid., xxxvi.
38. Ibid., xxxiv.
39. Greene, *Moira*, 305.
40. Eusebius, *Preparation for the Gospel*, trans. Edwin Hamilton Gifford (Eugene, OR: Wipf and Stock, 2002), bk. 14, chap. 26, 780c–d, 841–842.
41. See Robert Louis Wilken, *The Spirit of Early Christian Thought: Seeking the Face of God* (New Haven, CT: Yale University Press, 2003), 146.
42. Ambrose, "Hexameron," in Ambrose, *Hexameron, Paradise, and Cain and Abel*, trans. John J. Savage, *The Fathers of the Church*, vol. 42 (Washington, DC: Catholic University of America Press, 1961), 1.2.7, 7.
43. Wilken, *Spirit of Early Christian Thought*, 141.
44. Theophilus of Antioch, *To Autolycus*, 2.4, 2.10, as translated by Jaroslav Pelikan, *The Christian Tradition: A History of the Development of Doctrine*, vol. 1, *The Emergence of the Catholic Tradition (100–600)* (Chicago: University of Chicago Press, 1971), 36.
45. Ibid., 36.
46. Basil, *Hexaemeron*, 2.2, 1.7, 1.2 as translated and quoted by Wilken, *Spirit of Early Christian Thought*, 142.
47. Augustine, *On Genesis*, intro., trans., and notes Edmund Hill, OP, *The Works of Saint Augustine: A Translation for the 21st Century*, vol. 13 (Hyde Park, NY: New City, 2002), 21.42, 297
48. Ibid.

49. Ibid.
50. Ibid., 22.43, 298.
51. Ibid.
52. Ibid.
53. Ibid.
54. Ibid., 20.40, 296.
55. Though the full divinity of the Son and Holy Spirit would not be promulgated until the Council of Constantinople in 381, "there can be no doubt that he thought of both the Son and the Spirit as being divine in the full and proper sense of the word. Irenaeus was not particularly exercised by the problem of how one God could be three persons. His interest was directed far more to the activity of the Father, Son and Spirit in creation, and especially in the creation and redemption of humankind"; Denis Minns, "Truth and Tradition: Irenaeus," in *The Cambridge History of Christianity*, vol. 1, *Origins to Constantine*, ed. Margaret M. Mitchell and Frances M. Young (Cambridge: Cambridge University Press, 2006), 270.
56. Marcus Minucius Felix, Octavius, 11.6, as quoted in Robert Louis Wilken, "Free Choice and the Divine Will in Greek Christian Commentaries on Paul," in *Paul and the Legacies of Paul*, ed. William S. Babcock (Dallas: Southern Methodist University Press, 1990), 124.
57. Ibid., 126.
58. Ibid., 126. See Justin Martyr, "Justin's Apology on Behalf of Christians," in *Justin, Philosopher and Martyr: Apologies*, ed. Dennis Minns and Paul Purvis, Oxford Early Christian Texts (Oxford: Oxford University Press, 2009), 43.1–44.10, 191–195.
59. Justin Martyr, "Justin's Apology on Behalf of Christians," 42.1, 189.
60. Ibid., 44.11, 197. From this very first mention of free choice as a Christian teaching, God's foreknowledge was relied upon to uphold free choice
61. Wilken, "Free Choice and Divine Will," 128.
62. Romans 9:4–5 (NRSV).
63. Wilken, "Free Choice and Divine Will," 128.
64. Ambrosiaster, *Commentaries on Romans and 1–2 Corinthians*, trans. and ed. Gerald L. Bray, Ancient Christian Texts (Downers Grove, IL: InterVarsity Press, 2009), 75.
65. Diodore, "Pauline Commentary from the Greek Church," 15:99, in (ed.), *Romans*, ed. Gerald Bray, vol. 6 of *Ancient Christian Commentary on Scripture: New Testament*, ed. Thomas C. Oden (Downers Grove, IL: InterVarsity Press, 1998), 261.
66. The use of the terms "antecedent," "before," and "prior to" in reference to God's knowledge or will should not be understood in temporal terms because God is eternal; rather, they need to be understood in terms of a natural order of priority. An example of a natural order of priority is found in Trinitarian theology.

The one God is eternal and unchanging, yet it is constitutive of the nature of God that the Father is naturally prior to the Son because the Father generates the Son.

67. Augustine, *To Simplician—On Various Questions, Book 1 (De Diversis Quaestionibus)*, in *Augustine Earlier Writings*, ed. John H. S. Burleigh (Philadelphia, PA: Westminster, 1953), 2.12. 394.
68. NRSV translation.
69. See *To Simplician—On Various Questions*, 2.12. I reversed the phrase based on the NRSV translation.
70. Augustine, *The City of God*, introd. and trans. William Babcock, *The Works of Saint Augustine: A Translation for the 21st Century*, vol. 6 (Hyde Park, NY: New City, 2012), 5.1, 144; 5.8, 151–152.
71. Ibid., 5.9, 154.
72. Ibid., 5.9, 155.
73. Ibid., 5.9, 156.
74. Ibid.
75. Augustine, *Retractions*, trans. Sr. Mary Inez Bogan, RSM, *The Fathers of the Church*, vol. 60 (Washington, DC: Catholic University of America Press, 1968), 2.1 (27), 120.
76. Joseph A. Fitzmyer, *Romans: A New Translation with Introduction and Commentary* (New York: Doubleday, 1993), 542. See also James D. G. Dunn, *The Theology of Paul the Apostle* (Grand Rapids, MI: Eerdmans, 1998), 501, 411; N. T. Wright, "The Letter to the Romans," in *The New Interpreter's Bible*, vol. 10 (Nashville, TN: Abingdon, 2002), 603–604; Brendan Byrne, SJ, *Romans*, Sacra Pagina Series 6 (Collegeville, MN: Liturgical, 1996), 299n18; Ben Witherington III with Darlene Hyatt, *Paul's Letter to the Romans: A Socio-Rhetorical Commentary* (Grand Rapids, MI: Eerdmans, 2004), 246.
77. John H. Wright, *Divine Providence in the Bible: Meeting the Living and True God*, vol. 1, *Old Testament* (New York: Paulist, 2009), 5. See also John H. Wright, *Divine Providence in the Bible: Meeting the Living and True God*, vol. 2, *New Testament* (New York: Paulist, 2010).
78. Wright, *Divine Providence in the Bible*, 1:7.
79. John H. Wright, "The Eternal Plan of Divine Providence," *Theological Studies* 27, no. 1 (1966): 37.
80. Ibid., 37.
81. Wright, *Divine Providence in the Bible*, 1:5.
82. For an attempt to hold onto God's sovereignty and free choice, including some indications of how God's providence can be understood in terms of contingency in the natural world, see my "The Eternal Plan of Divine Providence and the God Who Dialogues: The Contribution of John H. Wright, S.J.," in *New Voices in Catholic Theology*, ed. Anna Bonta Moreland and Joseph Curran, 165–194 (New York: Herder and Herder, 2012).

Selected Bibliography

Ambrose, *Hexameron, Paradise, and Cain and Abel.* Translated by John J. Savage. *The Fathers of the Church*, vol. 42 (Washington, DC: Catholic University of America Press, 1961).

Ambrosiaster. *Commentaries on Romans and 1–2 Corinthians.* Translated and edited by Gerald L. Bray. Ancient Christian Texts (Downers Grove, IL: InterVarsity, 2009).

Augustine. *The Augustine Catechism: The Enchiridion on Faith, Hope, and Love.* Edited by Boniface Ramsey, translation and notes by Bruce Harbert. *The Works of Saint Augustine: A Translation for the 21st Century*, vol. 1 (Hyde Park, NY: New City, 1999).

Augustine. *The City of God.* Introduction and translation by William Babcock. *The Works of Saint Augustine: A Translation for the 21st Century*, vol. 6 (Hyde Park, NY: New City, 2012).

Augustine. *On Genesis.* Introduction, translation, and notes by Edmund Hill, OP. *The Works of Saint Augustine: A Translation for the 21st Century*, vol. 13 (Hyde Park, NY: New City, 2002).

Augustine. *Retractions.* Translated by Sr. Mary Inez Bogan, RSM. *The Fathers of the Church*, vol. 60 (Washington, DC: Catholic University of America Press, 1968).

Augustine. *To Simplician—On Various Questions, Book 1 (De Diversis Quaestionibus).* In *Augustine Earlier Writings*, edited by John H. S. Burleigh, 370–406 (Philadelphia, PA: Westminster, 1953).

Byrne, Brendan S. J. *Romans*, Sacra Pagina Series 6 (Collegeville, MN: Liturgical, 1996), 299n18.

Chadwick, Henry. *The Church in Ancient Society: From Galilee to Gregory the Great* (Oxford: Oxford University Press, 2001).

Cicero. *De Divinatione.* In *De Senectute, De Amicitia, De Divinatione*, translated by W. A. Falconer, 222–539. Loeb Classical Library (Cambridge, MA: Harvard University Press, 1923).

Colish, Marcia L. *The Stoic Tradition from Antiquity to the Early Middle Ages*, vol. 1, *Stoicism in Classical Latin Literature.* Studies in the History of Christian Thought, edited by Heiko A. Oberman, vol. 34 (Leiden: E. J. Brill, 1985).

Cumont, Franz. *Astrology and Religion among the Greeks and Romans* (New York: G. P. Putnam's Sons, 1912), 160.

Diodore. "Pauline Commentary from the Greek Church." In *Romans*, edited by Gerald Bray. Vol. 6 of *Ancient Christian Commentary on Scripture: New Testament*, edited by Thomas C. Oden (Downers Grove, IL: InterVarsity, 1998).

Dunn, James D. G. *The Theology of Paul the Apostle* (Grand Rapids, MI: Eerdmans, 1998), 501, 411.

Eusebius. *Preparation for the Gospel.* Translated by Edwin Hamilton Gifford (Eugene, OR: Wipf and Stock, 2002).

Fitzmyer, Joseph A. *Romans: A New Translation with Introduction and Commentary* (New York: Doubleday, 1993), 542.

Furley, David. "Cosmology," In *The Cambridge History of Hellenistic Philosophy*, edited by Keimpe Algra, Jonathan Barnes, Jaap Mansfeld, and Malcolm Schofield, 412–451 (Cambridge: Cambridge University Press, 1999).

Grant, Michael. *From Alexander to Cleopatra: The Hellenistic World* (New York: History Book Club, 2000), 214.

Green, Peter. *Alexander to Actium: The Historical Evolution of the Hellenistic Age* (Berkeley: University of California Press, 1990).

Greene, William Chase. *Moira: Fate, Good, and Evil in Greek Thought* (Cambridge, MA: Harvard University Press, 1944), 5.

Hegedus, Tim. *Early Christianity and Ancient Astrology*. Patristic Studies 6 (New York: Peter Lang, 2007).

Justin Martyr. *Justin, Philosopher and Martyr: Apologies*. Edited by Denis Minns and Paul Purvis. Oxford Early Christian Texts (Oxford: Oxford University Press, 2009).

Lucretius. *On the Nature of Things*. Translated by Martin Ferguson Smith (Indianapolis, IN: Hackett, 1969).

Miller, Richard W. "The Eternal Plan of Divine Providence and the God Who Dialogues: The Contribution of John H. Wright, S.J.," In *New Voices in Catholic Theology*, edited by Anna Bonta Moreland and Joseph Curran, 165–194 (New York: Herder and Herder, 2012).

Minns, Denis. "Truth and Tradition: Irenaeus." In *The Cambridge History of Christianity*. Vol. 1, *Origins to Constantine*, edited by Margaret M. Mitchell and Frances M. Young, 261–273 (Cambridge: Cambridge University Press, 2006).

Pelikan, Jaroslav. *Christianity and Classical Culture: The Metamorphosis of Natural Theology in the Christian Encounter with Hellenism* (New Haven, CT: Yale University Press, 1993), 160.

Pelikan, Jaroslav. *The Christian Tradition: A History of the Development of Doctrine*. Vol. 1, *The Emergence of the Catholic Tradition (100–600)* (Chicago: University of Chicago Press, 1971).

Plato. *Timaeus*. Translated by Donald J. Zeyl (Indianapolis, IN: Hackett, 2000).

Stead, Christopher. *Philosophy in Christian Antiquity* (Cambridge: Cambridge University Press, 1994).

Strodach, George K. *The Philosophy of Epicurus* (Chicago: Northwestern University Press, 1963).

Theodoret of Cyrus. *A Cure of Pagan Maladies*. Translated by Thomas Halton. Ancient Christian Writers 67 (New York: Newman, 2013).

Wilken, Robert Louis. "Free Choice and the Divine Will in Greek Christian Commentaries on Paul." In Paul and the Legacies of Paul, edited by William S. Babcock, 123–140 (Dallas, TX: Southern Methodist University Press, 1990).

Wilken, Robert Louis. *The Spirit of Early Christian Thought: Seeking the Face of God* (New Haven, CT: Yale University Press, 2003).

Witherington, Ben III with Hyatt, Darlene. *Paul's Letter to the Romans: A Socio-Rhetorical Commentary* (Grand Rapids, MI: Eerdmans, 2004), 246.

Wright, John H. *Divine Providence in the Bible: Meeting the Living and True God.* Vol. 1, *Old Testament,* (New York: Paulist, 2009).

Wright, John H. *Divine Providence in the Bible: Meeting the Living and True God.* Vol. 2, *New Testament* (New York: Paulist, 2010).

Wright, John H. "The Eternal Plan of Divine Providence." *Theological Studies* 27, no. 1 (1966): 27–57.

Wright, N. T. "The Letter to the Romans." In *The New Interpreter's Bible,* Vol. 10 (Nashville, TN: Abingdon, 2002), 603–604.

8

Thomas Aquinas on Natural Contingency and Providence

Ignacio Silva

Introduction: Aristotle, Neoplatonism, and Arabic Philosophy in Aquinas's Thought

Thomas Aquinas held a robust position regarding God's providential action in the universe, its relation to natural causes, and the fact that these natural causes were contingent in their causing, both chanceful and sometimes even random. For him, God's providential action was expressed as a primary cause accomplished through the actions of secondary created causes, which were in themselves contingent causes: for Aquinas, a providential God which allowed a world filled with contingent causes was more perfect than a purely deterministic world.

By the mid-thirteenth century, in the midst of the reception of Aristotelian philosophy in the High Middle Ages, Thomas Aquinas inherited the problem of God's causality within the created universe directly from the early Arabic philosophy of previous centuries. Until the twelfth century, Christian philosophy and theology had had mainly a Platonic character, following the Neoplatonic teachings of Pseudo-Dionysius and of Saint Augustine. The early thirteenth century, however, saw the arrival of the new philosophy of Aristotle, interpreted by Islamic commentators such as Ibn-Sina (or Avicenna, 980–1037) and Ibn-Rushd (or Averroes, 1126–1198), among others, for whom one of the most important topics of discussion was the relationship between God as an active agent in the world and natural causes. In this discussion they saw divine sovereignty over worldly events being clearly at stake.

Al-Ghazali (ca. 1058–1111), in his twelfth-century work *The Incoherence of the Philosophers,* held that those who adopted Greek philosophical views were unsuccessful in achieving a coherent theory of divine action. This position was held by the Mutakallimun theologians (of which al-Ghazali was the greatest proponent), within which the Kalam theology was the main stream of thought. Kalam theologians strongly held that if one were to take seriously the unchangeable nature of God's omnipotence and providence, then it was necessary to accept that there is no active power in creation, but that it is God who acts in every apparently natural event.

Following the core principles of Islamic religious teaching, Kalam theologians held that the universe is created out of nothing and that the universe had a beginning in time. They believed that God recreates the whole of the universe at every instant, rendering creation a succession of discrete, atomized events, and it remains rational and intelligible because God keeps its regularities constant. Hence, Kalam theologians believed that all things are complete and fulfilled at any given moment of their existence: any being's becoming other is entirely dependent upon an exterior agent, capable of effecting the change, and for every change it is God who acts. For Kalam theologians, then, all change involves a divine act of creation, since whatever change is effected represents the realization of a new being entirely. In this sense, in order to accept the Qur'anic teaching of God's constant involvement in the universe, they diminished the activities of created things to the point of denying them. In brief, they admitted that there was no causality at all in nature but divine causality. Were nature to act by itself, there would be no place at all for God to act. Given their theological premises, they needed to admit that creation had no active powers at all; God and God alone, by God's own command and power, was the direct cause of all events in the world. This doctrine was later known as occasionalism, and was adopted in the early modern period by some French Cartesian authors.[1]

Ibn-Rushd is the dominating figure in the second, contrasting school of Islamic thought in the later twelfth century. Ibn-Rushd is perhaps the main objector to occasionalism within the Arabic tradition. Affirming Aristotle's views, he claimed that nature was autonomous in its actions, which meant, first, that nature did not require the power of God to act, and second, that God's power was somewhat diminished. In fact, his position begins by rejecting the very idea of creation out of nothing because he thought that, if it were true, anything could come from anything, and there would be no congruity between effects and causes. Thus, for

Ibn-Rushd, the doctrine of creation out of nothing contradicted the existence of true natural causality in the universe, and hence, the science of nature would not be possible.[2]

This debate came to Aquinas's attention through the works of the Jewish philosopher Rabbi Maimonides (1135–1204), and the Latin translations of Ibn-Rushd's *Commentaries on Aristotle.* The significance of this debate for Aquinas can be seen in references and detailed analyses throughout his works, from the early *Commentary on the Sentences* to the later *Summa contra Gentiles, Quaestiones Disputatae de Veritate, De Potentia Dei,* and the mature *Summa Theologiae.*[3] Aquinas's own position recovers the better features of each of the two extremes within Islamic thought by affirming both the natural autonomy in causation together with divine action in the universe through secondary causes.

Aquinas bases his argument for providence on a very precise analysis of the notion of creation out of nothing. It is in this doctrine that one finds one of the clearest examples of Aristotelian philosophy conjugated with Neoplatonism in the High Middle Ages. In his exposition of the doctrine of creation out of nothing, Aquinas sought to affirm the radical and continuous dependence of all things upon God as their cause (a clearly Neoplatonic feature) and that this dependence is fully compatible with the discovery of causes in nature (one of the Aristotelian characters of his doctrine). God's omnipotence, for Aquinas, does not challenge the possibility of real causality for creatures. On the contrary, Aquinas would reject any notion of divine withdrawal from the world to leave room, so to speak, for the actions of creatures. Nevertheless, Aquinas does not think that God simply allows or permits creatures to behave in the way they do. Creation out of nothing means that creatures are what they are precisely because God is present to them as the cause of their being and their actions continually. That is, God causes creatures to exist in such a way that they are the real causes of their own operations, being present in every operation of nature. To support this doctrine, Aquinas emphasizes that divine causality and creaturely causality function at fundamentally different levels. While God's causality is causality of creation, creaturely causation is causality of change. Thus, since for Aquinas creation is not a change, these two different agents (God and creatures) differ radically in their causing. God is the complete cause of the whole reality of whatever is, and yet, there is in the created world a rich array of real secondary causes.

Before delving in the depths of Aquinas's thought surrounding the question of God's action in the world, it would be beneficial to revisit, even if briefly, his ideas on natural causality. Specifically, we should understand how this notion relates to the distinction between primary and secondary causality, and how, through his doctrine of creation, Aquinas can provide an account of God's providence through contingent natural causes. Following Aristotle, Aquinas affirms that natural things have certain causal powers which extend to the sphere of their own kind of being. Thus fire heats, water wets, and so on. In this sense natural things act according to a certain necessity which follows from their own kind of being, what medieval thinkers called their "nature." Thus, the effect of their action is produced regularly, so long as there are favorable circumstances for its production. Nevertheless, it is possible to think of a natural thing that is determined to produce a particular effect, which does so in the larger number of cases, but that, on some occasions, does not produce that particular effect. Today we can think of genetic mutations during embryonic development, for example, which occur around sixty times in each human being. Even though particular things come into being and tend to develop in consistent ways, there is always the possibility of accidental, contingent, or chance events which frustrate such tendencies and render them ultimately fruitless.

For Aquinas, then, the notion of causality does not imply a necessary relation between cause and effect. Instead, Aquinas's understanding of causality is better expressed in terms of a relation of dependence, in which the effect depends on the cause for its being or changing. This kind of causality as dependence opens the path to understanding causality as an analogical notion, where many different kinds of causality allow for several ways in which one thing can depend upon another for its being or change. All causes will thus share something in common, that is, the relation of dependence of their effects, and will also differ from each other, that is, the way they cause.

Following Aristotle, Aquinas teaches that the causes upon which something depends can be reduced to four different kinds, which explain both why something is what it is and why it can change and become something else. As previously mentioned, these four different causes will cause in different ways. Thus, each of them will be that upon which something else depends, even though this dependence will be with respect to different features of the thing caused.

Aquinas's four causes are well known: formal, material, efficient, and final. Two of these are extrinsic to the effects they cause, in the sense that they determine the existence of a new being from the outside.

The first of the extrinsic causes is the final cause, which receives its name because it is the last one to be accomplished—perplexingly, but logically, it is also the first cause because it is the one which starts and guides the action of the efficient cause or agent, which is the other extrinsic cause. The agent is that cause which produces the existence of the effect, by producing a new determination—the form—in an already existing matter. This new form is what constitutes the new being or effect. The form itself, on the other hand, is one of the intrinsic causes and the matter is the other one. These two, with their own being, constitute and cause the existence of the effect. Matter is the first intrinsic cause: it is the subject which receives the determination—the form—from the efficient cause. It is called first matter because it exists prior to the formal determination of the agent. The second intrinsic cause is the form, which is received in the matter and disposes the matter to be this or that different kind of being. Thus, the formal cause explains why a thing exists as this particular kind of thing and the material cause explains why it can cease to be what it is and become something else. Hence, the form is usually associated with the actuality and determination of a thing, while the matter is associated with its potentiality and indetermination, becoming thus the very source of chance and randomness in the natural world. The classical example of the sculptor and his making offers a good illustration of how these four causes cause together, the artist being the efficient cause, the marble the material cause, the shape the formal cause, and finally the idea that moved the sculptor to produce the work of art the final cause.

In sum, the essence of the causal nexus, for Aquinas, is the dependence of the effect—in its being or change—upon the cause, while the modes of causality and dependency vary greatly depending on the kinds of causes involved. Causality, understood in relationship to dependence, becomes greatly important in Aquinas's thought when considering God's creative and provident action. Before turning my attention to Aquinas's account of God's providential action in the world, I shall consider his views on contingency in nature.

Natural Contingency

For Aquinas, natural things have a tendency to act in a particular way, according to their particular kind of being. Thus (as before) fire heats, and water wets. Aquinas asserts, then, that natural things are somehow determined to act toward one single kind of effect. Nevertheless, Aquinas also teaches that a natural thing may or may not accomplish the effect which its nature has determined it to accomplish.[4] In saying this, Aquinas explicitly rejects a rigid determinism in nature, that is the position that whenever there is a cause a certain determinate effect necessarily follows. Because natural things are contingent in their being, that is, they either can or cannot be, Aquinas affirms that their actions are also contingent. Thus, they can fail in their natural actions.

Aquinas distinguishes between events which happen always (those which take place in the heavens), those which almost always happen, and those which happen almost never, but do happen.[5] Those events which almost always occur existed in their causes as being almost determined, and there were no impediments in the process of causing them. These events refer to the actions of every natural being that acts. The events which occur less frequently are those events which are not determined at all in their causes but happen by accident or due to some sort of deficiency. Aquinas usually referred to the strange occurrence of a sixth finger in a man's hand, but today we can speak of the random mutations that guide the process of evolution. Aquinas thus affirms a kind of mitigated determinism in nature, in that the expected effect may not be produced by the cause. Hence, although natural causes are necessary causes insofar as they are determined to cause one effect, they are nonetheless the source of contingency, which follows their own (limited) necessity. The root of this limited necessity is, for Aquinas, the material intrinsic coprinciple, which expresses the potency to be something else of every natural being. For Aquinas, the events which express this limited necessity, those which happen "less frequently," can occur for three reasons. He explains in his *Commentary on Aristotle's Metaphysics*:

> First, *because of the conjunction of two causes one of which does not come under the causality of the other*, as when robbers attack me without my intending this; for this meeting is caused by a twofold motive power, namely, mine and that of the robbers. Second, *because of some defect in the agent, which is so weak that he cannot attain the goal at which he aims*, for example, when someone falls on the road because of fatigue. Third, *because of the indisposition of the matter, which does not receive the form intended by the agent but*

> *another kind of form*. This is what occurs, for example, in the case of the deformed parts of animals.[6]

Thus, the three reasons reduce to (1) the encounter of many agents, (2) the weakness of the efficient cause in itself, and (3) the poor disposition of the patient on which the agent acts. I shall now briefly discuss each of these reasons.

1 Due to the Encounter of Many Agents

Aquinas identifies the fortuitous concourse of many independent causes with the "accidental being," which could be translated as an accidental complex or an accidental thing.[7] The accidental being cannot be called a "being as such" (a thing which is one by and of itself)[8] because the "being as such" occurs only where there is formal unity.[9] Hence, the encounter of independent causes in a particular time and place cannot be reduced, for Aquinas, to a cause as such,[10] simply because it does not have a cause of its own. Therefore, what comes out of this encounter is not by necessity, or determined in its causes.[11] That is, given that what is accidental is not properly speaking something with an internal unity, the event so produced can be considered as caused in a purely accidental way and thus, properly speaking, not having a cause. Aquinas speaks in these cases of an accidental cause.

In this fortuitous causal concourse, the plurality of causes is indefinite, and as such it behaves as the potentiality of matter. Aquinas's arguments teach that the different causal lines which coincide in a time and space are not determined to coincide with each other. Therefore, the causal concourse is accidental because it has no determinate cause. It is chance which brings about the material conjunction of causes.

2 Due to the Weakness of the Efficient Cause

As I mentioned in the introduction, Aquinas accepts that natural things are composed by two intrinsic coprinciples (two intrinsic causes of things), which are truly distinct and different: (1) the formal cause of a thing, which is the principle of being and actuality, of perfection, and of determination, which determines its nature and its ways of acting; and (2) the material cause, which is the principle of potentiality, of a passive capacity of being, which is by itself indeterminate, indifferent to being or not being, and indifferent to being this or that. Natural beings, for Aquinas, are thus a mixture of actuality and potentiality, of determination and indetermination. Following Aristotle, Aquinas teaches that the origin of the defectiveness or weakness in the action of natural agents should be found in the fundamental potentiality and indetermination of matter.[12]

Aquinas thus expresses the weakness of the efficient cause in terms of the passive principle of which the material being is composed. Due to this passive principle, the active potency of natural agents could sometimes fail to produce the determined effect. Thus, the material cause of natural things, which is their passive potency, generates in them the possibility of somewhat "escaping" from the active potency that would determine them.

3 Due to the Poor Disposition of Patient

Aquinas also refers to the disposition (or lack of) in the being receiving the action of the efficient cause as a reason for unexpected events happening in nature. In this respect, Aquinas affirms that even though the agent could act without any impediment from an external causal concourse or its own deficiency, there is still the possibility that the effect would not be produced because of the being, the "patient," which receives the action. Once again, the possibility of failing in the production of the effect arises from the material cause of this being. Since no natural form completely informs the potency of the matter of a natural thing, this material potentiality can be, partially, an independent cause allowing for unexpected effects to happen.

To summarize, although natural agents act out of necessity because they are determined by their natures to cause one kind of effect, at the same time they have in their internal composition the root of contingency, that is, their material cause. Since this cause always takes part in every natural action, it allows for the possibility that the effect which the agent determined to produce is not perfectly caused, bringing out instead some unexpected effect.[13] Thus, for Aquinas, the natural world, being composed by material beings, always includes a place for contingency and indetermination, the source of which is matter, which can make events to happen accidentally.[14] Thus, the action of natural beings, according to their formal active principle, being determined toward one kind of effect, enjoy at the same time and under a different aspect, a certain degree of indetermination.

Creation and Providence

It is now time to turn our attention to Aquinas's doctrine of providence, through his understanding of creation. Aquinas always begins his treatment of creation out of nothing by affirming that God can make something out of nothing and that God does so.[15] Since, he claims, every agent acts according to its own act and God is absolutely and totally being in each act, by His action God produces the whole subsistent being, or existence, of things from nothing. This is called "to create." In his *Summa Theologiae*, Aquinas makes use of Neoplatonic terminology to address the definition of creation, saying that "the emanation of beings [from God] is called creation."[16] This understanding of creation means that the creature depends for everything in its existence upon the creator, and given that the creature depends on the creator to exist at every moment, Aquinas argues that if the giving of being—creation—would stop, the creature would cease to exist.[17]

From this understanding of creation out of nothing, Aquinas affirms the distinction between primary and secondary causes. Causation of being absolutely belongs to the first universal cause—God in his creative action—whereas causation of all that is in addition to being (i.e., specific being) belongs to secondary causes, which act by information (i.e., by giving the form to the effect and by producing movements or changes in nature). This is, for Aquinas, the difference between the way God causes as primary cause and the way natural things cause as secondary causes. God is the primary cause of things because what God causes is the very existence of all things, without which things would simply neither exist nor act. Now, given that the very being of the secondary cause is caused by the primary cause, all that the secondary cause is, is caused by the primary cause. Therefore, its power to be a cause is also given by the primary cause; because a secondary cause has its own being from the first cause, it likewise has its power to act from the first cause. This line of thought allows for Aquinas a very detailed account of the relation between primary and secondary causes, to which I now turn my attention.

In one of his longest analyses of divine providence,[18] Aquinas holds that any explanation of why natural beings have causal powers requires referring to their dependence upon God's creative power. Natural things exist insofar as God gives them their being, so they act insofar as God provides them with causal power. This is the primary sense in which

Aquinas understands God being the cause of the action of natural agents. Nevertheless, Aquinas gives a more detailed account by arguing for four ways in which something can be said to be the cause of the action of something else.[19]

In the first place, something can be considered the cause of the effect of another thing when the former gives causal power to the latter. Aquinas holds the principle that every operation which follows a certain causal power is also attributed to the giver of that causal power as its effect. Since all natural causal powers are from God, Aquinas affirms that God causes all the actions of nature because God gives natural things the causal powers by which they act.

In the second place, God is said to be the cause of a natural action because God sustains the natural causal power in its being. Aquinas's premise for this argument holds that any action that cannot continue after the influence of some agent has ceased should be attributed to that agent. Hence, the preserver of a causal power is said to cause the action of that power—much the way a remedy which preserves health is said to make a man healthy. Since God not only gives existence to things, but also preserves them in existence, God is continuously causing the causal powers in them. Therefore, every operation of a thing can be attributed to God as its cause.

The remaining two ways allow Aquinas to account for providential divine action through secondary causes. Thus, in the third place, Aquinas holds that a thing is said to cause another's action when it moves that other thing to act by applying the other thing's causal power to action. Thus, much the same way a man causes the knife's cutting when he applies the blade of the knife to a loaf of bread, Aquinas argues in his *Summa Theologiae* that when natural things act, they do so by being moved by God.[20] Hence, the action of every natural thing is caused by God applying its power to action.

In the fourth and final place, Aquinas teaches that when a principal agent causes the action of an instrument, the agent's intended effect through the instrument is attributed to the principal agent. Thus, God causes every action of all natural things. Aquinas is here referring to the causation of being itself. Since every natural thing is a being, everything which acts in a certain way causes being.[21] Given that being is the most common first effect, it is an effect which belongs to God alone. Thus, God is said to be the cause of the action of natural things because in every action they somehow cause being.

Aquinas does not expand on the differences between these last two ways of causing. His analysis of instrumental causation, however, might shed some light on the matter. For Aquinas, when an agent uses an instrument, one can distinguish two different effects: the first one refers to the instrument's own causal power, while the second one refers to the agent's power, which goes beyond the power of the instrument. For example, cutting is the proper action of a knife by virtue of its own sharpness. Nevertheless, when someone is using a knife, the cutting is usually in such and such manner, in a way that the knife itself cannot cut: as when a man uses a knife to cut his loaf of bread in elongated slices, which the knife by itself cannot do. Yet the man could not cut the loaf of bread in elongated slices without the knife (or any other sharp instrument).

Aquinas observes, however, that it is through the first effect (the cutting) that the second effect (cutting the loaf in elongated slices) is achieved. Hence this instrument, and no other, is used to accomplish this particular effect. What is more, both effects are truly caused by the instrument because the agent moves it to cause. Thus, both effects (cutting, and cutting in such a manner) can be attributed to the instrument because it is through its power that they are achieved and to the agent because it is only by the agent's power that the instrument actually causes.

Aquinas constantly uses the analogy of instrumental causality when explaining his account of how God acts in nature through natural things, affirming that every agent in every action is an instrumental cause of God's action. That which goes beyond the natural agent's causal power is the instantiation of being, which is attributable only to God, because only God can cause being. Nevertheless, God causes being by acting as the primary agent in the actions of the natural created causes. Yet the instrumental cause is truly the cause of the second effect (the instantiation of being) while it causes its natural effect, by receiving the power to cause this second effect from the principal agent.[22] A knife truly cuts, but only by being moved by somebody who wants to have a piece of cake.

Therefore, both the first and second effects of the natural (instrumental) cause are achieved by receiving the power from the principal agent. The knife is moved by the man to cut, and to do it in a particular manner. Without the man's power, the knife could not cut, but without the edge of the knife, the man could not cut in this manner. In a similar way, God moves the natural agent to cause in its own natural way, thus achieving an effect that goes beyond the power of that natural agent. Aquinas therefore affirms that "the effect does not follow from the first cause, unless the secondary cause is present,"[23] and can also say that in some sense the secondary (instrumental) cause determines the action of the primary cause toward this particular effect.[24] Aquinas concludes that even though the divine will is unfailing, some of its effects are necessary while some are contingent.[25]

For Aquinas, then, God can be said to work in and through every natural agent inasmuch as God gives everything the causal power to act, preserves that causal power in being, and applies the causal power to action, and thus by divine power every other causal power acts. In a sense, for Aquinas the created causal powers of natural things require the divine power and, at the same time, are actors of their own account, since God and natural agents act on two different levels.[26] Like a craftsman gives his axe the sharpness as a permanent form but not his acting power, Aquinas argues that God gives natural things the power to perform their operations according to their own natures and moves them to act.

Finally, it is important to remark that Aquinas did not think that there are four *different* actions God has with respect to creation. On the contrary, Aquinas presents a fourfold account of God's unique and sole action. Ultimately, the dynamic moments present God's continuous providential involvement in the history of the universe. In this respect, Aquinas always frames his account as a doctrine that does not ask more than it can provide: the idea that the effect is completely produced by God and by the natural agent is articulately simple, just as a man using a knife producing two pieces of bread from just one is simple.

Providence and Contingency

Aquinas's doctrine of creation allows for a doctrine of providence that accounts for an autonomous natural causality that, while contingent in its actions to some extent, at the same time depends completely upon God's causal powers. Aquinas conceives of God as acting constantly, intimately, and providentially in and through every activity of natural agents, and as being fully involved in the development of the history of the universe and humanity. Given that God acts in each action of each natural agent and that God always acts according to God's reason and will, these actions are provident actions. This account, however, does not require denying or diminishing the action of natural agents. God providentially influences the course of nature by moving the secondary causes to cause and to achieve the goals that God seeks for the universe. Aquinas thus strongly argues for a God who is so powerful that secondary causes are indeed real causes, even contingent causes, of God's providential action.

Aquinas characterizes God's providential activity as having two main features: the planning and the execution of the divine plan. The planning, of course, belongs to God's intelligence, while the execution of God's will[27] is performed—as I have argued so far—in and through created natural causes. Yet since every action of natural agents can be attributed to God in the fourfold manner explained above, Aquinas affirms, "that which comes from the operation of the secondary causes is subject to the divine providence,"[28] meaning that it is God acting through every natural cause to achieve certain goals. For Aquinas, God is continuously and providentially active in the universe: "God acts in all secondary causes, and their effects are to be referred to God as their cause: thus anything which is done in these individuals is His own work."[29]

Contingent events relate to God's providential action in two different ways: (1) as ordered to themselves, that is to their created natures; and (2) as ordered to something else, that is to the effect of the divine providence. Events which happen as they were determined in their causes fall under both kinds of providence: they act according to what was expected from them and in doing so they are also guided by divine will and wisdom. On the other hand, events which happen due to the failure of the agent (those which Aquinas referred to as happening "less frequently") fall under only the second way of understanding the providential act.[30] In this case, the event was not determined in its cause but happened as a random event, truly contingent within the created natural world. Nevertheless, Aquinas argues that it is also guided by the divine providence because it is caused by God as its first cause in the four ways analyzed above. Thus, Aquinas affirms that God, even by means of a created, contingent in its action, natural agent (which can be described as a deficient instrument in the analogy used earlier), achieves his goals and intentions by causing it to cause contingently, or randomly. As in instrumental causality, the principal agent has goals which are not included in the causal power of the instrument but which are nevertheless achieved; God, as principal agent, even when acting through contingent causes, reaches his own goals.

As I alluded to in the introduction to this chapter, Aquinas's account of divine providence requires the created world to include some measure of contingency and randomness in the production of the effects of natural efficient causes. Aquinas sees the universe as a gradual hierarchy of being, in which all modes of being (and causing) should be included. Thus the universe would be imperfect if contingency were not included in it. Furthermore, there are beings which act out of necessity as well as beings which have a stronger inclination toward indeterminism in the production of their effects. As the final step of his argument, Aquinas affirms that God's providential actions through created natural causes do not exclude the contingent mode of causing.[31] Aquinas includes in this account not only the contingent activity of natural agents but also the doctrine of human free will. The basic idea is that even when God causes each natural action, these natural agents are truly contingent in their activity and in their causal capacities, being able, potentially, to fail in the realization of the determined effect of their natures. After all, the principal agent assumes the nature of its instrument to act with it.

Aquinas, then, argues that from a contingent, indeterminate, or random cause, God can accomplish something better in the universe. In fact, he also claims that even though the contingent effect was not determined in its causes (because it was caused by a failing natural cause), God's goals do include those effects, which are ordered to new good things in the universe. In this way, Aquinas's ideas help solve the theological question of why things happen outside the ordinary course of nature by explaining that even those which happen randomly or by chance are providentially guided by God's continuous action.

Conclusion

Aquinas inherited the discussions on divine activity in the world in relation to natural causes from his Arabic Aristotelian and anti-Aristotelian predecessors. Addressing this issue with a synthesis of Neoplatonic and Aristotelian philosophies, Aquinas was able to produce a sophisticated account of God's action and its relationship to the action of natural created contingent causes.

Yet in what can be seen an unexpected move, Aquinas affirms that the created universe is more perfect because it includes imperfect contingent causality, that is, natural causes which do not determine the effect in its totality. Nevertheless, Aquinas does not want to say that it is God who somehow completes this lack of efficient power. On the contrary, Aquinas is convinced that, given his account of primary and secondary causation, God accomplishes God's own intentions through the contingency of the created causes.

With his fourfold account of divine providence, Aquinas is able to sustain two of the most important and desirable ideas surrounding the issue of divine action: in the first place, he affirms the radical dependence upon God of the created universe and the things within it, also supporting God's direct and continuous involvement in the development of history of the universe and humanity. In the second place, Aquinas affirms that nature is autonomous in its operations, in the sense that natural things have their own powers to act and cause according to these powers in their own level of secondary causes. Thus Aquinas can maintain the fundamental distinction between divine and natural causality, concluding that within the natural realm, natural causes cause natural events.

Scholastic Aristotelian philosophy and theology were later dismissed during the sixteenth and seventeenth centuries. This reversal was motivated by a reaffirmation of divine omnipotence, which implied a rejection of Aquinas's analysis of primary and secondary causation. New approaches to causation rejected the notions of chance, random events, and contingent natural causes. In order to exalt divine sovereignty over worldly events, the theology of the Reformed Calvinist tradition—as Byung Soo Han explains in chapter 9 and Oliver Crisp exemplifies with the occasionalism of Jonathan Edwards in chapter 10—denied the existence of truly random and chanceful events in nature.

Adding to the pushback were those seventeenth-century champions of the mechanical philosophy of nature, who rejected the idea of "forms" of natural things in favor of an atomistic view of matter, therefore rejecting also Aquinas's ideas on primary and secondary causation. Nevertheless, far from following the tradition of atheism which was attached to atomism, as John Hedley Brooke explains in chapter 8, Descartes, Newton, and Kepler, in the company of many other natural philosophers, developed new views of divine providence and sovereignty over nature. Given their atomic view of nature, these views tended to deny real causal powers in natural things, allowing for God to govern the behavior of nature through eternal and immutable laws.

Notes

1. These included Louis de la Forge (1632–1666), Arnold Geulincx (1624–1669), Géraud de Cordemoy (1626–1684), and Nicolas Malebranche (1638–1715), as well as the English Newtonian Samuel Clarke (1675–1729) and the Reformed theologian Jonathan Edwards (1703–1758).

2. More details on the debates within the Islamic tradition can be found in Mustafa Ruzgar, chapter 6 in this volume.
3. *Scriptum super libros Sententiarum*, book 2 [*In II Sent*], d. 1, q. 1, a. 4; *Summa contra Gentiles* [*SCG*], 3, 65 and 3, 69; *Quaestiones Disputatae de Veritate* [*De Ver.*], q. 5, a. 2, ad 6; *De Potentia Dei* [*De Pot.*], q. 3, a. 7; and *Summa Theologiae* [*ST*], 1, q. 105, a. 5.
4. *SCG* 3, 64.
5. *SCG* 3, 39. See also *ST* 1, 63, 9, co; *Expositio Libri Peri hermeneias*, book 1 [*In I Peri Herm.*], 14, 172; *De Ver.* 3, 1, co; *De Malo*, 1, 3, 17; *Sententia de Caelo et Mundo*, book 2 [*In II De Caelo et Mundo*], 9, 4; *Sententia super Metaphysicam*, book 6 [*In VI Meta*], 2, 16; 3, 22; and *SCG* 3, 99. Aquinas also refers to events which are by no means determined in their causes, making reference to human, angelic, and divine free will. These types of events and their relation to divine primary causation, however, exceed the scope of this chapter.
6. *In VI Meta* l. 3. See also *SCG* 3, 99.
7. Cf. *SCG* 3, 74. The "accidental being" opposes to the "being as such," which in Aquinas's terms usually translate the ens per se and the ens per accidens.
8. Cf. *ST* 1, 116, 1, co.
9. *ST* 1, 115, 6, co.
10. Or a cause per se.
11. *ST* 1, 115, 6, co.
12. *In I Peri Herm.* 14, 183.
13. *In I Peri Herm.* l. 14.
14. *SCG* 3, 86.
15. *De Pot.* 3, 1, co. A similar statement is made in *ST* 1, 44, 1, co.
16. *ST* 1, 45, 1, co.
17. *De Pot.* 3, 14, ad 10. See also *De Pot.* 5, 1.
18. *De Pot.* 3, 7.
19. See also *SCG* 3, 67.
20. As explained in *ST* 1, 2, 3, co.
21. *SCG* 3, 67.
22. Aquinas also explains this relation by using the Neoplatonic language of participation. He argues that by participating in the power of the principal agent to produce the second effect, the instrument participates in the power of the principal agent to produce its own effect, which is what he means when saying that the principal agent applies the powers of the instrument to its own (the instrument's) effect. See *De Ver.* 5, 9, 7.
23. *De Ver.* 5, 9, 12.
24. *De Ver.* 5, 9, 10.
25. *In I Peri Herm.* 1, 14.
26. *De Pot.* 3, 7, 1, and *ST* 1, 105, 5, 2.
27. *SCG* 3, 71.

28. *SCG* 3, 77.
29. *SCG* 3, 75.
30. *De Ver.* 5, 4.
31. *SCG* 3, 72, and in 74: "It is against the notion of divine providence that there is nothing casual or random in things." And *SCG* 3, 74: "It would be against the perfection of the universe if there was nothing corruptible, or if no power would fail [in producing its effect]."

9

Chance, Sovereignty, and Providence in the Calvinist Tradition

Byung Soo (Paul) Han

Introduction

Is every creature unexceptionally and unavoidably dependent on the Creator, and does the being and subsisting of every creature depend on the Creator? Is every creature, as well as every accident and event in the world, entirely subject to the command of God? The apostle Paul writes that we have our being, live, and move in God because his word of power sustains us. The Reformed circle of Christians has maintained that God is not just the creator of all things, but has also been their sustainer and preserver since the very moment of creation, considering it "frigid and meager" to make God "a momentary creator" who made all things and thereafter allowed them to be sustained by the order infused in them from the beginning.[1] God by his providence sustains, cherishes, and superintends the whole creation and each of its parts. Thus, according to the Calvinist view, nothing exists or even happens by chance or fate independently of God's sovereignty and providence. This view, however, has been condemned by many as deterministic or fatalistic. As a scholar of Reformation and post-Reformation theology in the sixteenth and seventeenth centuries, I have studied whether such condemnations are reasonable by delving into historic Calvinism and the origin of Reformed tradition, among whose distinguished representatives are Calvin himself, Polanus, Twisse, and Turretin. This chapter intends to demonstrate that the Calvinistic view on chance, sovereignty, and providence, though diversely expressed, is not deterministic or fatalistic but biblically reasonable.

Providence in Calvin's Thought

Calvin clearly declares that the providence of God is not reconcilable with a secular understanding of worldly events as happening by chance or cosmic accident. The now-popular view of all events as merely fortunate or unfortunate happenings conflicts with the (biblically inspired) Calvinistic declaration that even the very hairs of each person's head are numbered, that the whole world and each of its parts belong to God, and that all events and every single creature are "governed by the secret counsel of God." To Calvin's eye, there is nothing that could be classified as "chance" and no event that could occur by the blind rotation of fortune—rather, all things are decreed by God's will. This is what divine providence means.[2]

Calvin's idea of providence leaves no room for chance or fate. Yet this does not mean that Calvin entirely denies any phenomenon or form of chance or fate occurring in the world. He states, "I do not . . . totally repudiate what is said of an universal providence, provided . . . it is conceded to me that the world is governed by God, not only because he maintains the order of nature appointed by him, but because he takes a special charge of every one of his works." Calvin does not deny that, if the eternal command of God leads some things to operate spontaneously, it must be true that each kind of thing moves by the motivation of its own nature. Yet Calvin goes on to say in support of his basic argument that every single event is so regulated by God and all events so proceed from his definite council that "nothing happens fortuitously." This argument is not necessarily charged with an utterly deterministic worldview—that is, Calvin would not say that God decides the outcomes of dice that are rolled in a gambling casino or in a children's game, since Calvin truly respects "contingency and real possibility at the level of secondary causes."[3]

To the eyes of common people, many worldly phenomena seem to happen by fate, natural law, or chance, which is another name for fate. Calvin, however, would assert that a drop of rain would not fall without the certain mandate of God. "A man's way is not in himself, nor is it in a man who walks to direct his steps but in God" (Jeremiah 10:23). It is nothing but "ridiculous insanity" that a man would do something by himself—even though the plans of the heart belong to man, the answer of the tongue is from God. The Bible provides many theological illustrations that make clear that even "the maximally fortuitous" belong to God's providence, and that there is nothing in the world that is not ordained by God. God is the preserver and governor of the whole creation who sustains, protects, and rears even the most inconsequential sparrow and who is in control of all the presumably fatalistic things by "a special providence." In his commentary on Amos, Calvin emphasizes that we should learn the vicissitudes of seasons do not belong to chance and that "the order of the whole nature refers to God's special providence"; what Calvin means by "special providence" is that the Lord wants to be seen "in daily events" so that "the tokens of his love may gladden us and also that the tokens of his wrath may humble us."[4]

It is possible to question whether Calvin's repugnance against chance—the belief that there is in all things and in history no event that does not depend on God's secret decision—is Stoic fatalism. Calvin, however, regards as bizarre the idea of "a necessity consisting of a perpetual chain of causes and a kind of involved series contained in nature," and he ascribes the eternal decree and its temporal execution to God alone.[5] Even when Augustine declared that all things are done partly by the free will of humans and partly by divine providence, he did not mean to deny the utter ascription of all events to God's providence because he shortly after clarified that "there cannot be any greater absurdity than to hold that anything is done without the ordination of God."[6] In full consensus with this great Church Father, Calvin declares that both the decree in eternity and its execution in time belong to God alone. It is interesting to note that Calvin, in his discussion of this issue, accepts the medieval distinction of absolute necessity and relative necessity, or necessity of the consequent and the necessity of the consequences. With this distinction, he asserts that what God decreed is by necessity carried on but not absolutely or by its own nature. For instance, Christ's bones were made subject to frailty, but God, according to the necessity of his counsel, did not make possible their actual fracturing that might have naturally taken place. The medieval distinction of the absolute and the relative necessity, acknowledges Calvin, was not blindly invented.[7]

Assuming the formal diversity in operation of God's providence—(1) it works at one time with means, (2) at another without means, and (3) at another against all means—Calvin observes that, "although the paternal favour and beneficence, as well as the judicial severity of God, is often conspicuous in the whole course of his Providence, yet occasionally as the causes of events are concealed." For this reason, people in hard times tend to complain by saying that all human affairs are controlled by the impulse of blind fate or they file a protest with God against God's arbitrary treatment of humankind. Calvin would recommend they keep in mind that there must be God's secret plan and cause behind all events in the world, preventing them from jumping with "excessive audacity and curiosity" into what God would leave hidden and belonging to God's self.[8]

Calvin draws our attention to what is necessary for us to recognize that God's providence must rule over fortune: We should mix fear of God as our creator and redeemer with humility. The fear makes our eyes open to see what is unseen. Calvin is convinced that no one could duly grasp the divine working in the world without fearing God. Those who, in Calvin's day, did *not* fear God were eager to tear apart this incomprehensible doctrine of divine providence "with envenomed teeth" or "assail it with their bark, refusing to give more license to God than their own reason dictates to themselves." But God-fearers would acknowledge that mysteries which far exceed the measure of our senses and are to be reverently adored are found in Scripture, as confessed by the Psalmist, who wrote God's "judgments are a great deep," and by Paul, who cried, "O! The depths of the riches of the wisdom and knowledge of God! How unsearchable are his judgments and his ways past finding out! For who has known the mind of the Lord, or who has been his counselor?" We see in Scripture that the whole world is not just ruled by the divine precepts of the law including God's will, but more broadly by God's other hidden will which Calvin compared to "a deep abyss."[9] The nonbelievers, however, would rather make sarcastic remarks: these unknowable things are just a theological invention of drunken affection. Indeed, no one can comprehend the mystery of law and gospel in God's divine method of governing the world unless enlightened by a spirit of understanding.

For his view of divine providence, Calvin appeals to Augustine's assertion that since God's providence is an unchangeable law, we have to work with good intention in accordance with the law, and all events in the world must take place "according to the law."[10] In this vein, Calvin underscores that we have to regard God's "right of governing the world unknown to us" as our "law of modesty and soberness," and God's will as our "our only rule of justice, and the most perfect cause of all things."[11]

Understanding Calvin's view in a distorted manner, the nonbeliever argues that, since all things and events are fixed by God's definite decree, human deliberation and effort must be useless, and that all evil deeds are a sort of virtue because they may be counted as obedient to God's unchangeable will. In response, Calvin contends that what the writer meant in Proverbs 16:9, "a man's heart devises his ways but the Lord directs his steps," is that "the eternal decrees of God by no means prevent us from proceeding under his will to provide for ourselves, and arrange all our affairs."[12] It, thus, would be sacrilegious to God if we ignore our human faculties of deliberation and caution with which we are endowed by God to serve God's providence and preserve our life.

Though all things are under God's unfathomable counsel—meaning there is nothing that happens by chance—we must consider the inferior causes to a certain degree. Although God works in and through all secondary causes, either good or evil, still it would be inappropriate to ascribe "the substance and responsibility of evil" to God. It differs little from the stench of a dead body which has been putrefied by the sun's heat: we do not blame the sun or its heat as the sole cause of such a stinking smell. According to Calvin, this reasoning does not abolish the fact that the source of the whole world and history is God's will; all plans, wills, efforts, and powers of humans, good or evil, are subject to the governing providence of God, who can direct them "like a watercourse wherever he pleases."[13]

As Isaiah wrote, God declares that "I form the light, and create darkness: I make peace, and create evil: I the Lord do all these things" (Isaiah 45:7). We often experience unfair and harmful events that are not our fault. Even in those events, the knowledge of divine providence advises us that it should not be our response to attack our enemies, thereby getting close to their wickedness that is liable to stimulate revengeful thoughts in us. Rather, we have to stay in the confidence of what God has in store for us, who "in all things works for the good of those who love him" (Romans 8:28), and, responding to God's divine attributes and works, become "partakers of divine nature" (2 Peter 1:4). We have to believe that, whatever evil our enemies have done, it was allowed by God as a part of God's just providence. The great comfort given by God to the pious lies in the fact, only revealed through faith, that their "heavenly Father so embraces all things under his power—so governs them at will by his nod—so regulates them by his wisdom, that nothing takes place save according to his appointment; that received into his favour, and entrusted to the care of his angels neither fire, nor water, nor sword, can do him harm, except in so far as God their master is pleased to permit." In other words, "the devil, and the whole train of the ungodly, are, in all directions, held in by the hand of God as with a bridle, so that they can neither conceive any mischief, nor plan what they have conceived, nor how much soever they may have planned, move a single finger to perpetrate, unless in so far as he permits, nay, unless in so far as he commands." This providence is, indeed, the foremost source of our comfort.[14]

However, the Bible clearly indicates that God repented of having made human beings (Genesis 6:6) and of having raised Saul to the kingdom (1 Samuel 15:11) and did not overthrow Nineveh but inclined to a more merciful sentence on their immediate repentance (Jonah 3:4–10). On these grounds, people like Origen argue that God's plan may be changed, that some of God's decrees may be annulled, and that God has not fixed human affairs by an eternal decree; rather, according to the merits of each individual and as God deems just and right, God disposes of each single year and day and hour.[15] Calvin opposes this argument, quoting Samuel's affirmation that "the Strength of Israel will not lie nor repent: for he is not a man, that he should change his mind or repent," contending that the use of the term "repentance" was made in a figurative way, as belonging to the modes of human expression concerning God and his works to accommodate our capacity. God's divine counsel or will, to Calvin's eyes, is not inversed, nor is his affection changed, but whatever God approved and decreed and foresaw from eternity is prosecuted as a part of perpetual tenor, even when the variation may seem sudden to human eyes. Given that "the LORD Almighty has purposed, and who can thwart him? His hand is stretched out, and who can turn it back?" (Isaiah 14:27), God's eternal decree and providence in time cannot be changed in any respect. Still, urges Calvin, we should acknowledge that this unchangeability of divine decree or providence remains an incomprehensible mystery.[16]

Amandus Polanus on Divine Providence

Calvin's view on God's providence became more firmly fixed as the Reformed tradition developed its understanding. Some methodological development and theological systematization were elaborated upon by eminent Reformed orthodox thinkers, particularly Amandus Polanus, William Twisse, and Francis Turretin.[17] Polanus (1561–1610) makes two distinctions of divine providence: into the internal and the external, and into the essential and the personal. According to his distinction, the generation of the Son by the Father and the procession of the Holy Spirit by the Father and the Son belong to the internal personal works of God, while divine counsel and decree belong to the internal essential works of God. In a slightly different way, Polanus also classifies God's counsel and decree made from eternity as "God's providence for internal works," and the execution of God's decree in time as "God's providence for external works."[18]

After making some distinctions, Polanus defines divine decree as wisest because it originated from God's wisdom, freest because it has God's most free will as its efficient cause, and absolute because it follows God's unchangeable counsel. The *finis* of divine decree is to glorify God and to complete God's will in all things, while its effect is the foreknowledge of God on all future things (all things and events in time), and on their causal order. Divine decree is divided into the general and the special: the former concerns all things as its object, while the latter concerns God's providence for his internal works. The special decree is part of general decree, having rational creatures as its object. Polanus posits the order of divine decree as follows: "*Finis* is prior to means in intention, posterior in execution." Accordingly, the glory of God is prior to the salvation of the elect and the means of salvation in intention, but in the order of execution the means of salvation comes to pass first and then the salvation of the elect and God's glory follow.[19]

The object of divine decree includes all things that exist and all events that take place in time so that there is nothing that goes beyond God's decreeing providence. It seems strange to us that God decrees even the evil things. To understand this strange argument, we need to observe a distinction of decree according to God's distinctive will: decree by the will of good pleasure and decree by the will of the sign. The former is the efficient one in which, before the creation of the world, God determines what he wants to do in accord with his good pleasure, while the latter decree is the one in which God reveals his will by means of precepts or promises. The decree of the sign is again divided into the preceptive and the permissive: the former is the decree in which God determines all things by precepts commanding and prohibiting, the latter by permitting. Sin or departure from divine laws is not determined in accordance to the efficient decree but to the permissive decree. It is notable here that, even though God decreed to permit human beings to sin according to the permissive decree, sin itself does not originate from any decree of God, either the efficient, the preceptive, or the permissive. It is one thing to come from the decree, and it is another thing to come according to the decree. If sin came from the decree, the decree is the cause of sin. Even though it is true that the decree is prior to sin, if sin came according to the decree, the decree is just adjunctive to sin, not its cause. In this way of speaking, the Reformed thinkers made their best theological endeavors not to compromise God's absolute sovereignty and holistic providence with any other pagan thoughts and not to ascribe the responsibility of sin to God.

The pagan notion of fate or chance has no place to lay its head in the Reformed tradition. It, nonetheless, does not mean that the terms of "fate" or "chance" themselves are not used at all. Polanus, for example, divides "fate" into the philosophical fate and the Christian fate. The former is subdivided into the mathematical, the physical, and the Stoic: the first is the fate that has ties with the movements and events which result from the power and position of stars; the second is the nexus of natural causes producing some results; the third concerns the natural necessity and order of all things and movements.[20] Different from these philosophical fates in terms of foundation, the Christian fate is "a theological and true fate."[21] Not like the Stoic fate, which makes God subject to itself, the Christian fate entirely depends on God, the most sovereign author of all things and the most sovereign *actus*, who has power and strength to see, know, and govern in himself, not allocating the power and strength to any others.[22]

The Reformed thinkers grant that divine decree is absolutely sovereign, but that it still does not destroy the contingency of effects and events. However, it does destroy such contingence if we impose the absolute or coactive to every future event. Opposing this, they argue that God decreed effects and events according to the necessity determined by themselves and let the secondary causes operate according to their natures. Thus, effects and events are necessary according to divine decree, but contingent according to secondary causes.[23]

William Twisse and the Westminster Confession of Faith on Divine Providence

The divines of the Westminster Assembly in the seventeenth century regarded divine providence as entirely dependent on God's will. A great prolocutor of the Westminster Assembly, William Twisse (1578–1646) confirmed that God, as the uncaused cause and unmoved mover, cannot be caused or moved to do anything by anything else but God's will alone. On the basis of Paul's phrase, "God hath mercy on whom he will" (Romans 9:18), Twisse raises the question, "What could be found in one to move God?" Nothing temporal can be the cause of the decree of God's eternal will.[24]

Twisse's conclusion is "All thinges are necessary in respect of the decree of God," not by their own nature. He makes the distinction that, while works of nature must come to pass necessarily by the decree of God, the actions of humans must come to pass by the decree of God contingently and freely. Twisse considers human actions to be contingent, for they are not from the decree of God but from the nature of God. However, it is impossible to say that "the world should not be of a contingent nature" because it is impossible in its own power to be so or not. It is still true that, for Twisse, God's decree cannot be caused from external causes such as contingent agents or their free actions.[25]

Concerning the argument that all things are produced by the necessity of divine nature, Twisse severely denounces it since it is "atheistical and utterly overthrowing all divine providence." The argument was at once employed by Jesuits to found the Christian fate depending only on God and God's decree. The Christian understanding of fate is, however, no more than the Stoic understanding. Both restrain God by the necessity of the truth determined from God's nature. Twisse reaffirms that God is free in the way that "He acts *in His will* according to His nature and the mode fitting for His nature."[26]

With regard to sin, Twisse basically agrees with Augustine, who says, "God is not the author of evil," and positively adapts Bradwardine's view that "God is the efficient, formal, and final cause of evil action, but not material." In this aspect, Twisse explains that Judas's betrayal of his master, Herod's mocking of Jesus, and Pilate's condemning Jesus were necessary for the divine ordinance, but were performed not necessarily but contingently and freely. Accordingly, God cannot be considered as the author of their sins, as contingent acts of their free will, but they themselves. However, one cannot find how Twisse understands and can explain the relationship between the material cause and the author of sin. That is, whether God, only if materially causing humans to sin, would be the author of sin. It is nevertheless clear for Twisse that God is the primary cause but not caused, or the first mover but not moved, by any kind of internal or external factor but by God's will. Twisse's view on divine providence is, thus, reflected in words of the Westminster Confession of Faith as below:

> God the great Creator of all things does uphold, direct, dispose, and govern all creatures, actions, and things, from the greatest even to the least, by his most wise and holy providence, according to his

infallible foreknowledge, and the free and immutable counsel of his own will, to the praise of the glory of his wisdom, power, justice, goodness, and mercy. Although, in relation to the foreknowledge and decree of God, the first Cause, all things come to pass immutably, and infallibly; yet, by the same providence, he orders them to fall out, according to the nature of second causes, either necessarily, freely, or contingently.[27]

Francis Turretin on Divine Providence

Known as a distinguished codifier of seventeenth-century Reformed theology, Francis Turretin (1623–1687)[28] maintains that the reality of God's providence is not just an assertion of the Christian church but also supported by the voice of nature, consensus of nations, and the wise among the gentiles. Plato, for instance, argues that "gods have a care for all things, small and great"; Aristotle maintains that "as the helmsman in his ship, as the charioteer in his chariot, as the leader in a chorus, as the lawgiver in a city, as the commander in a military camp, so is God in the cosmos"; and Seneca echoes Plato by writing that "Providence is over all and God takes care of us."[29]

Also for Turretin, divine providence neither destroys the contingency of things nor overthrows the liberty of the human will, allowing it to exercise its own movement "most freely, although inevitably." There is unchangeability or necessity in the providence of God. Turretin, however, argues that the species of necessity requires a distinction to be made in terms of God and things. Necessity in God is divided into two manifestations: (1) absolute necessity, which is grounded in the immutable nature of God, or the undeniability of God in nature; (2) hypothetical necessity, which relies upon the immutable will of God and in which anything intended by God in divine decree must come to pass. And Turretin divides the necessity of things into three as below:

(1) physical and internal necessity on the part of secondary causes which are so determined to one thing that they cannot occur otherwise, as in fire the necessity of burning;
(2) the necessity of coaction that arises from an external principle operated through violence;

(3) the necessity of hypothetical event or dependence through which a thing, although naturally mutable and contingent, cannot but be (on account of its dependence upon the ordination God whose will cannot be changed nor his foreknowledge be deceived).[30]

Turretin maintains that all things are ordained by God's eternal and unchangeable counsel. He puts even the most fortuitous and most casual of all things under the realm of divine providence. It is only in terms of the primary cause that the necessity and unchangeability of divine decree take away contingence, but not in terms of the secondary causes. Among the secondary causes, the necessary operate necessarily, the contingent contingently, and the free freely. Accordingly, the necessity of divine decree does not remove the liberty of spontaneity and indifference of things because it does not destroy the nature and propriety of the secondary causes.[31]

One event or result is said to be both necessary and free or contingent because the necessity of divine decree is consistent with the liberty or contingence of creatures. Although all things occur necessarily from divine decree or the primary cause, according to things themselves, they occur freely, contingently, and fortuitously. Turretin's reasoning enables us to say that Adam did not only necessarily sin but also did so voluntarily and contingently and freely: "the former with respect to the decree and the future existence of the thing; the latter with respect to his will and as to the mode." At this point, Turretin argues that the necessity of Adam's sin does not make God the author of sin since Adam did sin from the necessity of decree, but neither by the physical cause nor by the ethical cause. Adam's sin was the necessary result of divine decree but did not flow from it. Since the necessity in this case is extrinsic and hypothetical, divine decree does not cause evil but is of a permissive and directive character.[32]

As exemplified in Adam's sin, divine providence neither removes the contingence of things nor takes away the freedom of will. It is because God decreed things to occur, but through the secondary causes, leaving their spontaneity and contingence always preserved. Divine providence does not distort the rule of poetic justice since the necessity of following providence is not absolute, physical, or coactive but relative. The will of human beings always remains in a free and rational state.

We are often caught by doubt and confusion when we observe the prosperity of the unrighteous and the downfall of the righteous. Psalm 73 provides a typical case in which Asaph came so close to stumbling because he saw the nonsensical prosperity of the wicked: they are not in trouble as other people, nor are they plagued like humankind; the wicked are always carefree, they increase in wealth, but Asaph himself has been plagued all day long and punished every morning. Even in such a seemingly absurd providence of God, to Turretin's eyes, the splendid wisdom of God glitters. As to this, Jesus explains that God "causes his sun to rise on the evil and the good, and sends rain on the righteous and the unrighteous" (Matthew 5:45). Paul, in the same vein but with a different nuance, explains Asaph's experience as that providence in which God allows the unrighteous, on account of their stubbornness and unrepentant hearts, to store up wrath against themselves for the day of God's wrath (Romans 2:5). In this regard, see Augustine's comment that Turretin aptly quotes:

> If every sin should now be punished with manifest punishment, it would be supposed that nothing would be left for the last judgment. Again, if the divinity did not now openly punish any sin, it would be supposed that there is no providence. . . . It has pleased divine providence to prepare good things for the righteous hereafter which the unrighteous will not enjoy, and evils for the wicked with which the good will not be tormented. He wished, however, those temporal goods and evils to be common to both so that neither the good should be sought too eagerly, which the wicked also are seen to have, nor the ills be ignobly shunned, with which the good also are for the most part affected.[33]

In accord with Augustine, Turretin argues that it must be a secret providence of God and his sincere consideration of us that the wicked are not immediately punished and the good endure misery.

In his discussion of divine providence, Turretin also mentions fate, which he does not entirely deny, and, with reference to Pico della Mirandola (1463–1494), an Italian Renaissance philosopher, he makes four distinctions: physical, mathematical, Stoical, and Christian fate.[34] Turretin explains that *fatum* was employed in his day in a Christian sense actively to indicate "divine decree itself," not different from providence, but often passively to refer to "the very complexion and disposition of all causes to their own effects."[35] For him, fate is different from providence in three aspects: (1) in terms of the subject, providence is in God, while fate is from God in secondary causes; (2) in terms of the order, fate depends on providence, not the contrary; (3) in terms of the object, all things lie under providence but not under fate. Like the Christian fate understood in this way, Turretin acknowledges, the term *fatum* could be useful in a Christian meaning only if being properly used.[36] Following Calvin, nevertheless, he lists the several reasons for possibly abstaining from that term in the Christian school: (1) it is contaminated by heathenism, superstition, and impiety, and thus belongs to a number of those profane novelties Paul command us to flee; (2) it is too much exposed to the calumnies of opponents, who with its use charge us with receiving also the doctrine and so endeavor to fasten its odium upon the truth of God; (3) the word "providence" is handed down to us in Scripture itself, while fate by no means appears in Scripture.[37] Turretin concludes by quoting Augustine, who said that "If anyone calls the very power and will of God fate, let him hold the opinion, but let him correct the language."[38]

Everything without exception, confirms Turretin, is under divine providence, from which even the minutest and most trivial thing in the world is not free. With reference to biblical texts, he reckons as a part of divine providence the contingent and the fortuitous, which are seemingly out of divine control but still necessarily in the light of divine decree. Even those free and voluntary things which apparently pertain to human reason and power, argues Turretin, claim God's secret care and governance, since it is God who made heaven, the heaven of heavens, with all their hosts, the earth, and all things that are therein, and preserves them all (Nehemiah 9:6), by giving them life, breath, and all things necessary for their preservation, making possible their living, moving, and being (Acts 17:25, 28), and satisfying their desire (Psalms 145:15–16).[39]

In this context, Turretin argues that every creature should be regarded in relation to God not just in terms of being but also in terms of operating, as "the mode of operation follows that of being." Not just the indifferent and general, but also the particular and specific in the world, as well as the conservation of things and the sustenance of their operations, are governed by divine providence.[40]

Turretin keeps digging into the more detailed meaning of Paul's phrase: "in Him we live, move, and have our being."[41] A theological term that clarifies this matter is "concurrence," which, as Thomas Aquinas pointedly said, has five aspects: (1) God gives to secondary causes the strength and faculty to act; (2) God keeps and sustains them in being and vigor; (3) God excites and applies secondary causes to acting; (4) God determines them to act with respect to decree but only in a concursive sense; (5) God rules and directs them that they may accomplish the ends determined by himself.[42] Knowing these aspects, the Reformed thinkers especially emphasize that God's providence does not only reign over the conservation of things, but also in the concurrence of God, not only the indifferent and general but also the particular and specific.[43]

Concurrence describes the principle by which "God conserves the power of the secondary act and permits it to act" or by way of action, "inasmuch as God is the proximate principle of the operation put forth by the secondary cause so that the operation and action of God concurring is the very same as that which is included in the action itself of the creature." Concurrence has two expressions: the previous and predetermining and the simultaneous or concomitant. The former is "the action of God by which he, flowing into causes and their principles, excites and previously moves creatures to action and directs to the doing of a particular thing"; the latter is "that by which God produces the action of the creature as to its being or substance by which he is supposed to flow together with creatures into their actions and effects, but not into the creatures themselves." [44]

Acknowledging the diverse opinions of the Reformed thinkers, Turretin regards the simultaneous concurrence as "truer and safer." According to simultaneous concurrence, human beings exercise their will spontaneously, but with regard to providence and previous determination they are unable not to do so. It is not strange that there are two causes of different dimension in one and the same happening and also that one action produces an effect, in concomitant work with two causes. Notably, God stimulating secondary causes is different from God's producing their action, an action that belongs to God efficiently but formally and subjectively to the secondary causes.[45]

This reasoning, Turretin is convinced, is also applicable to evil actions; still its application does not make God the author of evil or the source of corruption, for God's concurrence is related to the substance of an act materially and naturally, but morally it has no relation to the ill will of the agent. Turretin also distinguishes the physical and the moral dimensions of an act. A similar distinction is that of a judge, who causes the death of a condemned criminal by executioner but is not the cause of cruelty shown in the execution. The created will, as physical agent, is the physical cause of an act and, as moral agent, the moral cause of wickedness. Since the human will produces not just an act but also an act of violation against the law that should be observed, the liability for that act is legitimately imposed on the human agent. The point made by Turretin is that, as moral wickedness is inherent or caused from deficient will, not in the transition of the nature of things into acts, we should not blame God for causing sin.[46]

Quite against Turretin's advocacy of divine concurrence, some contend that, if God concurs truly and efficiently with the material act of sin, he would be the cause of sin. In response, Turretin quotes scholars such as Aquinas and Cajetan, who wrote that, since "God in an action connected with deformity, does what belongs to the action, does not do what belongs to the deformity, he becomes the cause of the action but not of that deformity."[47] Therefore, we have to distinctively consider every good action as consisting of the action itself, which refers to the realm of being, and its good or evil, which concerns the morality of the action.

Some people argue that divine concurrence cannot be reconciled with the contingency and freedom of secondary causes, especially of human will. Against this argument, Turretin explains that God's providence concurs with all secondary causes, but it does not destroy any of them. Given that people act freely but still cannot do anything outside of the divine will and decree, he asserts that we have to confess "Oh, the depth of the riches of the wisdom and knowledge of God! How unsearchable his judgments, and his paths beyond tracing out!" (Romans 11:33). With reference to Scripture as the final judge and benchmark of all the mysterious and unaccountable, Turretin concludes that:

> God on the one hand by his providence not only decreed but most certainly secures the event of all things, whether free or contingent; on the other hand, however, man is always free in acting and many effects are contingent. Although I cannot understand how these can be mutually connected together, yet (on account of ignorance of the mode) the thing itself is (which is certain from another source, i.e., from the word) not either to be called in question or wholly denied.[48]

Conclusion

Divine providence provides us with the greatest comfort and peace of God. It is due to the knowledge of this providence that we are not disturbed but rather remain in an unshakable peace and rest, even when the most absurd things happen to us, when the cause of terrible things or events is unknown, or when an undeserved misfortune overwhelms us. God is the creator and preserver of all things and events, ruling over all things ranging from the minutest to the greatest. All things and events, righteous or unrighteous, good or evil, are under the providence of God and connected with God, as the means of divine revelation. Paul, in other words, depicts this by saying that "since the creation of the world God's invisible qualities—his eternal power and divine nature—have been clearly seen, being understood from what has been made" (Romans 1:20). Similarly, Calvin asserts that "wherever you turn your eyes, there is no portion of the world, however minute, that does not exhibit at least some sparks of beauty; while it is impossible to contemplate the vast and beautiful fabric as it extends around, without being overwhelmed by the immense weight of glory."[49] Kuyper, in the same vein, declares that "there is not a square inch in the whole domain of our human existence over which Christ, who is Sovereign over all, does not cry: 'Mine!' "[50]

This understanding of the Reformed thinkers did not allow any pagan concept of "fate" or "chance" to invade the Christian *truth*. Accordingly, even when we do not perceive or know any evident cause of things and events, that ignorance should not nullify the providential intervention of God in them. Even those happenings that possess seemingly free and contingent causality must be the actualization of God's infallible decree done in a mysterious way. Calvin was convinced of this, although he employed some medieval terms as necessary. Yet he did not entirely disregard the actual presence of fate-paved happenings in the world. Since Calvin, Christian thinkers have been quite antagonistic to the terms "fate" and "chance," but they are still being used, not in a sense of rhetorical flourish but of Christian modification. In line with Calvin, the Reformed orthodox of the sixteenth and seventeenth centuries took the term *fatum Christianum* to describe the mysterious things and events having causes unknown to human sense.

The Reformed thinkers of the post-Reformation era had to face sharp attacks from the opponents of their age and accordingly develop the theological themes of the Reformers like Calvin, not essentially but methodologically. Many sophisticated definitions and distinctions are found in the writings of orthodox Reformed scholars. These writings are not materially different from Calvin's standpoint on providence in the Reformed view, as previously examined in the Westminster Confession of Faith by Polanus, Twisse, and Turretin. They represent a methodological rather than a theological change—they continue to acknowledge God's absolute sovereignty, hold to the integral concept of providence as consisting of decree and its execution, advocate the concurrence of God in all things and events, and still argue that this divine concurrence does not make God the author of evil or the culprit of corruption. They argue that we should give honor and glory to God for God's unfathomable, inscrutable wisdom and knowledge in His amazing work of harmonizing divine decree, human freedom, and the contingency of nature. In the matter of divine providence, they aimed neither to go beyond the limit that Scripture draws nor to be silent of whatever Scripture says, so that the Reformed view of divine providence may not be endorsed by human discerning but by the testimony of Scripture.

Notes

1. John Calvin, *Institutio Christianae Religionis* (Lausanne, 1559) [hereafter *Institutio*], 1.16.1–4, Calvin, *Institutes of the Christian Religion*, trans. Henry Beveridge (Edinburgh: Calvin Translation Society, 1845) [hereafter Beveridge], 1: 230–237; Calvin, *Ioannis Calvini opera quae supersunt omnia* [hereafter CO], ed. G. Baum, E. Cunitz, and E. Reuss, vol. 24, *Commentarius Exodus et Praefatio in Legem et Lex* (Brunswick and Berlin: Schwetschke, 1863–1900), 43.
2. Calvin, *Institutio*, 1.16.2, Beveridge, 1: 232–233.
3. Calvin, *Institutio*, 1.16.2–4, Beveridge 1: 236–237; Richard A. Muller, *Christ and the Decree* (Grand Rapids, MI: Baker Academic, 2008), 22–27.
4. Calvin, *Institutio*, 1.16.1, 6, Beveridge 1: 231–232, 239; Calvin, *Praelectiones Amos ad Habacuc*, CO 43:62.
5. Calvin, *Institutio*, 1.16.8, Beveridge, 1: 241.
6. Augustine, *Quaestionum in Heptateuchum*, Migne, *Patrologia cursus completes: Series Latina* [*PL*], 34:601.
7. Richard A. Muller, *Dictionary of Latin and Greek Theological Terms: Drawn Principally from Protestant Scholastic Theology* (Grand Rapids, MI: Baker Academic, 1985), 200.
8. Calvin, *Institutio*, 1.17.1, Beveridge 1: 247–248; Calvin, *Commentarius Exodus et Praefatio in Legem et Lex*, CO 24:265.
9. Calvin, *Institutio*, 1.17.2, Beveridge, 1: 249–250.
10. Augustine, *De Civitate Dei*, 12.7, *PL* 41:355.
11. Calvin, *Institutio*, 1.17.2, Beveridge, 1: 251.
12. Calvin, *Institutio*, 1.17.3–4, Beveridge, 1: 252–253.
13. Calvin, *Institutio*, 1.17.5–6, Beveridge, 1: 254–256.
14. Calvin, *Institutio*, 1.17.11, Beveridge, 1: 262.
15. Origen, *De principiis* 3.1.17, Migne, *Patrologia cursus completes: Series Graeca* [*PG*] 11:283.
16. Calvin, *Institutio*, 1.17.12–14, Beveridge 1: 263–266.
17. Francis Turretin, *Institutio theologiae elencticae* (Edinburgh, 1847), 1:439.

18. Amandus Polanus, *Syntagma theologiae christianae* (Hanoviae, 1615), 4.1–6.
19. Ibid., 4.6.
20. Ibid., 4.6.
21. William Twisse, *Vindiciae gratiae, potestantis ac providentiae Dei* (Amsterdam: Joannem Janssorium, 1632), 29.
22. Johannes Heinrich Heidegger, *Corpus theologiae christianae* (Heidelberg, 1732), 246–248; Francis Turretin, *Institutio theologiae elencticae,* 1:446–448.
23. Amandus Polanus, *Syntagma theologiae christianae,* 4.6.
24. William Twisse, *The Riches of Gods Love* (1653), 1: 37, 188; Twisse, *The Doctrine of Synod of Dort and Arles* (1650), 40.
25. William Twisse, *A discovery of D Jacksons vanitie* (1631), 272, 288–290.
26. William Twisse, *Vindiciae gratiae, potestantis ac providentiae Dei,* 29.2.A–E; Twisse, *Doctrine of Synod of Dort and Arles,* 67.
27. *The Humble Advice of the Assembly of Divines, Now by Authority of Parliament Sitting at Westminster, Concerning a Confession of Faith* (London: Evan Tyler, 1647), 5. 1–2.
28. Francis Turretin, *Institutio theologiae elencticae,* 1:439–440.
29. Plato, *Epinomis,* 980b, trans. W. R. M. Lamb, Loeb Classical Library (Cambridge, MA: Harvard University Press, 1927), 12: 448–449 Aristotle, *On the Cosmos,* trans. E. S. Forster and D. J. Furley, Loeb Classical Library (Cambridge, MA: Harvard University Press, 1955), 402–403; Seneca, *De Providentia* 1.1, 2, in *Moral Essays,* trans. John W. Basore, Loeb Classical Library (Cambridge, MA: Harvard University Press, 1928) 1: 2–4.
30. Turretin, *Institutio theologiae elencticae,* 1:287.
31. Ibid., 1:288.
32. Ibid., 1:287–288.
33. Ibid., 1:443; Augustine, *De civitate Dei,* 1.8.2 (PL 41:20).
34. Pico della Mirandola, *Disputationes adversus astrologiam divinatricam* (1943), IV. iv (442–456).
35. Turretin, *Institutio theologiae elencticae,* 1:445–446.
36. The term *fatum* was often used by the fathers and its certainty and unchangeability were examined at full length by Thomas Aquinas in his *Summa Theologiae* (1, 116).
37. Calvin, *Institutio* 1559, 1.16.8.
38. Augustine, *De civitate Dei,* PL 41:141; Pico della Mirandola, *Disputationes adversus astrologiam divinatricam* (1943), IV.iv (442–456).
39. Turretin, *Institutio theologiae elencticae,* 1:448.
40. Ibid., 1:450–451.
41. Ibid., 1:450.
42. Aquinas, *Summa Theologiae,* 1, 83.
43. Aquinas, *Summa Theologiae,* 1, 83, 1; Turretin, *Institutio theologiae elencticae,* 1:450.

44. Turretin, *Institutio theologiae elencticae*, 1:454.
45. Ibid., 1:455–457.
46. Ibid., 1:457.
47. Thomas Aquinas, *Scriptum super libros sententiarum*, 2.37.2; Cajetan, *Commentaria in summam theologicam divi Thomae*, 1: 2.79.1.
48. Turretin, *Institutio theologiae elencticae*, 1:458–459.
49. Calvin, *Institutio*, 1.5.1. Beveridge 1: 66.
50. Abraham Kuyper, *Abraham Kuyper: A Centennial Reader*, ed. James D. Bratt (Grand Rapids, MI: Eerdmans, 1998), 488.

Selected Bibliography

Aquinas, Thomas. *Scriptum super libros sententiarum*, book 4.

Aquinas, Thomas. *Summa Theologiae*.

Aristotle. *On the Cosmos*. Translated by E. S. Forster and D. J. Furley. Loeb Classical Library (Cambridge, MA: Harvard University Press, 1955).

Augustine. *De Civitate Dei*. Migne, *Patrologia cursus completes: Series Latina*, vol. 41.

Augustine. *Quaestionum in Heptateuchum*. Migne, *Patrologia cursus completes: Series Latina*, vol. 34.

Calvin, John. *Ioannis Calvini opera quae supersunt omnia*, edited by G. Baum, E. Cunitz, and E. Reuss. Vol. 24, *Commentarius Exodus et Praefatio in Legem et Lex* (Brunswick and Berlin: Schwetschke, 1863–1900).

Calvin, John. *Institutes of the Christian Religion*. Translated by Henry Beveridge. 3 vols. (Edinburgh: Calvin Translation Society, 1845).

Calvin, John. *Institutio Christianae Religionis* (Lausanne, 1559).

Calvin, John. *Ioannis Calvini opera quae supersunt omnia*, edited by G. Baum, E. Cunitz, and E. Reuss. Vol. 43, *Praelectiȝones Amos ad Habacuc* (Brunswick and Berlin: Schwetschke, 1863–1900).

Cajetan, Thomas de Vio. *Commentaria in Summam theologicam divi Thomae* (Quebec: Laval University, 1948).

Heidegger, Johannes Heinrich. *Corpus theologiae christianae* (Heidelberg, 1732).

The Humble Advice of the Assembly of Divines, Now by Authority of Parliament Sitting at Westminster, Concerning a Confession of Faith (London: Evan Tyler, 1647).

Kuyper, Abraham. *Abraham Kuyper: A Centennial Reader*, ed. by James D. Bratt (Grand Rapids, MI: Eerdmans, 1998).

Mirandola, Pico della. *Disputationes adversus astrologiam divinatricam* (1943), IV.iv (442–456).

Muller, Richard A. *Christ and the Decree* (Grand Rapids, MI: Baker Academic, 2008).

Muller, Richard A. *Dictionary of Latin and Greek Theological Terms: Drawn Principally from Protestant Scholastic Theology* (Grand Rapids, MI: Baker Academic, 1985).

Origen. *De principiis*. Migne, *Patrologia cursus completes: Series Graeca*, vol. 11.

Plato. *Epinomis*. Translated by W. R. M. Lamb. Loeb Classical Library (Cambridge, MA: Harvard University Press, 1927).

Polanus, Amandus. *Syntagma theologiae christianae* (Hanover, 1615).

Seneca, *De Providentia*. In *Moral Essays*, translated by John W. Basore. Loeb Classical Library (Cambridge, MA: Harvard University Press, 1928).

Turretin, Francis. *Institutio theologiae elencticae* (Edinburgh, 1847).

Twisse, William. *A discovery of D Jacksons vanitie* (1631).

Twisse, William. *The Doctrine of Synod of Dort and Arles* (1650).

Twisse, William. *The Riches of Gods Love* (1653).

Twisse, William. *Vindiciae gratiae, potestantis ac providentiae Dei* (Amsterdam: Joannem Janssorium, 1632).

10

Jonathan Edwards and Occasionalism

Oliver D. Crisp

THE NEW ENGLAND theologian, pastor, and metaphysician Jonathan Edwards had some interesting and influential things to say about the relation of God to the created order, and about divine action in particular. In this chapter I set out what I take to be five key motifs in Edwards's thought, which collectively form the basis of a theologically and philosophically rich and interesting metaphysical picture of God's relation to the world. Having given some account of Edwards's views, I then offer some critical reflections upon them from the point of view of contemporary philosophical theology with an eye to the religion and science debate. Edwards is a very popular theologian partly because he was instrumental in the birth of evangelicalism and the Great Awakening in America—however, it happens that his views about divine action and creation are rather more exotic than some of his erstwhile followers might be willing to stomach, and they have some significant drawbacks that his contemporary defenders need to address. Chief among these are the difficulties his views have with accounting for the problem of evil in a world governed by a providential god, or "theodicy."

The Edwardsian Metaphysical Picture

Recent studies of post-Reformation thought have challenged received wisdom on the shape of Reformed theology, the tradition to which Edwards belonged.[1] It has often been thought that Reformed theology is inherently determinist in nature. God ordains all things from before the foundation of the world, electing some to salvation and passing over others that are damned. Even the minutiae of our lives are all ordered, arranged, and determined by divine decree. Not that we human beings are unfree—rather, our freedom of will must be construed in such a way that it is consistent with divine determinism.[2] Hence, in this traditional understanding, Reformed theology is synonymous with what we might call *theological compatibilism*: God's determination of all that comes to pass is consistent with my freedom to act as I so desire on a given occasion. More importantly, perhaps, my free actions are consistent with moral responsibility, so that for all actions I perform (where I am free in the relevant sense), I am morally responsible as well.

An example will make the point clear. Suppose I intentionally slap Jones. I desired to slap Jones; I desired to desire to slap Jones. That is, my first- and second-order desires were in accord so that (to borrow a term made famous by philosopher Harry Frankfurt[3]) I chose to slap Jones *wholeheartedly*. There were no conflicting first-order or second-order desires complicating my motivation for so acting. Not only that: in acting in this fashion, on the basis of such motivation, I am responsible for doing as I did—for slapping Jones rather than, say, shaking his hand—for I acted upon what I desired, and desired to desire; I was in my right mind at the time; I was not coerced or forced into action by others; and my desires were ordered toward this particular action. But clearly such a picture is also consistent with my being determined to act as I did—in this case, by God ordaining all that comes to pass, including my wholehearted desire to slap Jones.

This view, or something very like it, is said to be the Reformed view of the relation between divine ordination and human freedom. A significant reason for the widespread identification of this particular species of determinism with Reformation theology is the work of Edwards. Before Edwards, many Reformed thinkers who dealt with the topic of free will (they did not talk of "determinism," which was a term introduced later into the discussion) thought that human beings were free to do as they pleased with regard to mundane choices. More specifically, they thought that some sort of principle of alternate possibilities allowed for autonomy in many mundane creaturely choices, such as "Should I have porridge or corn flakes for breakfast?" or "Should I slap Jones or shake his hand?" At the moment of choice the agent in question really could have chosen otherwise; the choice she made was not determined in advance; her choice was unforced, uncoerced, and entirely up to her at the moment of choosing.

However, in matters pertaining to salvation, on this older Reformed view, God does determine every outcome because the effects of sin upon our intellectual capacities have effectively closed off such choices to fallen human beings absent divine intervention and grace. That is, we would never freely choose to turn to God for redemption because sin has blinded us, placing such choices beyond our reach rather like (we might think) the action of the alcoholic has placed beyond her reach the ability to sober up immediately and forthwith, without relapse. This thrall to sin and our inability to do anything about it in respect to our salvation was called "bondage to sin," a topic that several of the magisterial Reformers dealt with at length.[4]

Edwards's contribution was to take this central notion from his early modern forebears and transpose it into the language of the early Enlightenment. In effect, he sought to refound the Reformed position on the doctrines of sin and redemption using the tools fashioned by early Enlightenment philosophers like John Locke, Nicholas Malebranche, the Cambridge Platonists, and Isaac Newton and his disciples. Edwards was also well-read in the work of early modern thinkers whom he regarded as opponents of revealed religion, such as Thomas Hobbes and John Toland, and his mature views owe as much to those philosophers with whom he disagreed as it did to those with whom he had an affinity. His refashioned Reformed theology was decidedly deterministic in outlook. Indeed, he thought of the notion of an uncaused choice or action as utterly meaningless. Everything is caused by something else, going back in a chain of cause and effect that can be traced (in principle at least) to God's decision to create. Not only that, God's decision to create, which cannot be uncaused any more than creaturely choice can, is the necessary product of God's nature. That is, God must create given who God is and must create this particular world because it is the best possible.[5] Fallen human creatures are nevertheless free—provided that what we mean by "free" is that we choose according to our desires or according to the greatest apparent good. Naturally, given the disordered desires we often have as a consequence of sin, we will choose badly. But where we do make choices according to our desires, we are free in the relevant sense, and are morally responsible for the actions we perform to the extent that we are free. This, in a very pared-down form, is Edwards's theological compatibilism.[6]

These views about determinism and free will are a staple of the secondary literature on Edwards. However, they are only a part of a larger, and more exotic, whole. In addition to the above, Edwards held to a version of idealism and to the doctrine of occasionalism. The sort of idealism to which he ascribed is similar in many respects to that of Bishop Berkeley,[7] although it appears that Edwards came to his views independently of Berkeley. Like Berkeley, he thought that matter is a fiction. The world is a collection of ideas and created minds, which are sustained in being by God, who is an infinite mind. This view means that there is no mind-independent reality, for all that exists is the product of minds, either divine or creaturely. Hence, Edwards, like Berkeley, is a sort of metaphysical antirealist.

Such idealism was "in the air" in the early eighteenth century when Edwards was developing his views. The materialist philosophy of thinkers like Hobbes (whom Edwards mentions by name in his work) had sent shivers down the spine of many orthodox Christian intellectuals. For if the only substance is material substance, then God (if there is a god) must be a material object.[8] In reply, some had embraced the view that God is space. This notion, associated with the Cambridge Platonist Henry More,[9] was adopted by the young Edwards during his graduate studies at the nascent Yale College. He quickly rejected it, however, adopting a wholesale idealism instead. Rather than attempting to shore up Christian belief in metaphysical dualism (according to which there are two sorts of substance: immaterial and material), Edwards, like Berkeley, chose the path of monism opposite to that implied by Hobbes, denying that there are any material substances whatsoever. He even believed that God is the only true substance, strictly speaking, and that creaturely substances are only substances so-called, or in an attenuated sense.[10] There is much more to be said about the specifics of Edwards's idealism. But this sketch will do for now.

In addition, Edwards had particular views on the relationship between creation and the subsequent conservation of the created order by providence. In effect, he collapsed providence into his doctrine of creation. Or, to put it another way, creation-plus-providence is one seamless whole. That is, Edwards denied that the world God creates persists through time in order to be preserved at moments after its initial creation out of nothing. Instead, he maintained that God continuously created the world at each moment. Lest this view be mistaken for another, we must be clear that Edwards did not think that God, an eternal and timeless being, atemporally generates the world such that at every moment at which the world exists from its first to its last moment, God can be said to be continuously (that is, atemporally) creating it. Rather, Edwards's position was that God (atemporally) creates the world which immediately ceases to exist. God then creates a numerically distinct but qualitatively identical world with small incremental changes built into it. This process is repeated in a third and in subsequent worlds in an ordered sequence, which are really only momentary stages or (perhaps) temporal parts of a four-dimensional whole. The picture is rather like the numerous photographic exposures that are run together in one roll of film to make up a motion picture projected onto a cinematic screen. It is literally the case according to Edwards that no created thing persists through time, and that all created things are aggregates of temporal parts or (perhaps) stages that form one space-time whole.[11] God also creates the sequence of world-stages, segued according to God's infinite wisdom. He goes as far as to say that God "*makes truth,* in affairs of this nature,"[12] which leaves open the possibility that the deity may gerrymander the sequence of stages at any time (something that Edwards does appear to reconcile with respect to the doctrine of original sin—but that is another matter[13]). Of course, for Edwards, the created order, that is, the four-dimensional whole that is the series of world-stages created and ordered by divine intelligence, is an ideal order. It comprises ideas and created intellects that, says Edwards, God communicates moment by moment. We shall return to this point presently.

In addition to this doctrine of continuous creation, Edwards held to occasionalism, a much-misunderstood view according to which God brings about all that obtains in the world. Creaturely action is, at root, merely the occasion of God's action. So when I choose to slap Jones, both the basic act of forming the intention to slap Jones and the nonbasic physical changes that need to take place in my body in order to bring this action about (e.g., synapses firing, chemical and neurological signals being sent to my limbs, the kinetic movement of my hand, and so on) are the occasions of God's action. Strictly speaking, the claim is not that God is the *cause* of all creaturely action in the world, for causes are physical in nature.[14] God is not some physical entity that may affect the place, motion, and action of other physical entities in creation—for God is not a physical entity. Given that Edwards's ontology is idealist, there is an added complication in that there are no material objects to be accounted for in action theory. (There may be physical objects, of course—yet any physical object in Edwards's thinking cannot be composed of matter where matter is extended nonthinking, property-bearing substance. For Edwards, physicality boils down to the property of resistance, not extension in space.)

This understanding means that God ordains my created mind to form the intention it does and that the ideas of physical change and action between bodies coalesce such that I do, in fact, slap Jones. Importantly, for the occasionalist, God actualizes this state of affairs; we creatures may choose certain things consistent with our desires. But even these choices are regulated, ordained, and brought about by God. Indeed, for Edwards, God is not only the one who actualizes every event in the creation. God is the one who brings about every momentary world-stage that comprises the four-dimensional whole that is the cosmos from its inception to its extinction.

This picture of the world does have the advantage of solving the problem of special divine action, that is, God's action in the world in miraculous and supernatural ways at particular places and times.[15] Edwards's view means God does not need to "intervene" in the created world because the world does not persist through time as a numerically identical entity, wholly present at each moment of its existence. God is constantly creating it. God alone ensures that it, and all it contains, exists at particular moments in time. Edwards is very clear that nothing that existed a moment ago can cause what exists to exist now, for that which existed a moment ago no longer exists, and so cannot trouble the present one way or another. Only that which is present can affect other things present. Since nothing exists for more than a moment, nothing created exists long enough to be a true cause of any other created thing; God must be "causing," that is, bringing about, the obtaining of all that does obtain at any given moment in time.[16] There may be actions that are momentary in nature. But I suppose that Edwards thinks the momentary world-stages that comprise the four-dimensional whole of the created order are not of sufficient temporal length as to sustain action across time, even at very short intervals. (He does not go into detail about how short the momentary world-stages are, but his expressed views are consistent with the claim that these momentary stages are just that: stages of zero or near-zero duration, segued together in a densely ordered continuum.) God actualizes everything, every world-stage, and the content of every world-stage. Talk of *my* action is a way of speaking about the action of a four-dimensional entity that exists across time, comprising numerous temporal parts. Alternatively, it is a way of speaking about the aggregation of a series of numerically distinct, but qualitatively identical or near-identical person-stages. (This is consistent with stage-theory.) At each stage of my existence, God is actualizing my existence. Literally nothing would exist without this divine action.[17]

Although this position may be thought a rather extreme way of avoiding Hobbesian materialism, and deism, it does have two important features that commend it. The first of these is that it "saves the phenomena" as much as does a Berkeleyan view. Famously, Berkeley claimed his own idealism was really the commonsense view, a metaphysics for "the mob," or the common person.[18] When we reflect for a moment on our experience of the world, idealism seems much more plausible than it does in abstraction because it is constituted of perceptions, sensations, and other sense data. Although Edwards does not say his view is common sense as such, he does invoke the category of common sense in a variety of ways, and he does think that his position is able to account for everything the materialist and deist want—without sacrificing what he regarded as the theological sine qua non, namely absolute divine sovereignty over the creation.

The second attractive feature of Edwards's position is its account of action across time. We have already noted that his view does not introduce the problems posed in contemporary accounts of divine action that suppose God "intervenes" in creation, or "breaks the laws" in order to do so. If God determines all that comes to pass and if the creation comprises a series of world-stages segued together according to divine ordination such that God causes each world-stage to exist ex nihilo, as well as all that obtains in each world-stage, then there is no problem of special divine action to worry about over and above these metaphysical commitments. Yet such a world would look and feel exactly like the one we actually inhabit. What is more, from an Edwardsian point of view, these commitments "fit" with our commonsense view of the world. They explain both our freedom in choosing as we do, what that freedom consists in, as well as giving some account of the creation of the world, and the persistence of things across time in a cosmos governed by an absolute sovereign. It was, to Edwards's mind, a perfectly biblical picture, one in which God is responsible both for the rain that falls, the lot that is cast into the lap, and the resurrection of Christ from the dead. Even evil events are ordained by God, although Edwards maintains that creatures are morally responsible for the evil that they generate.

This position brings us to the final aspect of Edwards's metaphysical picture of the creation and its relation to the creator. Thus far we have given some account of his theological determinism, idealism, continuous creation, and occasionalism doctrines, as well as the related issue of his four-dimensionalist picture of the persistence of the world through time. To round out the whole view, we must now discuss his panentheism. This is an under-reported aspect of Edwards's thought, though it is an open secret in the Edwardsian scholarly community. Often in popular accounts of his work, Edwards is portrayed as a classical Christian theist, defending a robustly traditional account of divine nature. This is only partially true. Edwards did defend much of the classical view, but as with many other aspects of his thinking, his attempt to recast traditional Christian theism in the language and thought-forms of the early Enlightenment led him in directions that are, at the very least, in tension with his commitments to the more traditional Christian theistic picture. Earlier we noted that for Edwards, the world is the necessary output of divine creativity (though he denies God is psychologically or metaphysically dependent on the creation). As above, God must create a world—must create *this* world because it is the best possible. The Leibnizian[19] key to Edwards's doctrine of creation sits alongside his views about the emanation and remanation of creation, language that is Neoplatonist in origin.[20] These ideas require some explanation.

Panentheism is a slippery term that does not appear to have precise conceptual content.[21] However, a common metaphor often used to illustrate the doctrine is the relation between the human soul and body. Suppose humans are composed of bodies and souls, rightly related. In the panentheist scheme, God is to the world as the soul is to the body. Suppose this is right. Then it looks like the world is a proper part of God, though God has parts other than the world, that is, the correlate to the human soul in the example just given. Edwards seems to hold to something like this view, transposed into an idealist, four-dimensionalist key. That is, he thinks that the world (if we may call it that) is a four-dimensional whole composed of stages, or, perhaps, temporal parts organized according to divine wisdom. The whole and its parts are all ideal. That is, they are either created minds or ideas. God, in Edwards's way of thinking, emanates this world. In fact, if we place his views about creation beside his views about persistence, it seems like the world really is akin to the flickering images of a motion picture on the silver screen. God "projects" or emanates these ideal world-stages, "communicating" them as Edwards puts it. He communicates each world-stage and brings it about moment by moment. For, as he says (quoting the Apostle), "in him we live, and move, and have our being" (Acts 17:28).[22] This notion has potentially far-reaching theological consequences (it means God is literally bringing about everything in the creation, every moment). But it also sits within our commonsense perceptions of the world around us (the appearance of the world as we experience it moment by moment).

Prospects for the Edwardsian Position

Edwards's metaphysical vision was comprehensive, especially to the matter of divine action. While several aspects of his thought resonate with some of the contemporary science and religion literature, there are also significant drawbacks to the Edwardsian position, some of which we have already intimated.

Before discussing conflicts between Edwards's position and that of contemporary scholarship on theology and science, we should examine their unique resonances. First, Edwards's determinism fits with the Newtonian picture of the world with which he became familiar during his graduate studies at Yale. After Newton, the universe appeared to be a physically closed system, a grand machine that works according to physical laws that, by their very nature, admit of no exceptions.[23] Given such a picture of nature, the determinist must find some way of making sense of special divine action where it appears physical laws are fixed, immutable, and every action has an equal and opposite reaction. We have seen that Edwards has a rather interesting response to this sort of theological anxiety. Rather than trying to provide some reason for thinking God can "break the laws" and intervene in the world, Edwards posits (within idealism and the four-dimensionalist version of continuous creation yielding occasionalism) that physical laws are not exceptionless generalizations about certain physical constants in the world. Rather, they are more a sort of law-like framework within which God works, so that in every world-stage there appear to be the same sorts of physical constants at work.[24]

Another modern example from the film industry may help illustrate the point. Consider CGI, the computer-generated images that make up animated aspects of many live-action motion pictures, as well as cartoon feature-length films such as those produced by Pixar. Each frame in the digital sequence for a given scene of a movie must be composed by artists and compositors. In order to ensure the appearance of continuity of action across time, the artists must ensure that each frame works with the same "physical" principles. That is, in each frame, the artist seeks to ensure his characters act according to a facsimile of the same forces and laws as we see in the world around us. If they suspended these all the time or simply ignored these considerations in their work, the continuity of the movie would be destroyed. Nevertheless, strictly speaking, there are no exceptionless "laws" governing the artist's work.

It seems to me that this is a good analogue to the sort of view Edwards espouses. God is the artist creating each "frame," that is, each world-stage, ensuring continuity of physical constants across the different stages, even though these are not actually physical laws that persist through time, strictly speaking. Physical constants are simply a function of God's divine action, ensuring that things proceed in a way that is orderly and predictable. But like the CGI artist, such constants can be suspended on occasion for dramatic effect—as when a CGI character flies, or leaps tall buildings in a single bound. God does not "break the laws" on this view because there are no physical laws to break. What is more, this picture comports with the world as we see it. Edwards's view does not require any revision in our commonsense views of the world, or of the natural laws we commonly think govern it. In this way, his view "saves the phenomena" of the world in which we live. It would be a world that appears to be populated by entities that act in predictable and orderly ways, according to what appear to be physical laws. As philosophers Hugh McCann and Jonathan Kvanvig put it in their defense of a contemporary version of occasionalism:

> If the theological doctrines at issue are correct, then not only is it "in Him that we live, and move, and have our being," it is also through Him and by His power that the universe and the things in it have their own distinctive character at each instant. In certain ways, this claim is every bit as radical as it sounds. Nevertheless, it is a long way from it to a second claim associated with occasionalism: that scientific laws have no explanatory force, and that the apparent interactions among things in the world are illusory.[25]

Edwards could endorse this view wholeheartedly.

The four-dimensionalism Edwards espouses also resonates with those contemporary thinkers for whom the world is a densely ordered continuum of zero-duration temporal slices, a view that can be found in contemporary analytic metaphysics. But rather than offering some explanation of how causal action works across time, Edwards provides an elegant solution to questions of cause and effect: God does not deny to mundane causes some explanatory force—after all, God ordains that when the billiard ball is hit by another billiard ball, it moves in a certain direction, for a certain period, at a certain speed, and so on. However, it does mean that such "causes" turn out to be occasions of divine action. The phenomena are preserved, all right, but at a theological cost that may be too high for many.[26]

Finally, panentheism is a view that many in the current science and religion literature find appealing. Often this has been thought of as a move away from a traditional theistic conception of the God-world relationship. It is interesting that of all people Edwards, a fountainhead of modern evangelicalism and staunch defender of Christian theism against deism and materialism, should be sympathetic to such notions—normally associated with theological revisionism rather than theological conservatism. Admittedly, some contemporary panentheists, like Arthur Peacocke,[27] think of their view as more of an "emergent monism," or a "theistic naturalism," that is, a layered set of interlocking physical systems where certain properties or powers emerge from more basic or fundamental physical parts of the whole.[28] Unlike Edwards, Peacocke does not think of the world in terms of minds and their properties, but of events, processes, and the emergence of higher-order physical properties from simpler, lower-order ones. Yet Peacocke is clear that these physical processes are the actions of God who continuously creates them.

Edwards does not favor the language of emergence. His is the discourse of eighteenth-century natural philosophy and metaphysics. However, there are clear resonances with the sort of view espoused by modern thinkers like Peacocke—far more resonance than one might expect at first glance. The Edwardsian picture may yet provide a way for evangelical thinkers, who have been wary of the work of scientific theologians like Peacocke, to engage this recent literature in a more constructive manner than has been the case hitherto. That would certainly be a positive development.

However, I would be remiss not to give some account of the problems with Edwards's position.[29] Elsewhere, I have argued that occasionalism is a structural weakness for Edwards because it entails that God is the author of evil.[30] Suppose, with Edwards, that God does indeed actualize every state of affairs, so that creaturely action is only the occasion of God's action. This in and of itself does not necessarily place the Edwardsian position beyond the pale. One could argue that God in acting as God does is causally responsible but not morally responsible for all that obtains in the world. As we have noted, Edwards does use the language of causation with respect to God. But suppose we speak instead of God actualizing or bringing about a given state of affairs that has physical, causal consequences. My intention to slap Jones really is my action. I am the agent intending to do this; God is not. I am the one whose intention results in the morally inappropriate action of slapping Jones; God does not slap him. True, God actualizes the states of affairs that comprise this particular action-across-time. What is more, it transpires that any such action that takes time is in reality the aggregate of the action of numerically distinct stages or slices that God brings about ex nihilo and at each moment. But if one thinks that some sort of four-dimensionalism is true independent of these considerations, then this is not a particular problem for Edwards's view; it is just a cost of adopting such a metaphysical picture of persistence-through-time. The fact that God actualizes each world-stage and all it contains, including my action from intention to physical contact with Jones in slapping him, does not necessarily imply that God is morally responsible for what I choose to do. I form the intention. Yes, God actualizes it. But in this manner God is like the CGI artist that composites the frames that make up my action-across-time. The character in the story performs a particular action, the artist does not, although the artist generates both the character and the actions he performs. Nevertheless, it would be odd to ascribe responsibility for the actions of the CGI character to the artist that generates and composites them. We don't say that Walt Disney is responsible for the wickedness of Mickey Mouse, though he makes the character and "causes" him to do what he does. Similarly, according to the Edwardsian view, we should not ascribe to God moral responsibility for the actions of creatures, though he actualizes them and the states of affairs in which they obtain.

Does this position get God off the hook? That depends on whether one thinks an important factor in weighing moral responsibility for an action is the origin of the *conditions* that give rise to an agent choosing as she does, rather than choosing some other course of action. In this respect the contemporary Princeton philosopher Harry Frankfurt may come to Edwards's aid. Frankfurt thinks that the origination of the conditions that give rise to my choosing to choose an action, and my choosing it in an ordered hierarchy of desires and choice, is not relevant to either my freedom or my moral responsibility for the action in question. If I choose it and choose to choose it, then whether my first- and second-order desires were provided by some other agent or not, I am the one choosing as I do, and I am the one morally responsible for my action. As Frankfurt puts it:

> the only thing that really counts is what condition I am in. How I got into that condition is another matter. If I'm in the condition where I'm doing what I want to do and I really want to do it, i.e., I decisively identify with my action, then I think I'm responsible for it. It makes no difference how it came about that that is the case. If it *is* the case then it follows that I am fully responsible.[31]

Edwards can claim something similar. If the question is whether I am morally responsible for choosing according to what I desire, and desire to desire, the answer is: yes, I am. Provided my choice is wholehearted in the Frankfurtian sense, then I am responsible for the choice I made, irrespective of whether I could not have chosen otherwise and irrespective of whether the conditions for that choice originate outside me, in the action of God. The Edwardsian can affirm something very similar. Clearly this explanation does not do all the work necessary to get God off the theodicy hook. But such a view is commensurate with the biblical picture of a God intimately involved in his creation and its sustenance, where even the outcome of the throw of a dice into the lap is decided by God (Proverbs 16: 33).

Notes

1. Willem J. van Asselt, J. Martin Bac, and Roelf T. te Velde, eds. *Reformed Thought on Freedom: The Concept of Free Choice in Early Modern Reformed Theology* (Grand Rapids, MI: Baker Academic, 2010). An earlier foray into some of the same territory can be found in Richard A. Muller, "Grace, Election, and Contingent Choice: Arminius's Gambit and the Reformed Response," in *The Grace of God, The Bondage of The Will*, ed. Thomas R. Schreiner and Bruce A. Ware, vol. 2, 251–278 (Grand Rapids, MI: Baker, 1995).
2. A good recent restatement of this position can be found in Paul Helm, *The Providence of God* (Downers Grove, IL: InterVarsity Press, 1993).
3. Harry G. Frankfurt, "Alternate Possibilities and Moral Responsibility," in *The Importance of What We Care about* (Cambridge: Cambridge University Press, 1995), chap. 1. This essay has spawned an entire literature.
4. John Calvin, *The Bondage and Liberation of the Will: A Defence of the Orthodox Doctrine of Free Choice against Pighius*, ed. A. N. S. Lane, trans. G. I. Davies

(Grand Rapids, MI: Baker Academic, 1996), and Martin Luther, *The Bondage of the Will*, trans. J. I. Packer and O. R. Johnson (London: James Clarke, 1957).

5. Oliver D. Crisp, *Jonathan Edwards on God and Creation* (Oxford: Oxford University Press, 2012), chap. 3, and William J. Wainwright, "Jonathan Edwards, William Rowe, and the Necessity of Creation," in, eds. *Faith, Freedom, and Rationality: Philosophy of Religion Today*, ed. Jeff Jordan and Daniel Howard-Snyder, 119–133 (Lanham, MD: Rowman and Littlefield, 1996).
6. Jonathan Edwards, *The Works of Jonathan Edwards*, vol. 1, *Freedom of the Will*, ed. Paul Ramsey (New Haven, CT: Yale University Press, 1957). All references are to this edition of Edwards's works, cited as *WJE*, followed by volume number, and page reference, e.g., *WJE* 1: 150. The Yale edition is available online at http://edwards.yale.edu/.
7. George Berkeley, *Principles of Human Knowledge and Three Dialogues between Hylas and Philonous*, ed. Roger Woodhouse (Harmondsworth: Penguin Classics, 1988 [1710, 1713]). *Principles* was first published in 1710, *Three Dialogues* in 1713.
8. Thomas Hobbes, *De Corpore, Part I: Logic*, trans. A. P. Martinich (New York: Abaris, 1981), 3.4. *De Corpore* was first published in 1655.
9. C. A. Patrides, *The Cambridge Platonists* (Cambridge: Cambridge University Press, 1980).
10. This aspect of his position has a long history in Christian Platonist thought. For instance, Anselm in the *Monologion* maintains that God is the only true substance as well.
11. I argue this at greater length and with supporting evidence from Edwards's voluminous works in Crisp, *Jonathan Edwards on God and Creation*.
12. *WJE* 3: 405.
13. Thus Edwards, "And I am persuaded, no solid reason can be given, why God, who constitutes all other created union or oneness, according to his pleasure, and for what purposes, communications, and effects he pleases, may not establish a constitution whereby the natural posterity of Adam, proceeding from him, much as the buds and branches from the stock or root of a tree, should be treated as one with him, for the derivation, either of righteousness and communion in rewards, or of the loss of righteousness and consequent corruption and guilt." *WJE* 3, 405. Interested readers should consult Roderick M. Chisholm, *Person and Object: A Metaphysical Study* (La Salle, IL.: Open Court, 1976), appendix A; Oliver D. Crisp, *Jonathan Edwards and the Metaphysics of Sin* (Aldershot: Ashgate, 2005); and Michael C. Rea, "The Metaphysics of Sin," in *Persons: Human and Divine*, ed. Peter van Inwagen and Dean Zimmerman, 319–356 (Oxford: Oxford University Press, 2007).
14. Edwards does speak of God as a cause, and I suppose that occasionalism does entail that God's action brings about physical-causal changes in the world. It is just that, as far as I can see, God himself cannot be a physical cause like

a billiard ball can because he is not a physical entity, any more than a soul is a physical entity. In this respect I am "correcting" the Edwardsian view of occasionalism.

15. However, this "solution" will be regarded as a problem by some. See, e.g., Nicholas Saunders, *Divine Action and Modern Science* (Cambridge: Cambridge University Press, 2002). Saunders distinguishes between General Divine Action (which affects the creation as a whole), and Special Divine Action (which happens at particular times and places). Such a distinction dissolves given Edwardsian occasionalism. Saunders worries that by making God "directly responsible for causing every event within creation," the occasionalist denies "creation any functional integrity of its own and raises difficult issues of theodicy" (31). We shall return to these worries in evaluating Edwards's position.
16. Objection: what about simultaneous causation, where a cause and effect obtain at the same moment in time? Edwards does not really address this matter directly. However, even if cause and effect do obtain at the same moment, God brings about every state *within* a given world-stage directly. So there is no wiggle room here for efficacious mundane causation independent of divine action.
17. For a helpful introduction to four-dimensionalism, see E. J. Lowe, *A Survey of Metaphysics* (Oxford: Oxford University Press, 2002), chaps. 2–4; and Michael C. Rea, "Four-Dimensionalism," in *The Oxford Handbook of Metaphysics*, ed. Michael J. Loux and Dean W. Zimmerman, 246–280 (Oxford: Oxford University Press, 2003). The most comprehensive recent treatment of these issues is Theodore Sider, *Four-Dimensionalism: An Ontology of Persistence and Time* (Oxford: Oxford University Press, 2001). There are two theories of persistence consistent with four-dimensionalism: perdurantism, or the doctrine of temporal parts; and exdurantism, or stage-theory. Edwards's position is probably closer to a version of exdurantism, though there are aspects of his thinking that sound like perdurantism.
18. This is the title of John Russell Roberts study, *A Metaphysics for the Mob: The Philosophy of George Berkeley* (Oxford: Oxford University Press, 2007). He gets the title from Berkeley's claim that in all things he sides with "the mob."
19. (In)famously, Gottfried Wilhelm Leibniz argued that this world is the best possible in his *Theodicy: Essays on the Goodness of God, the Freedom of Man and the Origin of Evil*, ed. Austin Farrer, trans. E. M. Huggard (La Salle, IL: Open Court, 1985), originally published in 1710.
20. The Neoplatonic language of "emanation and remanation" can be found especially in the final section of the second chapter of his *Dissertation Concerning the End for Which God Created the World*, *WJE* 8: 527–536.
21. John W. Cooper, *Panentheism: The Other God of the Philosophers: From Plato to the Present* (Grand Rapids, MI: Baker Academic, 2006), for a survey of many different historic doctrines of panentheism.

22. In fact, there are aspects of Edwards's thought that press beyond panentheism in the direction of pantheism, that is, the identification of the creation with God. I have dealt with this matter elsewhere; see Oliver D. Crisp, "On the Orthodoxy of Jonathan Edwards," *Scottish Journal of Theology* 67, no. 3 (2014): 304–322.
23. I say the universe "appears" to be a closed physical system advisedly. As Alvin Plantinga has recently argued, Newton himself did not think the universe was a closed physical system, though this is often considered to be an implication of Newtonian physics, which, taken together with determinism, provides a reason for resisting theological claims about special divine action in the world. He ascribes the determinism + closed-physical-system view to Laplace, not Newton. See Alvin Plantinga, *Where the Conflict Really Lies: Science, Religion, and Naturalism* (Oxford: Oxford University Press, 2011), chap. 3.
24. There is disagreement amongst Edwards scholars here. Some think Edwards does believe there are physical laws because the world does persist through time. See, e.g., Sang Hyun Lee, *The Philosophical Theology of Jonathan Edwards*, expanded edition (Princeton, NJ: Princeton University Press, 2000). However, I think this view is mistaken and have argued against it in *Jonathan Edwards on God and Creation*. Much of this debate about how to interpret Edwards turns on one of his unpublished notebook entries, "Miscellany 1263: God's Immediate and Arbitrary Operation," which can be found in *WJE* 23: 202–212.
25. Hugh J. McCann and Jonathan L. Kvanvig, "The Occasionalist Proselytizer: A Modified Catechism," in *Philosophical Perspectives*, ed. James Tomberlin, vol. 5, *Philosophy of Religion* (Aterscadero, CA: Ridgeview, 1991), 598.
26. Such as Nicholas Saunders, see note 15. Today, idealism is not a particularly popular doctrine, although there are early signs of a comeback amongst analytically minded philosophers. But here too, there is something to be said for Edwards's view. A world composed of strings of matter or energy is rather closer to the idealist view than the world of inert material solidity of which many early modern materialists conceived. But that aside, Edwards is able to give a reason for resisting materialism that provides a powerful argument for the irreducibility of mind and of the presence of a divine intellect in the world.
27. Arthur Peacocke, *Theology for a Scientific Age: Being and Becoming—Natural, Divine, and Human* (Oxford: Blackwell, 1993).
28. Arthur Peacocke, *All That Is: A Naturalistic Faith for the Twenty-First Century* (Minneapolis: Fortress, 2007), 12, 14, 26, and especially chap. 4.
29. In fact, I have explored the problems with Edwards's views in a number of previous publications, e.g. Oliver D. Crisp, *Jonathan Edwards and the Metaphysics of Sin*, *Jonathan Edwards on God and Creation*, and *Jonathan Edwards among the Theologians* (Grand Rapids, MI: Eerdmans, 2015).
30. In Crisp, *Jonathan Edwards and the Metaphysics of Sin* in particular.
31. Ortwin de Graef, "Discussion with Harry Frankfurt," *Ethical Perspectives* 5, no. 1 (1998): 32.

Selected Bibliography

Berkeley, George. *Principles of Human Knowledge and Three Dialogues between Hylas and Philonous.* Edited by Roger Woodhouse (Harmondsworth: Penguin, 1988). *Principles* first published in 1710, *Three Dialogues* in 1713.

Calvin, John. *The Bondage and Liberation of the Will: A Defence of the Orthodox Doctrine of Human Choice against Pighius.* Edited by A. N. S. Lane, translated by G. I. Davies (Grand Rapids, MI: Baker Academic, 1996).

Cooper, John W. *Panentheism: The Other God of the Philosophers: From Plato to the Present* (Grand Rapids, MI: Baker Academic, 2006).

Crisp, Oliver D. *Jonathan Edwards among the Theologians* (Grand Rapids, MI: Eerdmans, 2015).

Crisp, Oliver D. *Jonathan Edwards and the Metaphysics of Sin* (Aldershot: Ashgate, 2005).

Crisp, Oliver D. *Jonathan Edwards on God and Creation* (Oxford: Oxford University Press, 2012).

Crisp, Oliver D. "On the Orthodoxy of Jonathan Edwards." *Scottish Journal of Theology* 67, no. 3 (2014): 304–322.

De Graef, Ortwin. "Discussion with Harry Frankfurt." *Ethical Perspectives* 5, no. 1 (1998): 15–43.

Edwards, Jonathan. *The Works of Jonathan Edwards.* Vol. 1, *Freedom of the Will.* Edited by Paul Ramsey (New Haven, CT: Yale University Press, 1957).

Frankfurt, Harry G. "Alternate Possibilities and Moral Responsibility." In *The Importance of What We Care about* (Cambridge: Cambridge University Press, 1998), 1–10.

Helm, Paul. *The Providence of God* (Downers Grove, IL: InterVarsity Press, 1993).

Hobbes, Thomas. *De Corpore, Part I: Logic.* Translated by A. P. Martinich (New York: Abaris, 1981). First published in 1655.

Leibniz, Gottfried Wilhelm. *Theodicy: Essays on the Goodness of God, the Freedom of Man and the Origin of Evil.* Edited by Austin Farrer, translated by E. M. Huggard (La Salle, IL: Open Court, 1985). First published in 1710.

Luther, Martin. *The Bondage of the Will.* Translated by J. I. Packer and O. R. Johnson (London: James Clarke, 1957).

McCann, Hugh J., and Jonathan L. Kvanvig. "The Occasionalist Proselytizer: A Modified Catechism." In *Philosophical Perspectives,* edited by James Tomberlin. Vol. 5, *Philosophy of Religion,* 587–615 (Aterscadero, CA: Ridgeview, 1991).

Muller, Richard A. "Grace, Election, and Contingent Choice: Arminius's Gambit and the Reformed Response." In *The Grace of God, The Bondage of The Will,* edited by Thomas R. Schreiner and Bruce A. Ware, vol. 2, 251–278 (Grand Rapids, MI: Baker, 1995).

Patrides, C. A. *The Cambridge Platonists* (Cambridge: Cambridge University Press, 1980).

Peacocke, Arthur. *All That Is: A Naturalistic Faith for the Twenty-First Century* (Minneapolis, MN: Fortress, 2007).

Peacocke, Arthur. *Theology for a Scientific Age: Being and Becoming—Natural, Divine, and Human* (Oxford: Blackwell, 1993).

Roberts, John Russell. *A Metaphysics for the Mob: The Philosophy of George Berkeley* (Oxford: Oxford University Press, 2007).

Van Asselt, Willem J., J. Martin Bac, and Roelf T. te Velde, eds. *Reformed Thought on Freedom: The Concept of Free Choice in Early Modern Reformed Theology* (Grand Rapids, MI: Baker Academic, 2010).

Wainwright, William J. "Jonathan Edwards, William Rowe, and the Necessity of Creation." In *Faith, Freedom, and Rationality: Philosophy of Religion Today*, edited by Jeff Jordan and Daniel Howard-Snyder, 119–133 (Lanham, MD: Rowman and Littlefield, 1996).

PART 3

The Complications of Science

II

Divine Providence in the Clockwork Universe

John Hedley Brooke

Introduction

Almost 150 years separated the great books of Nicolaus Copernicus (1543) and Isaac Newton (1687), a period traditionally described as the "scientific revolution." During those years, Earth was displaced from the center of a circumscribed cosmos as scientists and philosophers revised and expanded their view of the universe. New scientific instruments allowed for exciting discoveries—as when Galileo through his telescope observed the moons of Jupiter and a multitude of stars invisible to the naked eye. The microscope, too, gave exhilarating access to what had been an invisible world. Experimental methods began to gain priority over a long dependence on traditional authority, as when William Harvey demonstrated the lesser and greater circulation of the blood and Robert Boyle conducted original experiments on the physical properties of air.

Increasingly during the seventeenth century, nature came to be seen as a finely tuned machine rather than under the control of "final causes."[1] The doctrine of final causes, which arose out of Aristotelian philosophy, posited that change in nature occurred according to the ends or purposes that were achieved by the change. It was these ends that ultimately dictated the movements of bodies. When a stone fell to the ground it did so in order to return to its "natural place," where it would be reunited with earthly matter of its own kind. This was a very organic view of nature, Aristotle having suggested that, for example, the planets ought to be considered as partaking of life and as having initiative. By contrast, philosophers such as Descartes, Boyle, and Newton envisaged a universe operating according to *laws* of nature that could be expressed in the language of mathematics.[2] We refer today to Kepler's laws of planetary motion, to Galileo's law governing the acceleration of falling bodies, to Boyle's law which captured the inverse relationship between pressure and volume of a gas at constant temperature, to the laws of motion and universal gravitation, by which Newton explained the elliptical orbits of the planets.

These observable regularities of cause and effect helped make comparisons between the universe and machinery attractive and plausible during the seventeenth century. Both Descartes and Boyle liked to compare the universe to the spectacular clock of Strasbourg cathedral. But if the universe ran like a machine, what room was there for God's activity in the world? Was the Christian doctrine of providence compromised by this "mechanical philosophy"? It is tempting to answer "yes" to this last question, especially if one believes that scientific progress has invariably eroded the credibility of religious faith. This was a view—still influential today—championed in nineteenth-century Europe by philosophers Auguste Comte and Ernst Mach, and in America by the outspoken defenders of secular education John William Draper and Andrew Dickson White.[3] But did the scientific revolution achieve the emancipation of science from religious discourse and authority? There are good reasons to regard this familiar refrain critically.[4] Among them is the fact that some of the greatest scientific minds in late seventeenth-century Europe, such as Newton and his German critic Leibniz, developed philosophies of nature that were profoundly shaped by their theological commitments.[5]

In this chapter, I argue that the breakdown of a once-prevalent harmony between Christian theology and Aristotelian natural philosophy did indeed require and stimulate new thinking about God's relationship to nature, but that, far from destroying belief in providence, the consequence was the emergence of new syntheses of science with Christian belief. It is nevertheless undeniable that new metaphors applied to nature during the scientific revolution, such as "clockwork," "law-like," and "mechanical," while originally accommodated, even embedded, in theological literature, were later appropriated to justify deistic and other antiprovidentialist rhetoric.[6]

The Cosmos before Copernicus and Galileo

Although intimations of a sun-centered universe can be found in antiquity, the prevailing view until well into the seventeenth century was that a spherical (not a flat) Earth had a natural place at the center of a series of concentric spheres, which carried the moon and each of the planets around it. The outermost sphere was that of the fixed stars, beyond which was conventionally depicted the abode of God and a hierarchy of angels. An important distinction was made between the sublunary and superlunary regions. Beyond the moon, heavenly bodies moved in repetitive cyclic motion, a sign of immutability and perfection. Beneath the moon, the four elements earth, water, air, and fire had their own spheres, their own natural places, but were so intermingled that imperfection, corruptibility and noncyclic motions were everywhere visible. From a Christian perspective the Earth was at the center of corruption, both theologically (because of the consequences of Adam's "fall") and also physically, at the maximum distance from the perfect heavens.

For Aristotle there was a teleology, a purposiveness, immanent in nature that could be attractive to religious thinkers reflecting on divine will and providence. When interpreting natural phenomena, it was common practice to explore analogies between the human body (the microcosm) and the physical universe (the macrocosm). Here is Leonardo da Vinci: "We can say that the earth has a vegetative soul, and that its flesh is the land, its bones are the structure of the rocks . . . its blood is the pools of water . . . its breathing and its pulse are the ebb and flow of the sea."[7] Analogies of this kind reinforced images of the cosmos as an organism. In organic processes, seeds grew to become plants and trees, embryos developed to become living creatures, underlining the presence of goal-directed processes in nature, the end (Aristotle's final cause) dictating the course of development. One of Aristotle's major contributions to biology was his detailed observational study of the chick embryo and its development. When the intricate structures of living things were apparently so well adapted to their functions (the eye for seeing, the ear for hearing, a bird's wing for flying . . .) it was easy to see in nature a complex interweaving of means and ends.

When Aristotle's philosophy was translated into Latin from Arabic and Greek sources in the twelfth and thirteenth centuries it did, however, pose some problems for the Christian religion. This was because Aristotle had affirmed the eternity (not an original creation) of the world—a view that was also problematic for Jewish and Muslim scholars. Aristotle also affirmed the mortality of the soul. Moreover, the causes he adduced when explaining phenomena were always *natural* causes, immanent in nature, not instigated or directed supernaturally. Despite the high value placed on natural philosophy by the twelfth-century Jewish scholar Maimonides, his followers had to contend with more traditional voices who questioned whether Greek wisdom should have any place in Jewish scholarship.[8] Comparable concerns were sometimes expressed within Islamic and Christian cultures. (The response to the Aristotelian challenge by the Christian theologian Thomas Aquinas is discussed in detail in chapter 8 of this book). In brief, Aquinas argued that Aristotle's physics was incomplete because it could not fully account for the way in which physical bodies, which lacked knowledge, could act in concert with others to achieve certain ends. In his *Summa Theologiae,* Aquinas argued that whatever lacks knowledge cannot move toward an end unless directed by some being endowed with knowledge and intelligence. This was the fifth of the "five ways" in which Aquinas affirmed the rationality of belief in a transcendent deity. It was not so much a proof of the existence of God as a demonstration that Aristotle's philosophy was harmless to Christian theism, since it was ultimately incoherent without it. Even if the universe had always existed, a transcendent power would nevertheless be needed to sustain it. Aquinas showed that "an eternal world, one without a beginning to time, would be no less a created world."[9]

To the extent that Christian theology and Aristotelian philosophy achieved some harmony via Aquinas, the study of nature married faith in divine providence to the belief that final causes were to be sought in natural phenomena. This is clear from texts such as the *Religio Medici* (1642) of the pious physician Sir Thomas Browne, who argued that every created thing had a purpose in its being and operation. "This," he wrote, "is the cause I grope after in the works of nature; on this hangs the providence of God."[10] But by the middle of the seventeenth century, Browne's contemporaries faced a new challenge. The type of cause Browne had looked for in seeking to understand the natural world was being marginalized, even banished from scientific research. Final causes, according to Francis Bacon, were like "barren virgins"—they couldn't produce fruitful knowledge. They were also excluded from scientific study in the clockwork universe of Descartes. It was the immediate, mechanical causes of phenomena (the "efficient causes" in Aristotelian terminology) that had to be given precedence.[11] It is therefore time to look more closely at the theological anxieties raised by this mechanization of nature, and related scientific innovations, in seventeenth-century Europe.

Innovation and Anxiety

In 1605, Lutheran astronomer Johannes Kepler made a prophetic announcement of mechanistic thinking when he reported that his aim was "to show that the celestial machine is to be likened not to a divine organism but rather to clockwork."[12] Kepler was a convert to Copernican astronomy, in which the Earth orbited the Sun. Like Copernicus, Kepler was impressed by the greater mathematical harmony arising from this arrangement. When he spoke of the harmony of the world Kepler had in mind examples of both mathematical and musical harmony. He even suggested that each planet had a melody as it orbited the Sun, its pitch rising and falling as it gained and lost speed. It was Kepler who showed that the planets have elliptical orbits, accelerating as they approach their closest position to the Sun, decelerating as they move further away. Their music was to be perceived not by the ear but by the intellect. Kepler did, however, place the notes on a musical stave and suggested that, at the moment when God created the world, they would have combined in perfect harmony. In his desire to display the geometry of creation, Kepler believed he was thinking God's thoughts after him.

The Copernican innovation did, however, generate serious apprehension among both Catholic and Protestant thinkers. There were verses in Scripture, such as Joshua 10:12, which, if taken literally, implied that the Sun, not the Earth, was the body in motion. The Protestant astronomer Tycho Brahe found an ingenious, but cumbersome, solution to this inconsistency when he proposed that all the planets (but not the Earth) orbit the Sun, which, carrying the planets with it, in turn orbits a central, stationary Earth. This model proved attractive to several Jesuit astronomers and created a problem for Galileo because it was difficult to disprove. Galileo also had to contend with many common-sense objections to the Earth's motion. Why, if Earth is moving, does an object dropped from the top of a tower not hit the ground some way behind the foot of the tower? Surely, while the object was falling, Earth and the tower would have moved on? Galileo had to develop a concept of inertia to deal with the problem. But answering objections was not the same as providing definitive proof. This is why Galileo prized an argument based on the phenomenon of the tides.

He proposed that the tidal oscillations were analogous to what happened to the water carried by barges when they hit the dockside in Venice. The sudden jolt set up an oscillation. Galileo's argument was that Earth itself suffered a series of jolts arising from the combination of two motions: its daily rotation on its axis and its annual revolution around the Sun. We shall return to this argument later, but the Catholic Church did try to suppress it because it treated Earth's motion as a physical reality and not simply as a mathematical hypothesis. In disobeying Pope Urban VIII's prohibition on the use of the argument, Galileo, who always claimed to be a loyal Catholic, exposed himself to censure.[13] But scriptural objections also contributed to Galileo's downfall, since his innovative exegesis contravened what Cardinal Robert Bellarmine claimed was the consensual view of the Church Fathers.[14]

With specific reference to doctrines of providence, the new heliocentric astronomy could generate other anxieties. Displaced, disoriented, and demeaned, could humankind still plausibly believe that it was at the center of God's care and attention? As we shall see, this problem has been exaggerated, but it was potentially magnified by the magnification of the universe itself. If the Earth orbited the Sun, it should in principle be possible to detect stellar parallax—a consequential shift in the perceived position of one star relative to another in the same line of sight. The failure to detect this phenomenon was an early objection to the new astronomy, but was explicable if the distance to the stars far exceeded that previously supposed.

"What is man that thou art mindful of him?" was a question uttered in amazement by the Psalmist. Just *how* mindful was an issue raised by a further aspect of the new science. Following the Copernican innovation, the Earth was now a planet rather than a distinctive body at the center of a cosmos. This meant that analogies were quickly drawn between the Earth and other planets, leading to the supposition that intelligent life might exist elsewhere in the universe.[15] While theologians had been accustomed to the idea that God had the power to create other worlds, the belief that God had actually done so could be discomfiting. It was so for Philip Melanchthon, who took charge of Martin Luther's educational reforms. To imagine other inhabited worlds was to imagine that Christ might have died and been resurrected more than once, or that their inhabitants might be restored to eternal life without a knowledge of the Son of God.

Concerns of this kind were compounded by the notion that there was no divine providence in the world, only the natural motions and collisions of atoms as they moved through the void. Epicurus and other atomists of antiquity entertained the idea of the existence of an infinite plurality of worlds in an infinite universe. It was through the chance combinations of atoms that these worlds came into, and passed out of, being. The text of the Roman poet Lucretius, *De Rerum Natura* (*On the Nature of Things*), enshrined this view and had passed through many editions following its early 15th-century rediscovery in Europe. In many ways it presented the sharpest antithesis between chance and providence that seventeenth-century philosophers and theologians had to face. Not even the gods, according to Lucretius, could produce something out of nothing. Were it to be possible, it would be a recipe for disorder. The concept of divine providence was explicitly attacked, with particular reference to the permeation of the world by disease. Observing the incessant motions of dust particles in sunlight, Lucretius even gave empirical content to his atomistic worldview.

The most prominent seventeenth-century mechanist, René Descartes, was not strictly an atomist since he argued for the indefinite divisibility of matter and against the possibility of a vacuum in nature. But his philosophy of nature had much in common with that of the atomists. Space was filled with subtle matter, swirling vortices of which carried the planets around the Sun like corks floating on water. Even phenomena such as magnetic attraction, which at first sight might appear irreducible to mechanistic modelling, Descartes managed to explain by invoking the behavior of rotating screw-like particles. If they accumulated between the magnet and the iron, repulsion would ensue; if they were able to penetrate receptive channels in the iron they would leave a vacuum in their wake that caused attraction. Mechanical models of this kind conformed to Descartes's stipulation of clear and distinct ideas as prerequisites of scientific explanation.[16] Portentously he eliminated final causes from the study of nature, arguing that it was presumptuous to claim knowledge of divine ends and purposes.

This was to be troublesome for Boyle, who felt that Descartes was discarding the most powerful argument for God's existence—the argument from design. If this were not enough, Descartes's reduction of animals to machines, which he justified by their lack of reason and inability to speak, almost invited a materialistic understanding of humans, also. One who appeared to accept the invitation was the philosopher Thomas Hobbes, notorious for urging the corporeality of the soul. Moreover, in seeking to derive the qualities of bodies from the primary principles of matter in motion, Descartes created a particular problem for the Catholic Church, which could not see how to square his analysis with its understanding of the Eucharist, at which the bread and wine were believed to be transmuted into the body and blood of Christ.[17] A similar concern had been expressed behind the scenes when Galileo's atomism was made public in his *Assayer* (1623), though the suggestion of Pietro Redondi that this was the primary and ulterior reason for his condemnation has not found favor.[18]

In constructing mechanical models for the workings of nature, it was imperative for Descartes to consider how motion was transferred from one body to another. This was the context in which he proposed three "laws" of motion, one of which governed the exchange of motion when two bodies collided. This was central to a physics of impact, in which the total quantity of motion in the world remained the same. In another of his laws, Descartes anticipated Newton's first law of motion, the principle of linear inertia. In a letter of April 1630 to the Minim priest Marin Mersenne, he made it clear that "it is God who has laid down these laws in nature just as a king lays down laws in his kingdom."[19] Despite this theological reassurance, Descartes's mechanical philosophy could easily raise anxiety about the scope of divine providence. It was one thing for God to lay down laws, but was this an adequate account of a continued involvement with creation?

Providence in the Clockwork Universe: Strategies of Reassurance

Each of the concerns raised by these scientific innovations was addressed by natural philosophers themselves who, in their attempts to alleviate anxiety, reconstructed the relations between science and theology. In some cases it may have been their own doubts and anxiety that drove them, as they devised arguments to reassure themselves. Doubts, of course, are not foreign to faith, as Robert Boyle observed: "He whose faith never doubted, may justly doubt of his faith."[20] Nevertheless, in the construction of new syntheses between science and theology, the changes that took place resulted more from constructive attempts to reach mutual accommodation than from downright hostility between deeply polarized and impersonal forces.[21]

There were, for example, strategies to cope with the Copernican threat to Scripture. In his *Letter to the Grand Duchess Christina* (1615), Galileo appealed to the "accommodation" thesis to argue that biblical verses, which might appear to conflict with the new astronomy, had used language accommodated to the needs and perceptions of common folk. They were never intended to teach technical science and should not therefore be invoked to attack demonstrable scientific truths. The Bible teaches how to go to heaven not how heaven goes.[22] For many contingent reasons, including the politics of the Counter-Reformation and the breakdown of his once-cordial relationship with Pope Urban VIII, this argument was not sufficient to earn Galileo a reprieve.[23] It was, however, extensively and successfully invoked by Protestant astronomers.[24] Calvin had earlier stressed the accommodation of biblical language to the limitations of our fallen nature, asserting that those who wished to learn astronomy should not do so from Scripture: "He who would learn astronomy and other recondite arts, let him go elsewhere."[25]

Was belief in providence jeopardized by the displacement of humanity from the center of the cosmos? Contrary to a common mythology, it was possible to argue that humanity was not downgraded but actually elevated by being placed on a planet (i.e., in the heavenly region) instead of residing where all was imperfect and corruptible.[26] Kepler could claim that humans at last occupied their true place, as citizens of a planet occupying the central orbit in the solar system, revolving around what he believed was the largest sun in the universe.[27] It was also a question whether God's providential concern for humanity had to depend on physical location. This had already been denied by some Christian scholars, notably the fifteenth-century German theologian Nicholas of Cusa.[28] God's providential care was assured in Scripture and in having taken human flesh in the person of Jesus Christ.

How subversive was belief in the plurality of worlds? There was anxiety on this subject not least because of the execution of Giordano Bruno in Rome in 1600, as a political opponent of the Catholic Church and one who refused to renounce his heretical assertions. It was, however, possible to enlist theological arguments to support the idea of extraterrestrial life. Bruno had submitted that an infinite plurality of worlds was an appropriate expression of the infinite power of God.[29] Moreover, it was possible to argue that an omnipotent and loving God need not be prevented from caring for humankind by virtue of having other worlds to supervise. John Wilkins, the major popularizer of Copernican astronomy in England, insisted that life on other worlds need not be intelligent life; even if it were, it need not be human in its attributes; even if it were human-like, it might not have sinned and be in need of redemption; and even if it had, why should Christ's death not be so universally efficacious as to embrace them?[30] This left open the question how ETs would learn of their salvation, but was the situation so different from the situation of many on Earth who inhabited distant, inaccessible lands? Whether multiple incarnations were implied by multiple worlds would prove a divisive issue within Christendom,[31] but the affirmation of extraterrestrials was readily integrated into Christian natural theology, offering as it did a rationale for that myriad of stars revealed by Galileo's telescope.[32] They had the purpose of illuminating other worlds.

The atomism of antiquity, with its emphasis on the chance collision of atoms rather than divine supervision, was undoubtedly a challenge to a Christian doctrine of providence and was taken very seriously indeed. Rejoinders were, however, possible and one came from the great champion of experimental science Francis Bacon. In his essay *Of Atheism*, Bacon observed that a universe containing only atoms in motion was in far greater need of the guiding hand of providence than the traditional universe of Aristotle, where everything had its natural place and where final causes guaranteed an orderly system. In this way it was possible to baptize the atomist doctrine, as the French Catholic priest Pierre Gassendi soon showed.[33] Providence had played a foundational role in establishing the position, arrangement, and motions of the atoms that would guarantee a viable world: "Just as the clockmaker applies his intelligence to efficient causes to produce an elegant timepiece, so God utilizes efficient causes in designing the world."[34] Such was God's absolute power that any effect produced by secondary causes could be achieved directly if God willed it. Descartes, too, had ways of alleviating the anxiety occasioned by his mechanical philosophy. He did not believe that motion was intrinsic to matter. It was conserved in the world by the God who had been its source, the God, he asserted, who must recreate the world moment by moment. The laws of nature that Descartes formulated simply reflected God's constancy and immutability.[35]

But what of Descartes's exclusion of final causes from scientific enquiry, undermining attempts to demonstrate God's providence from the workings of nature? As an orthodox Christian and exponent of the mechanical philosophy himself, Robert Boyle felt compelled to respond. His reasons for favoring clockwork images of the universe included the fact that they created space for pious scientific inquiry. The task of the natural philosopher was to probe behind the clock face of nature to search out the most probable mechanisms at work.[36] At the same time, this need not preclude reflection on God's purposes in nature. Clocks and other machines, are, after all, designed and built for purposes. Boyle conceded that not all features of nature evince design and that there may be purposes in things we cannot discern; but, in an essay explicitly directed against Descartes, he insisted that in some cases final causes were transparent: the eye was surely designed to see with.[37] Questions about the functions and purposes of things could even be productive of new scientific knowledge. Boyle was pleased to report that William Harvey's research on the circulation of the blood had been advanced by asking what purpose was served by valves in the veins. It was important to Boyle that nature was not autonomous. For matter to obey the dictates of the divine will and to follow the laws of nature, there had to be a divine presence, a "preserving concourse." Matter, if left to its own devices, Boyle suggested, was too stupid to know what a law is!

Because the law metaphor resonated with belief in divine legislation, there was no real difficulty in synthesizing a mechanical philosophy with a theistic belief in "general providence."[38] But what of "special providence"? This was the belief that God had a more intimate relationship to individual human lives than to other living and nonliving creations. A life led in faith, in prayer and thanksgiving, was a life in which one looked to God for mercy and guidance in the details of one's earthly pilgrimage. The belief that prayers could be answered, or even that miracles had happened, suggested a powerful deity who could change the course of events from what they would otherwise have been without some form of intervention. Even here, however, the difficulty has been exaggerated. For Boyle, it was not a problem to have God taking an interest in human affairs, even controlling or responding to the minutiae of events. This was because Boyle saw an analogy between the exercise of the divine and human wills. Just as we can move matter by our minds, as when we move our limbs, so God as mental agency can move the matter in nature. Newton was to use a similar argument in his *Opticks*, claiming that God was more able to initiate events in the world than we are to move our bodies.[39] But why, if God can exert such control over the details of creation, is so much individual suffering permitted? Boyle's reply was that God had ordained some laws that were so fundamental to the general good of the universe that it was unrealistic to suppose they would be suspended to meet the needs, for example, of a man about to fall off a cliff. Striking a balance between the desiderata of general and special providence would remain a problem for Christian theologians, irrespective of whether the universe was a machine or not; but Boyle firmly believed that God could "intermeddle" with creation,[40] a fact most decisively shown by the miracles of Christ, especially his Resurrection. Thus Boyle protected a sense of providence that had deep personal meaning.[41] He believed, for example, that he had received guidance ("pregnant hints") from God in the execution of his scientific work.

There certainly were Christians troubled by the clockwork universe. The moderate puritan Richard Baxter complained that the mechanical philosophers "give so much more to mere matter and motion, than is truly due, and know or say so much too little of spirits, active natures, vital powers, which are the true principles of motion, that they differ as much from true philosophers, as a carcass or a clock from a living man."[42] Was Boyle then not a true philosopher? In fact he would have sympathized with Baxter's reference to "spirits," because central to Boyle's defense of providence was his restricting the scope of mechanism. Contrary to Hobbes, whose views on the materiality of the soul were widely regarded as idiosyncratic (albeit dangerously so), Boyle did not exclude spirit agencies from the world. He even believed that if the philosopher's stone of the alchemists could be found it might have the property of attracting spirits, hopefully angelic rather than demonic.[43] In the last analysis there was more to God's creation than clockwork machinery, a point on which Boyle's contemporary Henry More was even more insistent. In Newton's universe, too, "active principles" and "vital powers" enriched God's creation. It is a mistake to conflate Newton with Descartes when referring to the clockwork universe.

Choice Not Chance in Newton's Universe

For several reasons, Newton's philosophy of nature is commonly seen as the apotheosis of the clockwork universe. He subscribed to an atomic theory of matter and a particulate theory of light. His three laws of motion were an advance on those proposed by Descartes, and in his science he aimed to quantify the forces of nature such as gravity. This quantification introduced a new precision and sophistication into natural philosophy. For example, Newton showed that if the magnitude of the gravitational force between any two bodies was directly proportional to the product of their masses and inversely proportional to the square of the distance between them, he could explain the elliptical orbits of the planets with greater precision than had been possible for Descartes with his pictorial images of interlocking material vortices. Because Newton understood his laws to be universal, the entire creation could be interpreted as a single, unified, and homogeneous entity, quite different from the traditional cosmos of the scholastic philosophers with its division between sublunary and superlunary realms.

When, however, Newton's science is examined more closely, the image of clockwork fails to capture the richness of his theology of nature. Newton's universe is emphatically not the product of unguided atomic motions. It is the product of choice, not chance—choices made by the divine will, whose control over nature is expressed through the laws the creator has ordained, but which, by virtue of God's dominion, could in principle be changed.[44] In several respects Newton's universe was less remorselessly mechanistic than that of Descartes. The gravitational force was itself an example of an invisible agency in nature, seemingly acting at a distance in a manner that Descartes would have repudiated. Forces of attraction and repulsion banished in France were reinstated in England. When Newton discussed the sources of motion in the world, he explicitly invoked "active principles," as in Query 31 of his *Opticks*: "Seeing ... the variety of motion which we find in the world is always decreasing, there is a necessity of conserving and recruiting it by active principles, such as are the cause of gravity ... and the cause of fermentation. ... For we meet with very little motion in the world, besides what is owing to these active principles."[45]

Nature in other words is not dead like a machine. It has a vitality that transcends clockwork mechanism, as in the growth of vegetation. In this less mechanistic world, God is not remote from nature but omnipresent in it, even constituting space. This is a God not deprived of providential control but a "powerful ever-living Agent, who being in all places, is more able by his Will to move the bodies within his boundless uniform sensorium, and thereby to form and reform the parts of the universe, than we are by our will to move the parts of our own bodies."[46] For Newton there is an overarching providence at work that he believed could be demonstrated from history as well as nature, notably by the fulfillment of biblical prophecies.[47] Far from science invalidating conceptions of providence, it offered support. The setting up of the planetary orbits argued a cause "not blind and fortuitous, but very well skilled in mechanics and geometry."[48] An inverse-square law of gravitation would have been compatible with parabolic and hyperbolic trajectories for the planets, but in ensuring stable elliptical orbits, God had exercised choice. It was not a matter of chance.

Competing Conceptions of Providence: Newton and Leibniz

In framing discussions of the relations between science and religion it is easy to construct a narrative in which scientific innovation is the driving force for change: science impacts Christian theology, sometimes sympathetically, sometimes adversely. To some degree this is the model I have followed in this chapter, recognizing that scientists (then called "natural philosophers") occasionally took upon themselves the role of theologian. This switching of roles sometimes contributed to distrust from those who regarded themselves as safeguarding Christian tradition. Galileo suffered for trespassing on the prerogatives of theologians in the Catholic Church. In Protestant churches, where there was no comparably strong centralized authority, natural philosophers by and large (though not invariably) enjoyed greater freedom to develop new ways of integrating their science and religion.[49] In some cases, as with Boyle and Newton, this exercise was undertaken with a deep commitment to the study of Scripture. As befit one born on Christmas day, Newton aimed for nothing less than a definitive exegesis of two books—God's word and God's works. To achieve that end, he set down no fewer than fifteen rules for the correct interpretation of Scripture, placing a premium on simplicity.[50] Crucially, in the construction of new syntheses there was much more involved than the unidirectional impact of science on religion. Philosophical and theological ideas could influence the way the science was interpreted and, in some cases, even shape its content. Competing understandings of providence could eventuate in competing systems of natural philosophy.

The celebrated conflict between Newton and his German critic Leibniz illustrates this point. Newton's belief in the universality of his law of gravitation was grounded, at least in part, in his belief that the unity of the universe was a consequence of its creation by a single mind which sustained it. As he explained: "If there be an universal life and all space be the sensorium of a thinking being who by immediate presence perceives all things in it . . . the laws of motion arising from life or will may be of universal extent."[51] But Newton's principle of gravitational attraction failed to attract

Leibniz, who also protested against Newton's admission of a vacuum in nature. His protest was grounded in the theological consideration that the existence of a vacuum would mean that God must have stopped creating matter at a certain arbitrary point. This Leibniz could not admit, given his belief that "the more matter there is, the more God has occasion to exercise his wisdom and power."[52] Their controversy had many dimensions, personal, philosophical, and political. It was intensified by their respective priority claims for the invention of the calculus. But at the heart of their disagreements were divergent interpretations of the clockwork universe. These are visible in an extensive correspondence between Leibniz and Newton's defender Samuel Clarke.

In a letter of 1715 to Caroline, Princess of Wales, with whom he had been in correspondence since 1706, Leibniz complained that "Sir Isaac Newton, and his followers have ... a very odd opinion concerning the work of God. According to their doctrine, God Almighty wants to wind up his watch from time to time: otherwise it would cease to move."[53] This was a reference to Newton's suggestion that, over the course of time, the stability of the solar system would be threatened by a retarding of the planets in their orbits due to friction with the ether. Additionally, the sun would lose matter to evaporation. A periodic reformation of the system would be required, achieved perhaps by comets passing close to the Sun and transferring some of their matter to it through gravitational attraction. Although Newton looked to natural causes to explain how the restabilization occurred, he undoubtedly believed their action was under the guiding hand of providence. Hence Leibniz's jibe that "the machine of God's making is so imperfect according to these gentlemen that he is obliged to clean it now and then by an extraordinary concourse, and even to mend it, as a clockmaker mends his work."[54] Newton's God, according to Leibniz, was a second-rate clockmaker, whereas he, Leibniz, believed the world to embody a beautiful and inviolable preestablished order. Driving his point home, Leibniz asserted his belief that "when God works miracles, he does not do it in order to supply the wants of nature, but those of grace."[55]

Underlying this divergence were two contrasting understandings of providence. Newton's science was incorporated within a metaphysics in which God's freedom was celebrated—a freedom to choose how the natural world should be configured, including the freedom to create a world in which divine intervention might be necessary from time to time. For Leibniz it was more important to stress not divine freedom but the perfection of God's foresight. Even God must have been constrained, by virtue of having to create the *best* of all possible worlds, and it was hard to see how Newton's depiction conformed to that specification. In the ensuing exchange, Leibniz would accuse Clarke of holding a semideistic position, in which God intervened from outside the universe. Clarke in turn would accuse Leibniz of a fully deistic position in which the physical world, once created, had complete autonomy. Philosophically and theologically, their controversy was wide-ranging. Leibniz took exception to Newton's reference to space as God's "sensorium" in which all events in the world were perceived. Newton had written that God was all eye, all ear, all power to perceive. Leibniz protested that if God sensed and moved matter as we can with our bodies, this surely turned God into a corporeal (material) being with the universe as God's body. Newton emphatically rejected this inference, but the disagreement again shows how philosophical and theological preferences were finding expression in competing understandings of science and its implications for an understanding of providence. The tension between celebrating God's sovereign freedom and celebrating God's rational foresight would recur many times in Christian natural theology.

Conclusion: The Ambivalence of a Clockwork Universe

To study and interpret the universe as if it were a machine, or to see it as composed of many interlocking machines, posed no obvious threat to a Christian doctrine of *creation*. Machines are just the kind of thing that do not, and cannot, spring into existence by themselves. Even Descartes, who suggested how the solar system might have developed from the motions and impact of primordial matter, ascribed the creation of that matter to the God who conserved motion in the creation. In many ways the mechanical philosophy strengthened belief in a creator. The practice of comparing the universe and its components with well-designed clockwork would continue as a feature of Christian apologetics during the eighteenth century and was to underpin the famous design argument of William Paley.[56] Paley's *Natural Theology* (1802) is the subject of chapter 12 by Alister McGrath.

Historians have, however, argued that, by giving so much weight to arguments for design, Christian natural philosophers were in danger of praising God as creator rather than redeemer.[57] With specific reference to the doctrine of providence, the scientists we have been considering found ways of combining explanations in terms of natural causes with the belief that their causal potency derived from, and was continually sustained by, God's power. A tempting analogy, though not then available, might be with electric clocks! It was possible to acknowledge "chance" events in nature, as when otherwise independent causal chains intersected. Chance events of this kind would not be understood as undetermined. But the reification of "chance" as a causal agent itself was strenuously resisted, as when Newton set out to show that the laws and configuration of the universe were the product of divine *choice*, not chance. For some, including Galileo's French contemporary Marin Mersenne, the mechanical philosophy could even be a resource for the Catholic Church in upholding its belief in the reality of contemporary miracles against the skepticism of Protestant critics. If no mechanical explanation could be given of an unusual occurrence, it might qualify as a genuine miracle rather than a mere marvel.[58] Nor was there any specific threat to the belief that providence could make use of human agency in fulfilling the divine will. When the most famous of all diplomats for science, Francis Bacon, promised improvements in medicine and agriculture that would bring relief to humankind, it was not difficult to see in scientific progress itself the working out of God's providence.[59]

Nevertheless, clockwork metaphors for the universe were susceptible to many interpretations, not all as reverential as those we have considered. After all, once wound up, clocks run by themselves. Radical inferences to a deity no longer active could then prove irresistible to those with anticlerical leanings. When Boyle once referred to the physical world as a "self-moving engine," he almost invited the charge of deism, insinuated (though later rescinded) by his fellow naturalist John Ray.[60] An emphasis on the *laws* of nature, which in the philosophies of Descartes, Boyle, and Newton presupposed a divine legislator, could shift during the Enlightenment toward more radical ground when, as in the philosophy of David Hume, the "law" metaphor was recast to refer simply to regularities in nature as we experience them, not to divinely ordained powers. Even if the universe resembled a machine more than anything else (which Hume disputed), the analogy was too fragile to support proofs of God's existence. Nor could it show that the universe was the product of a single being, since machines were often the work of many hands.[61] Ironically, too, the reinterpretation of the doctrine of providence through the categories of science gave it more precision, making it an easier target for Enlightenment critics. It has been said that Newton's God was like a cosmic plumber who had a service contract with the universe. Despite the caricature, Newton's providential God was to prove vulnerable to the later science of Laplace, who showed mathematically how the planetary orbits could be self-stabilizing (Hahn 1986).[62] In such eventualities there is a useful lesson for all who might be tempted to overburden the latest scientific theories with vindications of their faith or (as with contemporary defenders of "intelligent design") to pin their hopes on what they believe current scientific theories cannot explain. Old analogies between nature and delicately designed clockwork could not be safe from future developments in science. During the nineteenth century, as the sciences of geology and evolutionary biology progressed, the natural world would be reconceived as an unfolding and unfinished historical process, with a challenging set of new implications for the understanding of providence.

Notes

1. Margret J. Osler, *Reconfiguring the World: Nature, God, and Human Understanding from the Middle Ages to Early Modern Europe* (Baltimore, MD: Johns Hopkins University Press, 2010), 77–93.
2. Friedrich Steinle, "From Principles to Regularities: Tracing 'Laws of Nature' in Early Modern France and England," in *Natural Law and Laws of Nature in Early Modern Europe*, ed. Lorraine Daston and Michael Stolleis, 215–231 (Farnham: Ashgate, 2008).
3. Margret J. Osler, "Religion and the Changing Historiography of the Scientific Revolution," in *Science and Religion: New Historical Perspectives*, ed. Thomas Dixon, Geoffrey Cantor, and Stephen Pumfrey, 71–86 (Cambridge: Cambridge University Press, 2010).
4. Ronald L. Numbers, eds., *Galileo Goes to Jail and Other Myths about Science and Religion* (Cambridge: MA: Harvard University Press, 2009), 90–98.
5. Denis Alexander, eds., *The Issac Newton Guidebook*. (Cambridge: Faraday Institute, 2012).
6. John Hedley Brooke, *Science and Religion: Some Historical Perspectives* (Cambridge: Cambridge University Press, 2014), 158–205.
7. Peter Burke, *Tradition and Innovation in Renaissance Italy* (London: Fontana, 1972), 208.
8. Noah Efron, "Early Judaism," in *Science and Religion around the World*, ed. John Hedley Brooke and Ronald L. Numbers, 20–43 (New York: Oxford University Press, 2011).

9. William E. Carroll, "Aquinas and Contemporary Cosmology: Creation and Beginnings," in *Georges Lemaître: Life, Science and Legacy*, ed. Rodney Holder and Simon Mitton, 75–88 (London: Springer, 2012).
10. Brooke, *Science and Religion*, 72.
11. Carolyn Merchant, *The Death of Nature: Women, Ecology and the Scientific Revolution* (London: Wildwood House, 1982), 192–235.
12. Robert S. Westman, "Magical Reform and Astronomical Reform: The Yates Thesis Reconsidered," in *Hermeticism and the Scientific Revolution* by Robert S. Westman and J. E. McGuire, 1–90 (Los Angeles: University of California, 1977).
13. Annibale Fantoli, *Galileo: For Copernicanism and for the Church*, trans. George V. Coyne (Vatican City and Notre Dame, IN: Vatican Observatory and University of Notre Dame Press, 1994), 310–311; William Shea and Mariano Artigas, *Galileo Observed: Science and the Politics of Belief* (Sagamore Beach, MA: Science History Publications, 2006), 140–142.
14. Maurice Finocchiaro, *The Galileo Affair: A Documentary History* (Berkeley: University of California Press, 1989), 67–69.
15. Steven J. Dick, *Plurality of Worlds: The Extraterrestrial Life Debate from Democritus to Kant* (Cambridge: Cambridge University Press, 1982).
16. Richard Westfall, *The Construction of Modern Science: Mechanisms and Mechanics* (Cambridge: Cambridge University Press, 1971).
17. Trevor McClaughlin, "Censorship and Defenders of the Cartesian Faith in Mid-Seventeenth Century France," *Journal of the History of Ideas* 40, no. 4 (1979): 563–581.
18. Pietro Redondi, *Galileo Eretico* (Turin: Einaudi, 1983); trans. Raymond Rosenthal as *Galileo Heretic* (Princeton, NJ: Princeton University Press, 1987); Maurice A. Finocchiaro, *Retrying Galileo, 1633–1992* (Berkeley: University of California Press, 2005), 362–363.
19. René Descartes, *Descartes: Philosophical Writings*, ed. and trans. Elizabeth Anscombe and Peter Thomas Geach (London: Nelson, 1954), 259.
20. Edward Davis, "Robert Boyle's Religious Life, Attitudes, and Vocation," *Science and Christian Belief* 19, no. 2 (2007): 120.
21. William B. Ashworth Jr., "Christianity and the Mechanistic Universe," in *When Science and Christianity Meet*, ed. David C. Lindberg and Ronald L. Numbers, 61–84 (Chicago: University of Chicago Press, 2003); Katherine Calloway, *Natural Theology in the Scientific Revolution* (London: Pickering and Chatto, 2014).
22. Finocchiaro, *Galileo Affair*, 87–118.
23. Ernan McMullin, ed., *The Church and Galileo* (Notre Dame, IN: University of Notre Dame Press, 2005).
24. Stephen Snobelen, "'In the Language of Men': The Hermeneutics of Accommodation in the Scientific Revolution," in *Nature and Scripture*

in the Abrahamic Religions: Up to 1700, ed. Jitse M. van der Meer and Scott Mandelbrote, vol. 2, 691–732 (Leiden: Brill, 2008).

25. Reijer Hooykaas, *Religion and the Rise of Modern Science* (Edinburgh: Scottish Academic Press, 1972), 118.
26. Dennis Danielson, "The Great Copernican Cliché," *American Journal of Physics* 69, no. 10 (2001): 1029–1035; Numbers, *Galileo Goes to Jail and Other Myths*, 50–58.
27. Keneth J. Howell, *God's Two Books: Copernican Cosmology and Biblical Interpretation in Early Modern Science* (Notre Dame, IN: University of Notre Dame Press, 2002), 109–135.
28. Dorothy Koenigsberger, *Renaissance Man and Creative Thinking: A History of Concepts of Harmony, 1400–1700* (Hassocks: Harvester, 1979), 103–133.
29. Westman, "Magical Reform and Astronomical Reform," 24–30.
30. Brooke, *Science and Religion*, 118.
31. David Wilkinson, *Science, Religion, and the Search for Extraterrestrial Intelligence* (Oxford: Oxford University Press, 2013), 150–171.
32. Dick, *Plurality of Worlds*, 151–156; Brooke, "Natural Theology and the Plurality of Worlds"; Michael Crowe, *The Extraterrestrial Life Debate, 1750–1900* (Cambridge: Cambridge University Press, 1986).
33. Margret J. Osler, *Divine Will and the Mechanical Philosophy: Gassendi and Descartes on Contingency and Necessity in the Created World* (Cambridge: Cambridge University Press, 1994), 36–57.
34. Ibid., 49.
35. Descartes, *Philosophical Writings*, 215.
36. Laurens Laudan, "The Clockwork Metaphor and Probabilism: The Impact of Descartes on English Methodological Thought, 1650–55," *Annals of Science* 22, no. 2 (1966): 73–104.
37. Robert Boyle, The Works of Robert Boyle, ed. Michael Hunter and Edward B. Davis, vol. 11, *Disquisition about the Final Causes of Natural Things* [1688] (London: Pickering and Chatto, 1999–2000), 79.
38. Richard Westfall, *Science and Religion in Seventeenth-Century England* (New Haven, CT: Yale University Press, 1958).
39. Isaac Newton, *Opticks* (New York: Dover, 1952), 403. First published in 1704.
40. Robert Boyle, *Selected Philosophical Papers of Robert Boyle*, ed. M. A. Stewart (Manchester: Manchester University Press, 1979), 155–175.
41. Michael Hunter, *Robert Boyle: Between God and Science* (New Haven, CT: Yale University Press, 2009).
42. Piyo M. Rattansi, "The Social Interpretation of Science in the Seventeenth Century," in *Science and Society, 1600–1900*, ed. Peter Mathias (Cambridge: Cambridge University Press, 1972), 26.
43. Lawrence Principe, *The Aspiring Adept: Robert Boyle and his Alchemical Quest* (Princeton, NJ: Princeton University Press, 1998), 203–205.

44. James E. Force, "Newton's God of Dominion: The Unity of Newton's Theological, Scientific, and Political Thought," in *Essays on the Context, Nature and Influence of Isaac Newton's Theology*, ed. James E. Force and Richard H. Popkin, 75–102 (Dordrecht: Kluwer, 1990).
45. Newton, *Opticks*, 399.
46. Ibid., 403.
47. Sarah Hutton, "More, Newton, and the Language of Biblical Prophecy," in *The Books of Nature and Scripture*, ed. James E. Force and Richard H. Popkin, 39–53 (Dordrecht: Kluwer, 1990); Frank E. Manuel, *The Religion of Isaac Newton* (Oxford: Oxford University Press, 1974), 83–104.
48. Isaac Newton, Letter to Richard Bentley, December 10, 1692, in *Newton's Philosophy of Nature*, ed. H. S. Thayer (New York: Hafner, 1953), 48–49.
49. John Hedley Brooke, *Science and Religion: Some Historical Perspectives* (Canto Classics) (Cambridge: Cambridge University Press, 2014), 110–157; Peter Harrison, *The Bible, Protestantism and the Rise of Natural Science* (Cambridge: Cambridge University Press, 1998); Peter Harrison, *The Fall of Man and the Foundations of Science* (Cambridge: Cambridge University Press, 2007).
50. Manuel, *Religion of Isaac Newton*, 116–125.
51. Richard Westfall, *Force in Newton's Physics* (London: Macdonald, 1971), 340.
52. H. G. Alexander, ed., *The Leibniz-Clarke Correspondence* (Manchester: Manchester University Press, 1956), 16.
53. Ibid., 11.
54. Ibid., 11–12.
55. Ibid., 12.
56. John Brooke and Geoffrey Cantor, *Reconstructing Nature: The Engagement of Science and Religion* (Edinburgh: T. & T. Clark, 1998), 176–206.
57. John Dillenberger, *Protestant Thought and Natural Science: A Historical Interpretation* (London: Collins, 1961); Michael J. Buckley, *At the Origins of Modern Atheism* (New Haven, CT: Yale University Press, 1987).
58. Robert Lenoble, *Mersenne ou la Naissance du Mécanisme* (Paris: Vrin, 1971); Peter Dear, *Mersenne and the Learning of the Schools* (Ithaca, NY: Cornell University Press, 1988).
59. Charles Webster, *The Great Instauration: Science, Medicine and Reform, 1626–1660* (London: Duckworth, 1975), 19–31.
60. H. R. McAdoo, *The Spirit of Anglicanism* (London: Black, 1965), 249.
61. Brooke, *Science and Religion*, 244–257.
62. Roger Hahn, "Laplace and the Mechanistic Universe," in *God and Nature: Historical Essays on the Encounter between Christianity and Science*, ed. David C. Lindberg and Ronald L. Numbers, 256–276 (Berkeley: University of California Press, 1986).

Selected Bibliography

Alexander, Denis, ed. *The Isaac Newton Guidebook* (Cambridge: Faraday Institute, 2012).

Alexander, H. G., ed. *The Leibniz-Clarke Correspondence* (Manchester: Manchester University Press, 1956).

Descartes, René. *Descartes: Philosophical Writings.* Edited and translated by Elizabeth Anscombe and Peter Thomas Geach (London: Nelson, 1954).

Ashworth, William B., Jr. "Christianity and the Mechanistic Universe." In *When Science and Christianity Meet,* edited by David C. Lindberg and Ronald L. Numbers, 61–84 (Chicago: University of Chicago Press, 2003).

Boyle, Robert. *Selected Philosophical Papers of Robert Boyle.* Edited by M. A. Stewart (Manchester: Manchester University Press, 1979).

Boyle, Robert. *The Works of Robert Boyle,* edited by Michael Hunter and Edward B. Davis. Vol. 11, *Disquisition about the Final Causes of Natural Things* (London: Pickering and Chatto, 1999–2000).

Brooke, John Hedley. "Natural Theology and the Plurality of Worlds: Observations on the Brewster-Whewell Debate." *Annals of Science* 34, no. 3 (1977), 221–286.

Brooke, John Hedley. *Science and Religion: Some Historical Perspectives* (Cambridge: Cambridge University Press, 1991).

Brooke, John Hedley. *Science and Religion: Some Historical Perspectives* (Canto Classics) (Cambridge: Cambridge University Press, 2014).

Brooke, John Hedley, and Geoffrey Cantor. *Reconstructing Nature: The Engagement of Science and Religion* (Edinburgh: T. & T. Clark, 1998).

Buckley, Michael J. *At the Origins of Modern Atheism* (New Haven, CT: Yale University Press, 1987).

Burke, Peter. *Tradition and Innovation in Renaissance Italy* (London: Fontana, 1972).

Calloway, Katherine. *Natural Theology in the Scientific Revolution* (London: Pickering and Chatto, 2014).

Carroll, William E. "Aquinas and Contemporary Cosmology: Creation and Beginnings." In *Georges Lemaître: Life, Science and Legacy,* edited by Rodney D. Holder and Simon Mitton, 75–88 (London: Springer, 2012).

Crowe, Michael J. *The Extraterrestrial Life Debate, 1750–1900* (Cambridge: Cambridge University Press, 1986).

Danielson, Dennis R. "The Great Copernican Cliché." *American Journal of Physics* 69, no. 10 (2001): 1029–1035.

Davis, Edward. "Robert Boyle's Religious Life, Attitudes, and Vocation." *Science and Christian Belief* 19, no. 2 (2007): 117–138.

Dear, Peter. *Mersenne and the Learning of the Schools* (Ithaca, NY: Cornell University Press, 1988).

Dick, Steven J. *Plurality of Worlds: The Extraterrestrial Life Debate from Democritus to Kant* (Cambridge: Cambridge University Press, 1982).

Dillenberger, John. *Protestant Thought and Natural Science: A Historical Interpretation* (London: Collins, 1961).

Efron, Noah. "Early Judaism." In *Science and Religion around the World*, edited by John Hedley Brooke and Ronald L. Numbers, 20–43 (New York: Oxford University Press, 2011).

Fantoli, Annibale. *Galileo: For Copernicanism and for the Church*. Translated by George V. Coyne (Vatican City and Notre Dame, IN: Vatican Observatory and University of Notre Dame Press, 1994).

Finocchiaro, Maurice A. *The Galileo Affair: A Documentary History* (Berkeley: University of California Press, 1989).

Finocchiaro, Maurice A. *Retrying Galileo, 1633–1992* (Berkeley: University of California Press, 2005).

Force, James E. "Newton's God of Dominion: The Unity of Newton's Theological, Scientific, and Political Thought." In *Essays on the Context, Nature and Influence of Isaac Newton's Theology*, edited by James E. Force and Richard H. Popkin, 75–102 (Dordrecht: Kluwer, 1990).

Hahn, Roger. "Laplace and the Mechanistic Universe." In *God and Nature: Historical Essays on the Encounter between Christianity and Science*, edited by David C. Lindberg and Ronald L. Numbers, 256–276 (Berkeley: University of California Press, 1986).

Harrison, Peter. *The Bible, Protestantism and the Rise of Natural Science* (Cambridge: Cambridge University Press, 1998).

Harrison, Peter. *The Fall of Man and the Foundations of Science* (Cambridge: Cambridge University Press, 2007).

Henry, John. *The Scientific Revolution and the Origins of Modern Science* (Basingstoke: Palgrave, 2002).

Hooykaas, Reijer. *Religion and the Rise of Modern Science* (Edinburgh: Scottish Academic Press, 1972).

Howell, Kenneth J. *God's Two Books: Copernican Cosmology and Biblical Interpretation in Early Modern Science* (Notre Dame, IN: University of Notre Dame Press, 2002).

Hunter, Michael. *Robert Boyle: Between God and Science* (New Haven, CT: Yale University Press, 2009).

Hutton, Sarah. "More, Newton, and the Language of Biblical Prophecy." In *The Books of Nature and Scripture*, edited by James E. Force and Richard H. Popkin, 39–53 (Dordrecht: Kluwer, 1990).

Koenigsberger, Dorothy. *Renaissance Man and Creative Thinking: A History of Concepts of Harmony, 1400–1700* (Hassocks: Harvester, 1979).

Laudan, Laurens. "The Clock Metaphor and Probabilism: The Impact of Descartes on English Methodological Thought, 1650–65." *Annals of Science* 22, no. 2 (1966): 73–104.

Lenoble, Robert. *Mersenne ou la Naissance du Mécanisme* (Paris: Vrin, 1971).

Manuel, Frank E. *The Religion of Isaac Newton* (Oxford: Oxford University Press, 1974).

McAdoo, H. R. *The Spirit of Anglicanism* (London: Black, 1965).

McClaughlin, Trevor. "Censorship and Defenders of the Cartesian Faith in Mid-Seventeenth Century France." *Journal of the History of Ideas* 40, no. 4 (1979): 563–581.

McMullin, Ernan., ed., *The Church and Galileo* (Notre Dame: University of Notre Dame Press, 2005).

Merchant, Carolyn. *The Death of Nature: Women, Ecology and the Scientific Revolution* (London: Wildwood House, 1982).

Newton, Isaac. "Four Letters to Richard Bentley." In *Newton's Philosophy of Nature*, edited by H. S. Thayer, 46–58 (New York: Hafner, 1953).

Newton, Isaac. *Opticks* (New York: Dover, 1952). Originally published in 1704.

Numbers, Ronald L., ed. *Galileo Goes to Jail and Other Myths about Science and Religion* (Cambridge, MA: Harvard University Press, 2009).

Osler, Margaret J. *Divine Will and the Mechanical Philosophy: Gassendi and Descartes on Contingency and Necessity in the Created World* (Cambridge: Cambridge University Press, 1994).

Osler, Margaret J. *Reconfiguring the World: Nature, God, and Human Understanding from the Middle Ages to Early Modern Europe* (Baltimore: Johns Hopkins University Press, 2010).

Osler, Margaret. "Religion and the Changing Historiography of the Scientific Revolution." In *Science and Religion: New Historical Perspectives*, edited by Thomas Dixon, Geoffrey Cantor, and Stephen Pumfrey, 71–86 (Cambridge: Cambridge University Press, 2010).

Principe, Lawrence. *The Aspiring Adept: Robert Boyle and his Alchemical Quest* (Princeton, NJ: Princeton University Press, 1998).

Principe, Lawrence. *The Scientific Revolution: A Very Short Introduction* (Oxford: Oxford University Press, 2011).

Rattansi, Piyo M. "The Social Interpretation of Science in the Seventeenth Century." In *Science and Society, 1600–1900*, edited by Peter Mathias, 1–32 (Cambridge: Cambridge University Press, 1972).

Redondi, Pietro. *Galileo Eretico* (Turin: Einaudi, 1983). Translated by Raymond Rosenthal as *Galileo Heretic* (Princeton, NJ: Princeton University Press, 1987).

Shea, William, and Mariano Artigas. *Galileo Observed: Science and the Politics of Belief* (Sagamore Beach, MA: Science History Publications, 2006).

Snobelen, Stephen. "'In the Language of Men': The Hermeneutics of Accommodation in the Scientific Revolution." In *Nature and Scripture in the Abrahamic Religions: Up to 1700*, edited by Jitse M. van der Meer and Scott Mandelbrote, vol. 2, 691–732 (Leiden: Brill, 2008).

Steinle, Friedrich. "From Principles to Regularities: Tracing 'Laws of Nature' in Early Modern France and England." In *Natural Law and Laws of Nature in Early Modern Europe*, edited by Lorraine Daston and Michael Stolleis, 215–231 (Farnham: Ashgate, 2008).

Webster, Charles. *The Great Instauration: Science, Medicine and Reform, 1626–1660* (London: Duckworth, 1975).

Westfall, Richard. *The Construction of Modern Science: Mechanisms and Mechanics* (Cambridge: Cambridge University Press, 1971).

Westfall, Richard. *Force in Newton's Physics* (London: Macdonald, 1971).

Westfall, Richard. *Science and Religion in Seventeenth-Century England* (New Haven, CT: Yale University Press, 1958).

Westman, Robert S. "Magical Reform and Astronomical Reform: The Yates Thesis Reconsidered." In *Hermeticism and the Scientific Revolution*, edited by Robert S. Westman and J. E. McGuire, 1–90 (Los Angeles: University of California Press, 1977).

Wilkinson, David. *Science, Religion, and the Search for Extraterrestrial Intelligence* (Oxford: Oxford University Press, 2013).

12

Chance and Providence in the Thought of William Paley

Alister E. McGrath

Introduction

Some readers may well express surprise at the inclusion of William Paley (1743–1805) in this volume. What justification might be given for devoting a chapter to a relatively obscure figure, who tends now to be remembered simply for one work, *Natural Theology* (1802), and whose claim to fame is arguably that Charles Darwin felt obliged to engage with it in developing and defending his own views on the origin of biological species, half a century later? More recently, of course, Paley has been adopted as a mascot by the Intelligent Design movement, perhaps most intriguingly illustrated by the foundation of the "William Paley Institute for Intelligent Design."[1] So why include him in this discussion?

It is a fair question. Yet Paley surely both demands and deserves to be included in this volume. The fact that Darwin felt obliged to engage with Paley—both explicitly and implicitly—in the *Origin of Species* is a telling indication of the extent to which Paley's approach to notions of design and order, especially within the biological domain, had permeated into nineteenth-century popular culture in England and beyond. As we shall see, Paley's ideas are largely derivative, perhaps best regarded (rather generously) as a reflection of the scientific and theological consensus of the early eighteenth century. Yet the manner in which Paley presented these ideas—above all, his use of Industrial Revolution–era technological imagery that would have been both familiar and engaging to his readers—was so effective that Paley's views on order and chance achieved a significant degree of cultural hegemony. Darwin realized that his own new theory would have to displace Paley's; it simply could not be ignored.

To study Paley is to inhabit a way of looking at the world that seemed self-evidently right to many in early nineteenth-century England. Although Paley thought appealing to the innate *complexity* of the biological world over its visible counterpart conferred significant apologetic advantages, *Natural Theology* still includes important astronomical sections reinforcing Paley's overall argument that the natural world, at every level, shows evidence of "contrivance"—that is to say, intelligent design and construction. "Contrivance, if established, appears to me to prove everything which we wish to prove."[2] Paley sets out an accessible and imaginatively plausible account of a stable, ordered universe, within which "chance" is to be seen as an unwelcome intruder, posing a threat to this order. By the end of the nineteenth century, the importance of chance or "disorder" was becoming increasingly clear in both biology and physics, forcing the popularizers of Darwinism and the "new thermodynamics" to develop strategies to popularize and rationalize the place of chance within this shifting scientific outlook.[3]

In this chapter, I propose to explore Paley's ideas, set within their complex intellectual and cultural context. We must begin, however, by introducing Paley himself.

Introducing Paley

Paley was born in Peterborough in 1743, the son of a clergyman of the Church of England who two years later went on to become the headmaster of Giggleswick school in Yorkshire. He began his career at the University of Cambridge at the age of sixteen. Like Darwin himself, Paley was an undergraduate at Christ's College.[4] In 1763, he graduated with distinction, having achieved the highest score in Cambridge University's final year mathematics examination, which won him the title of Senior Wrangler. At the time, this was seen as representing one of the greatest intellectual achievements in England, opening doors to future advancement in the academy, law, medicine, and church. Paley was elected a fellow of Christ's College in 1766 and in 1768 was appointed to a tutorship.

At Cambridge, Paley associated himself with a group of "Latitudinarians"—Anglican clergy inclined toward a rationalist understanding of faith and with an interest in natural theology, including John Jebb, John Law, and Richard Watson. This group shared a number of core beliefs developed by earlier writers within its tradition (such as John Tillotson),[5] including a natural religion based on an ordered creation, which witnessed to its divine origination, and a theologically informed utilitarian definition of virtue.[6] This emerging (though loose) alliance between Latitudinarianism and Newtonianism is known to have caused concern within some more traditionalist church circles in Cambridge and elsewhere.[7] During his time as tutor at Christ's College, Paley lectured on the philosophy of Samuel Clarke, Joseph Butler, and John Locke.[8]

Paley also delivered a course of lectures on moral philosophy, which subsequently formed the basis of his influential treatise *The Principles of Moral and Political Philosophy* (1785).

This work, which an uncharitable critic might suggest was distinguished more by its clarity of presentation than by its originality of argument, quickly became a "set text" for moral philosophy at Cambridge University—in other words, it was "required reading" upon which examination questions might be based.[9] It is certainly true that two of Paley's earlier works achieved this status—as above, his *Principles of Moral and Political Philosophy*, and also his later *View of the Evidences of Christianity* (1794). Yet, as Aileen Fyfe has convincingly demonstrated, *Natural Theology* enjoyed no such official status.[10] It was unquestionably discussed and debated, in that "natural theology" was a topic of no small interest at the time. At the same time, any suggestion that Cambridge was wedded to Paley's text or ideas needs to be treated with skepticism. While Charles Darwin was familiar with Paley's text, he probably did not study it in any detail until after he had left Cambridge.[11]

Few today read Paley's *Principles of Moral and Political Philosophy*. Yet it merits closer attention, not least because of its emphasis upon the importance of law in creating and sustaining a stable social order.[12] It is a somewhat startling work, mingling a well-argued defense of a utilitarian approach to ethics with what at times seems like a draconian enforcement of the civil code. For example, Paley defended the death penalty for the stealing of horses and sheep, arguing that, since juries rarely actually enforced the death penalty, the existence of the statute deterred potential thieves from committing such crimes. Yet it was, by the standards of the day, an enlightened work, which was regularly cited by moralists of a wide variety of political persuasions. Paley's fundamental point was that moral virtue was to be understood as "the doing good to mankind, in obedience to the will of God, and for the sake of everlasting happiness." The notion of virtue was thus rooted in divine order, even if its interpretation and application were open to a utilitarian reading.

Given the topic of this book, what needs to be noted in this early work is Paley's critique of any positive role of "chance" in the creation and preservation of a stable social order, and his clear anxiety about the possibility of "disorder" within society. Although the chaos of the French Revolution of 1789 lay in the future, it is easy to understand Paley's deep anxiety about the potential fragility of a stable social order, and his concern to ground it both in the will of God on the one hand and the practicalities of social existence on the other. Like many thinkers of the eighteenth century, Paley believed in a world created with a natural order, expressed in the physical, biological, and social domains.

It is perhaps worth noting that Paley dedicated his *Principles of Moral and Political Philosophy* to Edmund Law, bishop of Carlisle, who clearly took Paley under his wing when the situation required it. Law was himself a Cambridge man, who served both as Master of Peterhouse and as Knightbridge Professor of Philosophy in the University of Cambridge, before becoming bishop of Carlisle from 1768 to 1787. After leaving Cambridge, Paley moved to the diocese of Carlisle, serving first as rector of the village of Musgrave in Westmorland, then vicar of Dalston, and finally as archdeacon of Carlisle.[13] He left the diocese of Carlisle in 1795 and spent the final decade of his life in parishes in the dioceses of Durham and Lincoln. He was buried within Carlisle Cathedral.

Today, Paley is remembered chiefly as an apologist. Paley was drawn to the field of apologetics in the aftermath of the French Revolution. Aware of the rise of skeptical approaches to Christianity, Paley sought to reaffirm the public credibility of the Christian faith. His first major work of apologetics was *Horae Paulinae, or the Truth of the Scripture History of St Paul* (1790), followed by *A View of the Evidences of Christianity* (1794). Like the *Principles of Moral and Political Philosophy,* this latter work took the form of a reworking of older works, most notably Nathaniel Lardner's *The Credibility of the Gospel History* (1748) and John Douglas's *Criterion, or Miracles Examined* (1757).

Paley's Natural Theology

In 1802, Paley published the work of apologetics for which he is best remembered and which is to be considered in this chapter: *Natural Theology, or Evidences of the Existence and Attributes of the Deity collected from the Appearances of Nature,* based on a series of sermons apparently composed in the 1780s or 1790s. Here, as in his earlier works, Paley borrowed extensively from earlier writers, most notably John Ray's *Wisdom of God* (1691) and William Derham's *Physico-Theology* (1713). However, he also drew significantly on Bernard Nieuwentyt's little-known work *The Religious Philosopher* (1718), originally published in Dutch as *Het regt Gebruik der Werelt Beschouwingen* (The right use of world concepts) in 1715. Paley found himself accused of plagiarism by those who noted striking similarities, especially in relation to the deployment and application of the image of a watch, between Paley's *Natural Theology* and Nieuwentyt's *Religious Philosopher*.

Paley's extensive dependence upon apologetic writings of the period 1690–1720 means that his apologetic approach reflects the approaches and assumptions of early eighteenth-century British natural theologians, such as Ray and Derham. Some have criticized this dependency, suggesting that Paley's style and manner of argumentation are inferior to those found in earlier works, especially Ray's *Wisdom of God*.[14] Yet a more charitable judgment is not out of place here. Paley's formulation of these earlier arguments can be seen to represent a process of critical appropriation, sifting out what the passing of time had shown to be of permanent value in these earlier writing, and subtly reframing them within an intellectual framework that possessed a certain intuitive plausibility. Furthermore, the recognition of originality as an intellectual virtue still lay some distance in the future. Paley's respect for traditional views and approaches resonated well with the cultural milieu of his day.[15]

Yet the English intellectual landscape underwent massive changes in the eighteenth century, not least on account of the critiques directed against various forms of natural theology by David Hume and Immanuel Kant. While Paley was aware of Hume's significance, he does not engage explicitly with his arguments in his *Natural Theology*.[16] This absence does not mean that Paley was ignorant of these arguments. As Brooke and Cantor have pointed out, a Humean skeptic functions as an imaginary interlocutor in many natural theologies of the period, including Paley's apologetic work.[17]

Paley's failure to engage *explicitly* with such critiques is, of course, easily understood. The first edition of his *Natural Theology* would have been bought and read by a generally conservative readership, which would have been unlikely to have been too concerned with such issues.[18] During the "Augustan Age," natural theology appears to have played a role within English culture that extended beyond the realm of apologetics.[19] Although it is important not to overstate this role, a series of anxieties about the social stability of England during the late seventeenth century found some tenuous resolution through an appeal to the regularity of both the natural and political orders, expressed *scientifically* in the intellectual framework offered by Newtonian mechanics, *religiously* through the kind of natural theology expressed by John Ray and William Derham, and *socially* in a stable political order.[20]

Just as Newtonian natural theology offered reassurance to an English readership unsettled by the dramatic political uncertainties around the time of the Glorious Revolution in 1688, so Paley's natural theology offered reassurance to an equally unsettled conservative readership troubled by the Napoleonic war and increasing religious skepticism in English culture.[21] Where scientific advance seemed to lead to atheism in France, as the works of Laplace indicated, Paley established a context in which scientific advance was accommodated within a suitably generous natural theology. Paley's vision assuaged perceived internal and external insecurities by pointing to the fixed laws of science having counterparts in fixed laws of society, both of which were grounded in divine nature.

Paley thus offered a theological vision or "map" of the world in which the social and natural orders were seamlessly integrated with a framework that both rested upon and reflected the wisdom of God. As we shall see, ideas of "chance" and "disorder" in nature were thus seen as destructive of ordering—whether moral or scientific. Although Paley's *Natural Theology* has little to say about ethics, it is relatively easy to infer where Paley believes the intrusion of chance will lead. In responding to David Hume's suggestion that living systems could have arisen accidentally by means of unconscious generation, Paley argued that any such process could not easily be accommodated intellectually within a universe guided by the cosmic intelligence of a creator God.

Paley's *Natural Theology* is organized around a controlling analogy of considerable imaginative power. He developed what he and his peers clearly considered to be cogent arguments for the extreme rational difficulties attending any notion of an ordered world coming into existence by accident or chance. Paley's initial deployment of a controlling image—the watch—provides an imaginative framework within which his evidence and examples from the biological world are integrated. Paley's *Natural Theology* is a luminous example of the wisdom of Wittgenstein's famous aphorism: "A *picture* held us captive. And we could not get outside it, for it lay in our language and language seemed to repeat it to us inexorably."[22]

Paley asks his readers to imagine they are walking across a heath.[23] First, they encounter a stone. What explanation needs to be offered for its presence? Paley argues that it might have been lying there for ages. No special explanation is required. But what if they encountered a watch? The same response is inappropriate. Why? Because the watch stands out from its background on account of evidence of design and construction—what Paley famously termed "contrivance." The watch's case and mechanism cannot be accounted for on purely natural grounds:

> This mechanism being observed (it requires indeed an examination of the instrument, and perhaps some previous knowledge of the subject, to perceive and understand it; but being once, as we have said, observed and understood), the inference we think is inevitable, that the watch must have had a maker.[24]

Paley's fundamental theme in *Natural Theology* is that the natural world, like the watch, shows clear evidence of design, and that its existence cannot plausibly be attributed to chance. Showing a compendious knowledge of natural history, Paley sets out an accumulation of evidence for the "contrivance" of human beings and their constituent organs, particularly evident in the complex design of the human eye. Likewise, the human skeletal frame displays a precise mechanical arrangement of bones, cartilage, and joints, as does the manner the circulation of the blood and the corresponding disposition of the blood vessels. Paley's descriptive prose expressed both his delight in the complexity of the biological world and his fundamental conviction that only a wise and benevolent God can account satisfactorily for these marvels of mechanical perfection, purpose, and functionality. Such observations were, he declared, "proofs of contrivance."[25]

Does this amount to a "proof," in the strong sense of the term, for the existence of such a God? Paley's language certainly suggests that he thought so. For example, consider his important argument that each example of contrivance is to be valued, in addition to their collective cumulative force, on account of their interconnectedness.

> The proof is not a conclusion which lies at the end of a chain of reasoning, of which chain each instance of contrivance is only a link, and of which, if one link fail, the whole falls; but it is an argument separately supplied by every separate example.[26]

While Paley speaks of offering a "proof" of the existence of a creator, it is clear that he does not mean a *logical* proof, but rather a rhetorical demonstration according to familiar conventions, similar to that then encountered in a court of law.[27] Furthermore, Paley is better seen here as standing within an apologetic tradition going back to Joseph Butler, who argued that we can reflect on the created world using experience and reason, and compare this to the theory revealed in the Christian scriptures.[28] It is important not to overstate any resemblance between Butler's approach in *The Analogy of Religion* and modern formulations of "inference to the best explanation." Yet there is at least a parallel here, in that Butler's proposal is that Christianity commends itself as the most probable explanation of what is observed within the world.

Paley's overall approach, it seems to me, is best expressed not in terms of a "proof," despite his own use of this term, but in terms of the best available explanation of the complexities observed within the natural world. Paley's argument must be set against Hume's criticisms of natural theology, particularly his views on "probable reasoning";[29] Paley's approach can, I think, withstand those criticisms, if Paley is seen to argue that his is a more probable reason for the present ordering of the world than Hume's.

For example, in his posthumous *Dialogues Concerning Natural Religion* (1779), Hume had argued that any probabilistic inference to a divine design could be contested on several grounds, one of which was that there might exist some "original, inherent principle of order" within nature itself.[30] Hume thus suggests that nature shows order because of an internal ordering principle or mechanism, which requires no external explanation or cause.[31] Yet this is only a suggestion; it is not an argument. The question concerns how *probable* this explanation might be. Paley, clearly aware of Hume's attempted defeat of any argument from design, offers what he believes is a more probable explanation—namely, that such a "principle of order" is to be expected on the basis of his theistic framework, and is thus a more satisfying answer. For a start, Paley declares that Hume's proposal is flawed by conceptual vagueness and definitional uncertainty. "What is meant by a principle of order, as different from an intelligent Creator, has not been explained either by definition or example." For Paley, such a "principle of order" could "only signify the mind and intention which so adapts them."[32] There is a simple explanation of such principles of order, or laws of nature: "A law presupposes an agent"—which is God.[33]

Paley's most fundamental criticism is that such a "principle of order" is quite inadequate to explain how the "watch" of nature came into being. The postulation of some "principle of order" offers no plausible explanation to the observer of this celebrated watch as to how it came into existence in the first place.

> He never knew a watch made by the principle of order; nor can he even form to himself an idea of what is meant by a principle of order, distinct from the intelligence of the watch-maker.[34]

The imaginative power of this argument is obvious, and Paley returns to it later in his discussion. "Was a watch ever produced by a principle of order? and why might not a watch be so produced, as well as an eye?"[35]

Yet we must be careful not to portray Hume as Paley's enemy, in that Hume actually provides Paley with a theoretical framework which lends weight to his core argument. Hume's understanding of causality is such that the idea of anything being "caused" by chance is something of a contradiction in terms. Having postulated some "original, inherent principle of order" in his *Dialogues Concerning Natural Religion*, Hume argues that this has critical implications for any notion of "chance":

> Chance has no place, on any hypothesis, skeptical or religious. And were the inmost *essence* of things laid open to us, we should then discover a scene of which at present we can have no idea. Instead of admiring the order of natural beings, we should clearly see that it was absolutely impossible for them, in the smallest article, even to admit of any other disposition.[36]

Paley's genius lay in taking Hume's view that nothing is caused by chance, and declaring that Hume's own manner of conceptualizing this determinism is inadequate.[36] The idea of some "original, inherent principle of order" was vague and incapable of being formulated clearly; it failed to account for why things—whether watches or human eyes—existed at all, and it was, in any case, already implicit in a theistic way of thinking. On all three counts, Paley's readers would be likely to judge that his position seemed preferable to Hume's.

Paley on Chance and Providence

So what role does chance play in Paley's argument? Paley works with an essentially dysteleological definition of chance as "the operation of causes without design." How, he asks, could such a complex structure as the human eye arise by chance?

> I desire no greater certainty in reasoning, than that by which chance is excluded from the present disposition of the natural world. Universal experience is against it. What does chance ever do for us? In the human body, for instance, chance, i.e. the operation of causes without design, may produce a wen, a wart, a mole, a pimple, but never an eye.[37]

Paley's natural theology is based on the assumption—widely shared at that time—that the ordering of nature excludes chance, rather than recognizing that chance might be a means towards an ordered end. Paley is prepared to concede a "degree of chance which appears to prevail in the world";[38] this, however, is an *appearance*, reflecting our inability to grasp the full reality of the situation. There is no suggestion that chance might be a catalyst for the emergence of higher levels of order.

Paley develops the notion of "relation" to enhance the plausibility of his argument against chance,[39] meaning thereby something similar to what contemporary advocates of "Intelligent Design" have designated "irreducible complexity." Paley's own formulation of this idea merits attention:

> When several different parts contribute to one effect, or, which is the same thing, when an effect is produced by the joint action of different instruments, the fitness of such parts or instruments to one another for the purpose of producing, by their united action, the effect, is what I call relation; and wherever this is observed in the works of nature or of man, it appears to me to carry along with it decisive evidence of understanding, intention, art.[40]

Paley consistently emphasizes that both individual details of organisms and their broader "relations" within the biological world as a whole are too complex to be accounted for by anything other than contrivance. We must, he declares, recognize "the improbability of the present arrangement taking place by chance."[41] Since Paley precludes any idea that biological utility might *follow*, rather than *precede*, the origination of anatomical parts, the existence of such "relations" is to be interpreted as indicative of divine contrivance.[42] Complexity is explicable only in terms of a divine origination and superintendence of the natural world: "Such an exquisite structure of things could only arise from the contrivance and powerful influences of an intelligent, free, and most potent agent."[43]

This assertion naturally raises the question of what Paley means by "providence." If nature is governed by laws expressing the divine will and nature, what place is there for any kind of special divine action that might merit the term "providence"? Paley sets out his answer in *Natural Theology*, and it is entirely consistent with what has been said thus far. Providence is about a benevolent God constructing a world designed for our greater good, in which things are ordered for human well-being and happiness. God's providence creates a happy world, in which pain and suffering are to be seen as unintended intrusions. Perhaps Paley's discussion of toothache illustrates his approach to perfection:

> Contrivance proves design: and the predominant tendency of the contrivance indicates the disposition of the designer. The world abounds with contrivances: and all the contrivances which we are acquainted with, are directed to beneficial purposes. Evil, no doubt, exists; but is never, that we can perceive, the object of contrivance. Teeth are contrived to eat, not to ache; their aching now and then is incidental to the contrivance, perhaps inseparable from it: or even, if you will, let it be called a defect in the contrivance: but it is not the *object* of it.[44]

Other examples illustrate Paley's Panglossian reading of the natural world. One of the most startling concerns the providential design of the human epiglottis:

> In a city-feast, for example, what deglutition, what anhelation! yet does this little cartilage, the epiglottis, so effectually interpose its

> office, so securely guard the entrance of the wind-pipe, that whilst morsel after morsel, draught after draught, are coursing one another over it, an accident of a crumb or a drop slipping into this passage (which nevertheless must be opened for the breath every second of time), excites in the whole company, not only alarm by its danger, but surprise by its novelty. Not two guests are choked in a century.[45]

For Paley, the notion of providence thus affirms the benevolence of both the divine will and its created outcomes as seen in the structures of the world. "We never discover a train of contrivance to bring about an evil purpose. No anatomist ever discovered a system of organization calculated to produce pain and disease."[46] God does not need to act providentially in the present, in that God has already acted providentially to contrive structures appropriate to our well-being. God's providence "always rests upon final good."[47] We are invited to appreciate these "blessings of Providence,"[48] rather than anticipate their extension.

All of this leads ineluctably to the conclusion that belief in divine providence plays little role in everyday faith or life, being simply an extension of the notion that God created the world wisely and justly. Paley has no hesitation in declaring that this doctrine has no impact on our conduct:

> And if it be said, that the doctrine of Divine Providence, by reason of the ambiguity under which its exertions present themselves, can be attended with no practical influence upon our conduct; that, although we believe ever so firmly that there is a Providence, we must prepare, and provide, and act, as if there were none; I answer, that this is admitted: and that we further allege, that so to prepare, and so to provide, is consistent with the most perfect assurance of the reality of a Providence.[49]

A hostile critic could interpret this passage as indicating Paley's covert commitment to a fundamentally deist conception of God, who creates a good world and then stands back from its functioning. The lack of a Trinitarian understanding of God undermines any robust doctrine of divine providence as an active caring presence in the world. There is considerable truth in this; it is, however, perhaps important to appreciate that Paley and his Latitudinarian colleagues found the doctrine of the Trinity to be of questionable rationality and severely limited utility, and tended to articulate a theology that was attuned to the rational spirit of the age.[50] The theological rediscovery of the doctrine of the Trinity did not take place until the early twentieth century; Paley and his age belong to an earlier period in the history of Christian thought. It lies beyond the scope of this chapter to reflect on what difference an earlier rediscovery of this doctrine might have made.

Conclusion

Paley is not to be seen as a transitional figure, but as a figure of solidification and crystallization, in which the settled assumptions of the Newtonian age were expounded and illustrated with great clarity at the dawn of the nineteenth century. Although Paley focused on the biological rather than the physical or astronomical worlds, he saw both as governed by laws which precluded chance from the causal sequence. He wrote for an age which thought of the world in generally ordered, even determinist, ways. Whatever differences might have existed between Paley and Hume, they shared the view that explanation by processes of chance was ultimately conceptually incoherent. The Newtonian world was one governed by laws, not by chance.[51] There was simply no way in which chance could be seen as a causal agent, let alone something that might generate new order.

Those settled assumptions would be challenged in the later nineteenth century, as natural theology and natural science moved beyond Paley.[52] I find no hint of anticipation in Paley's writings of the radical ideas that would arise in the later nineteenth century, as indeterminist ideas began to take shape and take hold in the biological and physical realms. Paley cannot be blamed for this; we are all prisoners, to some extent, of what Paul Ricoeur called the "available believable."

Yet with the benefit of hindsight, it might be argued that Paley's popularization of the static and settled scientific worldview of the early eighteenth century perpetuated its influence on Victorian culture. Recent studies of the cultural history of the early Victorian age have noted its tendencies toward authoritarian and inflexible articulations of cultural normativity, in which certain ideas achieved a social hegemony that rendered them virtually immune to criticism.[53] Paley was part of that process of cultural solidification, which rendered the later acceptance of indeterminism more problematic.

With the passing of Paley and his age, the way was clear to think more radical thoughts—of indeterminist modes of conceiving natural processes and dynamic models of nature open to the idea of evolution. Perhaps this is best seen in the writings of Charles Darwin, who provided a new way of seeing the biological world in which chance played a real, and ultimately productive, role. It seemed to some that Darwin, in doing so, enabled a break with the *theological* as much as the cultural assumptions of early nineteenth-century England. Darwin's approach raised far more serious difficulties for a deistic notion of divine action than for its Trinitarian counterpart. The nineteenth-century Anglican theologian Aubrey Moore (1848–1890) famously argued that Darwin had done Christianity a favor by helping it to break free from the then culturally dominant but theologically defective vision of God.[54]

Notes

1. This institute is associated with the Liberty Park, USA Foundation, which promotes "the Freedom, Sovereignty, & Independence of America."
2. William Paley, *Natural Theology*, 12th ed. (London: Faulder, 1809), 408.
3. For this point, see especially the lines of scholarly exploration initiated in the 1980s by Ian Hacking, "Nineteenth Century Cracks in the Concept of Determinism," *Journal of the History of Ideas* 44, no. 3 (1983): 455–475; and Greg Myers, "Nineteenth-Century Popularizations of Thermodynamics and the Rhetoric of Social Prophecy," *Victorian Studies* 29, no. 1 (1985): 35–66.
4. For biographies, see Ernest Barker, *Traditions of Civility: Eight Essays* (Cambridge: Cambridge University Press, 1948), 193–262; M. L. Clarke, *Paley: Evidences for the Man* (London: SPCK, 1974); D. L. LeMahieu, *The Mind of William Paley: A Philosopher and His Age* (Lincoln: University of Nebraska Press, 1976).
5. Harvey Hill, "The Law of Nature Revived: Christianity and Natural Religion in the Sermons of John Tillotson," *Anglican and Episcopal History* 70, no. 2 (2001): 169–189.
6. See studies such as Frederick C. Beiser, *The Sovereignty of Reason: The Defense of Rationality in the Early English Enlightenment* (Princeton, NJ: Princeton University Press, 1996), 84–132 (with particular reference to the "Great Tew" circle); Patrick Müller, *Latitudinarianism and Didacticism in Eighteenth-Century Literature: Moral Theology in Fielding, Sterne, and Goldsmith* (Frankfurt: Peter Lang, 2009), 45–208 (with particular relevance to moral theology).
7. John Gascoigne, *Cambridge in the Age of the Enlightenment: Science, Religion and Politics from the Restoration to the French Revolution* (Cambridge and New York: Cambridge University Press, 1989), 171–173.

8. For an assessment of Paley's lingering influence at Cambridge in the first half of the nineteenth century, see Martha McMackin Garland, *Cambridge before Darwin: The Ideal of a Liberal Education, 1800–1860* (Cambridge: Cambridge University Press, 1980), 52–69.
9. Clarke, *Paley*, 126–7.
10. Aileen Fyfe, "The Reception of William Paley's *Natural Theology* in the University of Cambridge," *British Journal for the History of Science* 30, no. 3 (1997): 321–335. See also Aileen Fyfe, "Publishing and the Classics: Paley's *Natural Theology* and the Nineteenth-Century Scientific Canon." *Studies in the History and Philosophy of Science* 33, no. 4 (2002): 729–751.
11. In his autobiography, Darwin indicates familiarity with Paley's ideas while he was a student at Cambridge: *The Life and Letters of Charles Darwin*, ed. Francis Darwin (London: John Murray, 1887), 1: 47 "I did not at that time trouble myself about Paley's premises; and, taking these on trust, I was charmed and convinced by the long line of argumentation". However, a closer reading of the passage suggests that he was referring primarily to Paley's earlier works, *The Evidences of Christianity*, and *Moral Philosophy*. While Darwin mentions Paley's *Natural Theology* here, the context does not imply that Darwin knew this work at this stage.
12. For Paley's ideas in their historical context, see Robert Hole, *Pulpits, Politics and Public Order in England, 1760–1832* (Cambridge: Cambridge University Press, 1989), 73–82.
13. There is little doubt that Paley's Anglican theological roots are reflected in his apologetic approach: see the fine essay of Neil Hitchin, "Probability and the Word of God: William Paley's Anglican Method and the Defense of the Scriptures," *Anglican Theological Review* 77, no. 3 (1995): 392–407; Graham Cole, "William Paley's *Natural Theology*: An Anglican Classic?" *Journal of Anglican Studies* 5, no. 2 (2007): 209–225. For comments on the form of Anglicanism adopted by Paley and his circle, see A. M. C. Waterman, "A Cambridge 'Via Media' in Late Georgian Anglicanism," *Journal of Ecclesiastical History* 42, no. 3 (1991): 419–436.
14. See especially the perceptive comments at Charles E. Raven, *John Ray, Naturalist: His Life and Works* (Cambridge: Cambridge University Press, 1986), 455. Related concerns are expressed in Neal C. Gillespie, "Divine Design and the Industrial Revolution: William Paley's Abortive Reform of Natural Theology," *Isis* 81, no. 2 (1990): 214–229.
15. George J. Buelow, "Originality, Genius, Plagiarism in English Criticism of the Eighteenth Century," *International Review of the Aesthetics and Sociology of Music* 21, no. 2 (1990): 117–128.
16. LeMahieu, *The Mind of William Paley*, 30. Paley's strategy appears to be to deal with Humean concerns indirectly, without naming their source, through use of this controlling analogy.

17. John Hedley Brooke and Geoffrey Cantor, *Reconstructing Nature: The Engagement of Science and Religion* (Edinburgh: T. & T. Clarke, 1998), 196–198.
18. See especially Matthew D. Eddy, "The Rhetoric and Science of William Paley's *Natural Theology*." *Theology and Literature* 18 (2004): 1–22.
19. See Alister E. McGrath, *Darwinism and the Divine: Evolutionary Thought and Natural Theology* (Oxford: Wiley-Blackwell, 2011), 49–71.
20. For further comment, see Neal C. Gillespie, "Natural History, Natural Theology, and Social Order: John Ray and the 'Newtonian Ideology,'" *Journal of the History of Biology* 20, no. 1 (1987): 1–49; Brian W. Ogilvie, "Natural History, Ethics, and Physico-Theology," in *Historia: Empiricism and Erudition in Early Modern Europe*, ed. Gianna Pomata and Nancy G. Siraisi, 75–103 (Cambridge, MA: MIT Press, 2005).
21. This point is explored by John Hedley Brooke, *Science and Religion: Some Historical Perspectives* (Cambridge: Cambridge University Press, 1991), 210–213.
22. Ludwig Wittgenstein, *Philosophical Investigations*, 3rd ed. (Oxford: Blackwell, 1968), 48.
23. Paley, *Natural Theology*, 1.
24. Ibid., 3.
25. The important phrase "proof of contrivance" occurs five times in *Natural Theology*: see 7, 21, 269, 323, 417. Other phrases express a similar idea—such as the ordering of nature "demonstrates intention and contrivance" (82).
26. Paley, *Natural Theology*, 77.
27. For the importance of the socially constructed notion of "received opinion" in shaping such perceptions, see Douglas Lane Patey, *Probability and Literary Form: Philosophic Theory and Literary Practice in the Augustan Age* (Cambridge: Cambridge University Press, 1984), 3–13.
28. See Timothy Suttor, "Bishop Joseph Butler's Place in the English Tradition," *CCHA Study Sessions* 51 (1966): 11–23; James Rurak, "Butler's *Analogy*: A Still Interesting Synthesis of Reason and Revelation," *Anglican Theological Review* 62, no. 2 (1980): 365–381.
29. Lorne Falkenstein, "The Psychology and Epistemology of Hume's Account of Probable Reasoning," in *The Continuum Companion to Hume*, ed. Alan Bailey and Dan O'Brien, 104–130 (London: Continuum, 2012).
30. David Hume, *Philosophical Works of David Hume* (London: Fenton, 1824), 53: "How could things have been as they are, were there not an original, inherent principle of order somewhere, in thought or in matter?"
31. Hume's argument of such "ordering" extends to both mind and matter: see Miriam McCormick, "Hume on Natural Belief and Original Principles," *Hume Studies* 19, no. 1 (1993): 103–116.
32. Paley, *Natural Theology*, 71.
33. Ibid., 7.
34. Ibid., 6.
35. Ibid., 71.

36. [36] Hume, *Philosophical Works*, 53
36. On Hume's determinism and its modern scientific critics, see Barry Loewer, "Determinism," in *The Routledge Companion to Philosophy of Science*, 2nd ed., ed. Martin Curd and Stathis Psillos, 371–380 (London: Routledge, 2014).
37. Paley, *Natural Theology*, 62–63. Note that a "wen" is an abnormal growth or a cyst protruding from a surface, especially the surface of the skin.
38. Ibid., 527.
39. Francisco José Ayala Pereda, "In William Paley's Shadow: Darwin's Explanation of Design," *Ludus Vitalis* 12, no. 21 (2004): 53–66, especially 55–56.
40. Paley, *Natural Theology*, 261. The fifteenth chapter of *Natural Theology* (261–275) is given over to this idea, which Paley clearly regards as being of major importance for his argument.
41. Ibid., 383.
42. Ibid., 67.
43. Ibid., 404.
44. Ibid., 467.
45. Ibid., 179. For the link between Paley and Pangloss, see Mark Terry, "Pangloss, Paley, and the Privileged Planet," in *For the Rock Record: Geologists on Intelligent Design*, ed. Jill Schneiderman and Warren D. Allmon, 77–91 (Berkeley, CA: University of California Press, 2009), especially 80–82.
46. Paley, *Natural Theology*, 467–8.
47. Ibid., 523.
48. Ibid., 464.
49. Ibid., 524.
50. See especially Paul Chang-Ha Lim, *Mystery Unveiled: The Crisis of the Trinity in Early Modern England* (New York: Oxford University Press, 2012).
51. Lawrence Sklar, *Physics and Chance: Philosophical Issues in the Foundations of Statistical Mechanics* (Cambridge: Cambridge University Press, 1993); Toby Handfield, *A Philosophical Guide to Chance* (Cambridge: Cambridge University Press, 2012), 39–41.
52. For the move beyond Paley's natural theology in Britain during the first half of the nineteenth century, see McGrath, *Darwinism and the Divine*, 108–142.
53. A point made by Peter Garratt, *Victorian Empiricism: Self, Knowledge, and Reality in Ruskin, Bain, Lewes, Spencer, and George Eliot* (Madison, NJ: Fairleigh Dickinson University Press, 2010), 166–167.
54. McGrath, *Darwinism and the Divine*, 145–146.

Selected Bibliography

Ayala Pereda, Francisco José. "In William Paley's Shadow: Darwin's Explanation of Design." *Ludus Vitalis* 12, no. 21 (2004): 53–66.

Barker, Ernest. *Traditions of Civility: Eight Essays* (Cambridge: Cambridge University Press, 1948).

Beiser, Frederick C. *The Sovereignty of Reason: The Defense of Rationality in the Early English Enlightenment* (Princeton, NJ: Princeton University Press, 1996).

Brooke, John Hedley. *Science and Religion: Some Historical Perspectives* (Cambridge: Cambridge University Press, 1991).

Brooke, John Hedley, and Geoffrey Cantor. *Reconstructing Nature: The Engagement of Science and Religion* (Edinburgh: T. & T. Clarke, 1998).

Buelow, George J. "Originality, Genius, Plagiarism in English Criticism of the Eighteenth Century." *International Review of the Aesthetics and Sociology of Music* 21, no. 2 (1990): 117–128.

Clarke, M. L. *Paley: Evidences for the Man* (London: SPCK, 1974).

Cole, Graham. "William Paley's *Natural Theology*: An Anglican Classic?" *Journal of Anglican Studies* 5, no. 2 (2007): 209–225.

Darwin, Charles. *The Life and Letters of Charles Darwin.* Edited by Francis Darwin 3 vols. (London: John Murray, 1887).

Eddy, Matthew D. "The Rhetoric and Science of William Paley's *Natural Theology.*" *Theology and Literature* 18, no. 1 (2004): 1–22.

Falkenstein, Lorne. "The Psychology and Epistemology of Hume's Account of Probable Reasoning." In *The Continuum Companion to Hume*, edited by Alan Bailey and Dan O'Brien, 104–130 (London: Continuum, 2012).

Fyfe, Aileen. "Publishing and the Classics: Paley's *Natural Theology* and the Nineteenth- Century Scientific Canon." *Studies in History and Philosophy of Science* 33, no. 4 (2002): 729–751.

Fyfe, Aileen. "The Reception of William Paley's *Natural Theology* in the University of Cambridge." *British Journal for the History of Science* 30, no. 3 (1997): 321–335.

Garland, Martha McMackin. *Cambridge before Darwin: The Ideal of a Liberal Education, 1800–1860* (Cambridge: Cambridge University Press, 1980).

Garratt, Peter. *Victorian Empiricism: Self, Knowledge, and Reality in Ruskin, Bain, Lewes, Spencer, and George Eliot* (Madison, NJ: Fairleigh Dickinson University Press, 2010).

Gascoigne, John. *Cambridge in the Age of the Enlightenment: Science, Religion and Politics from the Restoration to the French Revolution* (Cambridge and New York: Cambridge University Press, 1988).

Gillespie, Neal C. "Natural History, Natural Theology, and Social Order: John Ray and the 'Newtonian Ideology.'" *Journal of the History of Biology* 20, no. 1 (1987): 1–49.

Hacking, Ian. "Nineteenth Century Cracks in the Concept of Determinism." *Journal of the History of Ideas* 44, no. 3 (1983): 455–475.

Handfield, Toby. *A Philosophical Guide to Chance* (Cambridge: Cambridge University Press, 2012).

Hill, Harvey. "The Law of Nature Revived: Christianity and Natural Religion in the Sermons of John Tillotson." *Anglican and Episcopal History* 70, no. 2 (2001): 169–189.

Hitchin, Neil. "Probability and the Word of God: William Paley's Anglican Method and the Defense of the Scriptures." *Anglican Theological Review* 77, no. 3 (1995): 392–407.

Hole, Robert. *Pulpits, Politics and Public Order in England, 1760–1832* (Cambridge: Cambridge University Press, 1989).

Hume, David. *Philosophical Works of David Hume* (London: Fenton, 1824).

LeMahieu, D. L. *The Mind of William Paley: A Philosopher and His Age* (Lincoln: University of Nebraska Press, 1976).

Lim, Paul Chang-Ha. *Mystery Unveiled: The Crisis of the Trinity in Early Modern England* (New York: Oxford University Press, 2012).

Loewer, Barry. "Determinism". In *The Routledge Companion to Philosophy of Science.* 2nd ed., edited by Martin Curd and Stathis Psillos, 371–80 (London: Routledge, 2014).

McCormick, Miriam. "Hume on Natural Belief and Original Principles." *Hume Studies* 19, no. 1 (1993): 103–116.

McGrath, Alister E. *Darwinism and the Divine: Evolutionary Thought and Natural Theology* (Oxford: Wiley-Blackwell, 2011).

Müller, Patrick. *Latitudinarianism and Didacticism in Eighteenth-Century Literature: Moral Theology in Fielding, Sterne, and Goldsmith* (Frankfurt: Peter Lang, 2009).

Myers, Greg. "Nineteenth-Century Popularizations of Thermodynamics and the Rhetoric of Social Prophecy." *Victorian Studies* 29, no. 1 (1985): 35–66.

Ogilvie, Brian W. "Natural History, Ethics, and Physico-Theology." In *Historia: Empiricism and Erudition in Early Modern Europe,* edited by Gianna Pomata and Nancy G. Siraisi, 75–103 (Cambridge, MA: MIT Press, 2005).

Paley, William. *Natural Theology.* 12th ed. (London: Faulder, 1809).

Patey, Douglas Lane. *Probability and Literary Form: Philosophic Theory and Literary Practice in the Augustan Age* (Cambridge: Cambridge University Press, 1984).

Raven, Charles E. *John Ray, Naturalist: His Life and Works* (Cambridge: Cambridge University Press, 1986).

Rurak, James. "Butler's *Analogy*: A Still Interesting Synthesis of Reason and Revelation." *Anglican Theological Review* 62, no. 2 (1980): 365–381.

Sklar, Lawrence. *Physics and Chance: Philosophical Issues in the Foundations of Statistical Mechanics* (Cambridge: Cambridge University Press, 1993).

Suttor, Timothy. "Bishop Joseph Butler's Place in the English Tradition." *CCHA Study Sessions* 51 (1966): 11–23.

Terry, Mark. "Pangloss, Paley, and the Privileged Planet." In *For the Rock Record: Geologists on Intelligent Design*, edited by Jill Schneiderman and Warren D. Allmon, 77–91 (Berkeley, CA: University of California Press, 2009).

Waterman, A. M. C. "A Cambridge 'Via Media' in Late Georgian Anglicanism." *Journal of Ecclesiastical History* 42, no. 3 (1991): 419–436.

Wittgenstein, Ludwig. *Philosophical Investigations*. 3rd ed. (Oxford: Blackwell, 1968).

13

Evolution, Providence, and the Problem of Chance

Peter Harrison

> The race is not to the swift, nor the battle to the strong, nor bread to the wise, nor riches to the intelligent, nor favor to the men of skill; but time and chance happen to them all.
>
> ECCLESIASTES 9:11

> What seems to us contingence, faith will recognise as the secret impulse of God.
>
> JOHN CALVIN, *Institutes*, 1.16.8

> They had clothed their belief of the workings of Providence in certain images; and they clung to those images with the persuasion that, without them, their belief could not subsist.
>
> WILLIAM WHEWELL, *Philosophy of the Inductive Sciences*, 1: 685.

IN DECEMBER 1859, in the immediate aftermath of the publication of Darwin's *Origin of Species*, Sir John Herschel rendered his verdict on the controversial work, dismissing Darwin's mechanism of natural selection as the "law of higgledly-piggledly."[1] A distinguished astronomer, mathematician, and chemist, Herschel was a bastion of the scientific establishment in England. Darwin himself had described him as "one of our greatest philosophers." Not surprisingly, Herschel's disparaging assessment of the book was a bitter disappointment to its author. Darwin was acutely aware that the two men shared a common belief in the natural origin of species—the "mysteries of mysteries," to use the phrase coined by Herschel and repeated by Darwin in the opening lines of the *Origin*. What made Herschel's rejection even more disheartening was the fact that Darwin had painstakingly sought to follow the prescriptions that Herschel had set out in his classic *Preliminary Discourse on the Study of Natural Philosophy* (1830)—one of the very first attempts to provide a systematic account of modern scientific method. Darwin had even sent Herschel one of the first copies of the book.

What could have motivated this emphatic rejection of Darwin's central doctrine by a figure we might expect to have been a significant ally? In a word, it was chance. Herschel was later to write:

> We can no more accept the principle of arbitrary and casual variation and natural selection as a sufficient account, *per se*, of the past and present organic world, than we can receive the Laputan method of composing books (pushed *a l'outrance*) as a sufficient one of Shakespeare and the Principia.[2]

The general point is clear. In spite of his commitment to the naturalistic origins of species and to the gradual and progressive variation of races of animals, Herschel could not bring himself to accept that chance lay at the heart of it all. To think that living things were all the result of natural selection working on chance variations would be akin to allowing that Jonathan Swift's "Laputan engine" might produce Shakespeare's plays or Newton's *Principia* by combining words selected at random. It was impossible, in his view, to have a science of nature based on chance. More than this, for Herschel and many of his contemporaries, the order of nature was a divinely imposed order, albeit one that was expressed in general laws. The fact that divine superintendence was a requirement for both a properly grounded scientific understanding and a true sense of human beings' place in nature made the Darwinian chance-based philosophy doubly unappealing.

In this chapter I trace the historical development of this collision between chance and providence. What I hope to show is that this apparent incompatibility between the Christian doctrine of providence and the chance elements of the Darwinian picture—an incompatibility that Herschel and many since have regarded as an acute difficulty—is to some extent an artifact of the peculiar historical circumstances in which Darwin's theory was first articulated.

Three historical factors are relevant here. First is the fact that while divine providence was traditionally understood to operate in the spheres of history and nature, in the realm of nature providence was regarded as conspicuous and demonstrable, whereas in the sphere of history it could be discerned only with the eye of faith. Second, during the period from the seventeenth to the nineteenth centuries, the nature-history boundary became blurred, as natural history was gradually transformed from a discipline that was concerned primarily with atemporal spatial and taxonomic relations to a genuinely historical discipline that was concerned with organic change over time. This transition was disguised to some extent by the paradoxical fact that at the very moment when natural history was becoming genuinely temporal, its practitioners adopted a new name for their activities—"biology." Moreover, the exponents of biology sought to align themselves with law-governed atemporal sciences such as physics. The important point, however, is that theological interpreters of evolutionary biology continued to carry with them a set of expectations about the perspicuity of God's providential activity *in nature* that were no longer appropriate for a discipline that had become essentially *historical*. (Evolutionary biology is thus numbered among the "historical sciences" that are based on evidence from past events. The historical sciences include cosmology, geology, paleontology, and archaeology.) These misplaced expectations are partly accounted for by a third factor, and that is the remarkable growth of natural theology from the seventeenth century onwards and, more specifically, a natural theology that was increasingly focused on the argument from organic design—that is, looking to the order and intricacy found in nature as arguments for a divine creator—to the exclusion of other kinds of design arguments. The refusal of Herschel and others to accept an evolutionary account that seemed completely devoid of overt design was the consequence of not wanting to trade theological views of a static and orderly nature for a dynamic and more chaotic history. The new status of evolution as a *historical science* was thus one of the key developments that exacerbated this clash between Christian ideas of providence and the Darwinian elevation of chance.

That said, Herschel's reluctance to attribute any significant role to chance in the operations of nature has an extended history that long predates the Darwinian controversies. Since the time of Plato, most Western thinkers had resisted the idea that chance might somehow be fundamental to how nature works or that chance might play a role in properly "scientific" explanations. There are four prominent reasons for this reluctance. First, it was difficult to imagine how the apparent design of living things and the orderly movements of the celestial bodies could possibly have arisen by chance. Second, and related to this, philosophers and religious thinkers up to the nineteenth century typically thought that nature was in some way imbued with purpose or teleology. Third, because cosmic purpose was generally thought to underpin human morality, chance was regarded as fatal to our coherent moral order. Fourth, because science presupposes a world that is intelligible and predictable, ascribing events to chance seemed incompatible with offering a scientific account of them. To say that something happened "by chance" is essentially equivalent to saying that it was inexplicable.

But in spite of longstanding and concerted resistance to granting contingency a central place in the natural world, chance has also had its champions, beginning with the pre-Socratic philosophers. These philosophers saw the undeniable fact of chance events, or at least what appear to be chance events, in everyday life and in the course of history. Even in the realm of organic life there are sufficient instances of less-than-optimal features that stand as challenges to the idea that all creatures have been purposefully designed. More generally, physical evils—disease, disabilities, and natural disasters—have always been in tension with notions of divine design. In response to this, advocates of design have often sought to explain how apparent instances of chance and gratuitous evils, particularly in the realm of human history, might be consistent with an overall design or intrinsic order.[3] More simply, however, teleology and design simply represented the most likely explanation of the order of nature.[4] Instances of chance and maladaptation may have posed a threat to the dominant position, but they did not in themselves constitute a systematic alternative explanation—thus teleology and design continued to dominate thought for most of Western history.

All of this was to change with the advent of a theory of natural selection which suggested that chance events could indeed play a significant role in determining the history of life and yield the *appearance* of design. Darwin's theory has rightly been accepted as revolutionary in this regard because it seems to make all the outcomes of evolution, including the arrival of human beings, a matter of chance. As John Beatty has expressed: "The multiplicity of possible outcomes of evolution by the natural selection of chance variations, and hence the contingency of the actual results (like us), is surely one of the most unsettling aspects of the Darwinian revolution."[5] The Harvard evolutionary biologist Stephen Jay Gould has highlighted these unsettling aspects of natural selection with his well-known analogy of "replaying life's tape." If we were to rewind the tape of life and run it again, "any replay of the tape would lead evolution down a pathway radically different from the road taken."[6] In this view, the appearance of human beings was a vastly improbable cosmic accident—something that Darwin himself admitted.[7]

Many religious believers could readily, and did, come to terms with the apparent inconsistencies between biblical creation narratives and the evolutionary account. Indeed, the fact that Darwin enjoyed significant support from prominent religious thinkers in the years immediately following the publication of the *Origin* is now often forgotten.[8] However, the apparent aimlessness of evolution, along with the implication that human beings were not an inevitable outcome of the evolutionary process—that the world exhibits "no design, no purpose, no evil, no good, nothing but pitiless indifference," as Richard Dawkins uncompromisingly puts it—seems radically at odds with traditional notions of providence.[9] It was this implication of natural selection that so shocked Herschel and many of his contemporaries, and which Darwin's most ardent religious supporters found impossible to accept.[10] Even today, it remains a significant obstacle to the reconciliation of evolution with traditional Christian belief. Religious believers continue to resist it. On the other side, religious skeptics posit lack of design in the natural world as a clinching argument against a purposeful creator. Darwin himself, while no advocate of atheism, admitted that natural selection was incompatible with design.[11] While contingency and chance had always been something of an irritation to proponents of providence and teleology, the elevation of the status of chance in Darwin's theory of natural selection represents for many an insurmountable challenge to Christian notions of providence, at least as traditionally conceived.

In order to understand fully the roots of this apparent incompatibility, it is helpful to consider in more detail how providence has traditionally been thought to operate in the distinct spheres of nature and history.

Augustine and Aquinas on Providence and Chance

In his *Commentary on Job*, written in 1260, Thomas Aquinas offered a helpful and concise history of Western ideas about chance and providence. It is worth repeating in full:

> Democritus and Empedocles attributed things to chance in most things. But by a more profound diligence in their contemplation of the truth later philosophers showed by evident proofs and reasons that natural things are set in motion by providence. . . . Therefore after the majority of men asserted the opinion that natural things did not happen by chance but by providence because of the order which clearly appears in them, a doubt emerged among most men about the acts of man as to whether human affairs evolved by chance or were governed by some kind of providence or a higher ordering. This doubt was fed especially because there is no sure order apparent in human events. . . . Some said that human affairs proceed by chance except to the extent that they are ruled by human providence and counsel, others attributed their outcome to a fatalism ruled by the heavens.

Aquinas went on to suggest that it was around this time that Jewish and Christian thinkers made a significant advance. They asserted that providence also operated in the sphere of human history. However, and this is a key point, they did not do so on the basis of their observations of history where, as Aquinas put it, no "sure order" manifests itself. Rather, this aspect of providence was revealed in the Hebrew Bible and the New Testament. It is significant that Aquinas's remarks occur not in the context of one of his numerous discussions of Aristotle's works, but in a biblical commentary. The whole aim of the book of Job, said Aquinas, is to "show how human affairs are ruled by divine providence."[12]

Earlier Christian responses to ideas of chance include longstanding philosophical critiques of Democritus and Epicurus, an extension of the operations of providence in nature, and a significant elaboration of the Jewish idea that God's providence operates in human history. Christian convert Dionysius of Alexandria (d. 264) devoted a complete work to an analysis and critique of Epicurean themes, introducing their doctrines in some detail before offering the standard criticism that the order that we observe in natural things is inconsistent with their being the products of "mere chance." He pointed out that these ideas are at odds with the Christian teaching that God created the world, saw that it was good, and continues to exercise providential care over it. In an intriguing anticipation of Darwin's own "horrid doubt" and Alvin Plantinga's evolutionary argument against naturalism, Dionysius went further to point out that ascribing the origin of the world and its inhabitants to chance is also difficult to square with confidence in our own intelligence and reason. If our minds consist only of the fortuitous arrangements of atoms, he suggests, we might as well give up philosophical speculation, along with "poetry, and music, and astronomy, and geometry, and all the arts and sciences."[13]

Subsequent Church Fathers also voiced concerns, mostly in connection with the doctrine of creation. Arnobius (d. ca. 330), noted that some philosophers "construct the whole fabric of the universe by chance accidents and by random collision, and fashion it by the concourse of atoms of different shapes', before dismissing these notions as 'perverse' and 'palpably foolish.' "[14] Lactantius (ca. 240–ca. 320) similarly condemned Democritus and Epicurus for having taught that "all things were either made or are governed by chance."[15] Basil the Great (330–379) agreed that the atomists had been "deceived by their inherent atheism" into thinking that "nothing governed the universe, and that all was given up to chance."[16] Jerome went so far as to offer an explanation for the supposedly counterintuitive views of the Epicureans, fathering an influential tradition according to which Lucretius had been driven mad by a love potion, and that *De rerum natura* had been composed during brief periods of lucidity before its author was eventually driven to suicide.[17]

A general Christian response to Epicurean notions of chance was to extend the scope of divine providence so that all events within nature and history fell within its remit.[18] This position meant both limiting the role of chance events and redefining classical notions of fate so that if fate were acknowledged at all, it was understood in terms of the will of God. Crucially, this thinking was extended to what transpired in human history. In *The City of God*, which was destined to become the classic treatment of divine action in history, Augustine of Hippo (354–430) dealt with the varying fortunes of the Roman Empire. Writing in the wake of the sack of Rome by the Visigoths in 410, Augustine insisted that the cause of the greatness of the empire "is neither chance nor fate." Rather, "it is by divine providence that human kingdoms are set up."[19] And it was by divine providence that they fell. As for the role of fate, it may be permissible to speak of "fate" in this context, but only if one means by that "the will or power of God."[20] Not only was there no genuine fate operating in the world, but for Augustine there were no chance events either:

> Whatever happens by chance happens without design. Whatever happens without design does not happen due to Providence. If therefore some things in the world happen by chance, then not all the world is governed by Providence. . . . Therefore nothing happens in the world by chance.[21]

For Augustine, whatever is done in the world is done "partly by divine agency and partly by our will."[22] Not everything that transpires in the world is directly attributable to the divine will, then, since human decisions (albeit permitted and foreseen by God) also play a role.

Augustine's attempts to restrict the scope of chance and expand that of providence are, as noted above, typical of a general trend among Christian writers. That said, the trend is more pronounced in the Latin Fathers.[23] Greek authors tended both to retain a place for chance events and to allow greater room for the operation of free will. This position is reflected in the West's adoption of a diluted form of Augustine's predestinarian views, and the East's profession of what the Western church was to refer to as "semi-pelagianism." Greek writers such as Basil the Great (330–379) and John of Damascus (676–749) also continued to rehearse, with approval, Aristotle's definition of chance events. According to Basil: "some events in life come naturally like old age and sickness, others by chance like unforeseen occurrences, of which the origin is beyond ourselves, often sad sometimes fortunate, as for instance the discovery of a treasure when digging a well, or the meeting of a mad dog when going to the marketplace. Others depend on ourselves, like ruling one's passions."[24] In the eighth century, John of Damascus revisited a number of these issues, noting a range of possible causes of events: God, necessity, fate, nature, chance, spontaneity. Necessity and fate he equated with the divine will. Generation, growth, corruption, plants, and animals belong to nature. To spontaneity belongs what befall inanimate things or brute beasts with the invention of nature or art. As for chance: "The unusual and unexpected belong to chance. For chance is defined as the accidental occurrence of two causes originating in deliberate choice but resulting in something other than was intended."[25]

Thomas Aquinas occupied a middle position between the more tightly constrained Augustinian world and the more free and spontaneous world of the Eastern theologians. According to Aquinas, God exercises immediate providence over things only in the sense of determining what kinds of things there will be. This belief allows a certain independence to nature, so that natural things move and develop in keeping with their inherent created powers. Moreover, insofar as God governs these things externally, angelic intelligences and demons act as intermediaries.[26] It follows that in governing the world, God does not exercise an immediate and direct control of every event.

Aquinas also allows a place for chance in the world, in keeping with his general deference toward Aristotelian doctrines, but emphatically denies that chance could ever give rise to harmony and purpose. Rather, harmony and purpose are intrinsic to nature, which is understood in Aristotelian terms as that which takes place "always or for the most part." Chance events are exceptions and are not part of nature per se:

> Whatever does not have a determinate cause happens by accident. Consequently, if the position mentioned above were true [i.e., that there are only material and efficient causes], all the harmony and usefulness found in things would be the result of chance. This was actually what Empedocles held. He asserted that it was by accident that the parts of animals came together in this way through friendship—and this was his explanation of an animal and of a frequent occurrence! This explanation, of course, is absurd, for those things that happen by chance, happen only rarely; we know from experience, however, that harmony and usefulness are found in nature either at all times or at least for the most part. This cannot be the result of mere chance; it must be because an end is intended.[27]

So chance events do take place, but they are sufficiently rare as not to interfere with the general harmony and purposefulness of nature.

There is one further area in which Aquinas also finds some space for events that are not directly willed by God. God, he suggests, also allows for "defects" in the operations of certain natural causes.[28] The occasional miscarriages of nature are an example of such defects, as when a person is born with six fingers on one hand. A further example is the whole arena of human sin, which is allowed—but not caused—by God. Sinful acts thus result from a deficiency in goodness that is permitted by God—permitted, since good may result from it. In a sense, then, sinful acts do not have a direct cause, but result from a defect of an essentially good tendency. This conception of evil as a deficiency of good had been a central feature of the theodicies of Plotinus and Augustine, and offered an explanation of how evil was consistent with the idea of God's having created a good world.[29] Related to this understanding is the case of divine reprobation where God *permits* individuals to fall away from their natural end and act contrary to his desire for their salvation.[30]

Famously, the Protestant reformer John Calvin was to demur from this position, insisting that God wills everything that takes place, including the reprobation of those not predestined to salvation. The post-Reformation period witnessed a number of realignments of Christian theology and natural philosophy through theological and philosophical movements that sought to tighten up the causal order of the world even further and to finally expel chance and contingency from their last redoubts. The key features of this repositioning were the magisterial reformers' emphasis on divine sovereignty and omnipotence, and a corresponding diminution of creaturely powers and freedoms; a new understanding of exceptionless and invariable laws of nature that rules out the "for the most part" clause of the Aristotelian understanding of nature; a baptism of some Epicurean ideas of matter theory, in which atoms or corpuscles became religiously respectable; a rejection of inherent teleology in the natural world and the human person. And, crucially, early modern thinkers continued to insist that divine providence, and not chance, ruled the sphere of history.

Chance and the Laws of Nature

The thought of John Calvin (1509–1564) is a good place to begin when considering a number of these programmatic shifts. In his account of the nature of divine providence, Calvin insists that God's omnipotence does not consist merely in general superintendence of the natural world, neither does it rest in the creation of particular kinds. God's power is "vigilant, efficacious, energetic and ever-active,—not an omnipotence which may only act as a general principle . . . but one which is intent on individual and special movements." God, then, is intimately involved in everything that takes place.[31] Opposing Thomas Aquinas's suggestion that God permits but does not directly will certain things, Calvin maintained that "God does not permit, but rules."[32] He concedes that there are many things that transpire in the course of history that might seem attributable to fate or fortune and that we can legitimately characterize as "fortuitous." But they are fortuitous *to us*, and only because their purpose and the mechanisms that brought them about are "hidden in the counsel of God."[33]

Calvin's idea of an ever-active divine power had significant parallels with key developments in natural philosophy. One of the distinctive characteristics of the new sciences lay in the idea that regularities in the natural world were to be understood in terms of laws of nature and that these laws are nothing other than divine volitions.[34] The order of nature, in this view, was not the outcome of the goal-directed natures of things working together in some teleological or purposeful way as Aristotle had taught. Rather, stripped of their intrinsic causal powers, natural things had to be moved by an external power that was typically identified as God. In *The World* (1633), French philosopher René Descartes argued that God's actions in nature are understood by us as laws of nature since those actions are so regular: "So it is that these two rules [of motion] follow manifestly from the mere fact that God is immutable and that, acting always in the same way, he always produces the same effect."[35] The immutability of the laws of nature, for Descartes, was grounded in the immutability of their divine author. It followed that the operations of nature were not to be understood, as Aristotle and Aquinas had maintained, as "what happens always or for the most part," but simply as "what happens always."

This Cartesian idea was taken up by English natural philosophers who, in spite of their differences with Descartes about how laws of nature could be derived, nonetheless accepted the basic idea that there were laws of nature and that these amounted to a description of the way in which God typically moves things around. Gravity, to take the most topical case, was understood to be "the immediate *fiat* and finger of God, and the execution of divine law."[36] Newtonian natural philosophers thus aligned the idea of laws of nature with what was essentially a Calvinist view of providence. Theologian and philosopher Samuel Clarke, who argued Newton's case in the celebrated controversy with Gottfried Leibniz, thought similarly that "the *Course of Nature*, cannot possibly be any thing else, but the *Arbitrary Will and pleasure of God* exerting itself and acting upon Matter continually."[37] It followed that miraculous events were of the same order as natural events, since both were the consequence of the immediate activity of God: it is just that miracles were unusual.[38]

Whereas Aristotelian teleology had once been the weapon of choice in the battle against the Epicurean worldview, laws of nature now assumed that role. Moreover, because laws of nature were conceptualized as immutable and universal—owing to their being grounded in either the divine nature or in divine volitions—they excluded even rare chance occurrences that had been allowed by Aristotle and Aquinas. While this had the "'advantage" of seeming to expel the very last remnants of chance from the natural world, it ran the opposite risk, incipient in Calvin's theology, of a thoroughgoing determinism. The danger of determinism (associated with Stoicism) was that it seemed to deny creaturely freedoms—including human choice—and make God the direct author of evil.

This chapter is not the place for an extended discussion of theodicy and the problem of evil in light of absolute determinism, but it is worth briefly considering the novel solutions proposed by Walter Charleton and Gottfried Leibniz, since they both grapple with the problem of contingency in history. Walter Charleton (1620–1707) was a philosopher and physician who played an important role in introducing Epicurean matter theory into England. He was concerned with finding a middle path between what he saw as the atheistic tendencies of Epicureanism and what in his view was just as bad—the fatalism and necessity of Calvin's double predestination. Epicurean atheists, he wrote, argue for "the conceived *Uncertainty and irregularity of Contingencies*, and the *unaequal dispensation of good and evill*; [that] all things seeming to fall out according to the giddy lottery of Chance, and as confusedly as if there were no Providence at all."[39] But the expulsion of *all* contingency from the world seemed to be equally problematic. Hence, the "absolute predestination" of the Calvinists was no better than "the *Fate* of *the Stoicks*."[40] In order to find some space between these equally unpalatable alternatives, Charleton devised an ingenious theory that represents free choice in terms of possible worlds (although he does not use that terminology).[41] In the late sixteenth century, the Spanish Jesuit Luis de Molina had sought to preserve human liberty in a world in which all events were divinely willed by attributing "middle knowledge" to God. This was knowledge of what human agents would freely choose in particular circumstances. If God knows these choices, he can determine that the relevant circumstances obtain, and thus will particular human decisions, but without compelling them.[42] In Charleton's version, God surveys the possible worlds represented by the various natural contingencies and choices of free agents and then actualizes the best of those worlds. In this way, God knows with certainty what will transpire in this world and wills everything that takes place in it, but does so without infringing free choice.[43] To employ Stephen Jay Gould's analogy, by knowing the full range of possibilities represented on all possible "tapes" of history, God knows the details of the one actually chosen to run.

Leibniz later adopted a similar stance in the *Theodicy* (1710). Before the moment of creation, God imagines the full range of possible worlds—as represented by various contingencies and human choices—and creates that which is best. This is the basis of Leibniz's well-known and much parodied doctrine that we live in the best of all possible worlds. Stated in terms of the principle of sufficient reason—a principle which stresses that there must be a reason for everything that takes place—the reason God created *this* world is because it is the best possible.[44] In this way, both human freedom, represented in alternative courses of action, and chance events could be represented in alternative possible worlds never actualized. These scenarios offered the prospect of preserving divine omnipotence and foreknowledge, of nullifying the impact of chance and contingency, and of preserving free will.

While the speculative solutions of Charleton and Leibniz offer possible mechanisms for reconciling divine providence with free will and the contingencies of history, they do not offer *evidence* for the providential guidance of history. This lack of an evidentiary basis for special providence had been a conspicuous feature of Calvin's theology.

Chance as Hidden Design

An important implication of Calvin's position, noted at the beginning of the previous section, is that divine providence cannot be directly inferred from the events of history. The interpretation of events as providential is not a matter of objective judgment but of training the mind, with the assistance of the gift of faith, to view all things as under God's control, unfolding according to the divine purpose: "What seems to us contingence, *faith* will recognize as the secret impulse of God."[45] This perspective, in turn, brings a kind of peace and assurance to the minds of the faithful (ironically, not unlike the "imperturbability" sought by the Epicureans): "But when once the light of Divine Providence has illumined the believer's soul, he is relieved and set free, not only from the extreme fear and anxiety which formerly oppressed him, but from all care."[46] So it is the eye of faith that enables us to declare that all things happen in accordance with divine purposes. Chance, in consequence, has only an epistemic status, as captured in the couplet that appears in the conclusion of Alexander Pope's "Essay on Man" (1732–1733):

> All Nature is but Art, unknown to thee;
> All Chance, Direction, which thou canst not see;[47]

William Paley, in a subtle but largely overlooked treatment of chance in *Natural Theology* (1802), similarly remarked that "the *appearance of chance* will always bear a proportion to the ignorance of the observer."[48] In this respect, the interpretation of history differed from the interpretation of nature, where divine providence was thought to be conspicuous in the design and purposeful behaviors of creatures and in the regularities of the motions of celestial bodies. If God's wisdom and providence were sometimes difficult to discern in the unfolding of history, it was, for all that, still apparent in the order of nature.

There is a curious coda to Calvin's treatment of providence in relation to "chance" events in human history, but it is one that is directly relevant to the present discussion. In the 1762 Glasgow edition of Calvin's *Institutes*, the hidden nature of God's oversight of history is described in terms of the operation of an " 'invisible hand":

> But those things which appear to us to happen by chance, faith will acknowledge to have been owing to a secret impulse of God. I grant there doth not always appear the like reason, but doubtless we ought to believe, that whatsoever changes of things are seen in the world, are brought about by the direction and influence of God's invisible hand.[49]

The idea of "the invisible hand" is now typically attributed to Adam Smith, who made the phrase famous in *The Wealth of Nations* (1776).[50] This earlier reference in Calvin's *Institutes* suggests that there was an existing tradition about " 'the invisible hand," which identified it with God's providential acts in history. This evidence offers some help in adjudicating competing contemporary claims about whether Smith's phrase was a purely secular device or was genuinely providential.[51] But more importantly, it points to the fact that divine providence, in the realm of history, was then understood to operate in ways that were inaccessible to human thought.

The invisible activity contrasted sharply with more conspicuous evidence of God's providence in the natural world. The full range of design arguments that flourished between the seventeenth and nineteenth centuries need not be rehearsed in detail here. But it is worth considering a few examples simply to contrast them with the more mysterious actions of God in history and to show how closely these arguments were connected to developments in what we would call "the new sciences." In his *Antidote again Atheism* (1653, 1655), Cambridge Platonist Henry More enumerated what would become over the next two centuries standard arguments for the existence and wisdom of God. In particular, he stipulated that the newly discovered laws of motion "very manifestly convince us of a Providence."[52] Robert Boyle, a key figure in the development of experimental science, similarly maintained that Descartes's discovery of the laws of motion provides us with "a double argument for the divine providence." The same could be said for the new experimentally based science, as practiced in the Royal Society: "a Belief of the Divine Providence . . . may be much confirmed by Experimental Philosophy."[53] Whereas God's providence in history was "secret," "hidden," "inaccessible," "not discernable," in the natural world such providence was "demonstrable," "very manifest," and "convincing." It was this clear distinction between the two kinds of knowledge of God's providence that was to become blurred when in the nineteenth century living things become subject to historical change.

History, Natural History, and the Demise of Design

While it is often thought that natural theology (understood as the attempt to provide support for religious belief from arguments based on reason alone) flourished in the Middle Ages, it was really only in the early modern period that it rose to prominence.[54] Of the so-called classical arguments for God's existence that form the core of natural theology—the ontological, cosmological, and teleological (design) arguments—it was the last that came to assume the main burden of offering independent support for religious belief. Henry More's *Antidote against Atheism* was one of the earliest examples of the genre, and it was followed by such popular works as John Ray's *Wisdom of God Manifested in the Works of Creation* (1691), Noël-Antoine Pluche's multivolume *Spectacle de la Nature* (1732), and William Paley's *Natural Theology*. In the later seventeenth century, the Boyle Lectures boosted the number of publications on these themes, and the topic enjoyed remarkable popularity until well into the nineteenth century. The Earl of Bridgewater made provision in his will for a series of books on "The Power, Wisdom, and Goodness of God, as manifested in the Creation," and the 1829 bequest made particular reference to "the variety and formation of God's creatures in the animal, vegetable, and mineral kingdoms; the effect of digestion, and thereby of conversion; the construction of the hand of man."[55]

There are a number of reasons for the popularity of the design argument in this period. It was widely regarded as more accessible than the "speculative" ontological and cosmological arguments. It was an argument for which there was a seemingly inexhaustible supply of relevant subject matter, to which the telescope and microscope made further contributions. Its logical structure was inductive, at a time when induction was coming to be regarded as the proper form of scientific reasoning. It provided an edifying framework for the popularization of scientific themes. It was an argument that even opponents of traditional Christianity supported, for it was as popular amongst deist writers as Christian apologists, as John Hedley Brooke has shown.[56] Finally, and related to a number of these points, it was the one argument that most closely drew upon the natural sciences. This intimate connection between natural theology, natural history, and natural philosophy had the dual advantages of establishing the religious legitimacy of scientific activity while at the same time reinforcing the rational credibility of religious belief.

A number of these features also served to distinguish natural history, in which these design arguments were embedded, from other kinds of history. Despite the fact that natural history has the word "history" in its title, it had never been historical in the sense of dealing with change over time. Thus, while classifications of the sciences traditionally placed natural history within a more general disciplinary category that included civil and ecclesiastical history, what was meant by "history" in this context was not a chronological account of the past, but something more like "a collection of particular facts."[57] Moreover, natural history was distinguished from other branches of history not just by its subject matter, but also by the fact that it was possible to organize that subject matter in a quite systematic way. Accordingly, those who argued that natural history provided evidence of God's providence took care to distinguish it from the more contingent sphere of human history. In his popular *The Historie of Foure-footed Beastes* (1607), Edward Topsell deployed the popular "book of nature" metaphor to point out that natural history was like a narrative dictated by God, and hence had a coherent plot. Unlike humanly authored chronicles, it was not like an account of "accidents of time past." Rather, it had the clear "appearance of design."[58] Indeed, design, or more strictly, "contrivance," was to become a unifying principle of natural history. Abbé Pluche maintained that nature was pervaded by "one universal Law of Harmony and Agreement," which consisted in the principle of design.[59] William Paley argued similarly that there was a "uniformity of plan" observable in the universe. What made the natural order "a system" was the fact that it had a coherent plan.[60] Thus the design principle was not so much a theological idea bolted onto a natural history as an apologetic afterthought: it was an underlying systematizing principle. It is not a complete surprise that Charles Darwin would recall that the logic of Paley's *Evidences of Christianity*, one of the set texts that he would have read as a Cambridge undergraduate, gave him as much delight as reading the *Elements* of Euclid.[61] The logic of design was what lent the discipline its coherence. And not only that, as an increasing emphasis was placed on arguments from organic design, natural history was moved even further away from the contingent realm of human history. But natural history eventually became truly historical, and Darwin's theory of evolution by natural selection would make this possible.

It is true that Darwin's theory came as something of a shock to his Victorian contemporaries—"like a plough into an ant-hill" as Andrew Dickson White put it.[62] Yet for all that, it had been a long time coming. Over the course of the eighteenth century, developments in geology made it apparent that the earth was much older than the 6000 years proposed in the well-known chronology of Archbishop James Ussher.[63] This conclusion was agreed upon by geologists and theologians alike. And while human history and geological history were not necessarily thought to be coterminous, nonetheless it seemed increasingly likely that the human race had a history that vastly exceeded the few millennia covered by the biblical record. In the late eighteenth and early nineteenth centuries, moreover, various thinkers had proposed schemes of organic transmutation.

Best known, perhaps, are the ideas of Jean-Baptiste Lamarck, who for generations of biology students has served as an example of how not to understand evolutionary development. In his *Philosophie Zoologique* (1809) Lamarck suggested that changes take place in species in accordance with a "tendency to progressive improvement." Species are propelled upwards in the chain of being, and the environment works to strengthen or weaken various characters that are preserved in subsequent generations. In 1844, Robert Chambers published a popular Lamarckian evolutionary account entitled *Vestiges of the Natural History of Creation,* which ran to numerous editions and enjoyed a very wide readership. He, too, invoked the idea of a guiding law, asserting that just as the physical world is ruled by a single law of gravity, so the organic world is governed by the law of development.[64] Other pre-Darwinian evolutionists maintained that biological change confirmed strict laws that were based on embryological development. (Indeed the term "evolution" as a scientific term originally derives from this embryological context.) These approaches tended to stress the law-like inexorability of the progression of species (and in the case of Haeckel, of races and cultures, too).

To a degree, the speculative accounts of Lamarck and Chambers prepared the way for the Darwinian account, in spite of the fact that neither was well received by the religious or scientific establishments. But they differed from the Darwinian theory of natural selection in a crucial way: both maintained that natural laws underwrote the purposeful and progressive nature of evolution. By way of contrast, as early as 1844, Darwin had declared that Lamarck's "tendency to progression" was "nonsense."[65] The Darwinian scheme was not one that invoked notions of purpose, progress, or direction. The *Origin* set out an evolutionary history that was genuinely open, with no guarantees of particular outcomes, progressive or otherwise.

If Darwin's embrace of contingency seemed unequivocal, the situation in regard to natural laws was more complicated. In the *Origin* Darwin spoke of the production and extinction of living things by secondary causes, in accordance with "the laws impressed on matter by the Creator."[66] This talk of laws of nature is superficially similar to that used by William Whewell in his Bridgewater Treatise and John Herschel in his *Preliminary Discourse*. Both of these authors had spoken of laws "impressed" upon nature, and Darwin sought to make his apparent reliance upon their conception explicit by using the relevant quotation from Whewell as one of the epigraphs for the *Origin*. In fact, the respective conceptions of laws of nature are quite different.[67] Whewell and Herschel had both thought that laws entail "intelligent direction," with Whewell insisting that "the intelligence by which the law is ordained . . . must be present at all times and in all places where the effects of the law occur." Herschel spoke of the "inevitable consequences" of the operations of natural law.[68] By way of contrast, Darwin had come to the view that what he was to call the "law of natural selection" was incompatible with design. This "law" also allowed a significant place to chance. Writing to Asa Gray in 1860, he wrote: "I am inclined to look at everything as resulting from designed laws, with the details, whether good or bad, left to the working out of what we may call chance."[69]

This is a very loose conception of "law." Darwin's "law of natural selection" could hardly be a law of nature in the usual sense. Crucially, it did not seem to provide a reliable basis for prediction. (As we would now express it, it was not the kind of law that could support counterfactuals).[70] Herschel, who had carefully set out how natural laws related to contingent events, perceived this with clarity, and it was his keen awareness of the disparity between his own notion of natural law and that of Darwin that led to his damning indictment of the Darwinian mechanism—the law of higgledy-piggledy, or, in reality, not a law at all. The problem was not just that the Darwinian scheme offended religious sensibilities but that it invited the long standing complaint that chance-based events "'can never be developed into a consistent system.'"[71]

Returning to the issue of what this all might mean for providence, we can conclude that if the history of nature were understood to be more akin to human history at the time Darwin published the *Origin*, no one would have expected to see conspicuous instances of purpose at every moment. What the doctrine of providence would dictate, then, would be that *in spite of* the prominence of apparent chance events, the faithful should be prepared to accept that God's hidden purposes were being fulfilled. Viewed in this light, the purpose behind the successions of species in the Darwinian framework would be no more obvious than the logic of the rise and fall of kingdoms in human history. Why so few read Darwinian evolution in this fashion is owing to a combination of historical factors—foremost among them the fact that the full implications of natural history's transformation into a temporal enterprise were not fully recognized at the time. Hence, the fateful collision between the expectation of design and the apparent randomness of the Darwinian theory.

The antiquity and persistence of "Epicurean" interpretations of the world suggest that there have always been those for whom the hypothesis of a universal purpose or design is unconvincing. To suggest that an intellectually coherent atheism became possible only in the wake of Darwinism does an injustice to previous thinkers for whom chance, contingency, and evils of various kinds were of sufficient weight to constitute an obstacle to the adoption of the design hypothesis. This is part of the import of Aquinas's earlier reflections on the history of ideas of chance. According to Aquinas, while the most acute philosophers eventually came to see that there were powerful arguments for purpose in nature, "most men" were still led by the contingencies of human affairs to doubt that there was some overarching superintendence of the course of history.[72] As Aquinas pointed out, what made the case for purpose in history was not a set of logical inferences from available facts, but the revealed tradition contained in the Hebrew Bible and New Testament. For those lacking privileged access to these sources, resorting to chance and fate to account for the shape of history was not unreasonable. Historically, the question of purpose in human history had never been one that could be resolved by appeals to the relevant facts. What I have suggested in this chapter is that after Darwin this became true for the history of life.

For some, the Darwinian revolution shifted the balance of probabilities back in favor of the Epicurean interpretation. This shift was particularly true for those disinclined to give much weight to the revealed truths of the Judeo-Christian tradition. For their part, those with religious commitments had three options. First, they could concede the ultimate incompatibility of an evolutionary view with the notion of underlying purpose, and reject one or the other. Second, they could seek empirical grounds for asserting that, contrary to appearances, evolutionary history was in fact purposeful. Or, third, they could accept the radical contingencies involved in evolutionary history and make the necessary epistemic adjustment to make it consistent with a belief in providence. That adjustment would involve an acceptance of the appearance of purposelessness in evolutionary processes, but would be accompanied by a fideistic commitment that hidden purposes were nonetheless at work. That the third option was adopted by so few, I have suggested, was to do with long engrained habits of thought about design in nature. Its "unthinkability" was largely an artifact of the historical predominance of design arguments over the preceding period.

The history that I have outlined here is not primarily intended to support any particular philosophical position on this issue. But this discussion goes beyond simply attempting to account for why one particular option for theistic evolution did not have much uptake. The meta-argument, as it were, is that the plausibility of certain philosophical positions is not a function of whether they are sound or valid but, rather, depends upon the historical context in which they are articulated. (Perhaps historians will not need to be persuaded of this conclusion.) What I hope to have shown is that knowledge of the relevant history helps us understand how philosophical arguments are received and that their reception is somewhat independent of their logic. A few philosophers have expressed similar views. There is a distant analogy to this idea at work in the Kantian antinomies of pure reason, some of which are directly to do with a rationally irreconcilable opposition between "Platonic" and "Epicurean" conceptions of the cosmos.[73] But Kant, of course, suggests that the contradiction between these apparently rationally coherent alternatives arises out of illicit attempts to apply reason beyond its legitimate bounds. What I am suggesting is closer to Charles Taylor's ideas about "the conditions of belief," according to which "all beliefs are held within a context or framework of the taken-for-granted, which usually remain tacit, and may even be as yet unacknowledged by the agent."[74] Closer still, perhaps, is Ludwig Wittgenstein, who offers these remarks in *On Certainty*:

> I did not get my picture of the world by satisfying myself of its correctness; nor do I have it because I am satisfied of its correctness. No: it is the inherited background against which I distinguish between true and false.
>
> The propositions describing this world-picture might be part of a kind of mythology.[75]

History offers one way into an understanding of these "inherited backgrounds," the way in which they change over time, and the power that they exert over what appears plausible to us. In a sense, then, the historical opposition between purpose and chance is not so much about the relevant arguments. These come later. And when they do, they are perhaps best understood as constituents of competing mythologies.

Notes

1. Charles Darwin to Charles Lyell, December 10, 1859, Darwin Correspondence Project, Letter 2575, http://www.darwinproject.ac.uk/entry-2575.
2. John Herschel, *Physical Geography*, 2nd ed. (Edinburgh: Adam and Charles Black, 1862),12 n. The slightly obscure mention of the "Laputan method" is a reference to a machine that Jonathan Swift's Gulliver encounters on his visit to the Grand Academy of Lagado. The machine is put to the unlikely task of composing whole books by randomly selecting words; "A Voyage to Laputa," *Gulliver's Travels* (Harmondsworth: Penguin, 1985), 227–229. This had become the now familiar "monkeys and typewriters generating Shakespeare" conceit.
3. I am distinguishing teleology (intrinsic order) from design, since the former is compatible with there being no Creator, as in the case of Aristotle's philosophy of nature.

4. This is where David Hume ends up, despite a tendency of some modern philosophical commentators to read his critiques of the design argument as responding to Paley, who wrote after him and in the full knowledge of the Humean objections. So, too, J. S. Mill, "in the present state of our knowledge, the adaptations in Nature afford a large balance of probability in favour of creation by intelligence"; "Theism" (originally published in 1874), in *Three Essays on Religion*, ed. Louis J. Matz (Peterborough: Broadview, 2009), 166.
5. John Beatty, "Chance Variation: Darwin on Orchids," *Philosophy of Science* 73, no. 5 (2006): 629–641.
6. Stephen Jay Gould, *Wonderful Life* (New York: W. W. Norton, 1990), 48–51.
7. "if any single link in this [evolutionary] chain had never existed, man would not have been exactly what he now is"; *The Descent of Man* (London: John Murray, 1871), 1: 213.
8. See, e.g., Jon H. Roberts, "Religious Reactions to Darwin," in *The Cambridge Companion to Science and Religion*, ed. Peter Harrison, 80–102 (Cambridge: Cambridge University Press, 2010); David N. Livingstone, *Darwin's Forgotten Defenders: The Encounter between Evangelical Theology and Evolutionary Thought* (Grand Rapids, MI: Eerdmans, 1987); James R. Moore, *The Post-Darwinian Controversies: A Study of the Protestant Struggle to Come to Terms with Darwin in Great Britain and America, 1870–1900* (Cambridge: Cambridge University Press, 1981).
9. Richard Dawkins, *River Out of Eden: A Darwinian View of Life* (New York: Basic Books, 1995), 133.
10. See, e.g., Asa Gray to Charles Darwin, July 7, 1863, Darwin Correspondence Project, Letter 4232F, http://www.darwinproject.ac.uk/entry-4232F. For the views of Gray and others, see Asa Gray, *Darwiniana: Essays and Reviews Pertaining to Darwinism* (New York: Appleton, 1889), esp. 142f, 153f, 361f, 368.
11. Charles Darwin, *The Autobiography of Charles Darwin*, ed. Nora Barlow (New York: Harcourt Brace, 1958), 87.
12. Thomas Aquinas, *Opera Omnia*, vol. 26, *Expositio super Iob ad litteram* (Rome: Commissio Leonina, 1965), 1.1.
13. Dionysius, "From the Books on Nature," 1–4, trans. S. D. F. Salmond, in *The Ante-Nicene Fathers: Translations of the Writings of the Fathers Down to A.D. 325*, ed. Alexander Roberts and James Donaldson, vol. 6, *Gregory Thaumaturgus, Dionysius the Great, Julius Africanus, Anatolius and Minor Writers, Methodius, Arnobius* (Buffalo: Christian Literature Company, 1886), 89. *Against the Epicureans* is not extant and only fragments survive. Cf. Charles Darwin to William Graham July 3, 1881: "But then with me the horrid doubt always arises whether the convictions of man's mind, which has been developed from the mind of the lower animals, are of any value or at all trustworthy"; Darwin Correspondence Project, Letter 13230, http://www.darwinproject.ac.uk/entry-13230. For Plantinga's argument and a discussion of his ideas, see James Beilby,

ed., *Naturalism Defeated: Essays on Plantinga's Evolutionary Argument against Naturalism* (Ithaca, NY: Cornell University Press, 2002).

14. Arnobius, "Against the Heathen," trans. Hamilton Bryce and Hugh Campbell, in *The Ante-Nicene Fathers: Translations of the Writings of the Fathers Down to A.D. 325*, ed. Alexander Roberts and James Donaldson, vol. 6, *Gregory Thaumaturgus, Dionysius the Great, Julius Africanus, Anatolius and Minor Writers, Methodius, Arnobius*, 413–539 (Buffalo: Christian Literature Company, 1886), 1.31, 421.
15. Lactantius, "The Divine Institutes," 1.2.1–2, trans. William Fletcher, in *The Ante-Nicene Fathers: Translations of the Writings of the Fathers Down to A.D. 325*, ed. Alexander Roberts and James Donaldson, vol. 7, *Lactantius, Venantius, Asterius, Victorinus, Dionysius, Apostolic Teaching and Constitutions, Homily, and Liturgies* (New York: Christian Literature Company, 1890), 11.
16. Basil the Great, "The Hexaemeron," 1.2, in *A Select Library of Nicene and Post-Nicene Fathers of the Christian Church*, ed. Henry Wace and Philip Schaff, second series, vol. 8, *St. Basil: Letters and Select Works*, ed. and trans. Blomfield Jackson (New York: Christian Literature Company, 1895), 53.
17. Ada Palmer, "Between Fits of Madness: Ancient References and Proto-Biographies," in *Reading Lucretius in the Renaissance* (Cambridge, MA: Harvard University Press, 2014), 97–139. For other patristic views see Origen, *Homilies on Genesis and Exodus*, trans. Ronald E. Heine, *Fathers of the Church*, vol. 71 (Washington, DC: Catholic University of America Press, 1982), 14.3, 198–201; John Chrysostom, "Homily 3," in *Homilies on Genesis 1–17*, trans. Robert C. Hill, *Fathers of the Church*, vol. 74 (Washington, DC: Catholic University of America Press, 1986) 45.
18. Origen and Augustine both make specific reference to those who limited the operations of providence to the supralunary realm. Origen, *Homilies on Genesis* 14.3, 198–201; Augustine, *Expositions on the Book of Psalms*, ed. A. Cleveland Coxe, *A Select Library of Nicene and Post-Nicene Fathers of the Christian Church*, ed. Philip Schaff, first series, vol. 8 (Grand Rapids, MI: Eerdmans, 1956), 148.8.
19. "nec fortuita est nec fatalis"; Augustine, *City of God*, trans. William M. Green, Loeb Classical Library (Cambridge, MA: Harvard University Press, 1961–1972), 5.1, 2: 132–133, 135.
20. Augustine, *City of God* 5.1, 2: 135; cf. 5.9.
21. Augustine, *Eighty-Three Different Questions*, trans. David L. Mosher, *Fathers of the Church*, vol. 70 (Washington, DC: Catholic University of America Press, 2010), question 24, 50–51.
22. Ibid.
23. One point of comparison lies in patristic commentary on Matthew 10.29, according to which not even a sparrow falls to the ground "apart from the Father." While exegesis of this passage is indicative of an extension of the scope

of providence to the most apparently trivial events, it is also suggestive of the different tendencies of East and West. The biblical phrase is ambiguous, but the Latin Fathers tend to slide from *sine patre vestro* ("without your father"), which is the Vulgate rendition, to *sine patris voluntate*—without the *will* or *permission* of your Father—implying that God wills every natural event. Cyprian, *Epistulae* (Corpus Scriptorum Ecclesiasticorum Latinorum, vol.3, pt. 1, 59.5, 672; Jerome, *Commentarium in Evangelium Matthaei*, 1.10 (Jacques-Paul Migne, *Patrologia cursus completes: Series Latina* [*PL*] 26:68–69); Augustine, *De agone Christiano*, 8.9 (*PL* 40:295–296); *Enarratio in Psalmum* 145 (*PL* 37:1893–1894); *Expositions on the Book of Psalms*, 146, 8: 663. See H. F. Stander, "The Sparrow's Fall: Mt. 10:29," *HTS Teologiese Studies/Theological Studies* 61, no. 4 (2005), 1071–1083.

24. Basil the Great, "Hexaemeron," 8: 62.
25. John of Damascus, "The Orthodox Faith," in *Writings*, trans. Frederic H. Chase Jr., 165–406, *Fathers of the Church*, vol. 37 (Washington, DC: Catholic University of America Press, 1958), 2.25, 255–256. Later he also asserts that God fore-knows, but does not predestine: 2.30, 263.
26. Aquinas, *Summa Theologiae* [*ST*] 1a, 22, 3.
27. Aquinas, *Quaestiones Disputatae de Veritate*, q. 5, a. 2: *Truth*, trans. Robert W. Mulligan (Indianapolis: Hackett, 1994), 1: 210. Cf. *ST* 1a, 115, 6; *Expositio libri Physicorum*, 2, 253. The view that Aquinas is critiquing—that there are only material and efficient causes—is the view attributed to the ancient atomists and Epicureans.
28. *ST* 1a, 22; 2, 49, 1; *Summa Contra Gentiles* 3, 3, 9; 3, 4, 3; 3, 99, 9.
29. Augustine, *The Augustine Catechism: The Enchiridion on Faith, Hope, and Love*, ed. Boniface Ramsey, trans. and notes by Bruce Harbert, *The Works of Saint Augustine: A Translation for the 21st Century*, vol. 1 (Hyde Park, NY: New City, 1999), 11; *City of God*, 3: 11.9.
30. Aquinas, *ST* 1a, 23, 3
31. John Calvin, *Institutes of the Christian Religion*, trans. Henry Beveridge (Edinburgh: Calvin Translation Society, 1845), 1.16.3, 1: 234.
32. Calvin, *Institutes*, 3.23.1, 2: 226.
33. Ibid.
34. For these developments see Eric Watkins, ed., *The Divine Order, the Human Order, and the Order of Nature: Historical Perspectives* (New York: Oxford University Press, 2013), chaps. 3–6; Peter Harrison, "The Development of the Concept of Laws of Nature," in *Creation: Law and Probability*, ed. Fraser Watts, 13–36 (Aldershot: Ashgate, 2008).
35. René Descartes, "The World or Treatise on Light," in *The Philosophical Writings of Descartes*, trans. John Cottingham, Robert Stoothoff, and Dugald Murdoch (Cambridge: Cambridge University Press, 1985), 1: 96.
36. Richard Bentley, *The Works of Richard Bentley D.D.*, vol. 3, *Theological Writings*, ed. Alexander Dyce (London: Macpherson, 1838), 74, 75.

37. Samuel Clarke, *The Works of Samuel Clarke, D.D.* (London: J. and P. Knapton, 1738), 2: 698.
38. ". . . absolutely speaking, in *This strict and Philosophical Sense*; either nothing is miraculous, namely, if we have respect to the Power of God; or, if we regard our own Power and Understanding, then almost *every thing*, as well what we call natural, as what we call supernatural, *is* in *this Sense* really miraculous; and 'tis only *usualness* or *Unusualness* that makes the distinction"; Ibid., 2: 697. See Peter Harrison, "Newtonian Science, Miracles, and the Laws of Nature," *Journal of the History of Ideas* 56, no. 4 (1995), 531–553. Not everyone accepted this notion of God as the immediate cause of natural events. Ralph Cudworth, against this general trend, maintained that it was unseemly for the Deity to "do all the meanest and triflingest things himself drudgingly"; *The True Intellectual System of the Universe* (London, 1678), 1.3.4, 149f. For alternative conceptions of natural order in this period, see Watkins, *Divine Order.*
39. Walter Charleton, *The Darknes of Atheism Dispelled by the Light of Nature. A Physico-Theologicall Treatise* (London, 1652), 99.
40. Ibid., 215.
41. I am grateful to Pete Jordan for drawing this feature of Charleton's thought to my attention.
42. Luis de Molina, *On Divine Foreknowledge: Part IV of the "Concordia"*, trans. Alfred J. Freddoso (Ithaca, NY: Cornell University Press, 1988); Thomas P. Flint, *Divine Providence: The Molinist Account* (Ithaca, NY: Cornell University Press, 1998). Charleton is clearly aware of Molina's work, although in *The Darknes of Atheism* (343) he appears to be dismissive of it.
43. Charleton, *Darknes of Atheism*, 242–243.
44. Gottfried Wilhelm Leibniz, *Theodicy: Essays on the Goodness of God, the Freedom on Man and the Origin of Evil*, trans. E. M. Huggard (La Salle, IL: Open Court, 1985), §414, 370–71; *Philosophical Essays*, ed. and trans. Roger Ariew and Daniel Garber (Indianapolis, IN: Hackett, 1989), 46. Unlike Charleton, Leibniz (*Theodicy*, 46–7) explicitly relies on Molina. Pt. 1, §§39–42.
45. Calvin, *Institutes*, 1.16.8 (my emphasis), 1: 241–243.
46. Calvin, *Institutes*, 1.17.11, 1:261–263.
47. Alexander Pope, "Essay on Man," in *Works of Alexander Pope*, ed. Joseph Wharton, vol. 3, 1–172 (London: 1797), section 10.
48. William Paley, *Natural Theology*, in *Paley's Works* (London: Henry G. Bohn, 1849), 514. For Paley on chance, see John Beatty, "Chance and Design," in *The Cambridge Encyclopedia of Darwin and Evolutionary Thought*, ed. Michael Ruse, 146–151 (Cambridge: Cambridge University Press, 2013).
49. John Calvin, *The Institution of the Christian religion: In Four Books*, trans. Thomas Norton (Glasgow, 1762), 1.16.9, 84.

50. Smith first used the phrase in *The Theory of Moral Sentiments* (1759), ed. D. D. Raphael and A. L. Macfie (Oxford: Oxford University Press, 1976), 4.1.10, 184f. For the later reference, see Adam Smith, *An Enquiry into the Nature and Causes of the Wealth of Nations*, ed. R. H. Campbell and A. S. Skinner (Oxford: Oxford University Press, 1975), 4.2.9, 2: 456.
51. On this point, and the history of the expression, see Peter Harrison, "Adam Smith and the History of the Invisible Hand," *Journal of the History of Ideas* 72, no. 1 (2011), 29–49.
52. Henry More, "An Antidote against Atheism," in *A Collection of Several Philosophical Writings of Dr. Henry More*, 2nd ed. (London: William Morden, 1662), 5.
53. Robert Boyle *The Christian Virtuoso* (London: Edward Jones for John Taylor, 1690), 34, 26.
54. See Peter Harrison, *The Territories of Science and Religion* (Chicago: University of Chicago Press, 2015), 71–74.
55. From the will and testament of Francis Henry Bridgewater, in the first Bridgewater Treatise, Thomas Chalmers, *On the Power of Wisdom and Goodness of God as Manifested in the Adaptation of External Nature to the Moral and Intellectual Constitution of Man*, 3rd ed. (London: William Pickering, 1834), ix.
56. John Hedley Brooke, *Science and Religion: Some Historical Perspectives* (Cambridge: Cambridge University Press, 1991), 262–264.
57. On the disciplinary category see Peter Harrison, "Natural History," in *Wrestling with Nature: From Omens to Science*, ed. Peter Harrison, Ronald L. Numbers, and Michael H. Shank, 117–148 (Chicago: University of Chicago Press, 2011). See also "Introduction," in *Historia: Empiricism and Erudition in Early Modern Europe*, ed. Gianna Pomata and Nancy G. Siraisi, 1–38 (Cambridge, MA: MIT Press, 2005).
58. Edward Topsell, *The Historie of Foure-footed Beastes* (London, 1607), Epistle Dedicatory.
59. Noël-Antoine Pluche, *The Spectacle of Nature on the Peculiarities of Natural History* (Paris : Frères Estienne, 1780), 3 : 112.
60. Paley, *Natural Theology*, 113.
61. Darwin, *Autobiography*, 59. Cf. Charles Darwin to John Stevens Henslow, July 2, [1848], Darwin Correspondence Project, Letter 1189, http://www.darwinproject.ac.uk/entry-1189.
62. Andrew Dickson White, *A History of the Warfare of Science with Theology in Christendom* (London: Macmillan, 1896), 1: 70.
63. James Ussher, *Annales Veteris Testamenti* (London, 1650).
64. Robert Chambers, *Vestiges of the Natural History of Creation* (London: John Churchill, 1844), 360, 156.

65. "I am almost convinced (quite contrary to opinion I started with) that species are not (it is like confessing a murder) immutable. Heaven forfend me from Lamarck nonsense of a 'tendency to progression' 'adaptations from the slow willing of animals,' &c,—but the conclusions I am led to are not widely different from his—though the means of change are wholly so"; Charles Darwin to Joseph Dalton Hooker, January 11, 1844, Darwin Correspondence Project, Letter 729, http://www.darwinproject.ac.uk/entry-729.
66. Charles Darwin, *On the Origin of Species* (London: James Murray, 1859), 488.
67. William Whewell, *The Bridgewater Treatises*, Treatise 3, *Astronomy and General Physics Considered with Reference to Natural Theology*, 7th ed. (London: William Pickering, 1839), 356–365; John Herschel, *Preliminary Discourse to the Study of Natural Philosophy*, new ed. (London: Longman, Brown, Green and Longmans, 1851), pp. 35–7.
68. Whewell, *Bridgewater Treatises*, Treatise 3, 361f. Herschel, *Preliminary Discourse*, 37.
69. "The old argument of design in nature, as given by Paley, which formerly seemed to me so conclusive, fails, now that the law of natural selection has been discovered'; Darwin, *Autobiography*, 87; Charles Darwin to Asa Gray, May 22, [1860], Darwin Correspondence Project, Letter 2814, http://www.darwinproject.ac.uk/entry-2814. In this same letter, Darwin also toyed with an alternative Leibnizian formulation: "I can see no reason, why a man, or other animal, may not have been aboriginally produced by other laws; & that all these laws may have been expressly designed by an omniscient Creator, who foresaw every future event & consequence. But the more I think the more bewildered I become." For Darwin on laws of nature see John Hedley Brooke, "'Laws Impressed on Matter by the Creator'? The *Origin* and the Question of Religion," in (eds.), *The Cambridge Companion to the "Origin of Species"*, ed. Michael Ruse and Robert J. Richards, 256–274 (Cambridge: Cambridge University Press, 2009).
70. Herschel comes close to using the language of counterfactuals; *Preliminary Discourse*, 36.
71. Gray, *Darwiniana*, 154.
72. William Paley had a similar view: "Natural theology has ever been pressed with the question; Why, under the regency of a supreme and benevolent Will, should there be, in the world, no much, as there is, of the appearance of chance?"; *Natural Theology*, 514.
73. Immanuel Kant, *Critique of Pure Reason*, trans. and ed. Paul Guyer and Allen W. Wood (Cambridge: Cambridge University Press, 1998), A471–2/B499–500.
74. Charles Taylor, *A Secular Age* (Cambridge, MA: Belknap Press of Harvard University Press, 2007), 12–14.

75. Ludwig Wittgenstein, *On Certainty*, ed. G. E. M. Anscombe and G. H. von Wright (New York: Harper and Rowe, 1972), §§94–95, 15e.

Selected Bibliography

Aquinas, Thomas. *Opera Omnia*. Vol. 26, *Expositio super Iob ad litteram*. Translated by Brian Mulladay (Rome: Commissio Leonina, 1965). http://dhspriory.org/thomas/SSJob.htm.

Aquinas, Thomas. *Truth*. Translated by Robert W. Mulligan. 3 vols. (Indianapolis, IN: Hackett, 1994).

Arnobius. "Against the Heathen." Translated by Hamilton Bryce and Hugh Campbell. In *The Ante-Nicene Fathers: Translations of the Writings of the Fathers Down to A.D. 325*, edited by Alexander Roberts and James Donaldson. Vol. 6, *Gregory Thaumaturgus, Dionysius the Great, Julius Africanus, Anatolius and Minor Writers, Methodius, Arnobius*, 413–539 (Buffalo: Christian Literature Company, 1886).

Augustine. *The Augustine Catechism: The Enchiridion on Faith, Hope, and Love*. Edited by Boniface Ramsey, translation and notes by Bruce Harbert. *The Works of Saint Augustine: A Translation for the 21st Century*, vol. 1 (Hyde Park, NY: New City, 1999).

Augustine. *City of God*. Translated by William M. Green. 7 vols. Loeb Classical Library (Cambridge, MA: Harvard University Press, 1961–1972).

Augustine. *Eighty-Three Different Questions*. Translated by David L. Mosher. *Fathers of the Church*, vol. 70 (Washington, DC: Catholic University of America Press, 2010).

Augustine, *Expositions on the Book of Psalms*. Edited by A. Cleveland Coxe. *A Select Library of Nicene and Post-Nicene Fathers of the Christian Church*, edited by Philip Schaff. First series, vol. 8 (Grand Rapids, MI: Eerdmans, 1956).

Basil the Great. "The Hexaemeron." In *A Select Library of Nicene and Post-Nicene Fathers of the Christian Church*, edited by Henry Wace and Philip Schaff. Second series, vol. 8, *St. Basil: Letters and Select Works*, edited and translated by Blomfield Jackson, 51–107 (New York: Christian Literature Company, 1895).

Beatty, John. "Chance Variation: Darwin on Orchids." *Philosophy of Science* 73, no. 5 (2006): 629–641.

Bentley, Richard. *The Works of Richard Bentley D.D.* Vol. 3, *Theological Writings*. Edited by Alexander Dyce (London: Macpherson, 1838).

Boyle, Robert. *The Christian Virtuoso* (London: Edward Jones for John Taylor, 1690).

Brooke, John Hedley. *Science and Religion: Some Historical Perspectives* (Cambridge: Cambridge University Press, 1991).

Calvin, John. *Institutes of the Christian Religion*. Translated by Henry Beveridge. 3 vols. (Edinburgh: Calvin Translation Society, 1845).

Calvin, John. *The Institution of the Christian religion: In Four Books*. Translated by Thomas Norton (Glasgow: Alexander Irvine, 1762).

Chalmers, Thomas. *On the Power Wisdom and Goodness of God as Manifested in the Adaptation of External Nature to the Moral and Intellectual Constitution of Man*. 3rd ed. (London: William Pickering, 1834).

Chambers, Robert. *Vestiges of the Natural History of Creation* (London: John Churchill, 1844).

Charleton, Walter. *The Darknes of Atheism Dispelled by the Light of Nature: A Physico-Theologicall Treatise* (London, 1652).

Chrysostom, John. "Homily 3," In *Homilies on Genesis 1–17*. Translated by Robert C. Hill, *Fathers of the Church*, 74 vols (Washington, DC: Catholic University of America Press, 1986) 45.

Clarke, Samuel. *The Works of Samuel Clarke, D.D.* 4 vols. (London: J. and P. Knapton, 1738).

Darwin, Charles. *The Autobiography of Charles Darwin*. Edited by Nora Barlow (New York: Harcourt Brace, 1958).

Darwin, Charles. *The Descent of Man, and Selection in Relation to Sex*. 2 vols. (London: John Murray, 1871).

Darwin, Charles. *On the Origin of Species by Means of Natural Selection, or the Preservation of Favoured Races in the Struggle for Life* (London: James Murray, 1859).

Dawkins, Richard. *River Out of Eden: A Darwinian View of Life* (New York: Basic Books, 1995).

De Molina, Luis. *On Divine Foreknowledge: Part IV of the "Concordia"*. Translated by Alfred J. Freddoso (Ithaca, NY: Cornell University Press, 1988).

Descartes, René. "The World or Treatise on Light." In *The Philosophical Writings of Descartes*, translated by John Cottingham, Robert Stoothoff, and Dugald Murdoch, vol. 1, 81–98 (Cambridge: Cambridge University Press, 1985).

Flint, Thomas P. *Divine Providence: The Molinist Account* (Ithaca, NY: Cornell University Press, 1998).

Gould, Stephen Jay. *Wonderful Life* (New York: W. W. Norton, 1989).

Gray, Asa. *Darwiniana: Essays and Reviews Pertaining to Darwinism* (New York: Appleton, 1889). First published in 1876.

Harrison, Peter. *The Territories of Science and Religion* (Chicago: University of Chicago Press, 2015).

Herschel, John. *Physical Geography*. 2nd ed. (Edinburgh: Adam and Charles Black, 1862).

Herschel, John. *Preliminary Discourse to the Study of Natural Philosophy*. New ed. (London: Longman, Brown, Green and Longmans, 1851).

John of Damascus, "The Orthodox Faith." In *Writings*, translated by Frederic H. Chase Jr., 165–406. *Fathers of the Church*, vol. 37 (Washington, DC: Catholic University of America Press, 1958).

Kant, Immanuel. *Critique of Pure Reason*. Translated and edited by Paul Guyer and Allen W. Wood (Cambridge: Cambridge University Press, 1998).

Lactantius, "The Divine Institutes." Translated by William Fletcher. In *The Ante-Nicene Fathers: Translations of the Writings of the Fathers Down to A.D. 325*, edited by Alexander Roberts and James Donaldson. Vol. 7, *Lactantius, Venantius, Asterius, Victorinus, Dionysius, Apostolic Teaching and Constitutions, Homily, and Liturgies*, 9–328 (New York: Christian Literature Company, 1890).

Leibniz, Gottfried Wilhelm. *Philosophical Essays*. Edited and translated by Roger Ariew and Daniel Garber (Indianapolis, IN: Hackett, 1989).

Leibniz, Gottfried Wilhelm. *Theodicy: Essays on the Goodness of God, the Freedom of Man and the Origin of Evil*. Edited by Austin Farrer, translated by E. M. Huggard (La Salle, IL: Open Court, 1985). First published in 1710.

Livingstone, David N. *Darwin's Forgotten Defenders: The Encounter between Evangelical Theology and Evolutionary Thought* (Grand Rapids, MI: Eerdmans, 1987).

Moore, James R. *The Post-Darwinian Controversies: A Study of the Protestant Struggle to Come to Terms with Darwin in Great Britain and America, 1870–1900* (Cambridge: Cambridge University Press, 1981).

More, Henry. "An Antidote against Atheism." In *A Collection of Several Philosophical Writings of Dr. Henry More*. 2nd ed. (London: William Morden, 1662).

Origen, *Homilies on Genesis and Exodus*. Translated by Ronald E. Heine. *Fathers of the Church*, vol. 71 (Washington, DC: Catholic University of America Press, 1982).

Paley, William. *Natural Theology*. In *Paley's Works* (London: Henry G. Bohn, 1849).

Palmer, Ada. *Reading Lucretius in the Renaissance* (Cambridge, MA: Harvard University Press, 2014).

Pluche, Noël-Antoine. *The Spectacle of Nature or Talks about the Peculiarities of Natural History* (Paris: Frères Estienne, 1780).

Pope, Alexander. "Essay on Man." In *Works of Alexander Pope*, edited by Joseph Wharton, vol. 3, 1–172 (London: 1797).

Richards, Robert J. *The Meaning of Evolution: The Morphological Construction and Ideological Reconstruction of Darwin's Theory* (Chicago: University of Chicago Press, 1992).

Roberts, Jon H. "Religious Reactions to Darwin." In *The Cambridge Companion to Science and Religion*, edited by Peter Harrison, 80–102 (Cambridge: Cambridge University Press, 2010).

Smith, Adam. *An Enquiry into the Nature and Causes of the Wealth of Nations*. Edited by R. H. Campbell and A. S. Skinner. 2 vols. (Oxford: Oxford University Press, 1975).

Taylor, Charles. *A Secular Age* (Cambridge, MA: Belknap Press of Harvard University Press, 2007).

Topsell, Edward. *The Historie of Foure-footed Beastes* (London, 1607).

Ussher, James. *Annales Veteris Testamenti* (London, 1650).

Whewell, William. *The Bridgewater Treatises*. Treatise 3, *Astronomy and General Physics Considered with Reference to Natural Theology*. 7th ed. (London: William Pickering, 1839).

Whewell, William. *The Philosophy of the Inductive Sciences, founded upon their History*, 2 vols. (London: John Parker, 1867).

White, Andrew Dickson. *A History of the Warfare of Science with Theology in Christendom*. 2 vols. (London: Macmillan, 1896).

Wittgenstein, Ludwig. *On Certainty*. Edited by G. E. M. Anscombe and G. H. von Wright (New York: Harper and Rowe, 1972).

14

Throwing Dice? Thoughts of God in a Quantum World

Shaun Henson

ONCE UPON A time, Albert Einstein found himself on the wrong side of a famous debate with fellow physicist Niels Bohr about what looked like a major gap in our understanding of the universe—quantum mechanics. The simple mathematical elegance with which Newtonian physics had explained and predicted seemingly all physical phenomena until that time was beginning to show cracks. The intuitive universality of "cause and effect" was not looking quite so universal. The beginning of the twentieth century, as the mysteries behind telescopes and microscopes were falling like dominos, was no time to suggest that the crucial operations of the universe at the subatomic level might—in dramatic contrast to the familiar world of ships, shoes, and sealing wax—defy cause and effect. Alongside the best physicists of the twentieth century, Bohr persisted in demonstrating that at its most fundamental and discrete level, the universe defied the organizational logic outlined by Aristotle, Newton, and eventually, Einstein.

Theologically, the "unknowability" of quantum physics creates interesting, if speculative, opportunities. If no scientific theory completely explains the actions of particles like electrons and photons, is the door not then open for God to influence particles to conform to the divine will? Are these phenomena merely a final gasp for divine providence, before science explains everything? Or does quantum mechanics deliver us to the place where, at nanoscopic scales, our world rests on randomness and unpredictability? Are the inexplicable operations of quantum particles just quaint puzzles for physicists, or are we peering into the abyss from which God moves, molds, makes, and mends a universe in which the future is not inexorably specified by the past?

These questions lie at the heart of this volume. For centuries, even millennia, we have marched progressively toward a *closed* universe. Does quantum mechanics—one of the best-established theories in physics—prove just the opposite, that we live in a universe that is, literally, at its core *open*? This chapter traces the remarkable history of the discoveries and debates surrounding the behavior of matter at its most fundamental level and then turns to the current debate about the implications of quantum mechanics for religion. Whether reluctantly or eagerly, physicists who peer into this abyss are forced to address questions that sound more like theology than physics. Einstein rejected any interpretation of the quantum world as random and indeterminate. He used the now legendary image of a game-playing deity in a rebuff that emblazons posters in physics departments everywhere: "God does not play dice with the universe." It is unlikely that Einstein intended to wax theological, but his quip frames the debate in precisely the manner that interests us here.

We now know that the considerable interpretative difficulties of quantum mechanics do not derive from mathematical trickery or incompleteness in the theory. The early conclusion of genuine quantum indeterminacy has survived all of its challenges, including the formidable ones launched at Bohr by Einstein. The consensus among quantum physicists is that the quantum world is full of random and unpredictable events. So what kind of room does this open up for thinking about divine action? We will explore this question by reviewing the history of this remarkable idea and then unpacking the complex dynamics of our universe at its most basic level.

Let There Be Light in Particles and Waves

Max Planck's (1858–1947) proposal for something he called *quanta* begins our story. As John Hedley Brooke showed chapter 11, the scientific revolution that began in the sixteenth century suggested that the natural world operated by predictable, rigid, cause-and-effect processes. A causally deterministic philosophy emerged, based on "laws of nature," understood as the creation of a law-giving God. The laws proposed by Isaac Newton (1642–1727) describe movement in terms of force, momentum, and acceleration. Newton's laws and formulas became the foundation of classical mechanics. Modern physical science emerged with the publication of his *Philosophiae Naturalis Principia Mathematica* (1687).[1] The physical universe seemed to act like a machine run by complex and interlocking parts, like the intricate gears of a watch. By the eighteenth century, the explanatory power of these laws and principles seemed boundless, and they were being extended successfully into new realms. Physicists turned away from "chance" as an explanation for any phenomena.

This development was not the end for those seeking to develop a theology of nature. In fact, when Einstein suggested that "God does not throw dice," he was affirming a theology of nature that had been proposed by William Paley (1743–1805). In his *Natural Theology* (1802), Paley affirms the work of God in the very structure of the mechanistic cosmos.[2] Paley's contemporary Pierre Simon Laplace (1749–1827), conversely, viewed predictability as evidence contrary to a designer "hypothesis." Laplace's take on the predictability enabled by determinism extended as far into the future—and into the past—as one might wish to project. He argued in *A Philosophical Essay on Probabilities* (1814) that the future could be determined by "an intelligence sufficiently vast," with complete knowledge of Newton's laws and the present state of the universe. Matters like the "revolutions of the sun" and even obscurities like the fortunes of nations; the happiness of societies; and the eventual outcomes of all human fears, hopes, and decisions were theoretically foreseeable as determinism was extended deep into human experience.[3] For Laplace, human society represented only a particularly complex manifestation of Newtonian physics. Beneath the vast number of variables was a system as clean as the gears of a watch; human lives, from God's view, would be as predictable as the motions of billiard balls or planets.

At the height of Newton's achievements, however, and despite his best efforts, the nature of light was unresolved. Newton hypothesized light in atomistic terms, proposing in *Opticks* (1704) that light beams consisted of tiny particles travelling in a stream. *Opticks* was influential, but a conceptual tug-of-war ensued after its publication, lasting for at least a century, before a grasp on the true nature of light was attained. Was light a stream of particles as conceived by Newton, or was light a wave, as some experiments indicated?[4]

Thomas Young (1773–1829), an English scientist experimenting with light, had observed (ca. 1801–1803) interference patterns of darkness and light whenever light passed through two slits in a specially constructed apparatus. What he saw was characteristic of waves combining. The pattern is like the ripples overlapping in water when two stones are dropped in side by side. Young saw "interference phenomena," as we call it today. How waves combine depends on their oscillations (wave-like undulations) in relation to each other. With light, if two oscillating waves are in step with each other ("in phase"), a bright band is created. When the waves are out of step ("out of phase"), the waves cancel each other out, creating a band of darkness. Newton had noted the alternating bands (later called "Newton's rings"), but not fully grasped their significance.

Hans Christian Oersted (1777–1851) and Michael Faraday (1791–1867) confirmed Young's wave behavior of light. James Clerk Maxwell (1831–1879) underscored what Young, Oersted, and Faraday had found. Maxwell's *Treatise on Electricity and Magnetism* (1873) showed electricity, magnetism, and optics to be so tightly linked as to form the basis for a new understanding of these previously separate phenomena called *electromagnetism.* Maxwell's equations for electromagnetism had wave-like solutions, the velocity of which was that of light itself. Maxwell showed that light is an electromagnetic wave. As physics approached the twentieth century, even the mysteries of light were giving way to scientific understanding.

Max Planck's Troubling Constant

Planck's discovery of the measure of energy he called *quanta* changed physics forever. The classical physics of giants like Newton and Maxwell began to weaken, and the noose that appeared to be tightening on chance and providence found a snag. Planck's proposal for quanta resolved a serious problem faced by early twentieth-century physicists regarding the behavior of radiation. Planck turned his attention toward the peculiar behavior of radiation, which defies the laws of thermodynamics in tests involving what physicist call a "blackbody." A blackbody is an object that absorbs 100 percent of the light that falls on it, reflecting nothing back. If the blackbody is visible at all, it is entirely from its emission of radiation. A black wire glowing in the dark—like the filament in a light bulb—is a good approximation to a blackbody.

Glowing objects should not have been hard to understand, but the theory describing them was disastrously wrong, predicting that such objects would give off infinite amounts of ultraviolet radiation. Clearly this was nonsense and Planck started exploring ways to make the theory match the observations. Planck realized that if radiation were composed of *quanta*—small packets of energy rather than spread out waves—the dilemma could be resolved. This solution required the radiation to behave in ways contrary to classical physics, however. Planck calculated the energy content of the proposed quanta to be the product of the frequency of the radiation and a new constant of nature, now appropriately called "Planck's constant."

Planck's calculations worked perfectly and brought the measured characteristics of glowing bodies into agreement with theory. The Planck constant (h, equal to the ratio of energy E of a quantum of energy to its frequency f, written as $E = hf$), was confirmed by others, opening the pathway to quantum mechanics. No one doubted the significance of Planck's findings, for which he was awarded the 1918 Nobel Prize in Physics. Uncertainty remained, however, for though the new "constant" could explain the behavior of radiation, it seemed inconsistent with Newtonian physics. Are Planck's energy quanta characteristic of everything in nature? Or does this new formula simply provide a placeholder for one part of reality until a deeper and more coherent understanding of light and subatomic matter can be developed? At the time Planck proposed his quantum idea, the interior structure of the atom was a complete mystery and some physicists were not convinced that atoms were even real. Nobody had any idea what was actually going on inside a blackbody that produced the radiation that was emitted.

Albert Einstein and the Photoelectric Effect

Albert Einstein (1879–1955) took another step toward quantum theory in 1905, linking Planck's findings to another puzzle, known as the photoelectric effect. The photoelectric effect occurs when a beam of light shining on a metal surface causes electrons to be ejected from the metal. The electrons, as was known from the study of electricity, freely moved around inside the metal, but they do not have enough energy to leave the metal spontaneously. Something holds them in place.

In the photoelectric effect, energy from the light falling on the metal is transferred to the trapped electrons. With enough energy, the electrons escape. The puzzle was why the individual light quanta needed to have a certain amount of energy, rather than simply the beam of light having enough energy. In the traditional picture the light should have simply energized the electrons until they could leap out of the metal, like popcorn starting to pop. But this was not the observed effect. If the light was below a certain frequency, the electrons never escaped, no matter how intense the light. Paradoxically, a beam of weak high-frequency light would cause electrons to be ejected while a much more powerful beam of low-frequency light would do nothing. This was very strange. Why would a powerful beam of red light—so bright it could burn a person—cause no electrons to come off a metal surface while a barely visible beam of blue light would cause electrons to be released? If light was currency, this would imply that one could buy more with a quarter than a thousand nickels.

Einstein, like Planck earlier, realized that the phenomenon would make sense if the light falling on the metal was composed of a stream of discrete energy packets—quanta. We now call these light packets *photons*. Einstein understood that high-frequency photons must have more energy than low-frequency photons. The critical point here is that a beam of light must be understood at two levels—how much total energy there is in the beam and how much energy there is in each photon in the beam. If an electron needs, say, ten units of energy to escape from the metal, hitting it over and over again with five units of energy will accomplish nothing. A person cannot jump a ten-foot fence with ten one-foot jumps. Newton's old idea of light as a stream of particles was being resurrected. There was reason to hope that the noose could yet close on the peculiar corner of the universe where Newtonian physics had been frustrated.

Experiments have confirmed photons to be real particles. They bounce off electrons, and conserve energy and momentum. Einstein won the 1921 Nobel Prize in Physics for his work explaining the photoelectric effect, which became an important foundation for quantum physics—ironic given Einstein's rejection of the ensuing findings of quantum indeterminacy. He recognized that Planck's findings challenged his preferred classical view of reality: "All of this was quite clear to me shortly after the appearance of Planck's fundamental work. . . . It was as if the ground had been pulled out from under us, with no firm foundation to be seen anywhere."[5]

A new and perplexing dilemma now appeared. When the experimental results from Young and Maxwell were considered with those of Planck and Einstein, a strange conclusion resulted: light behaved as *both* waves and particles. Eventually it would become clear that all photons, electrons, protons, neutrons, and so on, behave in these same paradoxical and perplexing ways. It seemed as if light and electrons were sometimes waves and sometimes particles, depending on the particular context in which they were being observed. These findings made no sense. Shouldn't the elements in nature be the same, regardless of how we are observing them? It was as mysterious as if birds suddenly appeared to be fish if we looked at them under the water.

Richard Feynman on Double-slit Experiments

Richard Feynman (1918–1988), another Nobel Prize-winner, called atomic-scaled matter and energy "particle-waves" to highlight their curious and seemingly duplicitous nature. Feynman was a brilliant communicator and taught a generation of physicists the new theory of quantum mechanics using familiar large-scale examples like bullets and water waves to highlight the apparent absurdity of what was actually happening at the level of electrons and photons. The classic example used to explain the strange indeterminacy of the quantum world uses a very simple example that is easy to visualize: a wall with two openings. Particles approach the wall, as a person might, and then pass through one doorway or the other. Feynman explained what would happen if we sent different objects through doorways onto a detector that would register which one they went through. The doors he had in mind were the slits of so-called double-slit experiments. These experiments are crucial for understanding the profound way that quantum mechanics forced a new view of reality on us. Of the experiments Feynman said,

> We choose to examine a phenomenon which is impossible, *absolutely* impossible, to explain in any classical way, and which has in it the heart of quantum mechanics. In reality, it contains the *only* mystery. We cannot make the mystery go away by "explaining" how it works. We will just tell you how it works. In telling you how it works we will have told you about the basic peculiarities of all quantum mechanics.[6]

An electron or photon fired at the double slits will go through one slit and not another in ways impossible to predict with precision, unlike the predictions made at larger scales in the everyday world of classical physics. This phenomenon is more peculiar than it sounds. Imagine a wall with two doorways at which a pitcher throws a baseball. Given that the openings are much larger than a strike zone, it would be trivial for any pitcher to throw the ball through one opening and not the other. But this is not true for photons. Shine a laser at one opening and some of the photons will go through the other one. It proves impossible to say why or how a quantum entity travels through one slit and not another and why in the most bizarre of events it sometimes seems to go through both slits simultaneously without splitting into two separate particles. In the face of these findings, Feynman famously stated, "I think I can safely say that nobody understands quantum mechanics."[7]

Double-slit experiments show that quantum objects like electrons and photons sometimes act entirely unlike anything else we have ever encountered.[8] Of great significance is the discovery that electrons, which were envisioned as particles at the dawn of the twentieth century, and light, which was envisioned as waves, do at least act similarly. We can therefore hearken back to the earlier light experiments of Young and Maxwell, as well as the quite different conclusions of Planck and Einstein, to inform the later findings with photons, electrons, and double slits.

The double-slit experiment has various versions, and physicists have struggled to create metaphors to bring it from the esoteric realm of mathematical physics to the more familiar world of our experience.[9] In one such metaphor we imagine a machine gun that randomly fires bullets. The gun is unsteadily mounted, firing in a cone-shaped arc as it sprays bullets. Opposite the machine gun, directly in the line of fire, is an armor-plated wall with two holes big enough for bullets to pass through. A piece of wood behind the armored wall will absorb every bullet that passes through the holes, creating a record of the events. The bullet holes in the wood provide a simple distribution pattern behind each hole.[10] None of this is surprising and the results feel familiar and intuitive.

A second experiment, using water instead of bullets, proves similarly unsurprising. The exception is that the results illustrate common wave behavior rather than projectile motion. An apparatus is set up similar to the machine-gun with backstop. But this apparatus works with water rather than bullets, measuring waves and their energy, which is proportional to their height. The source of the waves can be as simple as stones dropped into a pool of water. The screen in this case can be a jetty with two gaps, or slits, in it. The detectors can be a line of simple floating buoys, whose up and down motions will indicate the energy from waves striking them at their floating positions.

Gazing along the line of floating buoys, one will observe that when a stone is dropped, at points the crests of the waves going through the first slit will coincide with the arrival of crests from the second slit. The results will be larger up and down motions of a given buoy.[11] In other places crests and troughs will meet, cancelling each other out and producing no observable motion. At still additional places, the motions of a buoy will be between a full wave reaction and none at all. In contrast with our bullets embedded in the wood at fixed locations, the water wave energy is not in definite lumps since a water wave passes easily through both slits at the same time. Instead, the energy of each wave spreads itself out. The water is disturbed at a given position along the buoyed detectors by the sum of the disturbances of the waves passing through slits one and two. We further realize, by closing off first one and then the other slit, that the results in the case of our water experiment show definite interference. A similar result with light led Thomas Young to believe light to be wave-like. Young was seeing only part of the picture, however, just as Newton in viewing light as particles saw only part of the picture. We eventually appreciated that this was the case after continued experiments which, thanks to Planck and Einstein, helped us to understand light to be composed of discrete energy packets, or quanta.[12]

A third and final experiment using electrons illustrates the mystery to which Feynman referred. For this we use a gun that fires electrons instead of bullets. We recall here the earlier point that electrons and photons behave identically. We now know this to be true of all quantum objects, whether electrons, photons, protons, neutrons, and so on. The electron gun shoots electrons like the old-fashioned cathode-ray tubes that used to be used in televisions before the advent of flat screens. In front of the electron gun is a metal plate with two slits. Directly in the line of electron fire is a screen coated with a chemical that flashes whenever an electron strikes it, which was how televisions used to produce their images.[13] Counting the strikes will be similar to the experiment described above in which we counted bullets passing through the slits.[14] The quantum projectiles, whether they are electrons or photons, are like the bullets of the first experiment. They cannot split into two if, for instance, they were to hit the edge of a slit when passing through it. Electrons and photons cannot "break."

The mysteries of quantum behavior revealed by the double-slit experiments are several-fold. When an experiment detects which slit an electron goes through, we can say that it went through one or the other. If we arrange our equipment so we cannot detect which slit it goes through, the resulting interference pattern (the wave-like configuration) shows that the electron has somehow gone through both slits simultaneously, interfering with itself. This is a literal adding together of seemingly impossible situations—a bit of the electron is "here" and a bit of it is "there" and these two bits are added in a way that is simple mathematically but impossible to visualize physically. This is called the superposition principle, a central idea that embodies the rich strangeness of the quantum world.[15]

Superposition—which comes out of the equations that accurately describe the quantum world—says that a quantum object like an electron exists in every possible theoretical state simultaneously until it is measured ("observed"). So an electron will be in a state that combines the event of having gone through the slit on the left with an event of having gone through the slit on the right, as well as the interference of those two events. This collection of states is called the "wave packet," since it represents a bundle of options that interfere with each other like waves. Making the measurement causes the wave packet to "collapse" into just one of the options in the packet. Somehow an unmeasured, unobserved electron has more than one path, and therefore more than one past, present, and future. All at the same time an electron has multiple histories until the collapse of the packet occurs in the process of observation. Nothing like this is even hinted at in classical physics and this is so far removed from our experience of the world that it simply cannot be "understood" in any conventional sense. It would be like a baseball pitch being a curve, fastball, and knuckleball all at once and then inexplicably—and randomly—suddenly becoming just one of those when the ball made contact with a bat. The sudden "choice" being made here is referred to as the "collapse" of a package with many real possibilities suddenly becoming just one, with the other possibilities simply disappearing as if they never existed.

The collapse of the wave packet is at the center of quantum indeterminacy and it is here that Einstein thought he discerned claims that God was throwing dice. When the wave packet collapses, it can collapse into any of the options in the packet. Some options are more likely than others, but none is determined. In some mysterious way the electron "chooses" one available option. Next time round, an identical electron chooses a different option. Science finds itself up against a maddening paradox here—a paradox that threatens the Newtonian coherence of the universe. Compounding the problem is the puzzling role of observation in the collapse of the wave packets into a single option. This situation appears to render objective observation impossible. The phenomenon we want to understand is altered by the very act of measurement. Here, at the most crucial operation of matter, the cinching noose of scientific explanation has been halted. This is arguably the most profound insight in all of science.

The classical view of a future precisely determined by a particular past does not exist. The future is indeterminate, with an element of real randomness. Predictions at the quantum level are probabilistic, calculated from equations. And we can only calculate where a particle is *likely* to be when we observe it, although not where it will *definitely* be. Feynman called this kind of logic, imposed by the quantum world, the "logical tightrope" of quantum mechanics.[16] Physics was taking a serious detour from the structured universe physicists thought they had in their sights at the dawn of the twentieth century.

Interpreting Quantum Behavior

Planck's proposal for quanta and the subsequent murkiness about light behaving as both waves and particles created a tumultuous time for physics. Double-slit experiments were just the beginning. Clarifying insights began to arrive in 1925 in the form of successful equations, the true language of physics and, many would argue, the true language of nature. We will examine just two of the many advances during this era, the works of Werner Heisenberg (1901–1976) and Erwin Schrödinger (1887–1961).

Heisenberg discovered the *uncertainty principle* in 1925, which addressed the duality of the behavior of light as both particle and wave. Light had been shown to behave as both wave and particle, depending on the experiment. Heisenberg discovered that the uncertainty in the measurement of position (written as Δx) and the uncertainty in momentum (written as Δp) are linked. The Heisenberg uncertainty principle correlates these linked uncertainties in position and momentum to Planck's constant (h), and is expressed like this:

$$\Delta x \times \Delta p \approx h$$

This formula means, in English, that uncertainty in position multiplied by uncertainty in momentum is approximately equal to Planck's constant, the fundamental constant for quantum mechanics. When we tighten up the measurements on position, we widen the uncertainty on momentum, and vice versa. Like a teeter-totter, the suppression of uncertainty with one measurement elevates the uncertainty in the other.

If we analyze an electron or photon passing through a single slit, we see a pattern spread out in inverse proportion to the width of the slit. If we wish to more accurately determine the *position* of quantum objects as they pass through the slit—did it go through the middle of the slit or was it off to one side?—we do so by making the slit smaller and smaller. The smaller the slit, the more we can specify exactly where the particle was as it passed, just as a person passing through a narrow door has a more specified location than when passing through a wide door. As the slit narrows, we see the pattern on the other side of the slit spreading out as the particles pass through the slit and randomly strike the screen behind it. An individual particle will strike the screen somewhere within the pattern. Bafflingly, we remain unable to anticipate where it will strike the screen. Identical electrons arrive in different locations.

If anyone could ever "beat" such uncertainty, quantum mechanics would be invalidated.[17] But this result has never been achieved despite heroic and ingenious attempts by Einstein. Uncertainty and probability, rather than certainty and precision, are not quantum mirages or misunderstandings. They are inescapable aspects of reality encountered at the microscopic level, and they are binding and influential on everything that happens.[18]

In 1926, Erwin Schrödinger discovered an equation describing the mechanics of quantum waves. This equation allowed for clear predictions that could be compared with experiments, with the proviso that they focused on *probability* rather than determinacy. Schrödinger showed that quantum events cannot be accurately predicted, but a formula could predict the likelihood of any particular outcome of an experiment. The equation would predict, for example, how many out of 100 electrons would hit a particular spot on a screen. But it could not predict which ones.

The most famous of the many thought experiments of the quantum story involves "Schrödinger's cat." This strange illustration lays bare the bizarre implications of quantum theory, compelling us to believe that there is something amiss. A cat is placed in a box containing a quantum radioactive source with a 50–50 chance of decaying within an hour. The radiation resulting from the decay causes the release of a gas that kills the cat. Quantum principles say that, after an hour, the radioactive source must be in a superposition state of "decayed plus undecayed" since we don't know what happened in the box. This situation, strangely, implies that the cat is in a superposition of "dead plus alive." When an observer does an experiment to check on the radioactive source by opening the box, the superposition of the source collapses the possibilities into a particular reality. Prior to this collapse there is a "between period" of superposition in which the cat is simultaneously alive and dead. Shrödinger proposed this experiment to illustrate the strangeness of quantum mechanics, not to suggest that cats could be alive and dead at the same time. The deep and unresolved mystery of quantum mechanics is how and where the strangeness disappears as we move from the quantum world of the very small to the classical world of ordinary objects. And does it entirely disappear?

Interpreting Quantum Interpretations

The wave-particle duality and indeterminate behavior of quantum particles as revealed by double-slit experiments is in one respect all that one needs to know to grasp the implications of the quantum worldview.[19] From these examples and their interpretations we can gather what is implied by a notion like "quantum mechanics and the reality of randomness."

Quantum objects like electrons are basic constituents of all physical reality, including people and cats. Quantum phenomena is part of everything that happens; the strangeness seems to just get "averaged out" because ordinary objects have so many electrons. Feynman's sage advice to his students on how best to react to it all was:

> Just relax and enjoy it. If you will simply admit that maybe she [nature] does behave like this, you will find her a delightful, entrancing thing. Do not keep saying to yourself, if you can possibly avoid it, "But how can it be like that?" because you will get "down the drain," into a blind alley from which nobody has escaped. Nobody knows how it can be like that.[20]

Ideas contrary to our preconceptions and sensory experiences, however well evidenced they may be, are hard to accept. Galileo (1564–1642) faced this when he argued that the earth moved. How could this be? No one felt themselves to be moving—especially not at the tremendous speeds we now know to be true. But no educated person today doubts that Galileo was correct. Accepting the cloudy fitfulness of the quantum world, when everything around us on a larger scale seems quite stable, is somewhat like accepting that our planet hurtles through space even as we experience it as being reliably fixed and stationary.

No Greater Dialogue: Bohr and Einstein

"In all the history of human thought," physicist John Wheeler has remarked, "there is no greater dialogue than that which took place over the years between Niels Bohr and Albert Einstein about the meaning of the quantum."[21] Their debate offers two distinct approaches to the subatomic world while demonstrating a fundamental and deeply intuitive opposition when it comes to the possibility of nature possessing a real and unresolvable indeterminacy.

Bohr accepted the revolutionary classical-to-quantum changes of his lifetime. Einstein held to the classical line from which his own revolutionary work had flowered, pointing out problems and questions surrounding quantum theory. Both figures held considerable authority. Einstein had been an important forerunner of quantum theory, although in time taking a negative view toward the growing interpretation emphasizing randomness. Bohr, a Nobel Prize laureate in physics a year after Einstein's award, had given us a new image of the atomic world by applying similar principles to atoms that Planck had applied to radiation.[22] The Bohr atom operated by quantum principles, updating our understanding and modeling of the atomic world. It was in conversation with Bohr that Einstein made his legendary assertion, "God does not play dice with the universe."[23]

Einstein took his concerns about the reality of randomness at the quantum level to his grave, alienated from an important field of science that he had done much to create. His intuition was that there must be something missing. A couple centuries earlier the planet Saturn exhibited what looked like occasional random departures from its prescribed orbit. Some suggested that maybe Newton's laws were not truly universal—a reasonable speculation. The source of the randomness, however, turned out to be an undiscovered planet, now called Uranus. Einstein's gut told him that there must be something hidden, some missing part of the picture that, when discovered, would restore order to the world.

Einstein spent the final thirty years of his life resisting quantum randomness, searching for alternatives where God did not throw dice. "I could probably have arrived at something like this myself, but if all this is true then it means the end of physics," he lamented.[24] Physics did not end, of course, but the grand closed universe of Newton, where all events were part of a seamless whole linked forever by cause and effect, was gone.

Of Gods and Dice

Einstein's quip about God playing dice was metaphorical—a pithy way of affirming a law-like cosmos. But Einstein took the idea of God more seriously than is generally realized.[25] Some biographers have even declared its centrality for shaping his scientific views.[26] He once described his religious sense as "that deeply emotional conviction of the presence of a superior reasoning power, which is revealed in the incomprehensible universe, forms my idea of God."[27] Similarly, he said, "I'm not an atheist and I don't think I can call myself a pantheist." In any event, it seems that Einstein's view of the universe included an architecture that was sturdy all the way to the foundation, whatever his thought about an architect.

Einstein's fervent resistance to randomness underscores the significance of this scientific discovery about the quantum world. If quantum randomness were just a quaint sideshow, or if quantum uncertainty were not a massive interruption of conventional physics, would the subject have drawn such energetic and prolonged interest from Einstein?

Einstein never spoke of divine action in the universe and it is unlikely that his vague and unconventional references to God implied any notion of a transcendent realm containing any more than the source of the universe's grandeur. Certainly he never spoke of a God that acted in the world. But let us now raise the important question of divine action. If this baffling indeterminacy is a brute fact of our universe, what theological implications may we draw? What kind of deity might have made such a reality of randomness? The nature of this discovery lends itself to a vast array of interpretations. Quantum indeterminacy taunts physicists precisely because it straddles the boundary between physics and metaphysics. If someone were to suggest that quantum events are determined on the whims of capricious leprechauns, how could such suggestions be refuted? When classical physics loses its grip in the venerated endeavor to describe the world as a system of cause and effect, what metaphysic or theology steps into that gap?

Einstein once also said, "Subtle is the Lord," referring to the essential hiddenness of nature's secrets. As it is with nature, so it is with knowledge of God. Perhaps quantum uncertainty points beyond itself to a transcendent reality. If the world is constructed of particles whose behavior is, in some sense, "free," is it possible that a creator made it such, to provide space for divine providential interaction? No self-evident reason suggests that God would, or would not, have created nature with properties describable as probabilistic, cloudy, and fitful, or, in the language of this volume, random. But if a creator wanted a creation with "room" for ongoing interaction, then perhaps the world we find ourselves in fits that description.

Physicist John Polkinghorne has thought about this problem arguably more than any scientist or theologian (and indeed, he is both) over the past few decades. Attempting to bring contemporary physics into conversation with traditional Christian theology, Polkinghorne suggests that we might think of God as a cause among causes. He points to a kenotic theology, which emphasizes the way God moves and works otherwise than by classical causation. Rather than suggest that God is the hidden variable determining apparently random events, Polkinghorne suggests that the quantum world demonstrates the humility of God. Polkinghorne's God stirs the world gently, indirectly and outside of the classical articulations of causation and agency. A quantum world is critical to this theology, for it reveals to us that the universe rests not on the rock-solid pillars of determinacy but on a sea of uncertainty. The universe has the freedom to become more than the simple extrapolation of the present. Polkinghorne rightly understands that quantum uncertainty is not a pinhole gap in our understanding of the universe but a fundamental shift in the way we understand the nature of the universe at the deepest level. He proceeds tentatively, as befits a mathematical physicist, but presents a compelling case that when we peer into the abyss of quantum indeterminacy, we contemplate a theological mystery. Polkinghorne finds here a compelling connection to his understanding of Christianity, emphasizing a loving, gentle, and humble God.

Quantum mechanics interrupted the trajectory of a classical physics that threatened to expel freedom and even purpose from the universe. Einstein had faith that gaps in our knowledge would continue to close with discoveries in the classical tradition of cause and effect, that the inexplicable could be explained, and that the trajectory of philosophy and science pointed toward a closed universe. Neither physics nor philosophy has fully grasped the implications of quantum mechanics. Despite the preponderance of evidence, it will take both time and creativity to adjust to the idea that our universe is fundamentally open. Perhaps Einstein's principal mistake in rejecting the reality of the randomness revealed by quantum mechanics was also a theological error at some level, conflating his notion of "God" and a preference for a certain kind of natural order according to science, a determinism being overturned by the scientific revolution of quantum mechanics. Why can't God play dice? Or why can't God create a world filled with dice?

Niels Bohr's response to Einstein was especially apt, and a good final principle, however seriously or not one takes the notion of God. After all, the goal of science is not to impose upon nature what we wish it to reveal but to discover what is true. In this spirit Bohr gently chided his troubled debate partner: "Einstein, stop telling God what to do!"[28]

Notes

1. Isaac Newton, *Philosophiae Naturalis Principia Mathematica*, trans. I. Bernard Cohen and Anne Whitman (London: University of California Press, 1999).
2. William Paley, *Natural Theology*, ed. Matthew D. Eddy and David M. Knight (Oxford: Oxford University Press, 2008).
3. The full exposition of Pierre-Simon Laplace's views in each regard appear in his book *A Philosophical Essay on Probabilities*, trans. Andrew I. Dale (New York: Springer, 1995). First published in 1814.
4. Alan E. Shapiro, "Newton's Optics and Atomism," in *The Cambridge Companion to Newton*, ed. I. Bernard Cohen and George E. Smith, 227–255 (Cambridge: Cambridge University Press, 2002).
5. Albert Einstein, "Autobiographical Notes," in *Albert Einstein: Philosopher-Scientist*, ed. Paul Arthur Schilpp (La Salle, Ill.: Open Court Press, 1949), 46.
6. Richard P. Feynman, *The Feynman Lectures on Physics: Commemorative Issue*, vol. 3, *Quantum Mechanics* (Wokingham: Addison-Wesley, 1989), 1-1, "Quantum Behavior."
7. Richard P. Feynman, *The Character of Physical Law* (London: Penguin, 1992), 129.
8. Feynman, *Lectures on Physics*, 3: 1-1.
9. Ibid., 1-1–1-5. Others rely on Feynman's account, with various alterations. Cf. Tony Hey and Patrick Walters, *The New Quantum Universe* (Cambridge: Cambridge University Press, 2003), 8–15; Alastair Rae, *Quantum Physics: Illusion or Reality?* (Cambridge: Cambridge University Press, 1986), 1–15.
10. Feynman, *Lectures on Physics*, 3: 1-1–1-3.
11. Cf. ibid., 1–3, with Hey and Walters, *New Quantum Universe*, 8–12. The example of buoys from Hey and Walters is clearer than Feynman's account.
12. Hey and Walters, *New Quantum Universe*, 9–12.
13. Feynman, *Lectures on Physics*, 3: 1-4.

14. Hey and Walters, *New Quantum Universe*, 12.
15. Feynman, *Lectures on Physics*, 1: 25-2, defines and gives examples of the principle of superposition for linear systems.
16. Feynman, *Lectures on Physics*, 3: 1-9.
17. Ibid.
18. John Polkinghorne, *The Quantum World* (Princeton, NJ: Princeton University Press, 1989), 80–81; John Polkinghorne, *Quantum Theory: A Very Short Introduction* (Oxford: Oxford University Press, 2002), 85–86.
19. Feynman, *Lectures on Physics*, 3: 1-1.
20. Feynman, *Character of Physical Law*, 129.
21. Walter Isaacson, *Einstein: His Life and Universe* (London: Simon and Schuster, 2007), 325.
22. Polkinghorne, *Quantum World*, 10ff.
23. Isaacson, *Einstein*, 323–326.
24. Isaacson, *Einstein*, 325.
25. Shaun C. Henson, "Albert Einstein (1879–1955): 'A Rapturous Amazement at the Harmony of Natural Law . . ." or, "God Does Not Play at Dice with the Laws of Nature," in *God and Natural Order: Physics, Philosophy, and Theology* (New York and London: Routledge, 2014), 28–40.
26. See Max Jammer, *Einstein and Religion: Physics and Theology* (Princeton, NJ: Princeton University Press, 1999); and Isaacson, *Einstein*.
27. Isaacson, *Einstein*, 388.
28. Niels Bohr, "Discussion with Einstein on Epistemological Problems in Atomic Physics," in *Albert Einstein: Philosopher-Scientist*, edited by Paul Arthur Schilpp, 211 n. (La Salle, IL: Open Court, 1949).

Selected Bibliography

Bohr, Niels. "Discussion with Einstein on Epistemological Problems in Atomic Physics." In *Albert Einstein: Philosopher-Scientist*, edited by Paul Arthur Schilpp, 199–242 (La Salle, IL: Open Court, 1949).

Einstein, Albert. "Autobiographical Notes." In *Albert Einstein: Philosopher-Scientist*, edited by Paul Arthur Schilpp, 1–95 (La Salle, IL: Open Court, 1949).

Feynman, Richard P. *The Feynman Lectures on Physics: Commemorative Issue*. Vol. 3, *Quantum Mechanics* (Wokingham: Addison-Wesley, 1989).

Feynman, Richard P. *The Character of Physical Law* (London: Penguin, 1992).

Henson, Shaun C. *God and Natural Order: Physics, Philosophy, and Theology* (New York and London: Routledge, 2014).

Hey, Tony, and Patrick Walters. *The New Quantum Universe* (Cambridge: Cambridge University Press, 2003).

Isaacson, Walter. *Einstein: His Life and Universe* (London: Simon and Schuster, 2007).

Jammer, Max. *Einstein and Religion: Physics and Theology* (Princeton, NJ: Princeton University Press, 1999).

Laplace, Pierre-Simon. *A Philosophical Essay on Probabilities*. Translated by Andrew I. Dale (New York: Springer, 1995). First published in 1814.

Newton, Isaac. *Philosophiae Naturalis Principia Mathematica*. Translated by I. Bernard Cohen and Anne Whitman (London: University of California Press, 1999). First published in 1687.

Paley, William. *Natural Theology*. Edited by Matthew D. Eddy and David M. Knight (Oxford: Oxford University Press, 2008). First published in 1802.

Polkinghorne, John. *Quantum Theory: A Very Short Introduction* (Oxford: Oxford University Press, 2002).

Polkinghorne, John. *The Quantum World* (Princeton, NJ: Princeton University Press, 1989).

Rae, Alastair. *Quantum Physics: Illusion or Reality?* (Cambridge: Cambridge University Press, 1986).

Shapiro, Alan E. "Newton's Optics and Atomism." In *The Cambridge Companion to Newton*, edited by I. Bernard Cohen and George E. Smith, 227–255 (Cambridge: Cambridge University Press, 2002).

15

Darwinian Evolution and a Providential God

THE HUMAN PROBLEM

Michael Ruse

Introduction

Many writers and thinkers today believe modern science refutes the Christian religion totally and completely. For instance, Oxford chemist Peter Atkins writes: "Science and religion cannot be reconciled, and humanity should begin to recognize the power of its child and beat off all attempts at compromise."[1] While it may be true that one cannot reconcile modern science with claims about Noah's Flood and Jonah and the whale and the like, I would argue (with many others) that traditional Christianity has ways of dealing with such apparent conflicts—by recourse to metaphor and allegory—and that this still leaves the bulk of the Christian's claims unscathed.[2] I would go further and say that the basic claims of Christianity—for instance that God is creator and sustainer, and the reason why there is something rather than nothing—are quite untouched by science. Science does not even speak to issues such as this, and if the Christian wants to try to answer them, the Christian is free to go ahead.[3]

This is not to say that no criticism can now be offered of the Christian. One may not be able to use science to refute the Christian's answers. One can certainly use theology and philosophy to this end.[4] Moreover, obviously, Christianity wants to say more than just the very basic—why is there something rather than nothing and that sort of thing—and here science might indeed be relevant. For instance, there has been much discussion recently about the doctrine of original sin, specifically about the Augustinian interpretation of the doctrine of original sin, which puts it all down to the sin of Adam when he disobeyed God and took the fruit. As evolutionists point out, we now know a lot about the origins of humans and one thing we can say definitively is that there was no original Adam and Eve.[5] The human population never dropped below the thousands and even if you pick out a pair as the sinners, they would have had parents who would have been no less inclined to behave in ways we would judge wrong. In short, modern science shows here that, at the very least, Christianity needs substantial revision.[6] A problem of this kind is the topic of this chapter.

Human Beings

I start with the status of human beings in the Christian story. We are made in the image of God.[7] I take it that in some sense this is a bottom-level demand. It has to be true in a fairly literal sense. What is a literal sense here? Generally, following Augustine and his Platonic roots—actually, coming to him second-hand through Plotinus—we think in terms of intelligence. As Plato articulates in the *Republic*, humans are beings with souls (though he did not mean this as we do in the Christian sense) that include intelligence as a ruling force or part. We think and reason and our thinking and reasoning determines how we act. For Plato, and no less for Augustine, this means that we are moral beings. We know right and wrong and we have the power to decide and act upon this knowledge. That indeed is why we fell into sin.

I take that another bottom-level demand or claim is that God did not have to create human beings, however it was done. God is totally free to do as God wishes. We may depend on God, but not vice versa, setting aside the question of the degree to which we have created God in our image. However, just as a person does not have to have children, but decides to have them to love and to cherish, so God decided to create humans to love and cherish. In return, as children are expected to honor their parents, so we are expected to honor God. I am not sure how exact the analogy is here. Eventually you want your children to stop thinking about you and think instead about their children. But in a way you could say that there is no higher honor paid to parents than that their children follow them in having children of their own.

All of this being so, in some sense we surely have to say that for the Christian, human beings are necessary. Their arrival in this universe is not a matter of chance or whim—might have been, might not have been. We cannot paint God as an aspiring parent, trying desperately to have kids but with no firm guarantees. If God wanted to have kids, God was going to have kids. And here's the rub: evolution through natural selection makes all this very problematic. You can of course go the route of Augustine, followed by the great philosophers like Aquinas, distinguishing between primary causation and secondary causation. Primary causation is God's deciding that something is going to happen, like humans appearing. Secondary causation is the way in which it happens according to physical law, and God is a lot less preemptive here.

> In matters that are obscure and far beyond our vision, even in such as we may find treated in Holy Scripture, different Interpretations are sometimes possible without prejudice to the faith we have received. In such a case, we should not rush in headlong and so firmly take our stand on one side that, if further progress in the search of truth justly undermines this position, we too fall with it. That would be to battle not for the teaching of Holy Scripture but for our own, wishing its teaching to conform to ours, whereas we ought to wish ours to conform to that of Sacred Scripture.[8]

Basically, how things happen "down here" is up to law itself. Of course, the laws are created and sustained by God, but God cannot create any sort of law, because the laws have to work. God could not, for example, create laws prohibiting the formation of molecules and still have a universe with life in it. And here the rub continues. Can one find laws that will do what one wants—whatever God's role in making and sustaining them? Can we produce human beings in a way demanded by Christian theology? Actually, thanks to points made by atheist writer and popularizer Richard Dawkins, God might be a bit more constrained at this point than one suspects.[9] There is good reason to think that if we were produced by natural law, it was natural selection or nothing. Other putative mechanisms do not do what is needed. Those that supposedly can produce functioning organisms—like the Lamarckian inheritance of acquired characteristics—are largely false. Those that have some claim to being true—like large variations or macromutations, which certainly do occur on occasion—do not produce functioning organisms. They can at best be minor elaborations on a major theme. In short, if God created through law, it had to be through natural selection.

Producing Humans

We are not confined, of course, to humans appearing on Planet Earth. Somewhere in Andromeda would also do the trick. We don't have to have the skin color or finger number that we have. We could all be bright blue and have twelve fingers and still the Christian drama would occur. Instead of "I am black, but comely, Oh ye daughters of Jerusalem, As the tents of Kedar, As the curtains of Solomon,"[10] we could have "I am green, but comely, Oh ye daughters of Jerusalem, As the tents of Kedar, As the curtains of Solomon." If it were possible to have silicone-based life rather than carbon-based life that would also be okay. What about sex? Could we have only one sex or be hermaphrodites and have the Christian story still work? It would require some rethinking. Perhaps you have to have sex to have sophisticated organisms like humans, but even here there are possibilities. Charles Darwin discovered barnacles where there are normal-size females but the males are complemental—just little warty things that attach themselves to the females, being hardly more than sacks of sperm with very long penises. If nothing else, it would certainly give James Dobson's Focus on the Family much on which to think.

Let us leave such speculations for more worrying issues. We humans were produced by natural selection and so were all other humanoids, to use the term for human-like beings. We have to be rational beings. If we are not, then the Christian story is just not on. Jesus was not crucified for the eternal salvation of warthogs. We are not going to be moral beings unless we are social beings. Kant believed in duties to oneself, but it is hard to imagine the Christian story if we are all like orangutans who get together only briefly for mating. What price the Sermon on the Mount if we have nothing to do with each other? How could Jesus tell us to love one another if it simply is not in our nature to do so? To put it bluntly, if Jesus had told us all to go and eat feces, I doubt there would have been a Christian religion. But even if we are social, I am not sure that we are necessarily going to be moral. Perhaps we could do it all through discussion and calculation. I will help you not because it is right to help you but because of the payoff to me—I might need help or you will pay me or whatever. And even if we are moral, I am not sure that the morality we would have would be Christian morality. Darwin spoke of this in the *Descent of Man*.

> It may be well first to premise that I do not wish to maintain that any strictly social animal, if its intellectual faculties were to become as active and as highly developed as in man, would acquire exactly the same moral sense as ours. In the same manner as various animals have some sense of beauty, though they admire widely different objects, so they might have a sense of right and wrong, though led by it to follow widely different lines of conduct. If, for instance, to take an extreme case, men were reared under precisely the same conditions as hive-bees, there can hardly be a doubt that our unmarried females would, like the worker-bees, think it a sacred duty to kill their brothers, and mothers would strive to kill their fertile daughters; and no one would think of interfering. Nevertheless the bee, or any other social animal, would in our supposed case gain, as it appears to me, some feeling of right and wrong, or a conscience.[11]

Progress and the Lack Thereof

It all gets rather complex. But let us agree that since humans *did* evolve as they did, they *could* have evolved as they did. But did they have to evolve as they did? We must have humans, or humanoids, that are rational and moral, meaning that they have the capacity for morality even if they are not always themselves moral. How can this be? Traditionally evolutionary theory was thought of as progressive, from the monad to the man.[12] Listen to Charles Darwin's grandfather Erasmus Darwin.

> Organic Life beneath the shoreless waves
> Was born and nurs'd in Ocean's pearly caves;
> First forms minute, unseen by spheric glass,
> Move on the mud, or pierce the watery mass;
> These, as successive generations bloom,
> New powers acquire, and larger limbs assume;
> Whence countless groups of vegetation spring,
> And breathing realms of fin, and feet, and wing.

Thus the tall Oak, the giant of the wood,
Which bears Britannia's thunders on the flood;
The Whale, unmeasured monster of the main,
The lordly Lion, monarch of the plain,
The Eagle soaring in the realms of air,
Whose eye undazzled drinks the solar glare,
Imperious man, who rules the bestial crowd,
Of language, reason, and reflection proud,
With brow erect who scorns this earthy sod,
And styles himself the image of his God;
Arose from rudiments of form and sense,
An embryon point, or microscopic ens![13]

The trouble is that we don't believe this sort of stuff anymore. Darwin's theory scotched it. In the first place, natural selection is relative. It doesn't pick out one feature as superior for all time and place and head in that direction. It doesn't even pick out big brains as a prerequisite for intelligence. Apart from anything else, big brains need lots of protein, which means eating other animals. Twenty-first-century philosophy graduate students may be vegans but that was not an option for our ancestors. There were no soy substitutes out on the plains. But the trouble is that, out on the plains or back in the jungle, getting big chunks of other animals may not always have been feasible or even the best strategy. In the immortal words of the paleontologist Jack Sepkoski: "I see intelligence as just one of a variety of adaptations among tetrapods for survival. Running fast in a herd while being as dumb as shit, I think, is a very good adaptation for survival."[14]

Then in the second place, the raw building blocks of evolution—the mutations—are random, not in the sense of being uncaused (we know a lot about the causes) but in the sense of not occurring according to need. There is no direction and so evolution apparently can go whichever way; progress does not compute and is "[a] noxious, culturally embedded, untestable, nonoperational, intractable idea that must be replaced if we wish to understand the patterns of history."[15] Making facetious reference to the asteroid that hit the Earth sixty-five million years ago, wiping out the dinosaurs and making possible the Age of Mammals, Stephen Jay Gould wrote: "Since dinosaurs were not moving toward markedly larger brains, and since such a prospect may lie outside the capabilities of reptilian design . . . we must assume that consciousness would not have evolved on our planet if a cosmic catastrophe had not claimed the dinosaurs as victims. In an entirely literal sense, we owe our existence, as large and reasoning mammals, to our lucky stars."[16]

Theistic Evolution

So how are we going to get humans in the face of this? One way is to take it out of the range of science and to give a theological answer instead: God guides the mutations! God cannot afford to have things go wrong, so God intervenes in Creation. After the *Origin of Species* was published in 1859, this view was adopted immediately by Darwin's great American supporter Asa Gray. He supposed that God gives the variations a little shove every now and then and humans appear to order:

> We have only to say that the Darwinian system, as we understand it, coincides well with the theistic view of Nature. It not only acknowledges purpose . . . but builds upon it; and if purpose in this sense does not of itself imply design, it is certainly compatible with it, and suggestive of it. Difficult as it may be to conceive and impossible to demonstrate design in a whole of which the series of parts appear to be contingent, the alternative may be yet more difficult and less satisfactory. If all Nature is of a piece—as modern physical philosophy insists— then it seems clear that design must in some way, and in some sense, pervade the system, or be wholly absent from it.[17]

Darwin would have none of this. As far as he was concerned, this view of evolution—where God makes deliberate tweaks whenever needed to produce a certain end, in this case, humans—was simply no scientific answer and that is an end to matters.[18] However, this has not stopped a succession of theists down to the present offering variants of this argument. The so-called Intelligent Design (ID) theorists argue that every now and then we get a God-guided macromutation that moves evolution along its way.[19] They argue that life shows "irreducible complexity" and that without such interventions evolution itself could not proceed to its intended destination. Obviously when it comes to humans God is already on top of the job and so no great further effort is needed. The whole of life is intelligently designed. We are the climax.

Somewhat more scientifically plausible is physicist Robert J. Russell's argument that God puts direction into evolution at the quantum level.[20] By doing so, God takes control of things down among the random events undetectable by human observers, and does work both unseen and unknown to us. Russell calls his position NIODA—Non-Interventionist Objective Divine Action. He argues that God works in the Creation, objectively, on an ongoing basis. For this reason, he considers himself as a theistic evolutionist. The problem, as Russell knows, is that most people agree with Darwin in thinking that theistic evolution is a non-starter. Russell's clever maneuver is to fly beneath the radar, as it were, arguing that God could be working down at the subknowable level. Thanks to quantum mechanics, we know that the best that we can hope for in understanding such things as radioactive decay is a statistical result. In time *t*, *x* percent will go one way and *y* percent will go another way. But we cannot say for sure which exact time brackets (slices of *t*, as it were) will get the *x*-leaning effects and which the *y*-leaning effects. So God could get involved here. God is not intervening in the sense of breaking or altering the laws as best we can know or measure them, but God is at work nevertheless. And if, say, an *x* effect is needed to set off a mutation that will help keep evolution progressing toward humans, then God can and does do this. Thus a noninterventionist is *not* non-actionist. God is very active but is not breaking the laws of nature as best we know them. Thus, Russell has his cake and eats it too. He has the unbroken laws of nature and he has a progressive rise in evolution, from blobs to humans.

We can move on quickly from Gray. His problem was that he could not see how selection generally working on unguided variations could lead to adaptive functioning. Now, today, we have clear evidence that it can, so we need not invoke special guided mutations. Considerable experimental evidence shows how changes can be brought about—including some sophisticated and long-term experiments on microorganisms—and an even greater amount of work on animals and plants in nature leads back to this conclusion. One thinks, for instance, of the work of Peter and Rosemary Grant in the Galapagos on how weather conditions affect beak size on surprisingly short timescales,[21] or of the work of David Reznick in Trinidad on guppies and how predation affects life histories and breeding patterns.[22] We can move on equally quickly from the ID theorists. It has been shown in convincing detail that their claims about irreducible complexity are just not plausible. Their paradigmatic examples, the motor of the bacterial flagellum and the blood-clotting cascade have been shown to be reducible to smaller parts and selection has been demonstrated as the key causal factor in their nature and very existence.[23]

What about the theistic evolution of Russell? He stresses—and after much argument with him I am now inclined to think he is right—that this is not a traditional "God of the gaps" argument. He is not with Asa Gray and the ID theorists in wanting to bring God into science to mop up the missing moves. This does not mean however that he is off the hook. At one level, as the philosopher (and nonbeliever) Elliott Sober argues, Russell can probably get away with what he argues. Using the word "intervene" in a slightly different way from Russell—meaning "God being involved" rather than "breaking the laws of nature"—Sober writes:

> Biologists say they have abundant evidence that mutations are unguided. This seems to mean that God does not intervene in the evolutionary process, at least not by causing this or that mutation to occur. I'll argue that what biologists mean, or ought to mean, when they say that mutations are unguided says nothing about whether God ever causes a mutation to occur.[24]

Why is this? Because, as Sober stresses, we are dealing with probabilities. "The argument I'll give for thinking that evolutionary theory is logically compatible with this kind of divine intervention is simple; it relies just on the fact that evolutionary theory, properly understood, is a probabilistic theory." The point being made is very much that of Russell. Suppose, for example, that the evolutionist says that a certain gene in a certain population in a certain time has a 20 percent chance of mutating from one form to another. That means that if you have ten genes, numbered 1 through 10, two of them will change from A genes to B genes. Your theory does not say which of the two will change, just that two of them will change. Logically then, from the viewpoint of your theory, there is nothing to stop God from making the change occur in genes 1 and 10 rather than another combination, and that God does this knowing that these two changes will lead the population one way—the way that will lead to humans—rather than another, a way that will not lead to humans.

Sober is at pains to suggest that, unlike Russell, he does not actually think that God acts this way. But evolutionary theory does not preclude God acting this way. As a nonbeliever, I leave it to others to argue whether God would ever act this way. For myself, it seems almost to be cheating.

Perhaps God had to get into the miracle business for our salvation—the Resurrection for instance—but by and large stays out of it. However, you could argue that since God is immanent and upholds creation, there is nothing strange about God directing mutations, and that the creation of human beings is at least as significant theologically as their salvation. Despite all this, a major theological objection destroys the credibility of all forms of theistic evolution. Once God gets involved in the creative process, especially on an ongoing basis, why not make God work a bit harder? Why doesn't God prevent those horrendous mutations that lead to dreadful diseases? Why doesn't God bother to stop Huntington's chorea and Tay Sachs disease and sickle-cell anemia and a host of other awful afflictions caused by genes gone wrong? If God pushes mutations in the direction of producing humankind, why not push a mutation in the direction of producing healthy babies? In the end, the cost of theistic evolution—including NIODA—is just too high.

Arms Races

We turn therefore to other possibilities for producing humans via Darwinian evolutionary theory. I will discuss three. First, we argue that evolution through selection is indeed progressive. It leads to better and more efficient features and brains will win out. This was Darwin's own position.

> If we look at the differentiation and specialisation of the several organs of each being when adult (and this will include the advancement of the brain for intellectual purposes) as the best standard of highness of organisation, natural selection clearly leads towards highness; for all physiologists admit that the specialisation of organs, inasmuch as they perform in this state their functions better, is an advantage to each being; and hence the accumulation of variations tending towards specialisation is within the scope of natural selection.[25]

In the same mode, in the twentieth century, Darwinian evolutionists, especially Julian Huxley, developed the idea of evolutionary "arms races." Lines of organisms compete and their adaptations get better. The prey gets faster and so the predator gets faster. Eventually this all leads to brains and to humans. Huxley writes, "The leaden plum-puddings were not unfairly matched against the wooden walls of Nelson's day." Now however, "though our guns can hurl a third of a ton of sharp-nosed steel with dynamite entrails for a dozen miles, yet they are confronted with twelve-inch armor of backed and hardened steel, water-tight compartments, and targets moving thirty miles an hour. Each advance in attack has brought forth, as if by magic, a corresponding advance in defence." Likewise in nature, "if one species happens to vary in the direction of greater independence, the inter-related equilibrium is upset, and cannot be restored until a number of competing species have either given way to the increased pressure and become extinct, or else have answered pressure with pressure, and kept the first species in its place by themselves too discovering means of adding to their independence."[26]

Dawkins is an enthusiast for this kind of thinking. "Directionalist common sense surely wins on the very long time scale: once there was only blue-green slime and now there are sharp-eyed metazoa."[27] This is all thanks to arms races.

The "arms race" metaphor has much to recommend it—although the notion is much contested among some experts[28]—but it hardly guarantees, as Christianity requires, that humans appear.

Niches

The second approach to the possibility of producing humans via evolution was first mooted by Stephen Jay Gould, for all that he was against biological progress![29] Suppose that there are ecological niches that organisms seek out. Water, land, air are the obvious big ones. The existence of more refined and limited niches can allow for two apparently similar yet fundamentally different organisms to coevolve and exist. We see this in the way two completely different lines of saber-toothed tiger—one marsupial and one placental—evolved independently and sought out the same niche. Culture in some sense exists as an available niche, and had we humans not found it, some organisms some time somewhere would have found it. So intelligence (and presumably morality) would have evolved. The respected Christian paleontologist Simon Conway Morris endorses this line of thinking. About us he writes:

> If brains can get big independently and provide a neural machine capable of handling a highly complex environment, then perhaps

> there are other parallels, other convergences that drive some groups towards complexity. Could the story of sensory perception be one clue that, given time, evolution will inevitably lead not only to the emergence of such properties as intelligence, but also to other complexities, such as, say, agriculture and culture, that we tend to regard as the prerogative of the human? We may be unique, but paradoxically those properties that define our uniqueness can still be inherent in the evolutionary process. In other words, if we humans had not evolved then something more-or-less identical would have emerged sooner or later.[30]

Once again, a little cold water is not entirely inappropriate. Many biologists don't even think that niches are just waiting there to be discovered, but rather are created by their denizens; it is hard to imagine that the culture niche existed, just waiting for us to come and fit it perfectly. There is surely no necessity that the niche should ever be discovered at all. As it is, can we say that organisms have occupied all of the available niches? Or is it just the niches that we know about? Surely being in one niche might make getting into another niche much harder. Could the culture niche be like Brigadoon, open only once every hundred (or hundred million) years and if there are no takers, closed again for ages? My worry is that we could have things backwards. We know that there is a cultural niche because we are in it, but perhaps it did not exist without us and other beings might have been slightly different and gone slightly different ways and either missed our niche entirely or made a somewhat different niche—one that didn't make beings quite good enough for God. Again, you can try it repeatedly all over the universe to improve the odds but I don't quite see the guarantee that you need.

Complexity

A third option moves from biology to the characteristics of nature writ large and how it develops statistically. Perhaps nature just complexifies over time and humans naturally appear after that process has gone on long enough.

Darwin had some intimation of this, writing in one of his early (1838) notebooks:

> The enormous *number* of animals in the world depends on their varied structure & complexity—hence as the forms became complicated,

> they opened fresh means of adding to their complexity—but yet there is no *necessary* tendency in the simple animals to become complicated although all perhaps will have done so from the new relations caused by the advancing complexity of others—It may be said, why should there not be at any time as many species tending to dis-development (some probably always have done so, as the simplest fish), my answer is because, if we begin with the simplest forms & suppose them to have changed, their very changes tend to give rise to others.[31]

Leading science journalist Robert Wright argues this point in *Non-Zero: The Logic of Human Destiny.* Gould speculated along these lines,[32] and recently a philosopher (Robert Brandon) and paleontologist (Daniel McShea) at Duke University have floated a version of this line of thinking. They see a kind of upwards momentum to life's history. Offering what they call the "zero-force evolutionary law" (ZFEL for short), they write: "In any evolutionary system in which there is variation and heredity, in the absence of natural selection, other forces, and constraints acting on diversity or complexity, diversity and complexity will increase on average."[33] Of course, part of the problem here is what one means by complexity. Dawkins, as usual, has no qualms about providing a definition:

> We have an intuitive sense that a lobster, say, is more complex (more "advanced", some might even say more "highly evolved") than another animal, perhaps a millipede. Can we *measure* something in order to confirm or deny our intuition? Without literally turning it into bits, we can make an approximate estimate of the information contents of the two bodies as follows. Imagine writing the book describing the lobster. Now write another book describing the millipede down to the same level of detail. Divide the word-count in the one book by the word-count in the other, and you will have an approximate estimate of the relative information content of lobster and millipede. It is important to specify that both books describe their respective animals "down to the same level of detail". Obviously, if we describe the millipede down to cellular detail, but stick to gross anatomical features in the case of the lobster, the millipede would come out ahead. But if we do the test fairly, I'll bet the lobster book would come out longer than the millipede book.[34]

Does any of this make sense? Compare warthogs with millipedes. Does one count every warthog hair, or does the hair as a whole count as one? Does one count every millipede leg or do the legs collectively count as one? If you are comparing a bald man with a hairy man, then surely each active follicle counts as something at the same level of detail. This could make them very different with respect to complexity, even though the bald man may be a philosophy professor and by any intuitive measure far more complex and advanced than the hairy man, who is, say, a theologian.

Complexity is a very nebulous notion. Even if it does make sense, why it should equate to advancement, or in the biological world, to intelligence, seems entirely another matter. And even if it does all work, can one guarantee that it actually will work down here on this planet— or elsewhere in the universe for that matter?

Multiverses

Have we run out of steam? Let me try a more speculative hypothesis. What worries me about the suggestions thus far is that they crash either on the Charybdis of theology or the Scylla of science. We have a theological problem with the necessity of humankind. Either we flounder because we have offered a theological solution where it seems that science is needed or we flounder because we have offered scientific solutions and that theology wants more. Let's go back to the theology and see if we are missing something helpful there. A point already noted is that it is an essential part of Christian theology that God is outside space and time. God exists necessarily like the truths of mathematics, neither coming into being nor going out of being, and is not here or there or anywhere, but in some sense everywhere. In other words, God is not hanging around waiting for us to appear, growing impatient. In Augustinian terms, God has willed our being—primary cause—and in a sense is indifferent as to how long the secondary causes take to kick in. We are here thanks to evolution through natural selection. After enough tries it is bound to work. We know this because it did work. Whether things like arms races were involved is a matter for the science and not of great importance here.

So what we need are enough tries. The trouble with our universe is that it is finite. (If it isn't finite, then you can easily adjust what I am about to say.) We need an infinite or potentially infinite range of possibilities to guarantee that any particular probabilistic outcome will occur. Only then can we know that somewhere sometime we are going to hit the jackpot: humans. To deny this is to deny that evolution through selection could produce humans and this is simply not true. We are here! For us, it is no big surprise that we are here. If we were not here, we would not be here to comment on our absence. We are like people who have won the lottery ticket. There are a lot of losers out there—experiments in life that didn't make humans—but our ticket came up, our experiment succeeded, and because of this we can celebrate that fact.

How can we get an infinite range or potentially infinite range of possibilities? Multiverses! If there is an infinite number of universes, then somewhere, sometime, somehow humans are going to appear. Secondary causes have stepped up to satisfy God's primary intention to create humankind. Note that although this is a solution to a theological problem, it is not (unlike theistic evolution) a theological solution. Multiverses are scientific concepts. For this reason, take note that my position should not be confused with the philosophical thesis known as "modal realism." The author of this thesis, the late David Lewis, argued (following Leibniz) that probability should be understood in terms of possible worlds—to say that something is probable (or not impossible) is to say that there is some possible world where this thing obtains, is actually true. What Lewis argued was that we should consider each and every one of these possible worlds as in some sense real!

> I believe, and so do you, that things could have been different in countless ways. But what does this mean? Ordinary language permits the paraphrase: there are many ways things could have been besides the way they actually are. I believe that things could have been different in countless ways; I believe permissible paraphrases of what I believe; taking the paraphrase at its face value, I therefore believe in the existence of entities that might be called "ways things could have been." I prefer to call them "possible worlds."[35]

As one who resists mathematical Platonism—preferring to think of mathematics as relationships between things, rather than descriptions of an actually existing ideal world—I want to whip out Occam's razor at this point. I am quite happy to talk of probabilities in terms of possible worlds, but I see no reason to give them actual existence unless there are good scientific reasons for doing so, and that existence means really being there—Julius Caesar as opposed to David Copperfield. And that is what the appeal to multiverses is intended to provide.

I realize of course that multiverses are a highly contested notion in the scientific world.[36] That, I am afraid, is a topic for another essay. For now I am just going to have to rest with them as a given. But note the context of taking them as a given—my claim is that although appeal to multiverses is (like arms races and the others) a scientific solution, it is (unlike arms races and the others) also an adequate solution to the theological demands. Nevertheless, because they are a scientific given, if they are to make their way, it must be because of their scientific merits and not because of theological demands. That would not be acceptable. So I think I am on safer grounds than the modal realist, but this is because unlike the modal realist I cannot just conjure up my solution. I have to go out and find evidence to support it. And that is a good note on which to end this chapter.

Notes

1. Peter William Atkins, "The Limitless Power of Science", *Nature's Imagination: The Frontiers of Scientific Vision*. ed. by J. Cornwell (Oxford: Oxford University Press, 1995), 132.
2. Augustine, *The Literal Meaning of Genesis*, trans. John Hammond Taylor (New York: Newman, 1982).
3. Michael Ruse, *Science and Spirituality: Making Room for Faith in the Age of Science* (Cambridge: Cambridge University Press, 2010).
4. Michael Ruse, *Atheism: What Everyone Needs to Know* (Oxford: Oxford University Press, 2015).
5. Michael Ruse, *The Philosophy of Human Evolution* (Cambridge: Cambridge University Press, 2012).
6. John R. Schneider, "Recent Genetic Science and Christian Theology on Human Origins: An 'Aesthetic Supralapsarianism,'" *Perspectives on Science and Christian Faith* 62, no. 3 (2010): 196–212.
7. Alister E. McGrath, *Christian Theology: An Introduction*, 2nd ed. (Oxford: Blackwell, 1997).
8. Augustine, *Literal Meaning of Genesis*, 41.
9. Richard Dawkins, "Universal Darwinism," in *Evolution from Molecules to Men*, ed. D. S. Bendall, 403–425 (Cambridge: Cambridge University Press, 1983).
10. Song of Solomon 1:5.
11. Charles Darwin, *The Descent of Man, and Selection in Relation to Sex* (London: John Murray, 1871), 1: 73.

12. Michael Ruse, *Monad to Man: The Concept of Progress in Evolutionary Biology* (Cambridge, MA: Harvard University Press, 1996).
13. Erasmus Darwin, *The Temple of Nature* (London: J. Johnson, 1803), canto 1, stanza 11, lines 295–314.
14. Ruse, *Monad to Man*, 486.
15. Stephen Jay Gould, *The Flamingo's Smile: Reflections in Natural History* (New York: Norton, 1985), 319.
16. Stephen Jay Gould, *Wonderful Life: The Burgess Shale and the Nature of History* (New York: W. W. Norton, 1989), 318.
17. Asa Gray, *Darwiniana: Essays and Reviews Pertaining to Darwinism* (New York: Appleton, 1876), 379.
18. Michael Ruse, *The Darwinian Revolution: Science Red in Tooth and Claw*, 2nd ed. (Chicago: University of Chicago Press, 1999).
19. Michael Behe, *Darwin's Black Box: The Biochemical Challenge to Evolution* (New York: Free Press, 1996).
20. Robert John Russell, *Cosmology, from Alpha to Omega: The Creative Mutual Interaction of Theology and Science* (Minneapolis, MN: Fortress, 2008).
21. Peter R. Grant and B. Rosemary Grant, *How and Why Species Multiply: The Radiation of Darwin's Finches* (Princeton, NJ: Princeton University Press, 2008).
22. David N. Reznick and Joseph Travis, "The Empirical Study of Adaptation in Natural Populations," in *Adaptation*, ed. Michael R. Rose and George V. Lauder, 243–290 (San Diego: Academic, 1996).
23. Kenneth R. Miller, *Finding Darwin's God* (New York: Harper and Row, 1999); Michael Ruse, *Darwin and Design: Does Evolution Have a Purpose?* (Cambridge, MA: Harvard University Press, 2003).
24. Elliott Sober, "Evolutionary Theory, Causal Completeness, and Theism: The Case of 'Guided' Mutations," in *Evolutionary Biology: Conceptual, Ethical, and Religious Issues*, ed. R. Paul Thompson, and Denis M. Walsh (Cambridge: Cambridge University Press, 2014), 32.
25. Darwin, *On the Origin of Species*, 3rd ed., 134.
26. Julian S. Huxley, *The Individual in the Animal Kingdom* (Cambridge: Cambridge University Press, 1912), 115–116.
27. Richard Dawkins and John R. Krebs, "Arms Races between and within Species," *Proceedings of the Royal Society of London, Series B* 205, no. 1161 (1979): 508.
28. Geoffrey A. Parker, "Arms Races In Evolution—An E[volutionary] S[table] S[trategy] to the Opponent-Independent Costs Game," *Journal of Theoretical Biology* 101, no. 4 (1983): 619–648; Robert T. Bakker, "The Deer Flees, the Wolf Pursues: Incongruences in Predator-Prey Coevolution," in *Coevolution*, ed. Douglas J. Futuyma and Montgomery Slatkin, 350–382 (Sunderland, MA: Sinauer, 1983).
29. Gould, *Flamingo's Smile.*.
30. Simon Conway Morris, *Life's Solution: Inevitable Humans in a Lonely Universe* (Cambridge: Cambridge University Press, 2003), 196.

31. Paul H. Barrett et al., *Charles Darwin's Notebooks, 1839–1844* (Ithaca, NY: Cornell University Press, 1987), E 95–97.
32. Stephen Jay Gould, *Full House: The Spread of Excellence from Plato to Darwin* (New York: Random House, 1996).
33. Daniel W. McShea and Robert N. Brandon, *Biology's First Law: The Tendency for Diversity and Complexity to Increase in Evolutionary Systems* (Chicago: University of Chicago Press, 2010), 3.
34. Richard Dawkins, *A Devil's Chaplain: Reflections on Hope, Lies, Science and Love* (Boston and New York: Houghton Mifflin, 2003), 100.
35. David K. Lewis, *On the Plurality of Worlds* (Oxford: Blackwell, 1986), 84.
36. Max Tegmark, "Parallel Universes," *Scientific American* 288, no. 5 (2003): 40–51; George F. R. Ellis, "Does the Multiverse Really Exist?" *Scientific American* 305, no. 2 (2011): 38–43.

Selected Bibliography

Atkins, Peter W. "The Limitless Power of Science." In *Nature's Imagination: The Frontiers of Scientific Vision*, edited by John Cornwell, 122–132 (Oxford: Oxford University Press, 1995).

Augustine. *The Literal Meaning of Genesis*. Translated by John Hammond Taylor (New York: Newman, 1982).

Bakker, R. T. "The Deer Flees, the Wolf Pursues: Incongruences in Predator-Prey Coevolution." In *Coevolution*, edited by Douglas J. Futuyma and Montgomery Slatkin, 350–382 (Sunderland, MA: Sinauer, 1983).

Barrett, Paul H., Peter J. Gautrey, Sandra Herbert, David Kohn, and Sydney Smith, eds. *Charles Darwin's Notebooks, 1836–1844* (Ithaca, NY: Cornell University Press, 1987).

Behe, Michael. *Darwin's Black Box: The Biochemical Challenge to Evolution* (New York: Free Press, 1996).

Conway Morris, Simon. *Life's Solution: Inevitable Humans in a Lonely Universe* (Cambridge: Cambridge University Press, 2003).

Darwin, Charles. *The Descent of Man, and Selection in Relation to Sex*. 2 vols. (London: John Murray, 1871).

Darwin, Charles. *On the Origin of Species by Means of Natural Selection, or the Preservation of Favoured Races in the Struggle for Life* (London: John Murray, 1859).

Darwin, Charles. *On the Origin of Species*. 3rd ed. (London: John Murray, 1861).

Darwin, Erasmus. *The Temple of Nature* (London: J. Johnson, 1803).

Dawkins, Richard. *The Blind Watchmaker* (New York: Norton, 1986).

Dawkins, Richard. *A Devil's Chaplain: Reflections on Hope, Lies, Science and Love* (Boston and New York: Houghton Mifflin, 2003).

Dawkins, Richard. "Universal Darwinism." In *Evolution from Molecules to Men*, edited by D. S. Bendall, 403–425 (Cambridge: Cambridge University Press, 1983).

Dawkins, Richard, and John R. Krebs. "Arms Races between and within Species." *Proceedings of the Royal Society of London, Series B* 205, no. 1161 (1979): 489–511.

Ellis, George F. R. "Does the Multiverse Really Exist?" *Scientific American* 305, no. 2 (2011): 38–43.

Gould, Stephen Jay. *The Flamingo's Smile: Reflections in Natural History* (New York: Norton, 1985).

Gould, Stephen Jay. *Full House: The Spread of Excellence from Plato to Darwin* (New York: Random House, 1996).

Gould, Stephen Jay. "On Replacing the Idea of Progress with an Operational Notion of Directionality." In *Evolutionary Progress*, edited by Matthew H. Nitecki, 319–338 (Chicago: University of Chicago Press, 1988).

Gould, Stephen Jay. *Wonderful Life: The Burgess Shale and the Nature of History* (New York: W. W. Norton, 1989).

Grant, Peter R., and B. Rosemary Grant. *How and Why Species Multiply: The Radiation of Darwin's Finches* (Princeton, NJ: Princeton University Press, 2008).

Gray, Asa. *Darwiniana: Essays and Reviews Pertaining to Darwinism* (New York: Appleton, 1876).

Huxley, Julian S. *The Individual in the Animal Kingdom* (Cambridge: Cambridge University Press, 1912).

Lewis, David K. *On the Plurality of Worlds* (Oxford: Blackwell, 1986).

McGrath, Alister E. *Christian Theology: An Introduction*. 2nd ed. (Oxford: Blackwell, 1997).

McShea, Daniel W., and Robert N. Brandon. *Biology's First Law: The Tendency for Diversity and Complexity to Increase in Evolutionary Systems* (Chicago: University of Chicago Press, 2010).

Miller, Kenneth R. *Finding Darwin's God* (New York: Harper and Row, 1999).

Parker, Geoffrey A. "Arms Races in Evolution—An E[volutionary] S[table] S[trategy] to the Opponent-Independent Costs Game." *Journal of Theoretical Biology* 101, no. 4 (1983): 619–648.

Reznick, David N., and Joseph Travis. "The Empirical Study of Adaptation in Natural Populations." In *Adaptation*, edited by Michael R. Rose and George V. Lauder, 243–290 (San Diego: Academic, 1996).

Ruse, Michael. *Atheism: What Everyone Needs to Know* (Oxford: Oxford University Press, 2015).

Ruse, Michael. *Darwin and Design: Does Evolution have a Purpose?* (Cambridge, MA: Harvard University Press, 2003).

Ruse, Michael. *The Darwinian Revolution: Science Red in Tooth and Claw*. 2nd ed. (Chicago: University of Chicago Press, 1999).

Ruse, Michael. *Monad to Man: The Concept of Progress in Evolutionary Biology* (Cambridge, MA: Harvard University Press, 1996).

Ruse, Michael. *The Philosophy of Human Evolution* (Cambridge: Cambridge University Press, 2012).

Ruse, Michael. *Science and Spirituality: Making Room for Faith in the Age of Science* (Cambridge: Cambridge University Press, 2010).

Russell, Robert John. *Cosmology, from Alpha to Omega: The Creative Mutual Interaction of Theology and Science* (Minneapolis, MN: Fortress, 2008).

Schneider, John R. "Recent Genetic Science and Christian Theology on Human Origins: An 'Aesthetic Supralapsarianism.'" *Perspectives on Science and Christian Faith* 62, no. 3 (2010): 196–212.

Sober, Elliott. "Evolutionary Theory, Causal Completeness, and Theism: The Case of 'Guided' Mutation." In *Evolutionary Biology: Conceptual, Ethical, and Religious Issues*, edited by R. Paul Thompson and Denis M. Walsh, 31–44 (Cambridge: Cambridge University Press, 2014).

Tegmark, Max. "Parallel Universes." *Scientific American* 288, no. 5 (2003): 40–51.

PART 4

Closing Reflection

16

Abraham's Dice in the Flow of Life

THE EXPERIENCE OF THE TRAGIC AND ITS THEOLOGICAL INTERPRETATION

Reinhold Bernhardt

Introduction

This chapter does not deal—as most of the others do—with chance and providence in the *world*, that is, in nature and history, but in the experience of life. In the flow of life, we experience chance, randomness, and contingency all the time. As a pastor I often got involved in the life stories of parish members who were afflicted with a sudden disruption of their lives. In funeral services I sometimes quoted the verse from the Apocryphal book Sirach 18:26: "From the morning until the evening the time shall be changed." It is the "Book of the All-Virtuous Wisdom of Joshua ben Sira," commonly called the Wisdom of Sirach or simply Sirach, and also known as the Book of Ecclesiasticus.

To deal with the kinds of disruptive experiences we call "tragic," I first describe what tragedy is and then provide a theological interpretation that aligns these experiences with the providence of God.

If we assume that God's providence reigns over the life of each individual, how can there be contingency (that is, an unforeseen event or circumstance) in general and tragic contingency in particular? I will show that divine providence need not be understood as theological determinism; on the contrary, it can be understood as opening new possibilities for dealing with situations which seem to be desperate and dead-ended. Providence then means God breaks open the crusted earth so that the seeds of new life are able to sprout! Providence is the field of force of God's spirit which can be experienced in various forms: as spiritual guidance, as the power of resurrection in the midst of life, as a vigor of resilience, as the growing of new confidence and hope, and so on—especially in situations we experience as tragic. I intend for my reflections to be a contribution to the perennial discussion on theodicy (that is, the study of the problem of evil in the world) and as such, relevant for pastoral care.

What Does It Mean to Experience Something as "Tragic"?

The notion of the tragic is not an *empirical* category which is located on the level of facts but a *hermeneutical* category which is located on the level of understanding and interpretation. It is a pattern of meaning, but a pattern of meaning which paradoxically qualifies an experience as meaningless.

Not everything that is described in everyday language as tragic can be considered tragic in a philosophical way. The common use of the word "tragic" is too focused on the horror of an event. We need to clarify the concept first. I suggest differentiating between three dimensions of the tragic: the tragic as an external event, the tragic as an internal conflict, and the tragic as an unavoidable failure.

The Tragic as an External Event

A tragic situation can be experienced as a deeply shattering *external* event. We apply the notion of the tragic to those events which burst the regularities of our ordered flow of life. One could call them disruption-events, which break the more or less coherent nexus of experiences and expectations. They are contrary to what—on the basis of previous experiences—could be expected. But a tragic event is not an "event" as such but something that occurs in a specific situation at a certain time and place without necessity and has unpredictable destructive effects. At another time or place the same event would not have such consequential impact. In tragic situations, events are experienced as an avalanche of sheer contingency, making it impossible to ascribe any meaning to them. The concept of the tragic refers to those entanglements in sinister complex constellations of events that are experienced as a painful falling into meaninglessness and hopelessness. The disruption of a so-far-ordered situation can be caused by natural disasters but also through human actions, even actions motivated by good intentions.

Three examples will help illustrate what I mean:

- That death overtakes a person cannot be described as tragic. But we can call it tragic if it does so while that person is, for instance, in the process of completing her life's work, finishing the last chapter of a book which was meant to summarize all of her lifelong collected knowledge. It is not tragic to die, but to die at the wrong time can be described as tragic.
- The bursting of a truck tire is a purely physical event to which nothing tragic can be ascribed. However, when it bursts just before the exit to the Gotthard Road Tunnel in Switzerland and causes an accident that results in the gruesome death of eleven people (as happened in 2001), that is tragic.
- A bank robbery cannot and ought not to be interpreted as a tragic event. But if right at that moment a pregnant mother with a small child enters the bank, asks what is going on, and gets shot—that has the bitter quality of the tragic.

These three examples show that the tragic does not lie in the event itself, but rather in the setting of the event. In the first case the tragic relates to the *time* of the occurrence. In the second case it is the *place* of the occurrence. In the third case (as in the previous two examples) it is the unnecessitated connection between purposeful actions, unintended consequences, and their contingent devastating effects.

The notion of the tragic, however, is not exhausted in the dimension of *external events* that befall a person. It can also be applied to the impact of conflicts that lie *within a person.*

The Tragic as an Irresolvable Inner (Moral) Conflict

An inner conflict which is to be qualified as tragic can be either an unsolvable inner conflict between contradictory external demands that cannot be reconciled, or it can be a conflict between internal intentions and external compulsions to act in a particular way, or it can be a conflict between two or more opposing internal intentions. The external compulsion can be grounded in a natural necessity, a ruler's decree, a sacrosanct moral norm or a political law. The internal intention can be rooted in our values, or passions, or ethical responsibilities. In such cases the tragic is constituted by a grievous antagonism that places before the affected person the choice between two disastrous solutions; the conflict is thus irresolvable.

We find examples of such internal conflicts in the Greek tragedies. In Sophocles's *Antigone,* for instance, Creon's decree not to bury her brother Polynices brings Antigone into a conflict with the law of the gods. Not to obey Creon would result in imprisonment, and not to bury her brother would condemn him to eternal torment in the afterlife. No matter which of the conflicting commands Antigone followed, she would transgress against either Creon or the gods. A more current example could be the burial of a person's father who died of Ebola. According to cultural rules in many areas where Ebola is found, the father has to be buried in a dignified way, with the conduct of certain rites, which take a few days. But the health administration of the district—informed by the World Health Organization—requires that the corpse must be buried immediately by trained case management professionals using strong protective clothing and gloves.

The tragic as disruptive *external event* is experienced as subjection in sheer passivity, while the tragic as an *inner conflict* is felt as paralysis in the face of a grievous decision on how to act. While in the external case the tragedy has to do with suffering and mourning, in the second case the courage to become guilty and to sacrifice a value is required because no matter which option is chosen, it will be a culpable decision.

Those conflicts which are experienced as especially tragic involve a clash between contradictory equivalent goods or equivalent evils, so that it is not a conflict between good and evil but between good and good or between evil and evil.

The Tragic as Unavertable Failure

The notion of the tragic encompasses not only internal and external conflicts, but also the disparity between willing and executing, purpose and means, doing and consequence. In the above-mentioned inner conflicts, the tragic lay in the paralyzing alternative of two contrary imperatives—here it exists in the crucial connection of intention, action, and effect. The tragic as unavertable failure is neither a contingent external event nor an unresolvable inner conflict. It relates primarily to human action as motivated by inner intentions, using certain means of acting and having certain effects. Normally there is a continuity between intentions, actions, and effects: the effect correlates with the intention. But when that continuity becomes disturbed, when the effects get out of hand, it can come to a tragic failure. The failure is the result of the unstoppable internal dynamic of actions, which are experienced as fateful, because they overrun the human will.

Not every form of failure can be described as tragic—only those which arise out of one's own will and action and which lead to unintended destructive effects for oneself or others. It is tragic when a well-meant action gives rise to a devastating effect: when the means that are used not only fail to meet the goal but rather achieve the opposite of what was intended; when actors make themselves the prisoners of their own freedom; when one destroys one's beloved out of love; or when one restricts freedom in order to protect freedom. In such cases the striving for good brings about disaster as much as the renunciation of good. A trivial mistake has horrible consequences; that is to say, there is a crass incongruity between a definite guilt and indefinite suffering.

It is tragic when, out of a banal mistake, out of a misunderstanding, or out of an unlucky chain of individually harmless causes, catastrophic damage arises. It is virtually impossible to ascribe responsibility for such damages. Ludwig Wittgenstein sees in such circumstances an aspect of tragedy. "A tragedy could always, after all, begin with the words: 'Nothing whatsoever would have happened, had not . . .' (Had not a corner of his clothing caught in the machine?)."[1]

Theological Interpretation of the "Tragic"

The notion of the tragic was and is a challenge for theology because it seems to give the polarity of contingency and necessity a large space and thus could be considered as reducing the sovereignty of God. The Jewish, Christian, and Islamic understanding of reality sees the fundamental orderliness, rationality, and proportionality of the world as grounded in God's act of creation and sustained by God's providence. Even when this order is disturbed by sin, belief in God's graciously granted forgiveness and the restoration of the order of creation prevails (as seen at the end of the Book of Job). In contrast to this understanding of reality, tragedy could be described as (in the words of Ludwig Wittgenstein) experiences wherein the proverbial tree does not bow, it breaks.[2] The tragic event is *devastating*, the inner conflict is *irresolvable*, and the failure is *unavertable*. Thus in the notion of the tragic breathes an un-Jewish, un-Christian, and un-Islamic spirit.

"Tragedy" and "providence" seem to refer to different worldviews. According to its roots in Greek theater, the tragic doom leaves those entangled with it without any positive solution to their problems—no way out. Even if there is a concept similar to "providence," like the notion of *pronoia* in the Stoic school of philosophy, the difference is significant. *Pronoia* is more like an inescapable fate. In contrast, the Abrahamic religions hold fast to their hope in the will and power of God which can influence the flow of events, inspire decisions in the face of seemingly unresolvable inner conflicts, and help believers to cope with failure.

The difference of worldviews in which the tragic and the belief in God's providence are rooted, however, does not necessitate excluding the notion of the tragic from theological reflection and pastoral practice. "The 'tragic' . . . is one of those words, in which the suffering of humanity comes to expression"[3] and it is also used by many Christians to interpret crucial experiences in their existence. Therefore, this theme cannot be irrelevant for a theology which intends to address the experiences of human beings. It is necessary to draw the notion of tragedy into theology and to provide a space for it there.

In the next part of this chapter, I review the main theological interpretations of tragedy and critically discuss them. In one way or another, each of these schools of thought attributes some kind of divinely ordered meaning to tragic suffering. I will reject such attempts to endow the tragic with meaning and will suggest instead that "tragic" remains merely a descriptive notion of a particular type of situation and its consequences. Tragedy does not *give* meaning. Yet the description points beyond itself; using it provokes a *search* for meaning.

A person who has been afflicted with a tragic experience will ask for explanations. "Why did that happen to *me*?" If she feels that physical causes and/or a moral accounting are insufficient to explain the experience, she may be inclined to look for a "metaphysical" explanation, be it fate or the constellations or the effect of evil powers or divine providence. In the formulation of the question the answer can be implicit.

- If she asks: "What have I done wrong, so as to deserve suffering so much?" she assumes that her own behavior caused the suffering. This response may resonate with the basic idea that there is a necessary connection between deed and consequences: sin causes suffering.

- If she asks: "Why did God allow such a thing to happen to me?" the underlying assumption is that an act of God caused the tragic situation and the resulting suffering. The two questions combined—"What have I done wrong, so as to deserve suffering so much?" and "Why did God allow this to happen?"—suggest: "God did it to punish me for my sinful behavior." But the reasons for God's acting to punish does not require the human's sinful behavior—no necessary connection between deed and consequences need be insinuated. The Book of Job circles around this dilemma.
- If she adopts a more removed view, she might ask: "Why is there so much suffering in the world? Especially suffering of the innocent? Why do such bad things happen to good people? How long will it last?" Thus she might look for an explanation which does not refer to contingent human and/or divine action but to the basic structure of the world as a whole.

These three ways of seeking to reckon with tragedy resonate with three theological approaches to explain suffering in general and tragic suffering in particular. Theologians often attempt to make meaningless experiences meaningful by relating them to God's providence: they are thus understood either in terms of a divinely ordered general principle, according to which suffering is the result of sin, or in terms of special divine acts or as the consequence of original sin. I will point at those approaches, discuss them briefly, reject the first and the second completely and modify the third.

I think that theology has to be cautious about giving explanations which interpret the meaningless experience in terms of a "higher" volition or hidden divine purpose. This explanation can all too easily lead to what I would call a pious cynicism. If theologians like Laurence Michel proclaim with a view to the redemption in Christ, "the Gordian knot of the tragic has been cut,"[4] and infer from this that a Christian tragedy is a self-contradiction, then tragic experiences cannot be taken seriously.

(1) I reject the *moral solution*, that is, a theological interpretation of the tragic as sin (understood in moral terms as guilt) or as the immediate consequence of sin. Such an interpretation claims that the tragic is rooted in human action or at least in the freedom to act.

A theological interpretation, which considers tragic experiences to be the consequence of misconduct—be it a contravention of a divine command or of human moral (or even legal) imperative—misses the complex structure of tragic experiences, which are imbued with an overlapping network of situational context and human guilt. As per my analysis of tragic situations and experiences above, the tragic is a complex relationship of behavior and doom. It cannot simply be accounted for by the misconduct of the person afflicted by it nor explained as the result of wicked people doing wicked things. All these things may play a role, but none can be singled out as the one and only cause, sometimes not even as the "main" cause. The notion of "emergence" as opposed to "causation" is appropriate to understand tragedy. At best a tragedy can be understood—but never explained.

Thus, in contrast to the "moral solution," the tragic is to be more deeply anchored in the basic structure of human existence in the world. It cannot be interpreted as the result of a free act of humans. Tragic experiences mirror deep-rooted tensions of human life—tensions between freedom and compulsion, between contingency and necessity. Because tragic experiences are experiences of brokenness which cannot and may not (at least not completely) be traced back to guilty behavior against fellow human beings or against oneself or against God, its appropriate soteriological (that is, salvation-related) category for discussion is not forgiveness but rather redemption, salvation, and healing. If there is guilt or at least a sense of guilt involved (attributed to God or to other humans or to oneself), forgiveness of the actor can be an appropriate way to achieve healing. But this response remains only *one* aspect of the complex therapeutic process. Thus it would be a "category mistake" to apply only concepts of reconciliation—repentance, atonement, liberation of guilt, and so on—to ways of coping with a tragic experience. The entrapment by a person in a tragic situation and the wounds caused by it cannot be forgiven; they need to heal, in the sense of being made whole—and that takes time and care. That healing process may lead to empowerment in coping with the tragic situation itself or with its traumatic outcome, to restoration of integrity, to gaining a new foundation of trust, and to redirection in life. Salvific healing does not simply mean leaving behind the tragic experience as if it had not happened—restoring the status quo ante; rather, it means being able to integrate it into the whole of one's life-interpretation and life-orientation. In the sense of attempting "reconciliation" with one's own past, this term can be meaningful—but not in terms of "reconciliation" with God after sinful behavior. Reconciliation with one's own past can inspire new trust in the future.

(2) I reject the *divine-causation solution*, by which I mean interpreting the tragic as the result of a specific act of God for a certain purpose. The purpose can involve *disciplining, punishing*, or *reprobating* a person for her sinful conduct, but also in *educating* her, for instance, to grow more mature by coping with suffering or by developing deeper trust in God; it also could involve *testing* a person's moral strength or the strength of her faith in God.

Explaining the tragic as resulting from God's punishment can be easily combined with explaining it as a result of human sin, as in the "moral solution" I referred to above (1). It is explained then as God's punishment for human sin. But that is not a necessary connection. The tragic as a result of human sin can also be spelled out in terms of an inner dynamics of the sinful behavior itself which harms the actor, instead of a reacting act of God. Paul, for instance, indicates that suffering may be the result of sin which the sinner draws upon herself (Galatians 6:7–8). There is no action of God involved.

If the tragic experience becomes explained as a pattern of sin and guilt—like in the "moral solution"—the responsibility for the tragic situation is put on the sinful person. In this model, however, the responsibility is ascribed to God. This is also the case when divine punishment is interpreted as a reaction to human sin, for God is, of course, free to react in another way.

The interpretation of tragic situations as caused by special divine acts has roots in many biblical narratives, such as those in which God's express will is to cause obstinacy and harden hearts—after which God responds with reprobation. God obscures the human's view of what is right, puts within them the test of an inner conflict or an external experience of disaster. God himself orders these men's and women's sinful aversion to God and thus makes them guiltlessly guilty. Job finds himself in a God-decreed entangling network of despair that places him in an unresolvable tension to his own being as a creature of God—an experience that can truly be described as tragic.

When theologians refer sufferers of tragedy to the biblical testing, disciplining, punishing, and educating acts of God, they often are attempting to interpret the tragic in the light of the omnipotence and omnicausality of God. They make a direct inference from the tragic situation to its cause in God's purposeful intervention. The divine causality can be thought of either as a direct intervening act or as an indirect ordering act with which God constitutes the structural conditions for the occurrence of the tragic situation (in the Book of Job, God acts *mediated* by Satan). In both cases the tragic becomes elevated into the divine will. God is declared as the author of evil and suffering.

I want to raise at least three objections against explanations of the tragic as caused by acts of God. First, this interpretation implies a far too anthropomorphic understanding of God and God's activity, where God acts like a pedagogue (of former times), like a judge, or like a strict father. (In the last part of my chapter, I suggest an approach for conceptualizing divine action which refrains from anthropomorphism.) Second, I reject the "intervention model" of God's action in general, as I believe this leads to serious theological problems. One is the question of theodicy. If God is able to intervene in a specific situation and to change the state of affairs by performing a specific act, why did God not prevent all the horrors in the history of humanity and in the lives of individual human beings? Almightiness ought not to be understood as omnicausality but as the universal empowerment of the created beings. Third, I object to the belief that God is the author of evil and suffering. I find enough evidence in New Testament testimonies for claiming that God's very being is unconditional and universal grace. Therefore, God cannot be the one accountable for the suffering of God's creatures. If suffering is attributed to God as a painful means to achieve good aims, then the suffering cannot be seen as something which ought not be and that should be overcome, as I think it should be seen in the light of God's grace.

In the Book of Job, all the above interpretations are rejected. The three friends of Job suggest understanding the misery of Job as a result of God's punishment (for example, 8:20), education (33:14–25), or testing (36:21). Job protests in the name of God's justice against all those attempts to interpret his unjust suffering along those lines. He discovers that God's purpose for afflicting that misery on him is to show him the unfathomable mystery of God's being and will.

In contrast to the "divine-causation solution," I argue that the tragic ought to be described primarily as "secular" interaction between the external conditions of the situation and the person involved in this situation. Humans are guiltily guiltless victims of the disastrous experiences and entangling networks of their own world. God's providential activity is not the *cause* of the tragic but comes in as the power which heals the wounds of those who were afflicted with tragic experiences.

(3) I reject the *ontological solution,* by which I mean an interpretation of the tragic as an essential characteristic of the "fallen" creation

as a whole and as God-created human nature. Such an "essentialization" of the tragic can also be found in philosophy, for example, in Schopenhauer[5] and Nietzsche.[6] In their pessimistic ("pantragistic") worldview they see the tragic lying at the very foundation of being in general and of human being in particular. Humans are condemned to tragic failure. In addition, Miguel de Unamuno spoke of a "tragic sense of life."[7]

According to Schopenhauer, the tragic cannot be reduced to definable relationships of events primarily related to human challenges and failures; it is rather to be understood as the immediate outflow of the constitution of reality. There is an irreconcilable conflict running through every being. In his major work, *The World as Will and Idea,* he wrote that in tragedy "lies a significant hint of the nature of the world and of existence."[8] And he continues: "It is one and the same will that lives and appears in them all, but whose phenomena fight against each other and destroy each other."[9] Schopenhauer sees how close this philosophical interpretation of reality comes to the traditional theological doctrine of original sin: "The true sense of tragedy is the deeper insight, that it is not his own individual sins that the hero atones for, but original sin, *i.e.*, the crime of existence itself: 'Pues el delito mayor / Del hombre es haber nacido' ('For the greatest crime of man / Is that he was born') as Calderon exactly expresses it."[10]

Such a tragic worldview, in which the meaningfulness of being is denied, may find its confirmation in the multiplicity of meaningless suffering in human history. But it declares the deficits in creation to be its essence; in the end, there remains only a resigned aversion to this world, as Schopenhauer proclaimed. It is not possible to bring such a "pantragicism" into harmony with the fundamental convictions of the Christian belief in creation. The same applies to an understanding of original sin as ontological defect of reality as a whole. The original goodness of creation which reflects the goodness of God becomes obscured.

Opposing these philosophical and/or theological "ontologizations" of the tragic, we should again remind ourselves of the analysis of tragic experience as contingent external events or series of events, or as an inner conflict. None of these can be seen as the necessary expression of an original sin. The nonnecessity of the tragic cannot be ruled out by interpreting it as the result of an underlying cosmic necessity. It has to be taken seriously as real contingency. Just as the tragic is not to be understood as moral evil or physical evil, it cannot be interpreted as metaphysical evil in terms of a cosmic doom either.

But while I reject the "moral solution" and the "divine-action solution" more or less emphatically, I take up the "ontological solution" and wish to develop it further. In this view, it is the feature of necessity—that is, the tragic as a *necessary* and thus unavoidable feature of the fallen creature—that I find especially problematic. In contrast to that assumption, I argue that the tragic is not ontologically anchored in necessity but rather in an *omnipresent possibility*. Tragic situations can occur at any moment, but need not occur. The tragic is encountered paradoxically as nonnecessary necessity. At all times it is possible that a disastrous situation—in which one's own misconduct, the disorders of interhuman relationships, and disastrous external events interact with each other—will break in and lead to an experience of contingent brokenness.

How can we understand the contingent necessity of tragic (and other suffering-causing) entanglements? Already in medieval times, philosophers and theologians posited a distinction which is helpful for answering this question: the distinction between absolute and conditional necessity. The necessity inherent in tragic experiences cannot be conceived of as inevitable in terms of an *absolute* necessity—be it the corruption of human nature (which would correspond to an anthropological pessimism), a God-decreed necessity (which would correspond to a theological determinism), or a friction inscribed in the substance of reality (which would correspond to an ontological fatalism). The tragic is inevitable in terms of a *relative* or *conditional* necessity. According to an *absolute* necessity, it is to be assumed that the chain of events inevitably leads to the tragic constellation because it is determined by fate or the world order, or because it is decreed by God, or because human nature is defective. According to the *conditional* necessity, the tragic situation is not in *principle* but in *fact* inevitable. The necessity grows out of the interaction of influencing factors that work together in different chains of actions and events. The interaction of those chains is contingent. In looking back at the whole process, the tragic can be described with the words: "it could not have happened differently." However, this does not mean "it could not have happened differently because there was an absolute determination that the tragic occur." Rather, this insight comes retrospectively that, under the given circumstances, the tragic "must" have occurred and "It could have been different *if* . . ."

Thus, on the one hand, in tragic experience there is a necessity, which is rooted in an unstoppable dynamic within a process or conflict between opposing imperatives. On the other hand, it is precisely the nonnecessity which qualifies the experienced situation as tragic. If the necessity is conceived as absolute, grounded in a metaphysical causal network or in the action of God, humans would be released from their possible co-responsibility for the event and perhaps also from their responsibility for coping with the effects of it. It would be almost impossible to avoid ethical and existential indifference, that is, fatalism.

The Doctrine of Original Sin as an Interpretive Framework

Is there a basic conceptual framework for the tragic that accounts for the complexity of guilt and disaster, contingency, and necessity as described above? Can we view tragic darkness without, on the one hand, denying, marginalizing, or assimilating its reality into a higher purpose and not taking seriously enough its experiential quality as meaningless suffering and, on the other hand, without hiding it from God's light, thus declaring it to be a metaphysical principle elevated into a tragic worldview? The appropriate theological interpretative framework for the experience of the tragic appears to me to be, perhaps surprisingly, the doctrine of original sin. However, understanding tragedy this way will require a radical reinterpretation of that doctrine. In what follows I will not try to integrate the experience of the tragic into the traditional doctrine of original sin but work, instead, the other way round—indicating some features of an understanding of original sin that would result from my reflections on the tragic. I suggest the following twofold revision.

First, I would like to propose substituting an *ontological* with a *relational* understanding of original sin. It is not a defect of human nature but the permanent possibility of disaster in the four fundamental relationships of human life: the relationship with oneself, with the social world (i.e., fellow human beings), with the natural environment, and with the divine. The traditional understanding of original sin, which originated with Augustine, describes a corruption of human nature as a result of the sin of Adam and Eve according to Genesis 3. As opposed to such an ontological interpretation of original sin, the proposed relational (or social) understanding interprets "sin" as a disruption or destruction of relationships. Tragic situations can be seen as specific instances of such destructions and thus as an appearance of original sin in this broader metamoralistic and relational meaning of the concept. They can affect one or more of those four fundamental human relations. The ruin caused by an inner conflict mainly relates to the *relationship with one's self*; when a person is torn by the conflict of loyalties and the imperatives that flow from them, then the tragic happening mainly afflicts the *relationship to the social world*; a tragedy caused by a catastrophic experience mainly affects the human *relationship with the world.* All of those experiences can and probably will have an impact on the believer's *relationship to God.*

A second revision refers to the nexus of sin and guilt which is deeply rooted in Western Christianity. According to the traditional understanding, original sin is a notorious aversion to God resulting in "the fall" and causing a defect in human nature. Adam and Eve's aversion to God and their inability to live according to the will of God is inherited by all humans such that they are unable to experience a salvific relationship to God except through redemption in Christ. Even if individual persons are themselves not guilty of original sin, they participate in it, or rather, it participates *in them* since from the time of Adam and Eve the guilt of it has been rooted in the nature of humanity. Even newborn babies are guilty of it before they can perform any act. In contrast to individual acts of sin, this "possession of guilt" refers not only to the *acting* but to the *being* of humans in which their willing and acting are rooted. It is superior to the freedom of the individual.

The guiltless-guilty entanglement within a complex event-and-action network that is characteristic of tragedy mirrors this metamoralistic understanding of guilt. Without denying the (possible) active participation of the person in a "tragic" event, a theological interpretation of the tragic must speak of guilt in a supraindividual sense. But in contrast to an ontological or essential guilt, I suggest spelling it out existentially: less in the sense of "having guilt" or "being guilty," but rather in the sense that a person is always *somewhat* guilty (in terms of owing someone something) in that humans can never fulfill their relationships with themselves, with fellow humans, with nonhuman creatures, and with God. Even if they intend to do so, they are unable to completely do justice to these relationships. They are always in someone's debt.

Understood in this way, the tragic is the expression of the limitedness of human possibilities—however, not as an abstract or ontological attribute of human nature, but as mundane conditions of the boundaries of historical existence. These are boundaries of the basic relationships of the human being which I referred to above. In such a relational way

I suggest employing Leibniz concept of the "metaphysical evil." Leibniz sees the root of all evil in the last instance in the finitude of human existence.[11]

This supraindividual and metamoralistic understanding of guilt opens up the possibility of understanding "guilt" as a complex experience which can be seen from two perspectives: not only from the perspective of what a person remains guilty of in relation to God, the natural environment, other people, and themselves, but also what life possibilities are being withheld from that person in these relationships, that is, what she as a human being can expect to receive from God, from other people, from natural living conditions, and from herself. The Psalms of lament in the Old Testament articulate such a reversal of the attributing of "guilt" in an impressive form. For example, in Psalm 7 the enemies are accused of withholding or even destroying potentialities and opportunities of life, and God, on the one hand, is blamed for not intervening in the past and, on the other hand, is called to intervene now.

Original sin is accordingly understood as the interrelated complex of guilt and disaster in which human beings can be trapped time and time again and which brings deep wounds into the consummation of their existence. It is understood as a disturbance of the possibilities of their life that transcends their power to act and as the unavoidable failure of their projects with even the best will and cleverest actions. It is experienced and conceptualized as a *power* because it really exercises power over humans. But that does not allow us to demonize, objectivize, or personalize it as a metaphysical satanic force. More appropriately, "original sin" describes the destructive power inherent in the structures, conditions, relations, and situations of the particular "world" in which a human being lives. In a somewhat demythologized form, it is possible to theologically reappropriate the concept of "fate" and fill it with meaning when it is used to describe the situational circumstances that to a large extent debilitate the individual and significantly limit possibilities for positive action. Here the concept of "fate" can be a helpful interpretation of the experience of the tragic. But "fate" cannot be identified with "the tragic." It can be considered only an aspect of it: the aspect of necessity.

The tragic is constituted not in sheer necessity and passivity, as "fate" implies; rather, it is located in the intersection of action and effect, of guilt and disaster. It is the being drawn guiltless or guiltily into the disastrous breaking apart of human security, the abysmal experience of the fragility of one's life and the sensation of an ultimate loneliness in the world. It has to do with the fundamental experience of the loss of control and meaning and with the desperate struggle to find meaning.

In my modified understanding, original sin refers to the unavoidable deep shaking of the four constitutive relationships of humanity. It lies within the constitution of human existence—not in human nature or a divinely ordered necessity but as an omnipresent possibility. This omnipresent possibility is ultimately unexplainable and cannot in any way be referred back to an act of the divine will. It is a characteristic of the imperfection of creation, which according to Paul is still in the state of birth (Romans 8:22–25) and stands as such under the promise of being overcome eschatologically.

Freed from all moralistic connotations, original sin can be understood as the always and everywhere available possibility within creation of the guilty-guiltless transgression of the purpose of creation. The tragic is one mode in which this disruption is experienced. It is not simply the absurd (that is the absolute meaning*less*), rather that which is "empty" of meaning but longs for establishment of meaning. It *has* no meaning, but meaning *can grow* toward it.

Understanding the Providence of God in the Light of the Tragic

I understand God's providence as God's operative (or active) presence in the power of God's spirit. In interpersonal relationships we have analogies for the energy of pure presence. Without performing any specific actions at all, a person can alter a situation by simply being there. This effect can be experienced particularly in situations marked by suffering, mourning, and grief, or alternatively in situations where love, compassion, and caring predominate. Not only external actions, but also enacted relationships (for example, spending time with a person) have an effect on those who are afflicted with a tragic situation. I apply this analogy to the understanding of God's providential activity.

God's activity in the world is not to be depicted as a series of personal acts but as a spiritual influence. It resides in the circumstances of each creature and occasion so that there is no competition between God's activity and human action. Thus, creatures perform their free actions within a spiritual force field that nonetheless has an influence on them. This spiritual field does not exert an undirected energy but a purposive influence—aiming at the promised fulfillment of creation. (The analogy of a magnetic field, in which iron particles are directed according to the field lines, can be applied to illustrate it.) The Holy Spirit comes to be "the agent of providence" (*effector providentiae*)—as Calvin put it.[12] Calvin wrote: "Whatever happens in the world can quite rightly become attributed to the spirit of God."[13] That sentence can but need not be understood in terms of a theological determinism.

God's activity is *intrinsically* involved in human action; it does not go side by side with it. There is not a relationship of cooperation between them but of participation in divine life. The whole creation *exists* within—and humans *act* within—the activity of God, in the force field of God's Spirit, being more or less affected by it. "In God we live and move and have our being," according to Acts 17:28. I can summarize this position by saying: God acts by inspiration.

"Inspiration" cannot be assumed to *force* anything or anybody with irresistible power; its power is the "power of weakness," but there is the promise that this power will succeed in the end because of its everlasting durability. In 1 Corinthians 1:25 Paul says, "The weakness of God is stronger than man's strength." The proof of this, however, is eschatological. Therefore we cannot expect that reality as a whole is in accordance with God's providing and guiding activity. Tragic events happen. The spiritual force field of God's providence cannot prevent them. But it can help victims cope with tragic effects. It does not make the meaningless meaningful but creates new seeds of life and new patterns of meaning, seeds of resurrection in dead-end situations. God's operative presence has transforming effects on the awareness of people and communities, on their attitudes, and on their behavior. As the experience of the tragic is an omnipresent possibility, the power of God's spirit is an omnipresent healing power.

In God's spiritual force field a new life-orientation in the face of tragic experiences can emerge. This outlook can lead to an attitude of "faithful realism" (to use a term of Paul Tillich[14]) which in no way attempts to deny the reality of the tragic or to idealize it by attributing a metaphysical meaning to it. It is a realism which at first takes seriously the inscrutability of humans' existence in the world and their subjection to the omnipresent possibility of failure, a realism which secondly feels sympathy and solidarity with the suffering, and a realism which thirdly takes into account the reality of the transforming power of God. It is powered by the hope that God's healing and meaning-creating presence encompasses the tragic experience and places it in the light of God's promise that all suffering will eschatologically come to an end. This kind of realism provides the energy to look realistically at the inscrutability of the tragic experience yet not believe that the tragic disruption will lead to ultimate failure. With such an attitude a healing power in the processing of tragic experiences is at work, which helps sufferers to withstand the tragic experience and its effects.

The seeking of causal explanations for the tragic ("why did it happen?") provides no help in coping with tragic experiences; it paralyzes. Neither does the "what for?" question, in the sense of discovering some ultimate purpose of the tragic ("what was it good for?"). Meaning lies not in the event itself, nor in its effective or proposed final cause. However, the tragic experience can *gain* meaning when in the course of time it becomes possible to integrate it into a new pattern of meaning: when the affected person sees, for instance, a tragic accident retrospectively as causing a rearrangement of her life-orientation or her value-priorities, so that she experiences a disclosure of what seems to be *really* important in her life. Not as a general metaphysical explanation of the evil, but only in the retrospective interpretation of the affected person herself, the "what for?" question can become a means of healing the inflicted wounds. It is then not an attempt to *find* meaning in the past event, but to *attribute* meaning to it and to be open for a future creation of meaning. The question is not, "What *was/is* the meaning of the tragic experience?" but "Which meaning did and can grow out of it?"

"Faithful realism" takes into account the reality of the healing and transforming power of God. It trusts that those who were afflicted with tragic experiences will become empowered to cope with their suffering, to gain new hope, and, in so doing, to overcome the traumatic tragic experience and the wounds it has inflicted.

Notes

1. Ludwig Wittgenstein, *Public and Private Occasions*, ed. James C. Klagge and Alfred Nordmann (Lanham, MD: Rowman and Littlefield, 2003), 87.
2. Ludwig Wittgenstein, *Culture and Value*, ed. Georg Henrik von Wright, trans. Peter Winch (Oxford: Blackwell, 1998), 1/3: "You get tragedy where the tree, instead of bending, breaks. Tragedy is something un-Jewish."
3. Wilhelm Grenzmann, "Über das Tragische," in *Tragik und Tragödie*, ed. Volkmar Sander (Darmstadt: Wissenschaftliche Buchgesellschaft, 1971), 166 (my translation).

4. Laurence Michel, "Die Möglichkeit einer christlichen Tragödie," in *Tragik und Tragödie*, ed. Volkmar Sander (Darmstadt: Wissenschaftliche Buchgesellschaft, 1971), 208 (my translation).
5. Arthur Schopenhauer, *The World as Will and Idea*, trans. R. B. Haldane and J. Kemp, 7th ed. (London: Kegan Paul, Trench, Trübner, 1909), vol. 1, § 51.
6. Friedrich Nietzsche, "The Birth of Tragedy," in *Contemplating Music: Source Readings in the Aesthetics of Music*, ed. Ruth Katz and Carl Dalhaus, vol 1, *Substance*, 162–195 (Stuyvesant, NY: Pendragon, 1987); Friedrich Nietzsche, *Philosophy in the Tragic Age of the Greeks*, trans. Marianne Cowan (Washington, DC: Regnery, 1962.
7. Miguel de Unamuno, *Tragic Sense Of Life*, trans. J. E. Crawford Flitch (New York: Dover, 1954).
8. Schopenhauer, *World as Will and Idea*, 1: 326, § 51.
9. Ibid., 1: 327.
10. Ibid., 1: 328.
11. Gottfried Wilhelm Leibniz, *Theodicee* (1710). Translated into English by E. M. Huggard as *Theodicy: Essays on the Goodness of God, the Freedom on Man and the Origin of Evil* (La Salle, IL: Open Court, 1985).
12. Following the convincing interpretation in Werner Krusche, *Das Wirken des Heiligen Geistes nach Calvin* (Göttingen: Vandenhoeck & Ruprecht 1957), 14; Reinhold Bernhardt, *Was heißt "Handeln Gottes"? Eine Rekonstruktion der Lehre von der Vorsehung*, 2nd ed. (Berlin: LIT, 2008), 77.
13. John Calvin, *Ioannis Calvini opera omnia quae supersunt*, ed. G. Baum, E. Cunitz, and E. Reuss, vols 59 (Brunsvigae: C. A. Schwetschke, 1863–1900). Quotation: vol 44, p. 206. (my translation).
14. Paul Tillich, *The Protestant Era*, ed. James Luther Adams, 2nd ed. (Chicago: University of Chicago Press, 1957), 67. Other translations are: "believing realism" or "belief-ful" realism. James Luther Adams uses the term "self-transcending realism" as opposed to "self-sufficient realism."

Selected Bibliography

Bernhardt, Reinhold. *Was heißt "Handeln Gottes"? Eine Rekonstruktion der Lehre von der Vorsehung*. 2nd ed. (Berlin: LIT, 2008).

Calvin, John. *Ioannis Calvini opera omnia quae supersunt*, edited by G. Baum, E. Cunitz, and E. Reuss. Vols. 59 (Brunsvigae: C. A. Schwetschke, 1863–1900).

Grenzmann, Wilhelm. "Über das Tragische." In *Tragik und Tragödie*, edited by Volkmar Sander, 166–176 (Darmstadt: Wissenschaftliche Buchgesellschaft, 1971).

Krusche, Werner. *Das Wirken des Heiligen Geistes nach Calvin* (Göttingen: Vandenhoeck & Ruprecht, 1957).

Leibniz, Gottfried Wilhelm. *Theodicee* (1710). Translated into English by E. M. Huggard as *Theodicy: Essays on the Goodness of God, the Freedom on Man and the Origin of Evil* (La Salle, IL: Open Court, 1985).

Michel, Laurence. "Die Möglichkeit einer christlichen Tragödie." In *Tragik und Tragödie*, edited by Volkmar Sander, 177–208 (Darmstadt: Wissenschaftliche Buchgesellschaft, 1971).

Nietzsche, Friedrich. "The Birth of Tragedy", in *Contemplating Music: Source Readings in the Aesthetics of Music*, edited by Ruth Katz and Carl Dahlhaus. Vol. 1, *Substance*, 162–195 (Stuyvesant, NY: Pendragon, 1987).

Nietzsche, Friedrich. *Philosophy in the Tragic Age of the Greeks*. Translated by Marianne Cowan (Washington, DC: Regnery, 1962).

Schopenhauer, Arthur. *The World as Will and Idea*. Translated by R. B. Haldane and J. Kemp. 7th ed. 3 vols. (London: Kegan Paul, Trench, Trübner, 1909).

Tillich, Paul. *The Protestant Era*. Edited by James Luther Adams. 2nd ed. (Chicago: University of Chicago Press, 1957).

Unamuno, Miguel de. *Tragic Sense of Life*. Translated by J. E. Crawford Flitch (New York: Dover, 1954).

Wittgenstein, Ludwig. *Culture and Value*. Edited by Georg Henrik von Wright, translated by Peter Winch (Oxford: Blackwell, 1998).

Wittgenstein, Ludwig. *Public and Private Occasions*. Edited by James C. Klagge and Alfred Nordmann (Lanham, MD: Rowman and Littlefield, 2003).

Index